INSIDERS' GUIDE® SERIES

INSIDERS'
►GUIDE

CORPUS CHRISTI
AND THE TEXAS COASTAL BEND

by

Vivienne Heines

and

Scott Williams

INSIDERS'
►GUIDE®
AN IMPRINT OF THE GLOBE PEQUOT PRESS
GUILFORD, CONNECTICUT

•

Insiders' Guide is a registered trademark of The Globe Pequot Press

•

Front cover photo: air station, courtesy of Naval Air Station-Corpus Christi
Back cover photo: beach, courtesy of the Greater Corpus Christi Business Alliance
Photo band (left to right): beach, courtesy of the Greater Corpus Christi Business Alliance;
flamanco dancers, courtesy of the Greater Corpus Christi Business Alliance;
golfers, courtesy of the Corpus Christi Convention and Visitors Bureau;
windsurfer, courtesy of the Greater Corpus Christi Business Alliance;
bird hunters, courtesy of the Greater Corpus Christi Business Alliance
Spine photo: beach, courtesy of the Rockport-Fulton Chamber of Commerce

•

ISBN 1-57380-125-9

•

Manufactured in the United States of America

•

First Edition/Second Printing

Publications from The Insiders' Guide® series are available at special discounts for
bulk purchases for sales promotions, premiums, or fundraisings. Special editions,
including personalized covers, can be created in large quantities for special needs.
For more information, please contact The Globe Pequot Press at (800) 962-0973.

Preface

Early visitors to the Corpus Christi area called it the Texas Riviera, charmed by its shimmering waters, sea breezes, and abundant fishing.

Such ageless attributes still entice thousands of tourists and newcomers to this sunshine-filled hideaway on the Texas Gulf Coast, which is also known as the Texas Coastal Bend. This is where Texas' larger-than-life ranching heritage blends with the leisure of a beachfront lifestyle, where Stetson-wearing cowboys are as common as bronzed surfers and where a 10-minute drive takes you from a bustling fishing pier to vast acres of fluffy cotton fields.

It's a region rich in history, established by hardy pioneers who came seeking land and wealth and found instead a countryside as beautiful as it was demanding. The blessings of sunshine gave way to the curse of drought, and the cooling bay breezes could also bring deadly hurricanes. And as the settlers endured and flourished on this flat, rich landscape, they learned to appreciate the natural gifts from the land—the bounty of fish and wild game, the graceful shade of towering live oaks and the bright-pink splashes of bougainvillea flowers that accent the greenery.

Today, the area is far more civilized but no less alluring. It promises rest and relaxation, South Texas-style—from windsurfing and sailing to shrimp festivals and fiestas.

The region's largest city, Corpus Christi, boasts a population of more than 250,000, yet most residents and visitors find it has a small-town atmosphere. You'll find a spontaneous warmth and genuine friendliness among the natives, from the waitress at your restaurant to the park ranger who directs you to your campsite.

To say that we're off the beaten path is an understatement. The Coastal Bend is a destination unto itself, not a pit stop on the way to another locale. Still, we're located just hours from both the Mexican border and the big-city bustle of Houston and San Antonio.

To savor the character of our adopted homeland, first take a deep breath and relax.

Then take a drive down Corpus Christi's Ocean Drive and admire the showcase bayfront mansions set against a backdrop of sparkling blue-green water.

Travel to Padre Island National Seashore, the world's longest barrier island, a 55-mile refuge for world-weary visitors as well as more than 350 species of birds and wildlife.

Enjoy the saturated colors of a coastal sunset as you haul in a trophy marlin during a deep-sea fishing trip off Port Aransas.

Watch the *vaqueros*—Spanish for cowboys—corral longhorn cattle during a roundup at the world-famous King Ranch, where the region's ranching traditions meld seamlessly with the cultural heritage of nearby Mexico.

We who have chosen this lush and rugged paradise as our home have learned to celebrate its diversity. We have learned to embrace not only our longtime neighbors, but also the newcomers here and, yes, even the sometimes harsh geology and climate.

And we know that the hot summer sun of this semitropical land warms not only the Gulf waters but the hearts of those who visit here.

About the Authors

Vivienne Heines

Raised in New Orleans, Louisiana, Vivienne Heines is familiar with the Gulf coast lifestyle, culture, and climate. Her writing career, however, has been spent mostly in her adopted home state of Texas. She received a journalism degree from Trinity University in San Antonio and completed two college internships at the *Times Picayune-State Item* newspaper in New Orleans. She then was employed as a news reporter, features writer, and editor at various Texas newspapers including the *Houston Chronicle, Corpus Christi Caller-Times, Brazosport Facts, Brenham Banner Press, Wharton Journal Spectator,* and the *Colorado County Citizen.*

During her 16-year, full-time reporting career, she won nearly 30 awards and covered topics ranging from unsolved murders to historical profiles. She has tracked wild mountain lions and javelinas, been attacked by Africanized bees, flown in Navy jets, and exposed small-town corruption.

In 1996, Vivienne left full-time newspaper reporting and began a freelance writing career so she could spend more time with her three young children. Today, she writes articles for a variety of state and national publications on topics ranging from the military to economics. She is also active with volunteer work in her community, church, and school.

In her spare time, she enjoys jogging, tennis, reading, and caring for her children. She and her family share their home with two large dogs and a cat.

Scott Williams

A native Texan who grew up on the outskirts of Dallas, Scott Williams has lived most of his life far from the sandy shores of Corpus Christi. His lifelong dream of writing took him to the University of Texas at Austin, where he earned a journalism degree in 1985. He began his career at a weekly newspaper, the *Lockhart Post-Register*, where he covered everything from pee-wee football to county government. A year later he accepted a job as a business writer with *The Bryan-College Station Eagle*. In 1988, during his first visit to Corpus Christi, the sparkling green water and towering palm trees of Corpus Christi convinced Williams to accept a job with the *Corpus Christi Caller-Times.*

He began his *Caller-Times* career on the transportation and economic development beat before graduating to coverage of trials and legal affairs. He later became an area reporter, where he spent hundreds of hours on the roads between the tiny coastal hamlets of Rockport, Port Aransas and Portland. He spent his last four years at the *Caller-Times* as a features writer, profiling prominent South Texans and describing life in Corpus Christi. He has marveled up close at the Rockport hummingbirds, witnessed two open-heart surgeries by an acclaimed Corpus Christi surgeon, visited a privately owned lighthouse on a small

Gulf Coast island and flown with the Blue Angels. He left the *Caller-Times* in 1994 to care for his children full time and finish a novel.

Williams and his wife, journalist Libby Avery, live three blocks from Corpus Christi Bay with their two children, Avery and Grace. Williams and his family enjoy camping in South Texas parks, building sandcastles at the Padre Island National Seashore and relaxing in the laid-back South Texas lifestyle that accepts shorts and sandals almost everywhere.

Acknowledgments

Vivienne . . .

Writing this book was a learning experience for me. I discovered much about my community, and I also came to know dozens of people who shared observations, information and insight with me.

Among those who assisted me with this book are all the friendly folks at the Chambers of Commerce in Aransas Pass, Corpus Christi, Gregory-Portland, Ingleside, Port Aransas, Rockport-Fulton, Kingsville, San Antonio and South Padre Island. A special thanks goes to Dick Messbarger at the Kingsville Economic Development Council, who was never too busy to talk to us about his beloved city or to put us in touch with the right people.

Another special thanks goes to my loyal friend Libby Averyt Williams, who provided invaluable research assistance as well as enthusiastic support for this project.

I am indebted to my neighbors, Frank and Cindy Peterson, for their insight into the city's nightlife; to *Corpus Christi Caller-Times* columnist Rene Cabrera for his perspective on the city's Tejano music scene; and to *Corpus Christi Caller-Times* outdoor writer Buddy Gough, who patiently led me through the area's fishing and hunting terrain.

The local and area boards of Realtors helped by sharing their knowledge of the real estate scene, neighborhoods and available properties.

Many friends provided an invaluable resource—babysitting time—to help me conduct interviews and write on my computer. I owe a special thanks to Felisa Garza and Lisa Innins for the loving care they gave to my children during those busy times.

Last, but certainly not least, I owe a debt of gratitude to my family. My two sons, Zachary and Aaron, were great companions during much of the research for this book. When we went to visit all the bed and breakfast inns in the area, they cheerfully pointed out details and shared their opinions.

My daughter, Tessa, actually managed to exhibit patience—a rare attribute for a toddler—when she accompanied me on interviews or played semi-quietly while I talked on the telephone.

Also, I want to thank my co-author, Scott Williams, for his professionalism and his thoroughness in researching and writing this book.

And my husband, Andy, displayed a great deal of tolerance throughout my months of research. He supported, encouraged and generally endured as my files gradually took over most of our filing cabinet, bookshelf and home office.

To all of these people—this book is dedicated to you. Thank you.

Scott . . .

This book could not have been written without the assistance of several people in Corpus Christi who shared their knowledge and resources with us. I'd like to thank Ralph Goonan and Gretchen

Benkendorfer, both formerly of the Corpus Christi Business Alliance, for their help in acquiring information and some of the photographs for this book.

I'd also like to thank Diane Probst, executive director of the Rockport-Fulton Chamber of Commerce; Kathy Burge, assistant to the director at the Aransas Pass Chamber of Commerce; the Ingleside Chamber of Commerce; Rachel Munson, Ingleside city secretary; Linda Hodge and Santos Villarreal, Corpus Christi Park & Recreation Department; Dick Messbarger, executive director of the Kingsville Economic Development Council; and Lawanda Skrobarczyk, director of the Kingsville Convention and Visitors Bureau. Special thanks to *Corpus Christi Caller-Times* photographer George Gongora for the photograph of Selena Quintanilla-Perez; Francisco Tamez of the Laredo Convention & Visitors Bureau; and Gwen Spain, director of public relations at the Austin Convention and Visitors Bureau. I turned to many sources for the History chapter, but none was more helpful than Bill Walraven's *Corpus Christi: History of a Texas Seaport*.

Most of all I would like to thank my co-author, Vivienne Heines, for making this collaboration work without a hitch; friends Del Puckett and Sue Rothschild for babysitting my children while I worked; my wife, Libby, for her love and support and for assisting with research and proofreading; and my two children, Avery and Grace, who saw a lot less of their Daddy during the writing of this book.

Corpus Christi is one of the world's premier locations for windsurfing.

Photo: courtesy of the Greater Corpus Christi Business Alliance

Table of Contents

Directory of Maps

TEXAS COASTAL BEND

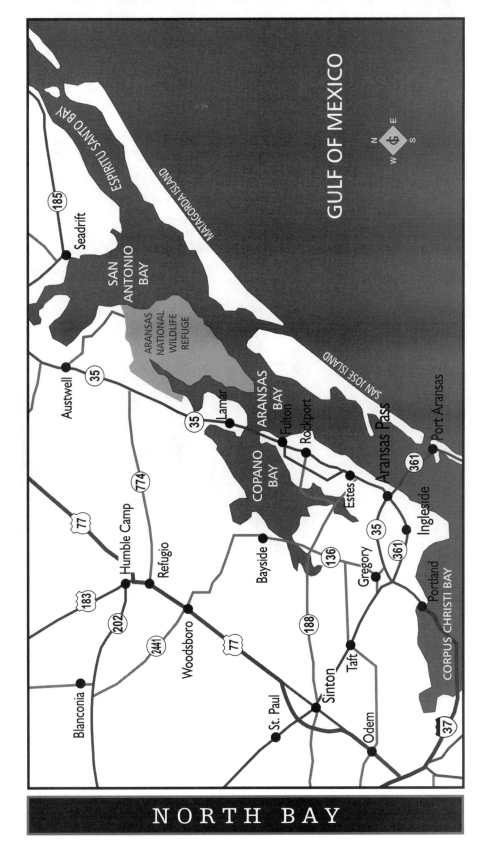

GULF OF MEXICO

ESPIRITU SANTO BAY

MATAGORDA ISLAND

SAN ANTONIO BAY

ARANSAS NATIONAL WILDLIFE REFUGE

SAN JOSE ISLAND

ARANSAS BAY

COPANO BAY

CORPUS CHRISTI BAY

Seadrift

(185)

Austwell

(35)

Lamar

(35)

Fulton

Rockport

Aransas Pass

Port Aransas

(361)

Estes

Ingleside

(35)

Gregory

(361)

Humble Camp

(774)

(77)

Refugio

Bayside

(136)

Portland

(183)

(202)

(2441)

Woodsboro

(77)

(188)

Taft

Odem

Blanconia

St. Paul

Sinton

(37)

N E S W

NORTH BAY

KINGSVILLE AREA

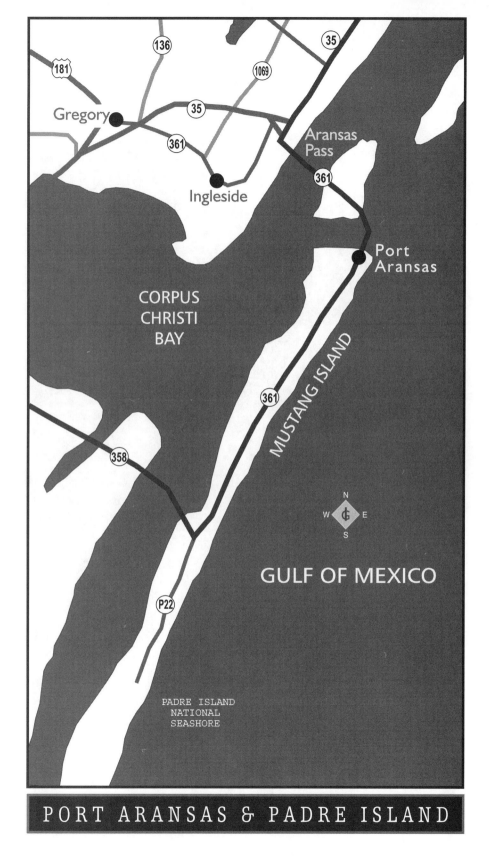

PORT ARANSAS & PADRE ISLAND

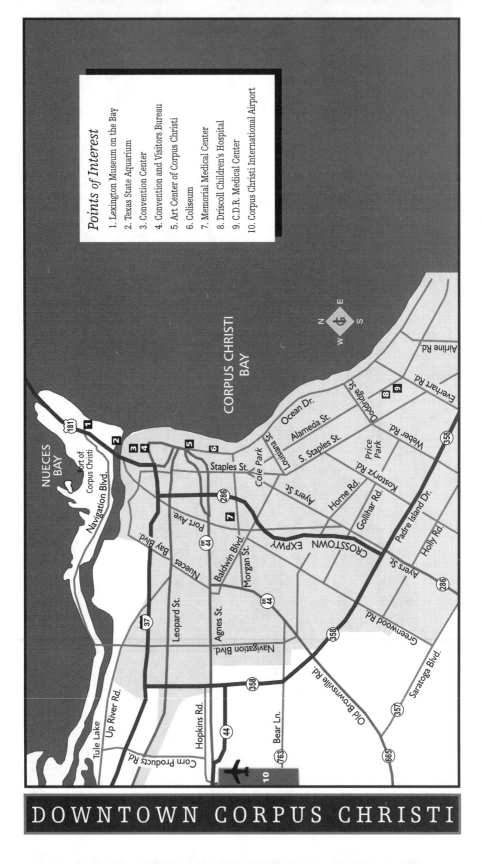

DOWNTOWN CORPUS CHRISTI

Points of Interest

1. Lexington Museum on the Bay
2. Texas State Aquarium
3. Convention Center
4. Convention and Visitors Bureau
5. Art Center of Corpus Christi
6. Coliseum
7. Memorial Medical Center
8. Driscoll Children's Hospital
9. C.D.R. Medical Center
10. Corpus Christi International Airport

CORPUS CHRISTI BAY

NUECES BAY

Port of Corpus Christi

Navigation Blvd.

181

1

2

3

4

5

6

286

7

Staples St.

Cole Park

Ocean Dr.

Alameda St.

S. Staples St.

Louisiana St.

Ayers St.

Horne Rd.

Price Park

Kostoryz Rd.

Weber Rd.

Doddridge St.

Everhart Rd.

Airline Rd.

8

9

358

CROSSTOWN EXPWY

Gollihar Rd.

Padre Island Dr.

Holly Rd.

Ayers St.

286

Port Ave.

Baldwin Blvd.

BR 44

Morgan St.

Nueces Bay Blvd.

Leopard St.

Agnes St.

37

Navigation Blvd.

BR 44

358

Greenwood Rd.

Saratoga Blvd.

357

Old Brownsville Rd.

665

Tule Lake

Up River Rd.

Corn Products Rd.

Hopkins Rd.

44

358

Bear Ln.

763

10

How to Use This Book

Like the early explorers who sailed these Texas coastal waters in search of treasure, we find living in the Corpus Christi area to be an ongoing adventure. There are so many nooks and crannies to explore, such varied recreational opportunities to experience and so many regional festivals and idiosyncrasies to savor.

Whether you're a summer visitor, a Midwesterner come to escape the chill of winter or a newcomer who plans to settle in and buy a home, we want this book to be your guide. Take along this book, and we'll journey with you to traverse the flora and fauna of state and national parks, to marvel at the minute perfection of a hummingbird in flight, to taste the seafood bounty at local restaurants and to feel the brush of salt spray against your face from a Jet Ski.

You can use the table of contents to flip quickly to the subject you're seeking, be it accommodations or watersports. Or you can use the index in the back of the book to find a specific topic, attraction, museum or shop.

The portion of the Texas Gulf Coast around Corpus Christi, also known as the Coastal Bend, begins northward at the Aransas National Wildlife Refuge and extends southward along the coast through Rockport, Fulton, Aransas Pass, Port Aransas, Ingleside, Portland and on to Corpus Christi, our largest city. We'll then travel southward along the coast to Padre Island National Seashore and inland to Kingsville, home of one of the world's largest ranches, the King Ranch.

We have grouped many of our listings by four geographic categories. The North Bay area includes the towns of Lamar, Fulton, Rockport, Aransas Pass, Ingleside, Gregory and Portland. The Corpus Christi area encompasses the city and its surrounding towns and communities. In the Port Aransas to Padre Island section, we provide information about the island city of Port Aransas and the area that extends through Padre Island National Seashore. Finally, the Kingsville area includes the city and its surrounding towns, such as Ricardo and Riviera.

In most of our chapters, the headings will be arranged in that same geographic order, from north to south, so you can look for a city name to locate, say, a restaurant or museum. And within each city, the listings will be alphabetical.

Entries for our most visible landmarks and attractions are listed in several different chapters, often cross-referenced for easy access.

We've included maps of this region to help guide you through the state highways and farm-to-market roads that intersect our landscape. The speed limit on interstate highways is 70 mph, not 75 mph. Although you might get away with driving 75, we wouldn't want to encourage law-breaking.

Scattered throughout the book are a host of Insiders' tips—interesting or informative tidbits about the Coastal Bend, its history, its people and its activities that you might not otherwise know or hear about.

In addition, we've included special close-up looks at topics that are particularly important or fascinating, such as the life and death of rising Tejana music star Selena or where to find the world's only flock of whooping cranes that is thriving in the wild.

We hope this book will help you appreciate this place we call home, and that you'll gain a deep insight into the past, present and future of this region. When you leave, we hope you'll take more than souvenirs and sunburn with you—you'll carry the imprint and memories of our sun-bleached land.

And while we have tried to acquaint you with the multifaceted aspects of the Corpus Christi area, we know you may have different opinions about where to go and what to see. Since the *Insiders' Guide to Corpus Christi* is updated frequently, we want to hear from you so we can include your tips in the next edition. Please contact us at Insiders' Guides, The Globe Pequot Press, P.O. Box 480, Guilford, CT 06437-0480. Or check out the Insiders' Guide website, at www.insiders.com.

Area Overview

In the vast expanse that is the state of Texas, the Corpus Christi area perches on the water's edge, curved like the inner chamber of a seashell. With its glistening waters, plentiful beaches, and year-round warmth, this sun-blessed region, also known as the Coastal Bend, has long been a favorite playground for Texans.

And no wonder. Natural wonders include coastal flats and saltwater marshes, wildlife sanctuaries and parks, epic ranches, and a colorful history. Camping, swimming, sailing, beach combing, birding, fishing, and hunting are among the myriad recreational activities that await visitors.

To help orient you to this region, let's consider the state as a whole.

Texas has 18 million people, with the humans only slightly outnumbering the state's 15 million cattle. Texas was the 28th state to join the union, and is the only state that was an independent nation (the Republic of Texas) before accepting statehood. The state's flag is red, white, and blue, like the U.S. flag. It features a single white star on a solitary blue, vertical stripe—thus earning Texas the nickname "Lone Star State"—and two wide horizontal stripes of red and white. As with the U.S. flag, the red stands for bravery, the white for strength and the blue for loyalty.

Texas is larger than all of New England, New York, Pennsylvania, Ohio, and Illinois combined—stretching 801 miles from north to south and 773 miles east to west. The state bird is the mockingbird, the state flower is the bluebonnet, and the state tree is the pecan. Texas is known for ranching, farming, and oil and gas industry, as well as fishing, hunting and beaches.

The Coastal Bend is a small, southern loop in the vast area of Texas, along a slight bend in the state's coastline, just a few hours from the Mexican border. The area has a semitropical climate with an average mean temperature of 71 degrees. The infrequent cold weather usually occurs in December and January, but seldom does it freeze. Summers can be hot, with July and August the hottest months of the year—and the temperatures have been known to exceed 100 degrees. However, breezes off the Gulf of Mexico generally keep even the hottest days from being too oppressive (see our Natural World chapter).

It takes about 2 ½ hours to drive from the north end of the Coastal Bend, beginning at the Aransas National Wildlife Refuge, to the southern tip of our region, ending below Kingsville along U.S. Highway 77.

Texans are known for their warmth, hospitality, ferocious pride, and independence. And in the Coastal Bend, residents are also known for their relaxed, no-fuss attitude and their friendliness.

When you drive along the coast, you'll encounter many communities, each varying from one another as much in size as in personality. Some towns are small, with a historical flavor; others are more industrial, developed because of the arrival of a petrochemical plant or the military. Some towns have been here for more than a century, while others are bedroom

LOOK FOR:
- North Bay Area
- Corpus Christi Area
- Port Aransas to Padre Island
- Kingsville Area

communities whose residents commute to their jobs in other cities. Some communities depend heavily on the waterfront for their livelihood—either in fishing, shrimping, or tourism. Others are largely agricultural communities, dependent on the vagaries of land and weather.

Corpus Christi, with a population of 257,453, is the region's largest city and serves as an economic and industrial hub for the rest of the area. Corpus Christi is also where many of the region's residents go to shop, dine out, or take in entertainment. But there's also plenty for tourists to see and do in surrounding communities.

In fact, tourism plays an increasingly large part in the region's economic fortunes. While Texans have always known about the Corpus Christi area's vacation charms, the area now draws many out-of-state visitors—lured here by the magnetic combination of salt air and gentle surf, sunshine and nature, fishing or boating, and fresh seafood.

Nonetheless, the Texas coast doesn't get nearly the publicity of the East and West coasts, which may be one of its charms. The Third Coast, as it is known, remains relatively undiscovered. The region offers miles of sandy stretches that rarely see human beings but that create a mecca for wildlife, including bird species rarely seen in other parts of the country.

In this chapter, we describe the communities in the Texas Coastal Bend for you, telling you a little about the present and the past of each. To make it easy for you to locate these towns on a map, we've arranged the communities into four categories: the North Bay area, which extends from the Aransas National Wildlife Refuge at the north to Portland at the south; Corpus Christi, the region's largest city, and surrounding communities; Port Aransas to Padre Island, which covers the beachfront; and the Kingsville area, including the mammoth King Ranch and surrounding small towns. Within each category, our descriptions of the towns move from north to south.

North Bay

Austwell

Just eight miles south of Aransas National Wildlife Refuge, Austwell is a small, tight-knit community on Hynes Bay. Founded in the late 1870s, its approximately 190 residents are surrounded by cotton fields and the bay waters. Once bustling with business, the town suffered bad harvests and devastation during the 1919 hurricane. Today, the main recreational activity is fishing for redfish and flounder in Hynes Bay or hunting.

Lamar

Continuing south on Texas Highway 35, you'll arrive at the town of Lamar. Named for Mirabeau B. Lamar, who in 1838 succeeded Sam Houston as president of the Republic of Texas, this community failed to develop into the bustling city that its settlers intended. In 1856, Samuel Colt and his brother, James L. Colt, known for their invention of the Colt revolver, purchased 14,000 acres here and planned a large-scale land promotion that never materialized.

To make matters worse, the city was shelled twice during the Civil War and was hit hard by the 1919 hurricane. In 1915, the post office closed and remained so for 30 years.

Today, the community contains several sites of interest to tourists. There's Goose Island State Park with the ancient live oak known as Big Tree, estimated to be about 2,000 years old. There's also the historic Lamar cemetery, Stella Maris Chapel, Schoenstatt Shrine, and the scenic drive along St. Charles Bay. Anglers and birders will find much to their liking here.

Fulton

This tiny coastal town with 812 residents is known for its wind-sculpted live oak trees and its fishing. Founded in 1866 and named for George Ware Fulton, Sr., who built a house on Aransas Bay in the 1870s, it sits side-by-side with the larger town of Rockport. In recent decades, Fulton residents have resisted annexation attempts by Rockport but have lost jurisdiction over some of their landmarks, including the Fulton Mansion, named after the town's first prominent citizen and operated today by the Texas Parks and Wildlife Department.

The waters surrounding the Corpus Christi area provide endless enjoyment.

Photo: courtesy of the Corpus Christi Convention and Visitors Bureau

The town is populated mostly by longtime residents and a few newcomers. It's less of a tourist destination than neighboring Rockport because it's less well known. Be sure to drive along lovely Fulton Beach Road, where you can watch shorebirds on the water and marvel at the beautiful trees shaped by the coastal winds.

Rockport

Known as a "sportsman's paradise," this city of 4,800 attracts those interested in fishing, birding, or waterfront living. A popular retirement home for many visitors and winter Texans,

Rockport is a place where many residents have their own boats. It's also an artists' colony and has a sizeable Vietnamese population.

Founded in the late 1800s, Rockport began as a port for cattle slaughter. Boat building and fishing emerged as important industries in the 1880s, and tourism became increasingly important as anglers came here to fish. The 1919 hurricane demolished many buildings, but the town rebuilt and the shrimping industry became a major enterprise. Today, shrimping and tourism, particularly birding tourism, are Rockport's largest industries.

Visitors come to see shorebirds and native birds as well as the hummingbirds that winter here and the endangered whooping cranes that spend the winter at the nearby Aransas National Wildlife Refuge.

The town has 11 art galleries and studios and is home to an estimated 100 artists. It was named for a rock ledge that underlies Rockport's shore.

Aransas Pass

Aransas Pass calls itself "the shrimping capital of Texas," because its livelihood is based on that small crustacean. It is home to several hundred shrimp trawlers, the largest fleet on the Gulf coast. It's also home to numerous shrimp processing plants and marinas, bait and tackle shops and public boat ramps.

The city is named for the entrance pass to Corpus Christi Bay that separates Mustang and San Jose Islands, 6 miles south. Its name, Aransas, has been traced to Spanish explorers who named the city after a shrine in Spain called **Nuestra Señora de Aranzazu** (Our Lady of Aranzazu).

The city got its start in 1909 with what some believe to be the largest and last land lottery in the United States. Tickets were sold for $100 apiece for 12,000 acres on Red Fish Bay that included the townsite of Aransas Pass. It was a lottery that no one could lose: 6,000 tickets were sold for 6,000 lots, with the only gamble being that you didn't know where your lot would be located. Interest was high in the lottery, because the U.S. government was about to finance the dredging of a port and everyone assumed it would be here, the closest outlet to the Gulf of Mexico.

INSIDERS' TIP

The city of Corpus Christi is actually built on two levels, with the older part lying along the bay at sea level and the newer section located on a 40-foot bluff.

However, the government chose Corpus Christi as the site for its port, not Aransas Pass—to the great disappointment of those who had bought the land lottery tickets. Nonetheless, the 7,600 current residents are ferociously proud of their community, particularly because Aransas Pass has always been confused with the larger, better-known, and nearby town of Port Aransas. But this town shouldn't worry; it has its own distinct personality. Long a favorite with winter Texans, this town often attracts retirees who want to settle in for peaceful coastal living.

Birders, too, are attracted here. The city bird is the brown pelican, and plenty of migrating species come through the area.

Ingleside

Developed as a resort area in the late 1800s, this community's early settlers grew grapes and bottled wines sent worldwide. Today, its main industries are major manufacturing plants such as Reynolds Aluminum, DuPont, OxyChem, and Aker Gulf Marine. The military is another mainstay of the town's economic growth. Naval Station Ingleside began with a groundbreaking in 1988, with government officials planning to develop the site as a homeport for battleships. Planners chose Ingleside as the location for the new base because of its quick access to the deep waters of the Gulf of Mexico, the well-protected waters inside the barrier islands, the existence of plenty of land for expansion and the area's potential for growth.

In 1991, military officials changed the base's focus to that of a headquarters for the Navy's mine warfare fleet and equipment. Most of the 25 ships to be ported at Ingleside have already arrived, and the town's population has swelled from 5,696 in the last census to an estimated 8,500. Today, the base is the town's largest employer, with 3,600 employees.

Nonetheless, Ingleside remains a small town, where everyone knows each other and the

Dairy Queen is the local gathering spot. And although a number of apartment complexes and new houses have been built, the town still experiences an occasional housing shortage for military newcomers and other residents, some of whom choose to live in neighboring communities or in Corpus Christi, a half-hour's drive away.

Corpus Christi Area

Gregory

Founded as a turnoff point on the railroad line to Corpus Christi, this town claims a population of about 2,500 people. Most of the residents are longtime citizens, retirees, refinery workers, and employees of the school district it shares with neighboring Portland. Many of the town's businesses were devastated by Hurricane Celia in August 1970.

The town was named after U.S. Attorney General Thomas Watt Gregory when it was established in 1886.

Portland

Situated on U.S. Highway 181 just 12 miles from Corpus Christi, Portland is a bedroom community of about 13,800. One of the town's passions is high school sports at Gregory-Portland High School, which has established a good reputation for a school its size.

The town was established by a land development firm from Wichita, Kansas, in 1891. Interest in the area dwindled until 1911, when the Coleman-Fulton Pasture Company constructed a wharf and railroad facilities to handle the emerging cotton business. The community prospered until it was hit by hurricanes in 1916 and 1919, but it rallied and continued to grow. Incorporated in 1949, Portland is known today for strong schools and churches—and it's one of the only local communities in which liquor by the glass is banned.

Corpus Christi

Just two hours from the Mexican border, the Coastal Bend's largest city is imbued with the influence of its southern neighbor—from its name, which means "body of Christ" in Spanish, to its Mexican restaurants and festivals.

The seventh-largest city in Texas, with a population of more than a quarter of a million, Corpus Christi is also South Texas's regional center for banking, retailing, healthcare, and business. It's an informal city, with a semitropical lifestyle that includes year-round access to golf, sailing, fishing, tennis, and sailboarding.

One of the city's most distinctive features is the seawall that lines the bayfront, starting in the downtown area. The seawall, which has steps that descend into the water, serves as a gathering place for visitors, strollers, joggers, bikers, and others. When city officials built the seawall, they also created the wide street known as Shoreline Boulevard at its northern end and as Ocean Drive as it progresses through the more residential section of the city. This lovely, scenic thoroughfare is one of the city's main attractions and has ensured that visitors have an expansive and unfettered view of the sparkling bay waters that have earned the city its nickname, "Sparkling City by the Sea."

Many residents take advantage of the natural amenities by making their homes on the waterfront—such as the showcase mansions that line the city's Ocean Drive—or on Padre Island, where you're likely to see fishing piers and boats in folks' backyards.

The bay was discovered by Spanish explorer Alonso Álvarez de Piñeda (see our History chapter) on the religious feast day of Corpus Christi in 1519, hence its name. The city eventually took on the same name. Three centuries later, colonists set up a frontier trading post near what is now downtown, and a community slowly developed. The city became a shipping point for Texas cattle and crops, but its greatest growth occurred when the U.S. government chose to turn the city into what is still the deepest port on the Texas coast. That, in turn, attracted the petrochemical and other industries, which are on the ship channel west of the city's downtown area.

For decades, the Corpus Christi area's main sources of revenue were oil and gas, shipping from its port, agriculture and ranching, and the military bases here. When the oil bust came in the 1980s, this region—like many others in the Lone Star State—had to reassess. Today, while oil and gas remain an important element of industry here, tourism plays an increasingly significant role.

Among attractions here are the Texas State Aquarium, the Lexington Museum on the Bay, Corpus Christi Botanical Gardens and the Columbus ships, copies of the vessels that Christopher Columbus used to discover the New World (see our Attractions chapter). The area also offers a wide variety of activities for those interested in the outdoors, from windsurfing and sailing to hunting and fishing, as well as miles of beaches to explore.

The military presence remains strong (see our Military chapter), with Naval Air Station Corpus Christi and the Corpus Christi Army Depot. The Naval Air Station is where the Navy trains student pilots to fly turboprop aircraft, many of whom then go on to fighter jet training in nearby Kingsville or at another Navy base in Meridian, Mississippi.

The Corpus Christi Army Depot is the largest tenant at the Navy base, and it's one of the world's largest helicopter repair facilities.

Violet

Continuing west on Texas Highway 44 past the airport, you'll soon arrive at the community of Violet. This is a tiny town, with an estimated population of about 160, established in the early 1900s by immigrant farmers of German descent. The town's population has gradually decreased as the community has been slowly swallowed up by the widening of the highway. Residents hold an annual Germanfest and Oktoberfest that draw visitors hungry for a taste of culture and history (see our Annual Events and Festivals chapter).

The town also contains the Violet Museum, built in 1910 and listed on state and national historic registers, inside the old St. Anthony's Catholic Church. Check it out to see candelabras, priests' vestments, and rosaries that date to the late 1800s. Named after the first storekeeper's wife, Violet Fister, the town is about 12 miles west of Corpus Christi.

Robstown

This farming community sits at the crossroads of two large highways, U.S. Highway 77 and Texas Highway 44—a stopping point for those headed to the Rio Grande Valley, Corpus Christi, Houston, or even Laredo. Established in 1907, it has about 13,000 residents and a high school baseball team, the Robstown Cotton Pickers, that's a source of fierce pride.

Many visitors may know Robstown for a famed barbecue restaurant, Joe Cotten's, which attracts folks from around the state. Celebrity patrons have included Lyndon Johnson, the Dallas Cowboys, Willie Nelson, and Robstown's own Olympic boxer, Lefty Barrera. (See our Restaurants chapter.)

Others may know the town as a political hotbed where the city council is constantly sparring and recall elections are commonplace. The area's U.S. representative, the county judge, a county commissioner and a district judge are all from this small, dusty town.

Port Aransas to Padre Island

Port Aransas

Known mostly as the "spring break capital" for thousands of college students, this island town of 2,268 residents has long played host to young vacationers. Its 18 miles of beaches have also long attracted surfers, beachcombers, anglers, and artists.

Sitting at the northern tip of Mustang Island, Port Aransas (rhymes with Kansas) is known to locals by the shortened name of "Port A." You can get here over the JFK Causeway from Corpus Christi or by the more scenic free ferryboat, which operates 24 hours a day.

Mustang Island was first called Wild Horse Island because of the wild horses called *Mestenos* that roamed its sandy shores. The horses were brought here by the Spaniards in the 1800s.

Settled in 1855, the town was first called Tarpon and Ropesville before townsfolk settled on

Miradores del Mar

The glittering white gazebos decorating the Corpus Christi seawall along the city's bayfront have more than one story to tell. Step inside these eight lighted "miradores" and discover an important moment from Corpus Christi's past. From the early days of the Spanish galleons to the formation of the King Ranch in 1853, these eight shaded overlooks recount the most crucial moments in this city's long history.

But there's more behind these small structures than meets the eye. They also serve as a tribute to a Corpus Christi resident who died in a fiery crash more than 20 years ago at the tender age of 19. The $1 million cost to build these concrete-and-tile "Miradores del Mar" came from the Devary Durrill Foundation, named for the daughter of William "Dusty" Durrill and his wife, Shirley.

Their daughter, the oldest of five children, died in 1978 when the Ford Mustang II in which she was riding burst into flames when it was hit from behind by another vehicle. The family eventually received a $12.3 million damage award from Ford Motor Co., an amount determined by a state appeals court after Ford challenged the $106.8 million jury award.

In 1984, the Durrills decided to honor their daughter by using the money to start a charitable foundation in her name. Over the years the foundation has contributed to several worthy causes, including the Art Center of Corpus Christi on Shoreline Boulevard and a Department of Public Safety program designed to teach children to avoid drugs.

Durrill, a former beer distributor, came up with the idea for the miradores after noticing similar structures in other coastal communities. His offer to do the same in Corpus Christi originally met with resistance from city officials, who considered proposed changes to the 2-mile-long historical structure as something akin to heresy.

But Durrill persisted and, in October 1991, the miradores were dedicated in a colorful and festive ceremony that included a wedding. Since that time, hundreds of weddings have been performed in the miradores, which look out over Corpus Christi Bay and nearby attractions.

These octagonal-shaped buildings are open to the sea breezes, offering passers-by a shady, cool retreat from the often harsh Corpus Christi sun. Water fountains and benches provide additional comfort to seaside travelers, who often bide their time reading the historical plaques mounted on pedestals near the center.

So step inside, enjoy the view and take a moment to pay tribute to a city's past—and to a young woman whose tragic end inadvertently made it all possible.

the name Port Aransas. Aransas comes from the Spanish word "aranzazu," which means "a place of thorny bushes." Apparently early explorers had to struggle across the dense brush on the island.

President Franklin Roosevelt fished here for tarpon, and thousands of others have hauled in trophy catches. Deep-sea fishing is big business, and there are lots of fishing tournaments (see our Fishing and Hunting chapter).

The atmosphere here is laid-back, as befitting a beachfront community, and you're likely to see residents dressed in shorts and sandals throughout most of the year. Surfing, not football, is the passion of students at the local high school—in fact, in this state where high school football is practically a religion, Port Aransas High School has no football team and doesn't want one.

Longtime residents include professors and graduate students at the University of Texas Marine Science Institute, a research and education facility. Some of the dwellings here are luxurious waterfront condos, while others are simple houses on pilings to prevent flood damage from a hurricane.

Plan to take the ferry across the Corpus Christi Ship Channel and visit some of the beach shops or seafood restaurants. Expect to wait in line at the ferry during the busiest summer months.

Kingsville Area

Bishop

Positioned along U.S. Highway 77 south of Corpus Christi, this coastal prairie community is named after founder Frances Zion Bishop, an ambitious insurance agent. Established in 1910 as an agricultural town, the community has since added a strong industrial base.

In 1945, Celanese Corporation of America opened a plant in Bishop. Now known as Hoechst-Celanese, it produces chemicals, plastics, polymers and pharmaceuticals. It also employs 1,100 full-time and 500 contract workers—nearly half the community's 3,337 residents. The plant also provides one of the town's two private swimming pools.

The community has a birding trail and a city park. The city-owned Bishop Airport has a paved, lighted, 3,200-foot runway.

The town's claim to fame is Ronnie Bull, a 1958 graduate of Bishop High School, who played football at Baylor University, then went on to the Chicago Bears. He was named Rookie of the Year in 1963 and played professional ball for about a dozen years.

Driscoll

Surrounded by maize and cotton fields, this community sits on U.S. Highway 77 about 30 miles south of Corpus Christi. Driscoll has about 700 residents, most of them farmers and workers at the Denton Petroleum Company. Those who live here tend to go to nearby Kingsville or to Corpus Christi for entertainment and shopping. Driscoll's claim to fame is native son and tennis champion Steve Denton, a two-time finalist at the Australian Open who was known for his powerful serve. His 139-m.p.h. serve still is listed in the *Guinness Book of World Records*. He played on the men's tour for 11 years, ranked No. 2 in doubles and No. 11 in singles in 1982.

Kingsville

Established by the bequest of ranch owner Henrietta King, this city boasts long ties with the state's cowboy heritage. The area was once known as the Wild Horse Desert and now serves as main entrance to the 825,000-acre King Ranch.

The ranch, itself a National Historic Landmark, is recognized as the birthplace of the American ranching industry. Its history is worth telling. When steamboat captain Richard King founded his ranch, he went looking for workers. He rode down to Mexico and into a small village, where he told the assembled residents that he would clothe, feed, and house anyone who came back with him. He returned with the entire village, and the people who lived on the King Ranch became known as *kiñenos*, or King's Men. Today, you can find third- and fourth-generation *kiñenos* still living and working on the ranch.

INSIDERS' TIP

Port Aransas has been through several name changes— originally known as Mustang Island, its name was changed to Ropesville in the 1890s, then Tarpon to celebrate the local fishing industry. It received the name Port Aransas in 1911.

Kingsville was created because King Ranch officials saw the need for a railroad terminal near the ranch. Today officials celebrate the day the first passenger stepped off the St. Louis, Brownsville, and Mexico Railway (July 4, 1904) as the town's birthday. The town incorporated in 1911, and its first businesses were also established by the King Ranch, including a hotel, an ice plant, a waterworks, a cotton gin, and a weekly newspaper.

Today, with approximately 26,000 residents, the town has a diverse economy based on manufacturing, ranching, tourism, aircraft maintenance, military and education. Historic mission-style buildings often sit beside newly built retail super centers. The town gained a little national infamy a few years ago when a resident began a campaign to get people to greet each other with the word "Heaven-o" instead of "Hello." He didn't like using the word "hell" so much. Thank heaven, the campaign fizzled.

The city also is home to Texas A&M University–Kingsville, a university that has long been known for producing some of the state's best teachers and engineers.

Yet another major source of income is the military. Kingsville is the proud home of the Navy's advanced jet training base, Naval Air Station Kingsville. This is where student pilots learn to fly fighter jets.

There's a quieter side to Kingsville, including its renovated downtown historic district and its plentiful parks. Birders flock here, particularly to see the green jay (the official city bird), which can be seen from Kingsville through South America.

Ricardo

This community began its life as a flag stop on the railway route from Riviera to Kingsville. In 1908, King Ranch officials laid out a town site christened Ricardo that was complete with a little park surrounding a flowing well. Its original park and well no longer exist, but it has its own school district, churches, and cotton gin.

The farmer's co-op is the main industry, but it's also a bedroom community for people who work in Kingsville. The community's estimated population is about 800.

Riviera

This agricultural town is the next stop when you travel south from Kingsville. This community also has its own school district, post office and telephone company, and there is even a small business district with a Dairy Queen restaurant. Although the town is unincorporated, the post office estimates that Riviera has about 600 residents.

Founded in 1907, the town received its name from a German developer who hoped it would equal its namesake on the Mediterranean. However, even the pronunciation didn't last—it's pronounced Ree-VAIR-a. And instead of becoming a watering hole for the wealthy, Riviera became a community too small to incorporate but too strong-willed to disappear. Landowners tried to promote the area as a travel destination, but their plans fell through, and hurricanes wiped out the biggest hotel. Today, Riviera is mostly popular with winter Texans and retirees, who bring their mobile homes here.

The area offers excellent fishing and hunting, as well as a high school baseball team that won three state titles in the past 20 years.

The best-known place in town is the King's Inn, a seafood restaurant that numbers patrons from around the globe, some of whom arrive in airplanes or helicopters. Famous guests include Governor George W. Bush, former Governor Ann Richards, and country-and-western singer George Strait. The restaurant, on Baffin Bay, was established in 1935 as a hamburger stand on the waterfront near the pier. Today, it specializes in excellent fried shrimp, fish, onion rings, and salads (see our Restaurants chapter).

Getting Here, Getting Around

Corpus Christi isn't exactly at the center of the universe. Come to think of it, Corpus Christi isn't at the center of anything. Many area residents, on the other hand, will tell you the city is located at the end of the earth. That's not true. It's actually at the end of Interstate Highway 37, which stops when it gets to Corpus Christi Bay. Because no interstate runs through the area, the only people who come here are those who planned to in the first place.

This is not necessarily a bad thing. Many Insiders like the area's out-of-the-way location and relatively sparse population. So do the thousands of tourists who visit each year. And despite the increase in tourism during the past decade, the area remains relatively uncrowded and undeveloped. Tired of crowded beaches and overdeveloped vacation spots? Then you'll love the Corpus Christi area, where you can still find secluded beaches and restaurants where you won't have to wait for a table.

Most people will arrive here by car or aircraft. A few will arrive by private boat. Others will fly their private planes to the area. No matter what your form of transportation, you'll find helpful information in this chapter on getting to the area. You'll also find out how to get around once you've arrived. Some things to consider before you arrive:

• The roads that bring you here are generally flat and straight, and the scenery is, well, repetitive. The stretch of road between San Antonio and Corpus Christi should be bottled as a cure for insomnia. You'll travel the entire 140-mile stretch of road without encountering a single city, although you will see several convenience stores and ranch and farmland. On a more positive note, Texans love to drive, so for the most part you'll find the highways wide and in good condition.

Visitors can travel on the Flagship for fun, panoramic tours of the Bay.

Photo: Daniel Fielder

• Don't misinterpret the finger-wave. In many parts of the country a single uplifted finger is grounds for a fist fight. Texans rarely get angry enough to make rude gestures to a fellow driver, especially motorists in Corpus Christi, although there are always exceptions. The finger-wave as it is used here is a single finger (usually the index finger) lifted from the steering wheel in acknowledgment of the passengers in an approaching car. Think of it as a nonverbal way of saying "Howdy." You're most likely to encounter the finger-wave on rural two-lane roads.

• Driving on the shoulders is OK in Texas when you're letting someone pass, provided it's an improved shoulder and isn't posted with signs prohibiting it. Someone crowding your bumper as you speed along the highway? Don't dig in your heels and make them pass in the oncoming traffic lane. Drive friendly, the Texas way, and move over to the shoulder. The motorist (or motorists) behind you will pass you with a friendly wave as their way of saying thanks. It's considered polite to say "you're welcome" with a finger-wave.

• Trucks, trucks, and more trucks. If you're from the Northeast or Midwest you'll see more trucks on a trip to Texas than you've seen in your entire life. Watch out for Suburbans, too, dubbed by Texas Monthly Magazine as "The National Car of Texas."

• Public transportation is rare in Texas. The only public transportation of note in the Corpus Christi area is the bus system based in Corpus Christi, which we discuss in the Getting Around section of this chapter. If you don't have a car, you'll find it hard to get around in the Corpus Christi area. But if you do, you'll find it amazingly easy to navigate the uncrowded roadways.

• All front-seat passengers of cars and light trucks must wear auto safety belts.

• Texas law makes it illegal for drivers to have an open container of alcohol in the cab of an automobile, and Corpus Christi law forbids anyone in the vehicle from having an open container of alcohol.

• Don't Mess With Texas: You can be fined as much as $1,000 for littering.

• The speed limit in Texas is 70 miles per hour on many rural roadways and rural sections of interstates.

Getting Here

Major Roadways

Interstate Highway 37 connects Corpus Christi and San Antonio, a distance of 140 miles. In San Antonio IH-37 connects with Interstate Highway 10 to Houston and West Texas and Interstate Highway 35 to Austin, Dallas, and Fort Worth.

In Corpus Christi IH-37 connects the Annaville, Calallen, Five Points, and Tuloso-Midway neighborhoods on the city's northwest side with the rest of the city. U.S. Highway 77 connects Kingsville and Corpus Christi and is the most direct route to and from the Rio Grande Valley on the Mexican border. U.S. 77 stretches as far south as Brownsville and as far north as Dallas, where it joins with IH-35. When traveling to the Rio Grande Valley, expect to stop at the Sarita checkpoint south of Kingsville. The purpose of the checkpoint, operated by the U.S. Border Patrol, is to stem the flow of illegal drugs and immigrants into the United States.

Another route to the border is Texas Highway 44 W. connecting with U.S. Highway 59 to Laredo. U.S. Highway 181 runs north from IH-37 near the Corpus Christi bayfront. It crosses the Harbor Bridge, Corpus Christi Beach and the Nueces Bay Causeway on its way to Portland. After passing through Portland, it veers northwest through several small towns until it reaches San Antonio, but this is not the preferred route to San Antonio. The quickest, most direct route to the Alamo city is along IH-37, although, as we mentioned earlier, the scenery leaves much to be desired.

Texas Highway 35 runs from U.S. 181 north of Portland to Aransas Pass and Rockport. There are two Texas 35s: Business 35 runs north from Aransas Pass along the water to Rockport, and the second bypasses Aransas Pass on its way to Rockport.

Texas Highway 361 runs east from Texas 35 to Ingleside, Aransas Pass, Harbor Island and the north ferry landing to Port Aransas. It then heads south down Mustang Island to Park Road 22 at the southern edge of Corpus Christi. Park Road 22 begins at the southeastern end of Texas Highway 358, known locally as South Padre Island Drive, and continues to the entrance to Padre Island National Seashore.

Texas 358 runs from west of the Crosstown Expressway (Texas 286) to Naval Air Station

Corpus Christi on the city's southeast side. The section of Texas 358 west of The Crosstown Expressway is referred to as North Padre Island Drive, while the section to the east is referred to as South Padre Island Drive, or SPID for short. The Crosstown Expressway connects IH-37 with South Padre Island Drive (also known as Texas 358) on a mostly north-to-south basis. The Crosstown Expressway is officially designated as Texas Highway 286, but if you ask for it by that name locals won't know what you're talking about.

Ocean Drive/Shoreline Boulevard runs along the Corpus Christi bayfront from north of Interstate 37 to Naval Air Station Corpus Christi. Shoreline Boulevard starts at the South Texas Institute for the Arts to the north and ends at the Furman Street intersection, where it becomes Ocean Drive.

Some visitors will be perplexed by the letters "F.M." seen on many rural road signs. The F.M. stands for Farm-to-Market, as in Farm-to-Market Road 3512. A Farm-to-Market road is simply a rural roadway originally constructed to help farmers and ranchers deliver their goods to nearby markets.

Bus Lines

Greyhound Bus Lines
702 N. Chaparral St., Corpus Christi
• **(361) 882-2516, (800) 231-2222**
• **www.greyhound.com**

Greyhound Bus Lines operates several buses per day from Corpus Christi to San Antonio, Houston, Dallas, Austin and other points throughout the state, nation, Mexico and Canada. It also provides bus service to Kingsville. For information in Spanish call (800) 531-5332.

Call for information on advanced purchase specials or visit the Greyhound Bus Lines web site.

Valley Transit Company
702 N. Chaparral St., Corpus Christi
• **(361) 882-2516, (800) 580-4710**
215 E. Monroe St., Harlingen
• **(956) 423-4287 or (956) 423-4288**
• **www.valleytransitcompany.com**

This company connects the Rio Grande Valley to northern Mexico, Corpus Christi, San Antonio, Austin, Houston and points in between. Valley Transit buses stop in the Corpus Christi-area towns of Kingsville, Corpus Christi, Aransas Pass, and Rockport. At the Corpus Christi terminal, Valley Transit Company passengers can connect with Greyhound Bus Lines

routes to destinations throughout the United States, Mexico and Canada. Call for route and fare information or go to their website.

Airports

Corpus Christi International Airport
1000 International Dr., Corpus Christi
• **(361) 289-0171**

There's good news and bad news when it comes to flying into Corpus Christi International Airport. The good news is the airport is small and easy to get around in. The bad news? Getting here may mean you'll have to fly on a bumpy, noisy turboprop airplane. Five airlines serve Corpus Christi International Airport, which opened in 1958, but only one uses jets on a full-time basis. Another uses a mixture of jets and turboprops, and the others use turboprops exclusively.

There's more good news/bad news. Construction has begun on a 40- to 50-year master plan to upgrade the airport's facilities at an eventual cost of $70 million to $80 million. The upgrade will eventually mean an additional 30 gates, more cargo planes, a new runway, and 1,400 acres added to the airport.

Short-term plans call for a redesigned terminal and a new control tower, which means you may have to endure detours, noise, and a certain amount of mess associated with any construction project. The redesigned terminal will have a larger, brighter ticket lobby and a spacious open area for artwork and a new food court and retail area offering more dining and shopping options for customers.

A new lounge, which may include a restaurant, will be twice the size of the present food court and would overlook the runway. The new terminal also would include a business center to allow travelers to conduct meetings and plug in their laptops. The plans call for a new baggage area closer to the exits and twice the space for ticket counters. All this comes immediately after a recent $12 million face-lift to expand and renovate the facilities. Improvements include a new food court, lounge and baggage claim area; renovations to the front of the building; and new restrooms, signs, and carpeting. The improvements are needed to keep local travelers from taking their business elsewhere. Airlines often charge a higher fare to fly from Corpus Christi than they do from other cities, because of its remote location, which prompts many travelers to drive to Houston or San Antonio to catch a plane.

The airport is located south of Texas Highway 44 on the west side of town. You can get there from just about anywhere in town in 15 to 20 minutes. From downtown take Interstate 37 toward San Antonio and head south on Texas 44. From the south side of town, take South Padre Island Drive (Texas 358) past the Crosstown Expressway (Texas 286) and veer to the east on Texas 44. Follow the signs and you won't get lost. The airport terminal runs east-to-west. The entrance is on the northern side of the building. You approach it via a parkway running from Texas 44.

Long-term parking is situated farthest from the terminal; hourly parking is closest. Airport parking lots are open from 5 AM to 1 AM daily. The long-term parking fee is 75¢ per hour, with a maximum of $7 per 24 hours; the charge is $7 per day if you lose your ticket. The fee for hourly parking is $1 per half-hour, with a maximum of $10 per 24 hours and a $10-per-day charge for lost tickets.

The four airlines serving Corpus Christi provide a variety of arrival and departure options:

• American Eagle/American Airlines, (800) 433-7300, offers seven arrivals and departures Sunday through Friday and six on Saturday to and from Dallas-Fort Worth International Airport via turboprop. Passengers board and unload at Gate 16 and Gate 1.

• Continental/Continental Express, (361) 883-3554 or (800) 525-0280, provides 11 arrivals and departures Monday through Friday, 10 on Saturday and eight on Sunday to and from Houston Intercontinental Airport via turboprop and jet. Passengers board and unload at Gates 12 for turboprops and 15 for jets.

• Atlantic Southeast Airlines/Delta, (361) 289-6893 or (800) 282-3424, providing connecting flights to Delta Airlines, offers two arrivals and departures each day to and from Dallas-Fort Worth International Airport via jets. Passengers board and unload at Gate 11.

• Austin Express, (888) 325-2879, offers four arrivals and departures Monday through Friday to and from Austin-Bergstrom International Airport via 19-seater turboprops. Passengers board and unload at Gate 7.

• Southwest Airlines, (800) 435-9792, offers eight arrivals and departures Monday through Friday, four on Saturday and six on Sunday to and from Houston's Hobby Airport via jets. Passengers board and unload at Gate 5.

For now, gates 1, 2, 5, and 7 are on the east side of the terminal. The Southwest and Austin Express gates are at the far end of that side. Gates 11, 12, 15, and 16 are on the west side of the terminal. And what about the other gates?

For now they don't exist, but with construction continuing well into 2001 all this could change by the time you get here. The single baggage claim area is in the middle of the terminal next to the rental car agencies.

Airline ticket counters are just inside the terminal entrance on the west side. Arrivals and departures are listed on the wall behind each airline's counter. Smoking is prohibited in all public areas. Inside the terminal you'll find the usual amenities—restrooms, courtesy phones, gift shop, lounge, and snack bar—and Riviera Reds, a seafood market where you can have local seafood packaged to take with you or shipped to an address.

Recent additions include a Whataburger hamburger restaurant, Pizza Hut Express, a delicatessen, and an ice cream shop. Prices here aren't as high as those in other airports we've visited, and they've maintained their small-town atmosphere. You'll find fewer surly employees and more smiling faces at the restaurants and elsewhere in the airport.

Rental car agencies with facilities at the airport include the following: Avis Rent-A-Car, (361) 289-0073; Hertz, (361) 289-0777; Dollar Rent A Car, (361) 289-2886; Budget Rent A Car, (361) 289-0434; and National Car Rental, (361) 289-0515.

You'll find taxicabs and shuttles through the doors opposite the baggage-claim carousel and between the rental car booths. You'll generally find several taxis waiting to take passengers to their hotels. Cab rates are $1.50 a mile with a minimum fare of $1.50. Flat rates are available for trips from the airport to surrounding communities.

Several hotels in the area provide free transportation. They include: Holiday Inn Airport, (361) 289-5100 or (800) 465-4329; Embassy Suites, (361) 853-7899 or (800) 362-2779; Drury Inn Airport, (361) 289-8200 or (800) 325-8300; Ramada Inn Bayfront, (361) 882-8100 or (800) 272-6232; Holiday Inn-Emerald Beach, (361) 883-5731 or 800-465-4329; Travelodge Airport, (361) 289-5666 or 800-531-1344; Omni Bayfront, (361) 887-1600 or (800) 843-6664; and Ramada Limited, (361) 289-5861.

Staff and students reporting to the Mine Warfare Training Center call 800-675-6982; Mine Warfare Commands, Ships Squadrons, Rotational Crews call the Mine Warfare Command Quarterdeck at (361) 961-4858; military personnel requiring transportation to Naval Station Ingleside and all others call (800) 577-6289.

Corpus Christi International Airport is a controlled airport with two runways. One is 7,500 feet long and 150 feet wide; the other is

GETTING HERE, GETTING AROUND

6,080 feet long and 150 feet wide. Jet fuel and low-lead fuel are available for private pilots. Tie-downs, hangar space, courtesy cars, pilots' lounge, avionics center, weather-briefing room and aircraft maintenance are available. For further information call Mercury Air Center at (361) 289-1881 or Signature Flight Support at (361) 289-0585.

Aransas County Airport
Texas Hwy. 35, Rockport
• **(361) 790-0141**

This uncontrolled airport north of town straddles the Fulton city limits on the west side of Texas 35. The airport, which serves private and Navy airplanes only, has three runways: one 5,600 feet long and 150 feet wide, and the other two 4,500 feet long and 150 feet wide. Jet A and 100 low-lead fuel is available.

The airport has a rotating beacon, automatic dusk-to-dawn lighting, lighted wind cone, tie-down area, pilots' lounge, and rental cars. There are no landing or tie-down fees, and there's a waiting list for hangar space. Pilots should watch out for Navy T-34 traffic. Navy student pilots practice touch-and-goes Monday through Thursday from 10 AM to 5 PM. The airport's unicom frequency is 122.8. A maintenance facility is located at the airport but is often closed.

T.P. McCampbell Airport
F.M. Rd. 3512, north of Ingleside
• **(361) 758-9910**

This airport owned and operated by San Patricio County is located south of Texas Highway 35, 3 miles west of Aransas Pass and 2 miles north of Ingleside. The airport has a 75-foot-by-5,000-foot runway with a full-length 40-foot taxiway capable of handling aircraft weighing as much as 30,000 pounds. The facility can handle single- and twin-engine aircraft and a limited number of business jets.

Other features include a rotating beacon, lighted wind cone, and a lighting system that must be keyed on at 123.0. Jet A and 100 low-lead fuel are available, but there is neither a maintenance facility nor hangar space. The unicom call frequency is 122.7. A paved tie-down area is available; there are no landing or tie-down fees. Amenities include a pilots' lounge (open from 8 AM to 5 PM), a pay phone, and rental cars from nearby Aransas Pass.

Mustang Beach Airport
Piper Blvd. and U.S. Hwy. 361,
Port Aransas
• **(361) 749-4111**

The runway at this uncontrolled airport 2.5 miles south of Port Aransas is 3,500 feet long and 75 feet wide. The facility has automatic dusk-to-dawn lighting and a rotating beacon but no fuel or maintenance facilities. Amenities are limited to a pay phone and a room where pilots can plan their trips. Rental and courtesy cars are not available, but a free shuttle comes by every 60 minutes from 10 AM to 5:30 PM every day except Thanksgiving and Christmas. The telephone number for a local taxicab company can be found on the door to the pilots' room. There are no tie-down fees during the day, but an overnight stay costs $5 each night on the tarmac and $4 a night on grass. Public hangar space is not available. The unicom call frequency is 122.9.

Kleberg County Airport
Texas Hwy. 141, 9 miles west of Kingsville
• **(361) 595-8540**

The runway at this uncontrolled airport is 5,999 feet long and 75 feet wide. It's equipped with automatic dawn-to-dusk lights as well as slope-indicator and runway-end lights. Pilots can increase the intensity of the lights with five clicks of the microphone; seven clicks will increase the intensity further. Jet A and 100 low-lead fuel are available. Maintenance and pilots' lessons also are available. Facilities include a pilots' lounge but no courtesy or on-site rental cars, although a rental car can be delivered to the airport from an agency in Kingsville, 10 to 15 minutes away.

Tie-downs are available, as is some hangar space. There are no landing fees. Hangar space goes for $10 a night for single-engine planes and $25 a night for twin-engine. There is no tie-down fee. The unicom call frequency is 122.7.

Marinas

Rockport Harbor
Downtown Rockport
• **(361) 729-6661**

From the Intracoastal Waterway head west at Marker 49 and go straight in along the marked channel. Rockport Harbor fronts the downtown area near the Texas Maritime Museum and the Rockport Center for the Arts (see our Attractions and Arts chapters). Restaurants, shops and a grocery store are within walking distance. Docking fees for vessels up to 29 feet in length are $10 a night without electricity and $12 a night with electricity. Other nightly fees are: 30 to 39 feet, $14 without electricity and $17 with electricity; 40 to 49 feet, $18 without electricity and $22 with electricity; more than 50 feet, $22 without electricity and $27 with electricity. Recent additions include showers and 30-amp breakers on transient slips. Fuel is not available but can be purchased nearby.

Dennis Dreyer Municipal Harbor
North of the south ferry landing,
Port Aransas
• **(361) 749-5429**

Boaters arriving from the north should follow the Intracoastal Waterway to Port Aransas, while those coming from the south should follow the Corpus Christi Ship Channel. The city harbor is just north of the south ferry landing and adjacent to Roberts Point Park (see our Parks chapter).

The marina has 20 spaces available for larger boats and six for smaller ones. Slip fees range from $8 to $30 a day, depending on the size of the boat. Showers, restrooms and laundry facilities are available. Fuel, groceries, and maintenance are available nearby.

San Patricio
County Navigation District Marina
1 mile southwest of Dale Miller Bridge,
Aransas Pass
• **(361) 758-1890**

Boaters arriving from the north along the Intracoastal Waterway should sail past Conn Brown Harbor and under the Dale Miller Bridge. Go about a mile, look to your right and you'll see the navigation district marina adjacent to public boat ramps and a public fishing pier. Boaters coming from the south will pass the Aransas Pass Community Park (see our Parks chapter) and a wastewater treatment plant.

Boat slips are available for $18 a day with electricity and water or $15 a day for slips without electricity. Large slips can accommodate boats from 38 to 50 feet long and 15 feet wide. Slips without electricity designed for smaller boats are available for $13 a day. Ice, fuel, bait, tackle, and snacks can be purchased nearby. Boat maintenance is available in Aransas Pass. A pump-out station has recently been added.

Corpus Christi Municipal Marina
Corpus Christi Bayfront,
 across from downtown Corpus Christi
• **(361) 882-7333**

The Corpus Christi Marina is one of the more eye-pleasing sites in the Corpus Christi area. Whitewashed sailboats with colorful rigging cluster along the perimeter of the T-shaped and L-shaped land masses jutting from the Corpus Christi Seawall. You can drive, bike, or walk down these man-made peninsulas or fish from the rock jetties forming a semicircle around the marina.

Boaters arriving via the Intracoastal Waterway should head west along the Corpus Christi Ship Channel toward the Harbor Bridge. From there you have two choices: cut across the bay and take the eastern entrance to the marina or continue farther along the ship channel before turning to port and enter via the northern entrance along the seawall. Deeper draft vessels will prefer the northern entrance.

On the Peoples Street T-Head, to the north, you'll find shrimping boats, fishing charter vessels, a seafood restaurant, paddleboat rentals, and tour boats. On the Lawrence Street T-Head, you'll find another seafood restaurant, the Bay Yacht Club, air-conditioned restrooms, showers and laundry facilities for boaters only, a fuel dock with gasoline and diesel for boats and automobiles, sanitary pump-out, marina offices, and marina rescue boats. The Cooper's Alley L-Head is home to the Corpus Christi Yacht Club, a newly built bait shop, air-conditioned restrooms, showers and laundry facilities available to boaters only, three public boat ramps, yacht sales, a haul-out facility, a sailing school, charter services, and boat storage.

More than 500 wet slips are available for pleasure or commercial vessels. The marina staff monitors the Coast Guard VHF Channel 16 and provides 24-hour patrols. Leasing rates are available on a visiting and long-term basis. Rates for visiting vessels are based on the length overall (LOA) of a vessel plus a minimum $2 per night utility fee. Electricity charges in metered slips will be calculated on a kilowatt-hour basis. See the gray box for visiting vessel rates.

> **Dockage Rates**
> **Wet slips** (minimums in parentheses):
> Daily, $.50/linear foot +$2 ($17/day)
> Weekly, $3/linear foot +$14 ($104/week)
> Monthly, $6/linear foot +$60 ($240/month)
> **Trailer/Boat Storage**:
> Daily, $5.50
> Weekly, $22
> Monthly, $64

Long-term slip lease rates are for a minimum of six months. The first and last month's rent is due when the lease is executed. Gate keys and security passes are issued to boat owners; a refundable $12 per key deposit is required on gate and restroom keys.

Floating and fixed piers are available. Monthly lease rates are based on the overall length of a vessel or slip, whichever is greater, plus electrical rates based on a vessel's overall length. Lease rates are $3.31 per linear foot for pleasure crafts and $4.40 per linear foot for commercial crafts.

Monthly electrical rates are charged according to the type and length of boat. For commercial boats, the rates are $7 up to 20 feet, $9.50 from 20.1 to 30 feet, $14.50 from 30.1 to 40 feet, and $23 for 40.1 feet and longer. Pleasure craft pay $3.75 for up to 20 feet, $6.87 for 20.1 to 30 feet, $13.12 for 30.1 to 40 feet, and $23.75 for 40.1 feet and longer.

Drinking water is available at each slip at no additional charge. Gear boxes rent for $3.75 to $5 a month, or a personal gear box may be installed with Marina Office approval. A flat rate of $50.74 a month is the fee for trailered boat storage, limited to boats 26 feet long or shorter. A flat rate of $12.98 a month for upper racks or $16.52 a month for lower racks is charged for board boat storage.

The marina offices are open from 8 AM to 5 PM every day.

Getting Around

As we mentioned previously, getting around in the Corpus Christi area is fairly easy, unless you're without a car. Roads are generally well maintained, and traffic is light except during rush hour and the Christmas shopping season.

Many downtown and uptown streets are one way, so watch the signs. Streets here are slightly narrower than in many parts of town, so RV drivers may want to avoid these areas.

Driving is allowed on most area beaches. The speed limit is 15 miles per hour, and Texas motor vehicle laws are enforced. For more information see our Beaches and Watersports chapter.

Public Transportation

The Regional Transportation Authority (RTA) in Corpus Christi operates the only public bus system in the Corpus Christi area. "The B," as the system is known, covers about 830 square miles from Port Aransas to far west Nueces County, carrying more than 18,000 people on an average day. The majority of its riders live in Corpus Christi, where the RTA provides 21 regular weekday and Saturday

INSIDERS' TIP

The Corpus Christi city council has voted to dredge a channel between the Gulf of Mexico and the Laguna Madre, a move that supporters say will be a boon for development and detractors argue will be detrimental to the environment.

routes and 10 Sunday routes. Sunday service connects the west and north sides with the southside shopping district. It also provides links to the city from the Calallen and Flour Bluff neighborhoods. Remember, service is limited on Sundays so check the schedules.

The B operates a reduced level of service or no service on certain holidays. Hours range from as early as 5 AM to as late as 10:30 PM. Check individual routes for times. Schedules for all routes are available at most H.E.B. Food Stores, or you can call the B RideLine at (361) 289-2600 to have one mailed to you. System maps outlining every bus route offered by the RTA also are available.

One of the best services the RTA provides is help in planning a trip. Let's say you need to get from your hotel to the Texas State Aquarium but have no idea which bus or buses to take. Simply call the B RideLine at (361) 289-2600 and they'll tell you how to get there and back.

To ride the B, look for a sign with red, blue and orange stripes and a large B on the top with the words "Bus Stop" below. The system has more than 15,000 bus stops. Buses are white with the same red, blue and orange stripes trailing from the B logo. Route numbers and names appear above buses' windshields. The RTA offers the following tips: Be at your stop at least five minutes before the scheduled departure time; have correct change; stay seated until the bus comes to a complete stop; and exit through the rear door.

Fares on weekdays are 50¢ for adults and 25¢ for seniors and the disabled (with a B I.D. or Medicare card) during peak hours (6 to 9 AM and 3 to 6 PM) and 10¢ during non-peak hours and 25¢ for students (with I.D.). Saturday fares are 25¢ per boarding for adults; children younger than 6 ride free. Fares on Sundays are 50¢ for adults and 25¢ for students, seniors, disabled and those on Medicare. Fares on Park & Ride routes are 75¢ to $1. Park and Ride routes are designed for commuters going to and coming from the Corpus Christi Army Depot and Naval Air Station Corpus Christi. Current service is Monday through Thursday. Transfers (good for unlimited transfers for two hours after issue) are free. If you board after 7 PM, your transfer slip will be good for the rest of the night.

Care-B/Paratransit service is public transportation designed for persons whose disabilities prevent them from using regular RTA buses. Care-B is a curb-to-curb service for certified riders. You must call 24 hours in advance to schedule a trip. Care-B services are available Monday through Saturday from 5 AM to 10 PM and Sunday from 11 AM to 7 PM. Fares are 75¢ per boarding plus $2 for trips that begin or end three-quarters of a mile outside the RTA's fixed-route service area. Call the RTA at (361) 289-2600 for details.

Don't want to mess with change and transfers? Then try a B Bus Pass for unlimited rides. A weekly pass is $5; monthly passes are $20. Monthly discount passes for a fixed route for disabled, senior citizens and students are $11 with proper I.D. Monthly Care-B passes must be purchased at the B Customer Service Center at 1806 S. Alameda St. from 8 AM to 5 PM Monday through Friday. Photo I.D. cards are free to seniors, Medicare riders and the disabled. They're available from 8 AM to 5 PM Monday through Friday at the B Customer Service Center, 1806 S. Alameda St. Students pay $3. Replacement I.D. cards are $3 for seniors and the disabled and $5 for students.

During the summer months (late May through early September) the RTA offers a number of services for tourists. Scenic Trail (No. 73), a bus designed to look like an old-time trolley, takes riders to Corpus Christi's historic sights; and Corpus Christi Beach Shuttle (No. 76) takes you to Corpus Christi Beach and the many attractions there. Regular and Saturday rates apply to the Scenic Trail, while the Corpus Christi Beach Shuttle is free.

For a $1 fare per boarding, Water Taxi (No. 77) ferries passengers from downtown Corpus Christi to Corpus Christi Beach and back via the ship channel.

Tourists will also be interested in the Port Aransas Shuttle (No. 94), a free ride offered daily from 10 AM to 5:55 PM in Port Aransas. It passes many, if not most, of the city's hot spots, including Roberts Point Park, University of Texas Marine Science Institute, Nueces County Park, Horace Caldwell Pier, the post office, Mustang Beach Airport, the public library, city hall, chamber of commerce and the offices of the Port Aransas police, EMS and county constable.

Taxis and Limousines

This is not New York City. You can't just step outside your hotel and hail a cab. Try it and you'll stand there so long that you could get arrested for loitering. The only place you'll find unoccupied cabs is at the Corpus Christi International Airport. Otherwise you have to call for your cab. Rates are $1.50 a mile with a minimum of $1.50 per trip.

Limousine service is available for $75 to $90 an hour depending on the size of the car. Flat rates are charged for trips from the airport to surrounding communities. For shuttle service between the Hampton Inn Hotel in Corpus Christi, 5209 Blanch Moore Drive, and the San Antonio airport or other San Antonio destinations, call Coastal Breeze Transportation at (361) 937-7079 or (800) 838-5577. Rates are $34 one way or $60 round trip for adults and $17 one way and $30 round trip for children.

Corpus Christi area taxicab and limousine services include the following:

In Rockport, Arrow Airport Taxi Service, (361) 729-8294; Rockport Fulton Taxi, (361) 729-8294 and Limo-Van Services, (361) 790-8294; and

In Aransas Pass, City Airport Limo and Taxi Service, (361) 758-5858 or (800) 874-0025.

In Corpus Christi, Admiral Limousines, (361) 225-3002; Classic Carriages Limousine Services, (361) 949-2527; City Cab, (361) 881-8294; Limousines Unlimited, 884-5466; The Limousine Company, (361) 814-5466; Liberty Taxi Service, (361) 882-7654 or (888) 520-7673; Pinkie's Taxi, (361) 881-5250; Star Cab Company, (361) 884-9451; United Taxi Cab Co., (361) 852-5555 and United Yellow Checker Cab, (361) 884-3211.In Port Aransas, Port A. Taxi Service, (361) 749-7678 or (888) 381-7287; American Cab Company, (361) 749-7678; and Island, Port Aransas, (800)-543-6467.

In Kingsville, Yellow Cab, (361) 592-3311.

History

At more than a quarter million people, Corpus Christi is by far the largest municipality in the region known as the Texas Coastal Bend, leading the way in population, commerce, and political clout. What began as a tiny trading post in 1839 has grown to the seventh-largest city in Texas.

Compared with other parts of the country, the Corpus Christi area is relatively young. The first Anglo-American settlers arrived here in 1828, more than 200 years after the first English colonists landed in Jamestown, Virginia. In the 172 years since those first settlers arrived, the Corpus Christi area has grown from a collection of rugged frontier outposts to a thriving mixture of metropolitan, rural and tourist communities. But to focus merely on Anglo-American settlers wouldn't be fair to the explorers, Spanish and Mexican colonists and Native Americans who came before them.

Early Inhabitants

The first people to settle in the area that now encompasses Corpus Christi arrived more than 8,000 years ago. They were descendants of North America's first inhabitants, who crossed the land bridge from Siberia to Alaska at the end of the Ice Age about 20,000 years ago. Little is known of these early settlers other than they used tools, hunted in groups, used flint spears and left during a drought 3,000 years after they arrived. A second group moved into the area 1,000 to 3,000 years later from the Edwards Plateau in West Texas. They ate shellfish, snails and small animals, and campsites uncovered by archaeologists revealed small spear points, large well-made knives and conch-shell tools. This second group abandoned the area during yet another dry spell 1,200 years ago. For the next century the Corpus Christi area remained uninhabited, until a fierce and cannibalistic tribe of Indians arrived on the scene.

The Karankawa Indians

The Karankawa Indians, who may have been descendants of the area's previous inhabitants, occupied a territory from what is now the eastern outskirts of Houston to Baffin Bay, south of Corpus Christi. History has generally painted the Karankawa with a disapproving brush, although it should be noted that they never had a chance to tell their side of the story. Because they were eventually exterminated by settlers, no descendants remain to defend their honor.

Since many of them were more than six feet tall, the Karankawa were considered giants by the more diminutive European explorers who came upon them. They had finely chiseled features, and tattoos covered their faces and bodies. They punctured their lips and breasts with slivers of cane and spoke in guttural tones without moving their mouths. Red-and-black war paint covered their faces, and they smeared their bodies with bear, shark, skunk, and alligator grease mixed with mud to repel mosquitoes (and anyone else who came too close).

The Karankawa roamed the Coastal Plain in small bands, hunting deer and javelina (a piglike mammal indigenous to the area) with giant bows made of cedar. They supplemented their diet with cactus fruit, berries, pecans, clams, oysters, and fish. European explorers and settlers described them as ferocious warriors and reviled them for their cannibalistic ways. Like other tribes the Karankawa practiced ceremonial cannibalism against enemies killed in battle in hopes of drawing magic from them. Settlers also described the Karankawa as an unlikable lot bent on stealing, robbing, and killing. But some evidence suggests the hostile actions taken by the Karankawa may have been prompted by the explorers and colonists and that they learned their cannibalistic ways from a Spanish exploration party, who ate their dead to keep from starving.

Although there were times when the Karankawa and their visitors got along well, in general they suffered from a severe case of culture clash, including one incident involving religion. The Spanish built missions in the area to convert the Karankawa from sun worship to Christianity. The Karankawa were receptive to their message as long as the missionaries gave them free food and clothing; however, as soon as the enticements ran out, so did the Karankawa, who preferred to continue worshipping the sun as they had for more than eight centuries. The Spanish never forgave them.

The Karankawas' beliefs caused more serious trouble when Texas settlers arrived and began building fences, planting crops, and raising cattle. No matter how hard the settlers tried to explain it to them, the Karankawa just couldn't grasp the concept of animal ownership. As skilled hunters they believed the animal belonged to the person who killed it, a belief Texans didn't particularly care for, especially when it was their animal that had been killed. Texans considered cattle theft a crime punishable by death, and it didn't matter to them that the Karankawa had settled the area first.

Empresario Stephen F. Austin, who brought some American families to Texas, ordered the Karankawa exterminated. (Empresarios were people who contracted with the Mexican government to bring Roman Catholic settlers to Texas in exchange for 9,300 hectares, or 23,000 acres, of land for each 100 families.) The Spanish missionaries had long ago given up on the tribe and were therefore unwilling to provide shelter to them. With nowhere to hide and no one to protect them, they eventually fled to Mexico, where they found more trouble. In 1858, at a place known as Tampacuas, 20 miles north of the Río Grande, a band of Mexican rancheros attacked and killed the last small band of Karankawa, extinguishing a culture that for a millennium called the Corpus Christi area home.

The Explorers

Although the Karankawa met their demise little more than a century ago, the beginning of the end may have come 360 years earlier, when Italian explorer Amerigo Vespucci sailed the Gulf of Mexico and made what is believed to be the first map showing the gulf's outline.

Twenty-one years later, Spanish explorer Alonzo Álvarez de Piñeda, who is generally credited with discovering the Texas Coastal Bend, sailed along the coast in search of a passage to the Spice Islands of the Pacific Ocean. Although the passage eluded him, he discovered the Mississippi River and landed at several sites along the Texas coast. Popular myth has it that Piñeda discovered and named Corpus Christi Bay, having supposedly discovered it on the day of the Roman Catholic Feast of Corpus Christi and therefore giving it that name.

The first Europeans to pass through the Corpus Christi area may well have been the survivors of the Panfilo de Narváez expedition that was stranded in Florida in 1528. With their sights set on Mexico, the 242 Spaniards on the expedition constructed crude barges and set sail across the vast gulf, hoping to reach settlements in Mexico where they could find transportation home. The barge commanded by Alvar Núñez Cabeza de Vaca came ashore near Galveston Island. Only four of the original 242 survived. They were immediately enslaved by the Karankawa, who held them captive for six years. They escaped in October 1534 and headed south toward settlements in Mexico, arriving 18 months later in Sonora in Northern Mexico.

Another group fared even worse than Cabeza de Vaca and his friends. They belonged to a treasure convoy sailing from Veracruz to Spain that wrecked on Padre Island in April 1554. The Karankawa, friendly at first, attacked without warning. The Spaniards fled toward Mexico, which they wrongly believed to be only a few miles away. A priest lost their package of crossbows as they rafted over an island pass, leaving them unarmed and unable to respond to the guerrilla warfare the Karankawa used against them. Arrows felled their leaders, and everyone suffered from hunger, thirst, exhaustion, and sunburn. Friar Marcos de Mena, wounded by seven arrows, was buried in the sand and left to die. But the warm sand renewed him and he arose, as if from the dead, to find his friends massacred.

Despite numerous expeditions to the area in and around what is now Corpus Christi, no one made serious inroads into the area until Frenchman René-Robert Cavelier, sieur de La Salle, landed on the shores of Matagorda Bay in 1685. He claimed for France all the lands that were drained by the Mississippi River and its tributaries and established a colony named Fort St. Louis. The Karankawa welcomed him with open arms until La Salle made the mistake of demanding the return of stolen items and compounded the problem by stealing their canoes. The Karankawa responded by destroying Fort St. Louis and killing many of La Salle's people.

H.M. King High School was a gift from Henrietta King to the city of Kingsville.

Photo: courtesy of the Greater Kingsville Economic Development Council

Spanish explorer Alonso De León left his mark on the area on April 4, 1689, while crossing a stream surrounded by a lovely pecan grove. He named the stream Nueces, Spanish for "nuts," a name eventually given to both the river that empties into Corpus Christi Bay and the county in which Corpus Christi is located.

Spanish Colonization

La Salle and other French explorers who visited the Corpus Christi area had little impact other than to frighten the Spanish into sending explorers and colonists of their own. The first was the Marquis de Aguayo, whom they sent to expel the French from the territory. Aguayo reached the ruins of Fort St. Louis on March 24, 1722, where he set up a presidio and mission named Nuestra Señora de Zuniga de la Bahía del Espíritu Santo.

It was the captain of that presidio and mission, Joaquín de Orobio y Basterra, who in 1746 made the first official record of Corpus Christi Bay when he discovered Nueces and Corpus Christi Bays in his search for possible settlements. He reported that the fresh water, fish, sources of salt, and fertile soil made the site ideal for settlement. His favorable reports convinced José Escandón, governor of the newly created Nuevo Santander state, to start a settlement and mission on Corpus Christi Bay. But the settlers enticed to risk the long journey were beset by a snowstorm, smallpox and the loss of their horses that ended their trip before they left Mexico, and the colony never materialized.

Despite such setbacks Spanish rancheros found the area's rich grasslands appealing and applied for land grants. Among the first Spanish landowners to arrive was Blas María de la Garza Falcón, who between the years of 1760 and 1764 established Rancho Santa Petronilla, 15 miles south of the mouth of the Nueces River. Other Spanish ranchers received grants and joined him, staking claim to vast stretches of grazing lands. In 1764 word of an English settlement on Padre Island brought Spanish Colonel Diego Ortiz Parilla and his troops to investigate. Blas Falcón's son, José Antonio, joined him. He explored the length of Padre Island, and later submitted a report under Colonel Parrilla's name. The report included a sketch of small tents labeled Camp on the Beach of Corpus Christi, the first time the site had been given that name.

Despite their efforts, the Spanish were destined to fail in South Texas. Corruption, government repression, and bureaucratic bumbling contributed to their downfall, as did the Lipan and Comanche Indians, whose periodic looting and killing drove the rancheros to seek safety south of the Río Grande.

The Irishmen

John McMullen and James McGloin, who in 1830 founded a colony a few miles northwest of what is now Corpus Christi, immigrated to the United States to escape conditions in Ireland. McMullen, who wound up a merchant in Matamoros, Mexico, met McGloin at an English port and convinced him to return with him to Matamoros. In 1828 the two men were granted an empresario contract to bring 200 families to the west bank of the Nueces River.

McMullen and McGloin accompanied the first 58 families that landed in October 1829 near the decaying mission of Our Lady of Refuge in Refugio. A short time later McMullen and McGloin led their party into the wilderness, where they established San Patricio de Hibernia on October 24, 1830. Within the year they had built a church, and the first Anglo-American colonists were here to stay. By 1834, San Patricio began to prosper: Crops flourished, wild game and cattle were plentiful, and there was a good supply of drinking water. The only trouble was the growing dissent between Mexico and Texas colonists.

The Texas Revolution

From 1821 to 1836 Texas's population jumped from 4,000 to between 35,000 and 50,000, with most of the settlers coming from the southern United States. Despite the fact that Mexico owned Texas at that time, these settlers refused to assimilate into Mexican culture and brought slaves to cultivate cotton. Mexicans, having fought recently for freedom from Spain, opposed slavery.

Tensions escalated in 1826 when the Fredonian Rebellion, a failed attempt to create a separate republic, aroused Mexican suspicions that Texas settlers were not loyal to Mexico. The Mexican government stationed troops in Texas and passed a law that both restricted further Anglo-American immigration and banned the importation of slaves. Texans petitioned Mexico to repeal the law, but Stephen F. Austin, their ambassador, was imprisoned when a letter he had written advising Texans to organize a separate state fell into Mexican hands. Mexico rejected the Texans' petition.

In 1834 the Mexican politician and soldier Antonio Lopez de Santa Anna deposed the Mexican government and assumed dictatorial powers, determined to crush the rebellion in Texas. Santa Anna consolidated his power by convincing his enemies that Texans, supported by the United States, were trying to steal Mexican territory. In October 1835 Mexican soldiers arrived in Gonzales, 50 miles east of San Antonio, to reclaim a cannon given to the settlers for use against the Indians. The settlers resisted, firing the first shots in what is considered the opening battle of the Texas Revolution.

A similar incident occurred in an area northwest of Corpus Christi, although with a different result, when Capt. Nicolas Rodrigues, Mexico's commander of Fort Lipantitlan across the Nueces River from San Patricio, confiscated the San Patricio colony's cannon. The colony responded by taking Fort Lipantitlan and repelling an attempt by Capt. Rodrigues to retake it. Meanwhile, a convention of Anglo-American settlers formed a provisional government, elected a governor and council, and declared that Texans were fighting for the rights due them under the Mexican Constitution of 1824.

The issue divided the area's Irish settlers. Some wished to remain Mexican citizens in the hope that a liberal government would prevail. Others believed the conservative government and its repressive policies, led by Santa Anna, would inevitably win. Even as they debated these issues, Texans elsewhere proceeded with efforts to break away from Mexico. Austin and two others went to the United States to borrow money, and a quickly formed Texas army marched to attack the Mexican garrison at San Antonio. In December a volunteer force led by Ben Milam defeated the Mexicans and forced them to retreat south of the Río Grande.

On February 23, 1836, Santa Anna's forces entered San Antonio, and the Texans withdrew

Old Nueces County Courthouse

Tourists approaching Corpus Christi's sparkling bayfront often are distracted by a mammoth, five-story building with a crumbling brick facade and boarded-up windows.

Opened in 1914, the old Nueces County Courthouse is one of the city's oldest structures and also one of the most debated. Since it closed in 1977, the building has stood in decay at the city's main entrance just a few blocks from the bayfront.

Some describe it as an eyesore that should be bulldozed. Others say its neo-classical style is a historic monument to justice that deserves preservation.

City officials are continuing to study whether the building is structurally sound. It has avoided the wrecking ball because of its designation as a historic site and the high cost of knocking it down.

Proposals for the building have ranged from a Tejano Music Hall of Fame to a satellite campus of Texas A&M University-Corpus Christi. A city councilman once suggested contacting a Hollywood movie mogul to offer the courthouse for a bombing scene.

The Justice Building Inc., a local nonprofit group, took control of the courthouse in 1992 to help raise private funds to restore the building. Several suggestions have been made, but little progress has occurred.

The Texas Historical Commission named the courthouse to the state's 10 most endangered historical properties and imposed a 40-year restrictive covenant on the building. The covenant, set to expire in 2018, mandates that the historical integrity of the building be preserved.

Designed by San Antonio architect Harvey L. Page, the building opened its

The Old Nueces County Courthouse sits at the entrance of Corpus Christi. Critics say the crumbling building should be torn down; others are working to find the funds to restore the landmark structure.

Photo: Ralph Goonan

HISTORY

doors more than eight decades ago to fanfare and applause. Columns and sculpted figures embellished the building, and the lush landscaping included palm and banana trees, oleanders, hibiscus, and violets. Goldfish swam in a pond out front.

Along with courts, the old building housed the county jail on its top two floors. Two dark and secluded "death cells" held prisoners awaiting the ultimate penalty.

The courthouse with the imposing steps leading to its front door survived the 1919 hurricane and Hurricane Celia in 1970. Whether it ultimately survives remains to be seen.

to the Alamo, a former mission building. William B. Travis, commander of the Texas forces, pleaded for reinforcements, but only 32 men from Gonzales, 50 miles to the east, answered the call. For 13 days the small force defended the Alamo against more than 5,000 Mexican troops until, on March 6, the Alamo fell and its defenders were killed. Among the dead were Tennessee frontier hero, pioneer and politician, Davy Crockett, and Georgia pioneer, James Bowie. Texans lost several other battles, too, including those in the Corpus Christi-area towns of San Patricio, Agua Dulce, and Refugio.

In a retreat from Goliad, 45 miles north of San Patricio, Col. James W. Fannin and his 283 men surrendered at Coleto Creek and were marched back to Goliad. A few days later, in what has come to be known as the Goliad Massacre, they were executed to serve as an example to other Texans.

On March 2, 1836, during the siege of the Alamo, a group of American Texans met on Washington-On-The-Brazos and declared their independence from Mexico. They also named Sam Houston commander-in-chief and adopted a constitution that protected slavery. The U.S. government supported Texas independence but did not intervene.

Houston retreated toward the coast to entice Santa Anna away from his supply lines near San Antonio. Meanwhile, his army increased daily as volunteers from the United States came to help. He had almost 800 men under his command when he camped at San Jacinto, opposite Santa Anna's force of about 1,600. Santa Anna failed to post guards, and with shouts of "Remember the Alamo! Remember Goliad!" the Texans attacked on the afternoon of April 21, 1836. Most of Santa Anna's troops were killed, wounded, or captured in battle. The Texans suffered nine dead and 30 wounded, including Houston, who was shot in the ankle. Captured the next day, Santa Anna eventually recognized Texas' independence and withdrew south of the Río Grande after his release.

Annexation and the Mexican War

Texas became an independent nation following the war with Mexico and remained one for the next 10 years. Houston defeated Austin to become the Republic's first president, but a host of problems, principally financial, plagued his and subsequent administrations.

The first problem involved a border dispute. Mexico insisted the Nueces River should be the border between the two countries. Texans disagreed. The debate that followed grew so heated that Mexican soldiers invaded Texas, captured and imprisoned a Texas trading expedition, and briefly occupied San Antonio, Goliad, and Refugio.

Despite problems with Mexico, the population of Texas continued to increase, climbing about 300 percent by 1836. Most came from the United States to claim free land, and most joined Houston and his political supporters, who wanted the United States to annex the republic. Other Texans argued against U.S. annexation, preferring to live in an independent republic. Eventually those favoring annexation won out, and on December 29, 1845, Texas joined the union. Mexico immediately broke diplomatic relations with the United States.

U.S. General (and future president) Zachary Taylor marched to the Río Grande to enforce it as the southern U.S. border, camping in Corpus Christi. The site, now known as Artesian Park,

HISTORY

is in downtown Corpus Christi. Mexico considered Taylor's arrival an act of aggression and sent troops across the Río Grande. President James K. Polk accused Mexico of invading U.S. soil, and on May 13, 1846, Congress declared war on Mexico.

Taylor and other U.S. generals made quick work of the Mexican army, capturing several cities and putting an end to the war by taking Mexico City. Mexico begrudgingly acknowledged defeat and on February 2, 1848, signed the Treaty of Guadalupe Hidalgo, establishing peace between the two countries. Under the treaty the Río Grande was made the southern boundary of Texas, and Mexico ceded California and New Mexico to the United States. In return, the United States paid $15 million and agreed to settle all legal claims of U.S. citizens against Mexico.

The Birth of Corpus Christi

Corpus Christi profited greatly from the Mexican War, serving as a supply point for Taylor's men. When the war ended, it continued as a supply point, shipping goods for operations in the West. The city had begun as a trading post in 1839 on land that Colonel Henry L. Kinney purchased from the former commandant of Fort Lipantitlan. Although subject to raids by Indians, Texas cattle thieves and Mexican troops who suspected Kinney of harboring border pirates, Kinney prevailed, and a colony slowly grew up around the post. In 1846 the Texas Legislature authorized the formation of Nueces County and a year later—six years before it incorporated as a city—Corpus Christi became the county seat.

The 1850 Nueces County census reported 689 people living in 151 dwellings. There were no schools or churches. More than half of the residents had been born in Mexico and 53 had been born in Texas. Of the others, 51 were from Germany, 32 were from Ireland, 47 were black slaves, and one was a freedman. In 1852 immigration peaked with the founding of Nuecestown west of Corpus Christi by settlers from Scotland, Wales, England, Ireland, and Germany. That same year Corpus Christi incorporated, and B.F. Neal was elected mayor.

The town entered a brief growth period, which ended in 1854 when a yellow-fever epidemic hit town. Later that year Kinney left town for unknown reasons, and the leaders who remained turned their attention to improving the city. They formed a school and established Catholic, Methodist, Presbyterian, and Episcopal churches. But the city's future depended on gaining access to deep water so that large cargo ships could dock there. The problem lay in the Aransas bar, a long ridge of sand near the surface that prevented heavily laden ships from sailing to Corpus Christi. Two attempts to dredge a pass through the bar failed, and the problem persisted for the next 72 years.

The King Ranch and North Bay Development

The King Ranch is one of the largest privately owned ranches in the world, covering 825,000 acres southwest of Corpus Christi and the adjoining the city of Kingsville. The North Bay is an area north of Corpus Christi encompassing Aransas County and parts of San Patricio and Nueces Counties.

The year 1852 was an eventful one in the Texas Coastal Bend, for it was then that Captain Richard King started a ranch—the King Ranch—on Santa Gertrudis Creek. King spent most of his early life as a seaman, a job that brought him to the Río Grande at the age of 23 to captain one of the river steamboats that supplied Taylor's army. In 1852 he quit his job, bought part of a Spanish land grant and started what would become one of the largest ranches in the world.

The town of Kingsville sprung up around the King Ranch, thanks largely to the efforts of King's widow, Henrietta, who donated a large amount of land to help finance the St. Louis, Brownsville and Mexico Railroad. One provision of her financing was that Kingsville be named the railroad's headquarters. The railroad, the King Ranch and the sinking of water wells in 1899 that provided drinking water allowed Kingsville to prosper.

The King Ranch continues to play a major role in Kingsville's economic and political circles. The city also is home to a pilot-training facility, Naval Air Station—Kingsville and Texas A&M University—Kingsville.

In the mid-1850s, Englishman R. L. Mercer and his family came to the tip of Mustang Island to fish and raise cattle. Mercer set up a small dock and warehouse for servicing visiting ships.

Miradores line Corpus Christ's seawall and give visitors glimpses of local history.

Photo: Daniel Fielder

Others followed, and a tiny community, which later became known as Port Aransas, sprouted. In 1870 a New Yorker bought San Jose Island, a few miles north of Mustang Island, and those who had settled there were forced to leave. Many joined Mercer's settlement, where they made money fishing and catching sea turtles weighing as much as 500 pounds.

Harsh storms have devastated the town twice, but its proximity to the water and the beaches keeps people coming back. Access to Port Aransas was limited to boats and ferries until 1954 when a highway running the length of Mustang Island linked the town with Corpus Christi. The causeway from the town of Aransas Pass to the ferry landing opened in 1960, and three years later the first condominium opened its doors. Port Aransas is now a popular tourist destination for anglers, beachgoers and watersports enthusiasts.

The city of Aransas Pass, a few miles to the west, got its start in a most unusual way. In 1909 a man named T. B. Wheeler and his partner, Russell Harrison, son of former president Benjamin Harrison, decided to hold a lottery to sell 13,000 acres on Red Fish Bay, including the townsite of Aransas Pass. Buyers were attracted to the lottery because the U.S. government was about to finance the dredging of a port in the area, and, because the waterway known as Aransas Pass was the closest outlet to the gulf, everyone assumed it would be chosen over Corpus Christi or Rockport.

Lottery tickets sold for $100 each, and buyers from as far away as Kansas and Nebraska arrived on special trains. It was called a lottery although everyone who bought a ticket received land. One ticket was sold for each of the 6,000 lots, and the only gamble concerned the location of the land each ticketholder would receive. As it turned out, they all wound up losers when the U.S. government chose Corpus Christi as the location for a deep-water port.

The town of Rockport came into prominence when the Coleman-Fulton cattle companies contracted with the Morgan Steamship Company of New York to supply at least $1,000 worth of hides, tallow, bones, and horns every 10 days. As the cattle industry developed after the Civil War, huge herds were shipped to Rockport to be slaughtered, turning the port into one of the largest in the state. But the city's packing industry died as the great cattle drives to the Midwestern railheads became more common. Although the city suffered, residents soon turned to the water for their jobs. Fishing became the major industry and tourism followed. Throughout the years Rockport and its smaller neighbor, Fulton, have grown together to the point that visitors see them as one community. Both continue to serve as major fishing and resort communities.

The Civil War and Beyond

Texans owned slaves, and most sided with the South on the issue of slavery. The Texas Legislature voted to secede from the Union in 1861, and local residents enthusiastically supported the decision at a local meeting. But with the exception of a few cannonballs fired on the city and an occupation by Union troops of less than six months, Corpus Christi escaped the Civil War unscathed.

After the war, Corpus Christi became a shipping point for Texas cattle moving to eastern markets, and for crops including cotton, which was first shipped from Corpus Christi in 1883. In 1874 a channel through Corpus Christi Bay was dredged to a depth of eight feet, deep enough to allow steamships to dock at Corpus Christi. In the latter part of the century, the city formed a fire department and acquired a daily newspaper, a hospital and a water system. In 1909 the Texas Legislature formed the Corpus Christi Independent School District, and a year later, trolley cars replaced horse-drawn cars on Corpus Christi streets.

In 1911 the first causeway was built across Nueces Bay, linking Corpus Christi with the North Bay area. Streetlights were installed in 1912, and in the following year, a major natural gas field was discovered across Nueces Bay. Gas, electricity, and paved streets made life better in Corpus Christi, and the discovery of another gas field assured there would be enough natural gas to supply residents and industries.

At the turn of the century, the city began to attract tourists with tales of cool breezes and a healthful climate. Piers were built along the bayfront, and pavilions offered bowling, dancing, drinking, dining, fishing, bathing, and entertainment. Saloons and motion-picture houses popped up everywhere. Drinking establishments became so abundant that in 1915 the City Council passed an ordinance requiring all saloons on three downtown streets to move to the east side so that ladies could walk the sidewalks without having to see inside them.

Hurricanes took a major toll on the city in 1916 and again in 1919. The 1916 hurricane destroyed the Nueces Bay Causeway, damaged the bayfront and left 20 dead. The 1919 hurricane devastated the city, killing 287 people. For the next few years, the tourist industry suffered because tourist facilities had been destroyed and investors were reluctant to invest money in an area vulnerable to hurricanes. At that point Corpus Christi residents decided two things: They wanted to protect themselves from future hurricanes and they wanted a deep-water port to bring prosperity to the region. Corpus Christi residents petitioned the federal government for a 21-mile ship channel.

The federal government eventually agreed, and on January 16, 1925, dredge boats began

The Fulton Mansion, overlooking Aranasas Bay, was built in 1874
during the time of cattle barons in South Texas.

Photo: courtesy of the Rockport-Fulton Chamber of Commerce

HISTORY

digging the channel while harbor facilities were built with local and state funds. The Port of Corpus Christi opened on September 14, 1926, and Corpus Christi was on its way to becoming a major center for the oil refining and petrochemical industries.

The Modern Era

The deep-water port and an oil boom quickly ushered Corpus Christi into the modern era. By late 1935 Nueces County had 60 oil wells in two oil fields. Two years later there were 894 wells in 15 fields. The boom attracted people from all over, and the city's population jumped from 27,742 in 1930 to 57,301 in 1940. Farmers and ranchers with new oil wealth built expensive homes in Corpus Christi, and young men left jobless by the Depression came from all over the country to work.

Changes came quickly to Corpus Christi during the modern era. The city's first skyscraper, the 12-story Nixon Building (later renamed the Wilson Building), opened in 1927. City voters approved the sale of bonds to finish the $2.5 million seawall along the bayfront, providing storm protection along the downtown area. The 14-foot-tall, 2-mile-long project was completed in 1940, 20 years after it began.

In 1929 the League of United Latin American Citizens (LULAC) formed, with Ben Garza as chairman and president. The group held its first convention in Corpus Christi. Since its inception almost 90 years ago, LULAC has grown from a Texas organization to a national one, and has done much to advance causes important to the Hispanic community.

City residents voted in 1935 to create Del Mar Junior College, now Del Mar College, and U.S. Highway 77 opened through the King and Kenedy ranches south of Corpus Christi. In 1938 Ada Wilson established the Ada Wilson Crippled Children's Hospital, and a year later workers completed the majestic Corpus Christi Cathedral, an architectural and spiritual icon to tens of thousands of South Texas Catholics. The cathedral, as impressive as ever, overlooks downtown Corpus Christi and Corpus Christi Bay.

In 1938, as World War II approached, the U.S. Navy began looking for a site for an airplane training base. The Navy needed 2,000 acres on a sheltered bay with land that sloped to the water for a seaplane base. A citizens' committee met with the Navy and guaranteed roads, water and housing if the Navy would locate its $44 million base in the city. The Navy dedicated the Naval Air Station in 1941 as the largest naval flight-training center in the world. By 1944 more than 20,000 civilians worked at the base, with another 20,000 employed at satellite fields. The city's population almost doubled between 1940 and 1950, rising from 57,301 to 108,287. In 1945 a 12-foot-deep Intra-coastal Canal opened from Galveston to Corpus Christi, allowing trade to move quickly between the two cities.

INSIDERS' TIP

The Confederate Army used Centennial House, 411 N. Broadway, as a hospital during the Civil War. Following the attack and seizure of Corpus Christi by Union soldiers, it served as headquarters for the Quartermaster Corps.

Two years later the Clara Driscoll Foundation bought land for a free clinic and children's hospital that continues to serve sick children throughout the Corpus Christi area. In that same year the Baptist Foundation established the University of Corpus Christi (now Texas A&M University–Corpus Christi) at a former Navy facility on the city's southern end. In 1949 the Intracoastal Canal opened from Corpus Christi to Brownsville, and a year later, the 4-mile-long Padre Island Causeway (later renamed John F. Kennedy Causeway) connected the city with Padre and Mustang Islands. Del Mar Junior College became integrated in 1952 after the local NAACP challenged school racial policies. The Corpus Christi school district began integrating three years later following the U.S. Supreme Court ruling that separate but equal schools were unconstitutional.

The 1950s ended with a local recession after the Navy Overhaul and Repair Department at the Naval Air Station closed down in 1959, leaving 3,000 people jobless. In that same year, workers completed the towering Harbor Bridge over the Corpus Christi Ship Channel, putting an end to long drawbridge delays.

The 1960s dawned with the dedication of the Corpus Christi International Airport. A year later, the Army Maintenance Center (now called the Corpus Christi Army Depot) opened in space formerly occupied by the Navy Overhaul and Repair Department. In that same year the city annexed Flour Bluff, a subdivision on the city's south side, and in 1962 President Kennedy authorized the purchase of 80.5 miles of Padre Island for a national seashore. Construction began on Interstate Highway 37 connecting Corpus Christi to San Antonio and work also got under way on Corpus Christi Museum. The museum was the first building in the Bayfront Arts and Science Park, a collection of facilities dedicated to art, theater and science. The Art Museum of South Texas opened there in 1972, and in 1976, the city celebrated the bicentennial with a performance of *1776* in the city's new Harbor Playhouse.

INSIDERS' TIP

The Galvan House in Corpus Christi's Heritage Park is named for Rafael Galvan, who became Corpus Christi's first Mexican-American police officer.

By 1970, the population had doubled again to 204,525. Hurricane Celia lashed the city, causing considerable damage and killing 11. In 1972 the state bought land for Mustang Island State Park, and in 1977 county officials moved from the old courthouse near the bayfront to a new one farther inland. The old courthouse, empty and crumbling, continues to greet visitors as they near the bayfront. For the past 20 years residents have debated whether to demolish the building or try to restore it. See our Close-up on the old Nueces County Courthouse in this chapter.

The 1980s began with bad news when the H.E.B. Grocery Company, founded in Corpus Christi in 1939, announced it would move its headquarters and 450 employees to San Antonio. Hurricane Allen soaked Corpus Christi that year, driving an estimated 100,000 people from their homes. Like many other Texas cities, Corpus Christi suffered in the early 1980s when the oil and gas industry on which it depended suddenly faltered. Fortunately for the city the oil refineries that had located along the port continued to operate near top capacity as imported oil flowed in to take advantage of sophisticated new equipment. Other industries built facilities along the port and helped make it the sixth largest in the nation in terms of tonnage.

Concerned about the city's overdependency on oil and gas, city leaders began looking for ways to diversify the economy. Although they had always known Corpus Christi was a nice place to visit, city leaders had never thoroughly explored the tourism market. As a new convention center opened in 1981, city officials began looking for ways to attract more tourists. In the meantime, the area's infrastructure received needed improvements; several new public amenities made the Corpus Christi area a better place to live.

One of the most important improvements came in 1981 when workers completed the 140-mile IH-37, linking Corpus Christi with San Antonio, a project that was 22 years in the making. A year later officials dedicated the $112 million Choke Canyon Reservoir northwest of the city, establishing a more reliable source of water to the city while creating recreational opportunities for residents and visitors.

In 1985 the U.S. Navy chose the city of Ingleside across Corpus Christi Bay as the home port for the battleship USS *Wisconsin*, and Corpus Christi voters approved a half-cent sales tax to fund a regional bus service. A new $4 million Corpus Christi Public Library opened in 1986, and in 1988 the twin towers known as One Shoreline Plaza opened on the downtown bayfront. Other improvements included a new six-story City Hall and, at the Bayfront Arts and Science Park, the $2.38 million Watergarden, a dancing water sculpture that serves as the park's centerpiece.

The 1990s

By 1990 the population had grown to 257,453. Tourism, the port, and the military continued to be the major legs on which the economy stood. Investors bet that greyhound racing would become a popular attraction and, under a recent state law allowing it, opened the Corpus Christi Greyhound Race Track. In that same year the Texas State Aquarium opened to large crowds with exhibits of fish and other marine life indigenous to the Gulf of Mexico. Local military installations were threatened by federal budget cuts, and Navy officials said they doubted Naval Station Ingleside would ever become a homeport for the USS *Wisconsin*. A reprieve came in 1991 when it was announced that several mine-sweeping vessels would be stationed at Ingleside, and in 1992 when the Atlantic Fleet designated Naval Station Ingleside as its mine warfare command headquarters. See our Military chapter for more information.

Several tourist-related attractions came to Corpus Christi in the 1990s, including the decommissioned USS *Lexington* aircraft carrier. The *Lexington* now serves as a museum on the north side of the city in an area known as Corpus Christi Beach.

The international spotlight hit Corpus Christi on March 31, 1995, when Tejano music singer Selena Quintanilla-Perez was fatally shot at a Corpus Christi hotel by the founder of her fan club. The city built a memorial statue in her honor along the bayfront and renamed the city's auditorium after her. For more information, see our Close-up on Selena in the Attractions chapter.

In 1997 the city began work on the Gateway Project to add a parkway and landscaping to the city's entrance. The first phase created a 6-acre greenbelt from the old Nueces County Courthouse to Shoreline Boulevard, where a new $22 million federal courthouse has been built. But the City Council later abandoned plans to create a bayfront park adjacent to the seawall when citizens protested.

Henry L. Kinney wouldn't recognize the trading post he founded 161years ago or the surrounding towns that have grown up throughout the years. But many of the qualities that attracted him to the area—warm weather, blue-green water, and a laid-back lifestyle—continue to draw people to the area to this day.

The Natural World

LOOK FOR:
• Weather
• Flora
• Fauna
• Insects

The Corpus Christi area stretches out along a graceful curve of the Gulf of Mexico, its flora and fauna nurtured by the very remoteness that attracts thousands of visitors each summer. However, despite this annual influx of sun worshipers and nature lovers, the area retains much of its unfettered natural beauty, thanks to measures taken to preserve wildlife for future generations. The area is home to the Aransas National Wildlife Refuge—winter nesting grounds of the endangered whooping crane—and the Padre Island National Seashore. See our Parks chapter for more information on both areas.

The North Bay alone has three major areas where the public can view the local flora and fauna in a mostly natural state: Goose Island State Park north of Rockport, described in our Parks chapter; the Fennessey Ranch, 40 miles northwest of Corpus Christi (see our Attractions chapter); and the Rob and Bessie Welder Wildlife Refuge north of Sinton (see our Attractions chapter). You can even get a close-up view of bottle-nosed dolphins with the Dolphin Connection tours based in Ingleside (see our Attractions chapter).

In Corpus Christi you'll find nature hasn't been forgotten. Hans Suter Park on the city's south side and Blucher Park near downtown are popular birding sites, and Hazel Bazemore Park west of town is a popular site for migratory hawks. The King Ranch has 825,000 acres where both cattle and wildlife thrive, and, like many ranches in the area, offers guided tours of native flora and fauna (see our Attractions chapter).

Corpus Christi and the surrounding area, known officially as the Texas Coastal Bend, has several sites on the Great Texas Coastal Birding

Orchids bloom in the tropical wing of the Exhibit House at Corpus Christi Botanical Gardens.

Photo: MaryJane Crull, courtesy of Corpus Christi Botanical Gardens

Trail. Each year thousands of people travel to the area in hopes of spotting many of the more than 500 species of native and migratory birds that can be seen here. Birding is such a popular attraction that we've devoted a separate chapter to it. For information on everything else— weather, plants, animals, and insects—read on.

Weather

Whatever lasting impressions of Corpus Christi weather you take with you will depend in large part on when you visit. And although that's true no matter where you visit, it seems especially so when speaking of Corpus Christi's weather. Arrive in the winter or spring and you'll leave dreaming of a tropical paradise where the temperature rarely dips to uncomfortable levels and a cool, dry wind soothes your body on even the sunniest of days. But plan your trip for summer or early fall and you'll quickly learn why local residents refer to air-conditioning as "life-support." There's no way to sugarcoat it: It's hot and humid down here from late May or early June until late October or early November. The first cool front that arrives each fall is cause for celebration, allowing residents to venture outdoors again without breaking into a sweat. Don't misunderstand: You can enjoy the outdoors in the early morning and late evening without succumbing to heat stroke, but exercising or even taking a short walk in the middle of the day is masochistic. Thank heaven for the beach, swimming pools, and water sprinklers.

Corpus Christi has an average mean temperature of 71.2 degrees and an annual rainfall of 27.5 inches. That sounds quite pleasant until you consider that the temperature is often well above 71.2 degrees. July and August are the warmest months, with mean temperatures between 85 and 86 degrees and highs in the low to mid 90s. In an average year Corpus Christi has 106 days with temperatures of 90 degrees or above and no days with temperatures of zero or below. January is the coldest month of the year, with a mean temperature of 55.2 degrees. The mercury rarely dips below freezing, and then only for a day or so. Snow is a rarity, occurring for a few hours every seven or eight years, and the chances of seeing snow where you live or stay is remote. It's not unusual to encounter shorts-and-T-shirt weather even in the dead of winter.

Monthly mean temperatures and average monthly rainfall show the seasonal variations: January 55.2 degrees, 1.60 inches; February 58.0 degrees, 2.02 inches; March, 63.5 degrees, 1.36 inches; April, 71.0 degrees, 1.91 inches; May 76.3 degrees, 3.13 inches; June 81.0 degrees, 2.88 inches; July 85.7 degrees, 1.93 inches; August 85.9 degrees, 2.34 inches; September 81.1 degrees, 4.82 inches; October 72.9 degrees, 2.59 inches; November 65.3 degrees, 1.81 inches; and December 58.4 degrees, 1.68 inches.

Fortunately, Gulf breezes are constant here. Humidity is almost always present, too, (except during drought conditions) making summer and fall temperatures seem even hotter. There's a saying down here that goes: "It's not the heat, it's the humidity." Texans do not consider 95 degrees particularly hot for the middle of a summer day. At that temperature—and with a mild breeze—you should be able to sit in the shade without breaking a sweat. But when the humidity reaches 50 percent or more, you can't walk from your house to your car without feeling like you're walking through a sauna. The heat index chart is to Corpus Christi residents what the wind/chill factor is to Minnesota's inhabitants. Combine the temperature with the relative humidity and you come up with a number for how hot it feels. For instance, when the temperature is 90 degrees and the relative humidity is 70 percent, it feels like 106 degrees.

Hurricanes

Hurricanes are as much a part of Corpus Christi as sea gulls and shrimp boats. Its proximity to warm Gulf waters makes the area vulnerable to these great storms, and the region's history is replete with hurricanes that have killed hundreds and caused millions of dollars in damage. Hurricane season begins June 1 and runs through November 30. August and September are the most active months, with the peak coming September 10. September has seen more major hurricanes than all other months combined.

Several major hurricanes have made landfall along the Corpus Christi area, and many that have landed elsewhere along the coast have caused major flooding and wind damage here. Atlantic hurricanes generate off the African coast and move toward the United States along east-west trade winds. As they gain strength they grow into tropical depressions, then tropical storms and finally into hurricanes. Atlantic hurricanes occur when storm cells migrate over warm tropical waters. If the water is warm enough it will feed the storm cells, causing them to release heat into the atmosphere and form a tropical depression. As the trade winds blow the system westward, barometric pressure begins to drop in the vortex of the storm and winds begin to rotate counterclockwise around it.

INSIDERS' TIP

The lightning whelk, found throughout Corpus Christi-area beaches, is the official state shell of Texas.

When the wind speed reaches 38 mph, the system becomes a tropical storm, with spiral bands of rain clouds extending for more than 100 miles. When the storm's wind speed reaches 74 mph, it becomes a hurricane. Many turn north and either dissipate in the Atlantic or slam into the Atlantic Coast. Others hit Florida, the Caribbean Islands or Mexico's Yucatán Peninsula. Some move into the Gulf of Mexico, where they often gather strength before making landfall. Tropical storms with winds in excess of 39 mph are given names.

Hurricanes are classified into five categories based on strength:

• Category 1—Winds of 74 to 95 mph with a storm surge of 4 to 5 feet. Damage is minimal with signs, tree branches and power lines blown down.

• Category 2—Winds of 96 to 110 mph with a storm surge of 6 to 8 feet. Damage is moderate with larger signs and tree branches blown down.

• Category 3—Winds of 111 to 130 mph with a storm surge of 9 to 12 feet. Damage is extensive. Minor damage to buildings, and trees are blown down.

• Category 4—Winds of 131 to 155 mph with a storm surge of 13 to 18 feet. Damage is extreme with almost total destruction of doors and windows.

• Category 5—Winds of more than 155 mph with a storm surge higher than 18 feet. Damage is catastrophic. Buildings, roofs and structures are destroyed.

The first recorded hurricane to make landfall here slammed into Padre Island in 1791, flooding it and killing an estimated 50,000 cattle. The cattle were believed to have belonged to José Antonio de la Garza Falcón, whose family established Santa Petronila Ranch 15 miles southwest of the Nueces River. There were no human casualties. Another major hurricane struck Corpus Christi on August 18 and 19, 1916, killing 20 people and causing $1.6 million in damage. Winds reached 130 mph, and wind and rising tides destroyed many boats and every pier in the city.

On September 14, 1919, another unnamed hurricane hit south of Corpus Christi, killing nearly 300 residents and causing $20.3 million in damage. Winds reached 110 mph, and water ran 10 feet deep on downtown streets. Nueces Bay, north of Corpus Christi, was littered with bodies. Initial estimates placed the death toll as high as 600, but only 287 bodies were recovered. The Corpus Christi seawall, which extends 2 miles along the bayfront, was built as a result of this hurricane.

In more recent history, Hurricane Celia came ashore between Corpus Christi and Aransas Pass on August 3, 1970, killing 11 and causing $453.7 million in damage. Wind gusts reached 184 mph, damaging 66,000 homes. Almost 4,000 people crowded into shelters around the city. Hurricane Allen hit near the King Ranch on August 9 and 10, 1980, before moving north to Corpus Christi. Although winds diminished to 90 mph by the time it arrived, the storm surge that hit Corpus Christi Beach killed two people. Fifteen thousand homes lost power, and 3,000 residents lost telephone service.

A hurricane watch is issued for a coastal area when there is a threat of hurricane conditions within 24 to 36 hours. A warning is issued when the threat of hurricane conditions will exist within 24 hours or less.

• When a hurricane watch is issued, you should take action on a number of fronts. First, listen to NOAA Weather Radio or local radio or TV stations for the latest on storm information.

• Prepare to bring indoors any lawn furniture, decorations, trash cans, hanging plants, and anything else that can be picked up by the wind.

• Prepare to cover all windows. If shutters have not been installed, use precut plywood. Apply long strips of masking tape to exposed glass to keep it from shattering; draw drapes across windows and doors for protection against flying glass.

• Fill your car's gas tank.

• Check batteries and stock up on canned food, first-aid supplies, drinking water, and medications. These are the first items to disappear from store shelves when a hurricane threatens, so don't wait until the last minute to replenish your supply.

• Plan an escape route early. Check with emergency management personnel for low points and flooding history of your route. The best road on which to leave Corpus Christi is Interstate Highway 37.

• Tune to 1440 KEYS/KZFM 95.5 or 620 AM as you leave Corpus Christi, then change to WOAI 1200 AM as you near San Antonio.

• Put irreplaceable documents in waterproof containers and store in the highest possible spot. If you evacuate, take them with you.

Flora

The Corpus Christi area is home to a wide variety of plant life, ranging from the scattered, low-lying vegetation found on sand dunes to densely wooded thickets in the North Bay. Plants that grow in the Mustang and Padre Islands sand dunes play an important role in slowing dune erosion by providing a buffer against high winds. Plants that thrive here not only are wind resistant but tolerant to shifting sand and salt spray. They survive by spreading their roots over wide areas, retrieving nutrients and water from the sand. Among the more notable plants found here are sea oats grass, fiddleleaf and beach morning glories, cattails, prickly pear, beach evening primrose and sunflowers.

The tall, wispy strands of sea oats grass act as windbreaks, slowing breezes and forcing the wind to release its load of sand onto the dunes. Fiddleleaf and beach morning glories are flowering plants that cling to the dunes and send runners across the surface of the sand. Their brightly colored blooms offer a splash of color to the white sand. The fiddleleaf blooms are pink, funnel-shaped flowers, while beach morning glories are white with yellow-tinted centers. The prickly pear grows on both the dunes and the flats between and behind the dunes. It produces large, colorful flowers of yellow, orange or red, along with a red or purple berry. The beach evening primrose is common throughout the summer, but its yellow blooms appear only between the early evening and the late morning.

Grasslands cover the central, flat part of Mustang and Padre islands behind the dunes, an area known as the barrier flats. Here you'll find a greater variety of grasses than those found on the dunes, including seacoast bluestem, Gulf cordgrass, Indiangrass, and windmill grass. Various types of rushes and sedges—grasslike plants that are often confused with grasses—also inhabit the barrier flats. The white-topped umbrella sedge (so named because of the white flower that grows atop its slender stem) and goldenrods also are common.

The Corpus Christi area's wooded territory north of the city will never be confused with America's Great Northwest timber region. The trees that grow here are shorter and less abundant than those found in the Northwest or most other wooded areas. They have adapted to this dry, wind-swept region by hunkering close to the ground and developing a tenacious spirit that refuses to succumb to the elements. Goose Island State Park offers a good example of this with its dense forest of live oaks and mesquites, interspersed with paths of coastal prairie grass. Drive along Fulton Beach Road in Rockport/Fulton and you'll see live oak trees that have adapted to the elements. Buffeted by constant breezes from Aransas Bay, they lean in the opposite direction, their branches bowing to the wind's relentlessness.

The live oak tree can grow as high as 65 feet and spread its branches as wide as 70 feet. It is a wide-crowned, evergreen species of oak native to the southeastern United States and northern parts of South America. It has a short trunk and leathery leaves and produces acorns. Its branches often are covered with Spanish moss. Live oaks are widely cultivated as shade trees in coastal regions.

The Corpus Christi landscape and that of other area cities has been changed by the availability of water to irrigate lawns and other plants not native to the area. Here you'll find plants popular in other parts of the country, native plants and exotics such as bougainvillea and towering palm trees. Among the native plants you'll find here and throughout the Corpus Christi area is the mesquite, an attractive, shade-producing tree found in many yards. Its light, airy appearance produces dappled shade, allowing lawns to grow right to the tree's base, which makes it an attractive choice for landscaping. It has deep and far-reaching roots, and its numerous crooked

Kemp's Ridley Sea Turtles

Watching an endangered species struggle to survive isn't on most vacation itineraries—unless your travel plans take you to the Corpus Christi area at the right time of year. Each summer, biologists at the Padre Island National Seashore release endangered Kemp's ridley sea turtle hatchlings into the Gulf

of Mexico in an effort to expand their nesting grounds, thereby increasing their chance of survival. The public is usually notified of the releases, giving those who attend the rare opportunity to watch science help one of nature's imperiled creatures.

Virtually the entire Kemp's ridley population now nests on a 14-mile stretch of beach near the village of Rancho Nuevo, Tamaulipas, Mexico. Biologists hope to establish a second nesting site on Padre Island as insurance against an environmental or human catastrophe at the Mexico site. In 1997 fewer than 1,500 females nested near Rancho Nuevo, a decrease from an estimated 40,000 in 1947.

Legislation has slowed the killing of turtles—the total adult turtle population is estimated at around 3,000—and shrimpers now use devices on their nets to prevent the creatures from becoming entangled and drowning. Recently a bi-national effort to save the species from extinction has begun to show promising results.

The Kemp's Ridley Sea Turtle Restoration and Enhancement Project organized in 1978 to establish a secondary breeding population at Padre Island. Participants include the Instituto Nacional de Pesca of Mexico, U.S. Fish and Wildlife Service, National Marine Fisheries, National Park Service, and Texas Parks and Wildlife Department. They chose the national seashore

Each year endangered Kemp's ridley sea turtle hatchlings are released into the wild at the Padre Island National Seashore. Biologists are trying to establish a second breeding colony on the uninhabited island.

Photo: courtesy of the Greater Corpus Christi Business Alliance

because Kemp's ridleys had been known to nest there and because its remote location would provide some protection to the species.

Each summer from 1978 to 1988, biologists collected about 2,000 eggs at Rancho Nuevo and sent them to Padre Island National Seashore. Once they hatched, the tiny turtles were released on the beach and allowed to enter the surf before being recaptured with aquarium dip nets. During those 10 years almost 16,000 recaptured hatchlings were transported to the National Marine Fisheries laboratory in Galveston, Texas, where they were allowed to grow for a year until they were large enough to avoid most predators.

About 13,450 survived and were tagged and released, primarily offshore from Padre Island. Biologists hoped the released females eventually would return to Padre Island to lay their eggs. Beach patrols (including many volunteers) for nesting turtles began in 1986, with a number of nests found. Increasing numbers of Kemp's ridley nests have been found along the Texas coast. The greatest reward came in 1996 when two females that hatched on Padre Island in 1983 and 1986 returned to nest.

National seashore officials collect eggs laid each year to protect them from predators. They place the eggs in boxes of sand and monitor them for 48 to 53 days until they hatch. When the hatchlings are deemed strong enough, they're released on the beach and guided into the surf.

Baby Kemp's ridleys measure 1 to 1½ inches in length and are black on top and bottom. Adult Kemp's ridleys, which take 10 to 15 years to mature, weigh 80 to 100 pounds and reach lengths of 2½ feet. The age at which Kemp's ridleys mature is unknown, but estimates range from eight to 15 years. When mature they are olive green on top and white on the bottom.

Biologists don't know how sea turtles find their way back to the beaches where they were born. One theory is that they remember the smell or texture of the nesting sand; another theory suggests the Earth's magnetic field guides them.

Efforts to educate the public about the Kemp's ridleys continue. Padre Island visitors often help with reporting turtles, and some get the chance to see them released into the wild. There, scientists hope they will begin their long, perilous journey back from the brink of extinction.

limbs grow close to the ground. The mesquite is common in pasture and rangeland, growing in such density that measures have to be taken to control it. It reaches a height of about 30 to 35 feet and produces a yellowish-green flower and a shiny brown legume that is eaten by horses, cattle, goats, white-tailed deer, and javelina (a pig-like animal that inhabits the area).

Another popular landscaping fixture here is the century plant, which stands as high as 6 feet tall with several long, thick gray leaves shooting up from the ground and fanning outward. It is also known as the agave or American aloe, a type of plant native to desert regions of the western hemisphere. The end of each leaf is tipped with a sharp spine that can produce painful jabs if you get too close. It lives for 10 to 25 years before flowering once and then dying. Before it flowers, a long stalk grows quickly upward to a height of 40 feet. It has large, thick and fleshy leaves that store large amounts of water.

The fruit of the Texas prickly pear cactus, aside from being a favorite javelina meal, may be eaten raw or made into a preserve, and the cactus leaves (nopalitos) may be cooked and served with a peppery dressing when young and tender. During droughts farmers burn off the spines so that hungry cattle can graze on the whole cactus plant. Javelina, white-tailed deer and other species of wildlife eat the leaves and fruit. They serve as both a food source and water reservoir for wild animals.

The pecan tree is the Texas state tree, and although it's more abundant in other parts of the state, you will find it represented here. The pecan is a large tree that grows as tall as 150 feet. The

THE NATURAL WORLD

THE GOOSE ISLAND OAK
(Live oak)
Quercus virginiana Mill.

For centuries these gnarled limbs have stood in their silent vigil of man's passing. Estimated to be in excess of 1000 years old, this mighty oak was already a giant when Cabeza de Vaca and Sieur de la Salle explored the Texas coast during the 1500's and 1600's.

The occasionally used name of "Lamar Oak" probably stems from the small village of Lamar. Established here in 1838 by a group of Irishmen, the village received its name in honor of Mirabeau Lamar, the second president of the Republic of Texas. Later, with the Civil War at hand, the "Big Tree" was witness to the burning of most of Lamar.

In 1966 the Texas Forest Service recognized this weathered veteran as the state champion live oak. As you pass in review before this grand old oak, consider those who have gone before you and those who may follow.

CIRCUMFERENCE	421-3/4 inches
CROWN SPREAD	89 feet
HEIGHT	44 feet

This oak tree at Goose Island State Park is believed to be the oldest in the state.

Photo: courtesy of the Greater Corpus Christi Business Alliance

THE NATURAL WORLD

trunk is often large. The tree flowers in the spring and produces fruit (the pecan) in the fall. It is widely cultivated for its fruit, and many forms of wildlife depend on it as a part of their diet.

The Texas palm, which reaches a height of 50 feet, has a large trunk and fan-shaped leaves that form a rounded crown. As the leaves die, they fall toward the trunk, where they cling unless trimmed away. Texas palms, also called Texas palmetto, are often used in residential landscaping in coastal communities. These are not to be confused with the giant palm trees seen throughout the Corpus Christi and neighboring towns, including the Corpus Christi Bayfront. These palms, imported from other parts of the world, thrive in the warm climate, although some succumb to the occasional freeze.

Visitors who arrive in Texas in the spring may be surprised by the large number of wildflowers they see along roadways. Texas is more than the cactus and sagebrush often depicted in the movies. Almost 400 wildflowers are known to bloom in Texas. Many can be found in the Corpus Christi area, including the bluebonnet (the official state flower), phlox, Indian paintbrush, Indian blanket, winecup, evening primrose, spiderwort, flax, brown-eyed Susan, common sunflower, lazy daisy, and Queen Anne's lace.

In recent years Texans have taken it upon themselves to promote the planting of wildflowers along public roads. With the help of former First Lady Ladybird Johnson, Texans founded the National Wildflower Research Center in Austin. Wildflowers bloom mostly between February and May, and the display varies depending on environmental conditions during the spring and fall. Many wildflowers reproduce by seed and require freeze-thaw, wet-dry cycles, or passage through an animal's digestive system before they can germinate and grow.

Each year, the Texas Department of Transportation, (361) 886-6000, extension 7468, operates a wildflower line telling motorists where to find the best display of wildflowers in a 10-county area. The Texas Wildflower Hotline, (800) 452-9292, provides statewide wildflower information in case you're planning a trip during the spring display.

Fauna

The sea holds the most abundant variety of creatures. Blue crabs, stone crabs, ghost crabs, and ghost shrimp populate the intertidal zone along the beach, while oysters and shrimp live in local waters in large numbers. Redfish, speckled seatrout, flounder, and red and black drum attract anglers to the Gulf and bays, where stingrays, nurse sharks, groupers, sea turtles, and barracuda also reside. Other fish common to Gulf of Mexico waters include sheepshead, Atlantic spadefish, tarpon, ladyfish, snook, yellowtailed snapper, amberjack, Bermuda chub, sandtiger shark, pork fish, cobia, and trigger fish.

Among the animals you can spot in the area are white-tailed deer, javelinas, raccoons, wild turkeys, armadillos, opossums, bobwhite (quail), ducks, geese, squirrels, and hundreds of bird species. The back dunes on the barrier islands are home to picket gophers, ground squirrels, lizards, snakes, and coyotes, among other creatures. Mustang Island State Park is home to grasshopper mice, rice rats, cotton rats, cottontail rabbits, jackrabbits, skunks, snakes, and lizards. Take the Grasslands Nature Trail, south of the entrance to Padre Island National Seashore, and you might be lucky enough to spot a Padre Island kangaroo rat, a tiny long-tailed mammal found only on Padre and Mustang Islands. And it's the rare visitor who gets the chance to see a nesting Kemp's ridley sea turtle scramble ashore to lay her eggs in the sand. Efforts have been under way for 20 years to help the endangered species establish a second nesting ground on the island (see the Close-up in this chapter).

You're more likely to catch a glimpse of the unusual-looking javelinas native to the area. The javelina, not to be confused with the feral hogs that also can be found here, is a nocturnal wild pig-like creature also known as the collared peccary. These squat little creatures with bristly hair roam in groups of two to 50, feeding on insects, roots, fruit, and reptiles. A favorite food is prickly pear cactus, although many have taken to accepting handouts from picnickers at the Aransas National Wildlife Refuge (much to the displeasure of park rangers).

You can often spot bottle-nosed dolphins from Roberts Point Park in Port Aransas or from the ferry that shuttles people and cars across the Corpus Christi Ship Channel. A favorite dolphin pastime is to swim in the bow wave created by huge oil tankers and barges. On rare occasions they have even been spotted inside the breakwater along the Corpus Christi bayfront.

Alligators and western diamondback rattlesnakes inhabit the area. Alligators can be found in

THE NATURAL WORLD

wetlands like those at the Aransas National Wildlife Refuge, while rattlesnakes make their homes in dry places such as sand dunes and the South Texas brush country.

Around the house or outside your hotel room (and sometimes inside) you're likely to run into lizards.

The Mediterranean gecko is a harmless, nocturnal lizard that grows to 4 to 5 inches long. It was brought to Texas on ships from the Mediterranean, the Middle East and India. It is pale to translucent in color with small spots and large, lidless eyes.

The anole, commonly called a chameleon, is a harmless lizard active during the daytime. It grows to 5 to 8 inches long and its color varies from deep green to dark brown. It eats insects and spiders.

Insects

Insects enjoy the warm Corpus Christi-area weather as much as the people who live and visit here. Why, the bugs even love it during the dog days of summer. Flies, moths, butterflies, roaches, spiders, crickets, and all manner of caterpillars crawl, fly, and hop here.

The most pesky insect to inhabit the region is the mosquito, whose bloodsucking propensities can ruin a picnic or camping trip. Mosquitoes can do more than leave a tiny red mark that makes you itch. They can also spread viruses like dengue fever and St. Louis encephalitis, although such occurrences are rare. The best way to deal with mosquitoes is to prevent them from breeding. Remove or empty all containers with stagnant water so that mosquitoes cannot lay their eggs there. Puddles, leaky pipes, potted plants, and blocked gutters are common culprits. Insect repellent, bug zappers, and citronella candles will deter some mosquitoes, although nothing is 100 percent effective. Visitors to the Aransas National Wildlife Refuge will want to take special precautions. The refuge's marshlike setting makes it a stellar insect breeding ground. Visitors are advised to wear protective clothing such as long pants, long-sleeved shirts, hats, and boots.

Mosquito season lasts from early March to early December. They're most active at dawn and dusk, and the only thing that seems to stop them is a long drought.

Fifty to 60 types of mosquitoes live in the Corpus Christi area. Some can be found in fresh water, others in salt water. Some live in holes in trees, and others can be found in holes that crabs make at the beach. Mosquitoes can fly 20 miles in search of blood. Their eggs can lie dormant in dry fields for as long as a year, and once covered with water can hatch in 10 minutes. It takes seven to 10 days for the mosquito larva to mature.

Another common pest—and one that may surprise, fascinate and gross you out—is a species of giant cockroach that lives here. Most people just call them "giant roaches." Others call them "tree roaches." Whatever the name, they are big. Really big. We're talking 2 to 3 inches in length and an inch or so wide. Step on one and you'll hear a loud "snap." They appear in warm weather and disappear when it turns cold. You'll most likely run into them outside, although they do venture indoors through cracks and holes. They're also fairly swift and will skitter to safety before you can say "rolled-up newspaper."

Females lay an egg case with 35 young every 25 days. To control them, keep rooms clean and dry, don't leave dirty dishes out overnight, do not leave water or food out for pets, don't overwater plants and throw out old newspapers and paper bags, which make good hiding places.

Another insect you may encounter on a trip here is the June Bug, so named because it appears around the month of June. These round, dark brown bugs don't stay long or appear in great numbers, but their lack of flying ability makes them genuine pests while they're here. June bugs are horrible pilots, flying helter-skelter and into everything and everyone in their vicinity. Like many other insects, they seem to congregate near porch lights.

Red imported fire ants are another Corpus Christi-area pest you'll want to watch out for. In fact, fire ants can be downright dangerous. Texas ranchers tell tales of fire ants killing and devouring injured cattle and newborn calves.

This native of South America made its way to Texas in the late 1950s. These reddish brown ants grow up to a quarter inch long and inflict painful, burning stings. They build large, hard dirt mounds up to 2 feet high that can house hundreds of thousands of fire ants.

By the way, that shrill sound you hear during spring and summer is produced by cicadas. Males produce that sound by means of vibrating membranes on the underside of the abdomen.

Hotels and Motels

Finding a place to stay in the Corpus Christi area shouldn't be difficult, especially if you reserve your room in advance. In our Hotels and Motels chapter you'll find a variety of both types of lodgings divided into our four geographic areas: North Bay Area, Corpus Christi, Port Aransas to Padre Island, and Kingsville Area. Tourists and business travelers alike will find plenty to choose from among our listings.

The Corpus Christi area has experienced remarkable growth in its tourist industry during the past decade, including the addition of several accommodations. You'll find many of the major hotel/motel chains represented here, along with a few locally owned establishments. We've tried to offer you choices in a variety of locations, styles, and price ranges. Those of you planning to stay for more than a few days, or anyone who prefers to stay in a condominium, will want to turn to our Weekly and Long-term Rentals chapter. There you'll find information on several condominium complexes that cater to guests needing long-term rentals, along with those who plan stays of as short as a day.

Hotels and motels in the area generally fall into four categories based on their surroundings and the people who visit. In the North Bay, fishing is a huge draw, luring anglers from all over Texas and the nation for some of the best fishing in the state. Accordingly, accommodations in that area sometimes skimp on creature comforts in exchange for accessibility to the water and the fish that live there. Fish-cleaning stations are common in the North Bay Area but less so in other areas. This is not to say that the North Bay Area is lacking in luxurious accommodations: Homes for rent in Rockport's Key Allegro subdivision rival many found along Corpus Christi's prestigious Ocean Drive, and several leasing agencies rent medium- to high-end condos and homes in the North Bay Area.

The Corpus Christi lodging scene caters to both business people and tourists with a healthy mix of accommodations along Corpus Christi Bay as well as the industrial corridors of Interstate 37 and Padre Island Drive. Lodgings here range from the very basic to luxurious, with a good number of medium-priced accommodations available. You'll have to clean your fish elsewhere, but you'll most likely enjoy more amenities here than you would if you stayed in the North Bay motels and cottages.

The Port Aransas to Padre Island section caters to tourists whose main reason for staying in the area is its proximity to the beach. This is a good area for people who want to swim in the Gulf of Mexico, walk on the beach, lounge around the pool, and enjoy recreational activities not found in urban lodgings.

Kingsville's motels and lodges generally cater to hunters and anglers. Hunters are drawn to the wide-open spaces to bag deer, quail, or dove, while anglers come to hook a redfish or speckled trout.

The least expensive lodgings can be found in Kingsville, but choices there are limited. North Bay Area prices are slightly higher, followed by

LOOK FOR:
• North Bay Area
• Corpus Christi
• Port Aransas to Mustang Island
• Kingsville Area

Price Code

Prices are for high season, double occupancy per night for one-bedroom units or, when a one-bedroom is not offered, the smallest unit available. Some offer a variety of rooms for two adults and the range in prices is reflected in our listing. Prices do not include the 13 percent to 15 percent hotel/motel tax.

$	Less than $50
$$	$51 to $75
$$$	$76 to $100
$$$$	$100 to $150
$$$$$	More than $150

rates in Corpus Christi and Port Aransas to Padre Island. Summer (late May through early September) is the high season for the area, with some accommodations also charging high rates in March, when the area is inundated with high school and college students on spring break. You can expect higher rates on weekends, holidays, and on dates that coincide with special events. Other seasons are the regular season (roughly September, October, early November, April and part of May) and the winter season (mid-November to the end of March), with winter the least expensive. Winter rates can be less than half of summer rates, with regular-season rates somewhere in the middle. Weekends, holidays, and special-event dates will generally run you an additional $10 to $30 a night.

The closer you are to the water the more you will pay; and the better your view of the water the higher your rates will be. Discounts are available for active military, seniors, groups, and for extended stays. Daily, weekly, and monthly rates are available at many places; most, if not all, accommodations in the Corpus Christi area are open year round. Remember to add between 13 and 15 percent to the room price for the hotel/motel tax.

The listings are arranged alphabetically in the Corpus Christi section and north to south by city in all other sections.

You can assume that all accommodations have televisions, telephones, and maid service unless otherwise mentioned. You can also assume that a lodging accepts major credit cards unless otherwise noted. Pet policies vary. Some accept them, some don't. Some charge a fee. Smoking and nonsmoking rooms are available in most places, as are wheelchair-accessible rooms. Check before making reservations.

North Bay Area

Best Western Inn by The Bay
$$ • 3902 Texas Hwy. 35 N., Fulton
• (361) 729-8351, (800) 235-6076
Nestled among shady live oak trees, this 72-room Best Western offers quiet accommodations just east of Texas Highway 35 and a half mile west of Aransas Bay. It looks more like a quiet apartment complex than a motel. Live oak trees mute traffic noise, and the rooms are divided into two buildings separated by a courtyard with gazebo, benches, and picnic tables.

Amenities include a free full breakfast, screened recreation patio, swimming pool, guest laundry, television with HBO, free boat hook-

ups, fish-cleaning station and fax and copy service. Guests can choose from a room with two double beds or one king-size bed. The hotel has facilities for bus tours, banquets, meetings, and conferences of fewer than 100 people. The hotel does not have its own restaurant, but eating establishments are close by. The Best Western's Seahorse Recreational Vehicle and Motor Home Park is next door.

Days Inn, Rockport
$$–$$$ • 1212 Laurel St., Rockport
• (361) 729-6379, (800) 329-7466
This three-story motel at the corner of Laurel Street and Texas Highway 35 looks out over the Texas Maritime Museum and the Rockport Marina. Downtown shopping and restaurants and the beautiful Key Allegro neighborhood are a short drive away. The grounds and swimming pool area are beautifully landscaped, and the white stucco exterior gives the hotel a tropical look appropriate to the warm climate.

Rooms come with a surprising number of decorator touches such as ceiling fans, sofas, fireplaces in some rooms and mirrored walls. You can choose a room with two double beds or one king.

Holiday Inn Express
$$$ • 901 Texas Hwy. 35 N., Rockport
• (361) 727-0283, (800) 465-4329
This motel on the city's main thoroughfare opened its doors in the summer of 1997. The 50 rooms have peach walls; hardwood floors and crown molding add elegant touches to the lobby. The motel is across Texas Highway 35 from Rockport Beach Park; the Texas Maritime Museum and Rockport Marina are nearby. Amenities include cable television with HBO and a free continental breakfast. Children 19 and younger stay free. Meeting rooms can accommodate as many as 25 people.

Laguna Reef Hotel
$$$$ • 1021 Water St., Rockport
• (361) 729-1742, (800) 248-1057
The Laguna Reef Hotel offers a great view and a convenient location two blocks south of downtown overlooking Aransas Bay. This modern four-story complex offers one- and two-bedroom suites and hotel guestrooms. All suites come with fully equipped kitchens, queen-size beds, and double sofa beds. Two-bedroom suites come in small and large floor plans. The second bedrooms in the small floorplans come with two twin beds, while the second bedroom in the large floorplan is equipped with two double

beds. Hotel guest rooms come with one king-size bed, one queen-size bed or two double beds. Some rooms are on the bay side, while others overlook the parking lot. Hotel amenities include balconies, cable television, meeting rooms, a swimming pool, a 1,000-foot lighted fishing pier, free continental breakfast, picnic and barbecue area and a putting green.

Sandollar Resort
$$ • 919 N. Fulton Beach Rd., Fulton
• (361) 729-2381

The Sandollar Resort combines a motel with a 100-space recreational vehicle-park set amid wind-swept oak trees between Texas Highway 35 and Fulton Beach Road. The RV spaces are on the highway side; the motel faces Fulton Beach Road and Aransas Bay. Motel rooms come in two sizes: the smaller size is a regular motel room with two double beds and a bath; larger rooms come with two double beds and kitchenettes equipped with small dinettes, refrigerators, and stoves. Children six and younger stay free.

Outside you'll find two swimming pools, shuffleboard, horseshoes, volleyball court and a fishing pier and marina. Across the street the Sandollar Pavilion serves burgers, steaks, and seafood. The resort office is open 24 hours.

Days Inn Suites
$$–$$$ • 410 Goodnight Ave.,
Aransas Pass
• (361) 758-7375, (800) 325-2525

The 32-unit Days Inn Suites in Aransas Pass is only a few years old but the rooms are already being remodeled to keep the place looking sharp. The hotel's white walls and red-tile roof echo South Texas's Spanish heritage, and its location in the middle of town along Texas Highway 361 places it close to local attractions. The old-fashioned downtown shopping district is just down the street, and Conn Brown Harbor, where the shrimp boats dock, is a short distance away. Port Aransas, Ingleside, and Rockport are within driving distance.

The hotel offers a choice of a single room with two queen-size beds or a suite with a king-size bed and a queen-size sofa sleeper in the living area. Each suite comes with two cable televisions (with HBO and Cinemax), two telephones, a hairdryer, microwave, and refrigera-

INSIDERS' TIP

Accommodations in Corpus Christi are geared more toward business travelers and tourists staying a few days. Rockport, Port Aransas, and Padre Island tend to cater to travelers staying for several days to several months.

tor. Other features include a swimming pool, exercise room and conference rooms for as many as 40 people.

Super 8 Motel, Aransas Pass
$$ • 500 E. Goodnight Ave., Aransas Pass
• (361) 758-7888, (800) 800-8000

This tan-and-white, 49-room motel near the Days Inn Suites is a recent addition to Aransas Pass and still has that new sparkle to it. A small but clean heated swimming pool is on the east side of the motel in front of a covered, lighted picnic area for motel guests. Amenities include two whirlpool suites, guest laundry, free coffee, and toast in the morning and cable television with HBO.

The Super 8 is a short walk from Aransas Pass's downtown shopping district and is just around the corner from Conn Brown Harbor. Port Aransas, Ingleside, and Rockport are a short drive away.

Best Western–Ingleside
$$$ • 2025 Texas Hwy. 361, Ingleside
• (361) 776-2767, (877) 776-4440

This beige-and-plum, two-story motel is popular among the military and laborers brought in to work on ships stationed at Naval Station Ingleside. Tourists are more common in summer months. Each of its 37 rooms comes with one king- or two queen-sized beds, a microwave oven, coffeepot, and a refrigerator. A free continental breakfast is served every morning in the enclosed breakfast area next to the lobby. Non-smoking rooms are available. The motel has an outdoor pool.

Comfort Inn
$$ • 1703 Texas Hwy. 181 N., Portland
• (361) 643-2222

If you don't mind driving a few minutes, this moderately priced hotel on Portland's main thoroughfare may be the place you're looking for. Only 10 minutes from downtown Corpus Christi, this recent apricot-and-seafoam-colored addition to Portland is convenient to both Corpus Christi, Port Aransas, and much of the North Bay Area.

Each single room comes with one king-size or two queen-size beds, a microwave, refrigerator, and cable television. Other amenities include a swimming pool and VCR and movie rentals. A VCR and one movie can be rented for a day; a VCR and unlimited movies also are available. Guests also receive a free continental breakfast.

Corpus Christi

Radisson Beach Hotel
**$$$$–$$$$$ • 3200 Surfside Blvd.,
Corpus Christi**
• (361) 883-7456, (800) 242-5814

You won't find a hotel more convenient to Corpus Christi's major tourist attractions than the Radisson Beach Hotel on Corpus Christi Beach. This 250-room hotel is within walking distance of the Texas State Aquarium and the Lexington Museum on the Bay (a decommissioned aircraft carrier). It's also a five-minute drive across the Harbor Bridge to downtown Corpus Christi, the South Texas Institute for the Arts, The Museum of Oriental Cultures, The Corpus Christi Museum of Arts and Sciences, and several other attractions (see our Attractions chapter).

Hotel amenities include a swimming pool, whirlpool, business center, on-demand movies, and cable television which includes HBO. Rooms come with microwave ovens, refrigerators, ironing board and irons, and coffeepots. All you have to do is step outside the Radisson's doors to see the sun and surf on Corpus Christi Beach or the Corpus Christi skyline to the southeast.

You'll find a restaurant inside the Radisson along with a full-service bar. Banquet and meeting space also is available.

Corpus Christi Residence Inn
**$$$$ • 5229 Blanche Moore St.,
Corpus Christi**
• (361) 985-1113, (800) 331-3131

Shopaholics will love the location of the Corpus Christi Residence Inn, owned by the Marriott hotel chain. It sits smack dab in the middle of the Blanche Moore Shopping Center and across the highway from Corpus Christi's two malls. It's a block from the city's main thoroughfare, South Padre Island Drive (SPID), and right behind Barnes & Noble Booksellers, a favorite hangout for those who love books and Italian coffee.

Inside this traditional-style brick building you'll find a heated indoor swimming pool and spa, exercise room, breakfast area, and guest laundry facilities. What you won't find is a restaurant, but that's no problem because several fine restaurants are along SPID. Amenities include a free continental breakfast, HBO, a social hour Monday through Thursday with free food and drinks, fax and copy services and a sports court where you can play basketball, tennis, or badminton.

Corpus Christi Residence Inn offers one bedroom, two bedrooms, and studios. All rooms come with king-size beds and fully equipped kitchens.

Drury Inn Airport
**$$ • 2021 N. Padre Island Dr.,
Corpus Christi**
• (361) 289-8200, (800) 325-8300

Chief among the Drury Inn's main selling points is its proximity to the airport, the Port of Corpus Christi, the city's industrial district, and Corpus Christi Greyhound Racetrack. Corpus Christi International Airport is a mere five minutes away from this four-story motel. Amenities include a free continental breakfast served in an area adjacent to the lobby, free evening cocktails and snacks from 5:30 to 7 PM Monday through Thursday, a swimming pool, cable television with HBO and The Disney Channel, free fax service, computer dataports in all rooms, coffee makers, exercise room, guest laundry, and almost 1,000 square feet of meeting space.

The lobby is cozy and well-lighted thanks to the four-story glass wall on the room's eastern side. Cushy armchairs and sofas abound. Rooms come in several sizes. The single deluxe has a living area with a work station, armchair, microwave, refrigerator, and coffee maker. The main drawback? There aren't any eateries within walking distance, but the price keeps business travelers and summer tourists coming back.

Embassy Suites
**$$$$ • 4337 S. Padre Island Dr.,
Corpus Christi**
• (361) 853-7899, (800) 362-2779

Embassy Suites has the biggest lobby in the Corpus Christi area. Rooms in this three-story hotel open onto the cavernous lobby where you can lounge in a sofa or armchair or have a bite at the hotel snack bar. Keep walking and you'll come across the hotel lounge and, beyond that,

INSIDERS' TIP

Most places charge a fee, typically $5, for each extra person who stays in the room.

the swimming pool. Each two-room suite has a separate living room with a sofa bed, coffeemaker, refrigerator, microwave, wet bar, two telephones with voice mail and data port capabilities, two televisions with cable and in-room movies, and an iron and full-size ironing board. Each room is furnished with either a king-size bed or two double beds.

Amenities include a free newspaper every weekday morning, a free shuttle to the airport and to anywhere within 5 miles of the hotel, a free continental breakfast, free evening beverages and snacks, indoor heated swimming pool, whirlpool, sauna, and exercise facilities. The Embassy Suites has more than 4,300 square feet of meeting/banquet space.

Holiday Inn Emerald Beach
$$$$ • 1102 S. Shoreline Blvd.,
Corpus Christi
• (361) 883-5731, (800) 465-4329

The Holiday Inn Emerald Beach has two things that no other Shoreline Boulevard hotel can claim: a site right on the water and a beach. This 600-foot public beach is outside its back doors, at the end of the seawall a half-mile south of the city marina. Many of its 368 rooms have bay views; others open onto the indoor recreation area that's outfitted with a swimming pool, sauna, whirlpool, Ping-Pong tables, and a children's Playport similar to those found at Discovery Zone or McDonald's restaurants. Other amenities include cable television with Showtime, coffeemakers, a fitness center and more than 10,000 square feet of meeting space.

The hotel has a full-service restaurant, a grill serving a breakfast buffet and sandwiches and a bar. Children younger than 12 eat free if dining with an adult.

Holiday Inn Padre Island Drive
$$$ • 5549 Leopard St., Corpus Christi
• (361) 289-5100, (800) 465-4329

The Holiday Inn Padre Island Drive is only three miles from Corpus Christi International Airport and five minutes—via Interstate 37—from downtown and the bayfront. Its proximity to Padre Island Drive also makes it fairly convenient to Padre and Mustang Islands, which on a good traffic day (and in Corpus Christi most days are good traffic days) is only a 20-minute drive.

This 247-room hotel offers free airport transportation 24 hours a day, six two-room suites with oversize whirlpool baths, coffeemakers, an indoor heated swimming pool, whirlpool, sun deck, business center, exercise facility, and

11 meeting rooms for as many as 700 people. An in-house sports bar offers nightly specials and appetizers and the Atrium Cafe serves breakfast, lunch, and dinner. There's also a multilevel lounge with a fountain that's decorated with greenery.

Knights Inn
$–$$ • 3615 Timon Blvd., Corpus Christi
• (361) 883-4411, (800) 883-0424

The Knights Inn can't match the luxury found in Corpus Christi's more expensive hotels, but you can tell by the way the place is kept that the owners take pride in their establishment. Located one block from Corpus Christi Beach, the hotel features attractive and well maintained grounds. Rooms come with private balconies (some with bay views) and cable television with HBO. Suites with kitchens are available. Outdoor amenities include a swimming pool, grills, volleyball, swings, and shuffleboard.

La Quinta Inn South
$$$ • 6225 S. Padre Island Dr.,
Corpus Christi
• (361) 991-5730, (800) 531-5900,
(800)687-6667

La Quinta Inn's rooms have been upgraded in recent years to "Gold Medal" status, which means they're a lot nicer than they used to be and a good value as well. Included in the 129 rooms are crown molding, built-in closets, and wood furniture. The bathrooms have been enlarged and decorated with ceramic tile floors, designer vanities, angled mirrors, and better lighting. Each room has a coffeemaker, a work area, and dataport phones for visitors needing to use a laptop computer.

The inn is near Corpus Christi's main shopping area. Two malls and several shopping centers are within a few miles. Amenities include a free continental breakfast, first-run movies, video games, messaging and fax service, same-day laundry and dry cleaning and a swimming pool. La Quinta visitors also have access to exercise facilities at the Corpus Christi Athletic Club, a short drive away. Children younger than 18 stay free in their parents' room.

The Omni Bayfront
$$$–$$$$ • 900 N. Shoreline Blvd.,
Corpus Christi
• (361) 887-1600, (800) 843-6664

The Omni Bayfront may be the finest hotel in the Corpus Christi area. It boasts a good location as well. The hotel overlooks Corpus

HOTELS AND MOTELS

The Omni Bayfront is the largest hotel on Corpus Christi's Shoreline Drive.

Photo: Daniel Fielder

tures prime beef and seafood and a great view of the bay. The Republic of Texas is open beginning at 5:30 for dinner.

The Omni Marina
$$$–$$$$
• **707 N. Shoreline Blvd., Corpus Christi**
• **(361) 882-1700, (800) 843-6664**

The Omni Marina is one block from the Omni Bayfront and shares something with its sister hotel: both provide excellent rooms and phenomenal service at reasonable prices. They are so popular with tourists one concierge told us that they don't have to charge more for their rooms. They make up for it with volume. The outside of this high-rise hotel is brown brick with teal accents on top of the first-floor lobby, lounge, outdoor terrace, and restaurant. Its 346 guest rooms, including 19 suites, come with private balconies and bayfront views. The view from the swimming pool, located on the roof above the lobby, is spectacular.

The Corpus Christi Marina is just across the street and the rest of the bayfront stretches out to the north and south. Amenities include a complete health club with dry sauna and whirlpool, indoor/outdoor heated swimming pool, meeting rooms, and conference space. The Omni Marina has a lounge and a cafe serving breakfast, lunch, and dinner.

Christi Bay and the seawall where tourists and locals walk, jog and glide along on in-line skates. Omni has taken two hotels a block apart and combined operations into one hotel, designating the two separate buildings as the Bayfront and Marina. Its 475 guest rooms, including 29 suites, were completely renovated in April 1999. Each comes with a bayfront view.

Amenities for all guests include free airport shuttle, health club, sauna, indoor/outdoor heated swimming pool, more than 38,000 square feet of meeting and banquet space and two restaurants. The Glass Pavilion on the second floor offers casual dining for breakfast, lunch or dinner, while the multilevel Republic of Texas Bar and Grill on the 20th floor fea-

Railway Inn Suites
$$ • 4343 Ocean Dr., Corpus Christi
• **(361) 225-3946, (888) 729-7245**

The Railway Inn Suites is somewhat of an oddity in this world of chain hotels. This 40-room hotel on scenic Ocean Drive is privately owned and touts itself as "dedicated to God and family." But what really sets it apart is its railroad theme. Inside this dark brick building you'll find all sorts of railroad paraphernalia, and outside you'll find a railroad track encircling the building and surrounding property.

The owners have a small train for use by hotel guests and pre-arranged groups.

All rooms are suite-size with either two queen-size beds or one king and one queen-size sleeper sofa. Each room has a refrigerator and microwave. A free continental breakfast is served in a room adjoining the lobby. The Railway Inn has two swimming pools, including one for tots.

Best Western Marina Grand
$$$ • 300 N. Shoreline Blvd.,
Corpus Christi
• (361) 883-5111, (800) 578-7878

The Best Western Marina Grand is a new entry in our guide, although the hotel itself, under different names, has overlooked Corpus Christi Bay since 1967. The hotel opened its doors as the Sheraton Marina Inn, operating as a four-star hotel for many years before falling into some decline after ownership changed hands several times. The current owners, who purchased the hotel in 1997, spent approximately $2 million upgrading the 172-room hotel to meet the needs of modern business and vacation travelers.

The hotel offers single rooms with king-size beds or two double beds. It also has one 3-bedroom suite and three 1-bedroom suites. Amenities include a free continental breakfast, coffeemakers, in-room safes, microwaves and refrigerators in some rooms, an outdoor pool, exercise room, business center and meeting rooms for as many as 200 people. Private balconies overlook Corpus Christi Bay.

Port Aransas to Mustang Island

Tarpon Inn
$$–$$$ • 200 E. Cotter Ave., Port Aransas
• (361) 749-5555, (800) 365-6784

Named for the abundant trophy fish in the nearby Gulf of Mexico, the Tarpon Inn is one of only two accommodations in the Corpus Christi area to be listed on the National Register of Historic Places. Built in 1886 by Frank Stephenson, a boat pilot and assistant lighthouse keeper, the Tarpon Inn has survived fire, hurricane, and tidal wave to become one of the area's most interesting lodgings.

Many famous people have stayed here in the more than a century since the founding of the Tarpon Inn, near the Port Aransas wharf. Franklin D. Roosevelt, who disdained the inn in favor of his private yacht, left behind an autographed tarpon scale that is now framed and displayed prominently in the motel lobby along with 7,000 others caught by former guests.

The Tarpon Inn offers 24 small guest rooms filled with an eclectic blend of antiques. One two-room suite is available. All rooms open onto a shady porch where you can rock the day away while watching traffic roll by when you're not busy enjoying the ambiance of the town. Rooms do not have telephones or TVs. Beulah's, one of the best restaurants in the Corpus Christi area, is in back of the Tarpon Inn (see our Restaurants chapter). Eat inside or on the porch overlooking the Tarpon Inn courtyard. The beach is less than a mile away. For more on the Tarpon Inn, see the Close-up in this chapter.

Captain's Quarters Inn
$$–$$$ • 235 W. Cotter Ave, Port Aransas
• (361) 749-6005, (888) 272-6727

This 40-room motel built in 1996 is located on one of the two main thoroughfares in Port Aransas, a short distance from the ferry landing. It's within walking distance of the municipal harbor, Roberts Point Park and many shops and restaurants. Walk across the street and you can check out the catches brought in by the fishing boats. The major drawback? It's quite a walk from the beach. But, like everything else in Port Aransas, it's less than a five-minute drive from your room to the water.

Rooms come with one king-size or two queen-size beds, 25-inch color TVs with cable, microwaves, and refrigerators. Other amenities include a free continental breakfast, swimming pool, conference room, and free trolley service.

Alister Square Inn
$$$ • 122 S. Alister St., Port Aransas
• (361) 749-3000, (888) 749-3003

If you like your rooms to have that new-motel cachet, you might want to check out the Alister Square Inn on Port Aransas's main drag, also known as Texas 361. Only a mile from the beach (and just about everything else in town), this recent addition to the Port Aransas lodging scene offers space-efficient rooms with queen-size beds, microwaves, refrigerators, and cable televisions. Rooms with kitchenettes are also available.

Amenities include a free continental breakfast of coffee, juice and donuts, guest laundry, swimming pool, voice mail, computer outlet jacks, fax service, and a meeting room for as many as 150 people. A free trolley service is

Tarpon Inn

The Tarpon Inn in Port Aransas is as much a lesson in history as it is a place to stay. This 24-room hotel at 200 E. Cotter Avenue is a throwback to an era when anglers came from all over the country to fish for tarpon in the Gulf of Mexico.

The more than 7,000 autographed tarpon scales tacked onto the lobby's walls testify to the former abundance of this coveted trophy fish, which is now scarce in local waters. For decades anglers left a record of their catch by writing their name, home city, the size of the catch, and the date on a two- to three-inch tarpon scale that was then attached to the walls.

So prized was the tarpon that celebrities the world over came to Port Aransas, and many stayed at the Tarpon Inn. Movie star Heddy Lamarr stayed there. So did evangelist Aimee Semple McPherson, aviator Douglas "Wrong Way" Corrigan, and gourmet Duncan Hines, who was married at the hotel.

During his visit to Port Aransas in May 1937, President Franklin D. Roosevelt opted for his private yacht rather than the Tarpon Inn's small rooms. But a souvenir of his visit can be found on the hotel's back wall, where his framed, autographed tarpon scale is displayed prominently behind protective glass.

The inn's ties to history have landed it on the National Register of Historic Places and designation as a Texas Landmark. Frank Stephenson, a boat pilot and assistant lighthouse keeper, built the hotel in 1886 from lumber taken from Civil War barracks on nearby San Jose Island.

The Tarpon Inn in Port Aransas is listed on the National Register of Historic Places.
One lobby wall is covered with autographed tarpon scales,
including one signed by Franklin Delano Roosevelt.

Photo: courtesy of the Greater Corpus Christi Business Alliance

During the next 100-plus years, the inn endured fire, hurricanes, and several changes in ownership. In 1991 Houston-area businesswoman Priscilla Conoley bought it with plans to restore it.

Work included painting the building, installing new wallboard and rebuilding the bathrooms, railings, and supports. Conoley had the 200-foot-long porch overlooking Cotter Avenue rebuilt, and refurbished the rooms by ripping up carpeting, refinishing the hardwood floors beneath them, and decorating the rooms with area rugs and antiques.

Beulah's Restaurant, behind the Tarpon Inn, is one of the Coastal Bend's finest restaurants, serving international cuisine with an island flair. Take a seat inside or dine on the porch overlooking the Tarpon Inn courtyard.

The Tarpon Inn's rooms are small and lack many amenities found at other lodgings (the rooms have no telephones nor televisions), but you won't find a hotel in the Coastal Bend with more charm—or history—than this 19th-century inn. For more information see our Hotels and Motels chapter.

available for city and beach travel and for transportation to and from the Island Moorings Airport. The motel's second-story rear balcony is a great place to catch the sunset.

Best Western Ocean Villa
$$$–$$$$ • 400 E. Ave. G, Port Aransas • (361) 749-3010, (800) 528-1234

This 49-room Best Western is a recent addition to Port Aransas. It's best feature? It's within walking distance of the beach. Just step outside this two-story building, head east and you'll find yourself in the Gulf of Mexico in five to 10 minutes. Rooms come with one king-size bed or two or three queens. Rooms come with refrigerators, microwaves, hair dryers, and free cable TV with HBO. The motel also offers a free continental breakfast, swimming pool, and game room with a pool table. Rooms are reached from the outside.

This is an attractive motel with white and beige walls and red-tiled roof. The tropical landscaping is also attractive.

Holiday Inn Sunspree Resort
$$$$ • 15202 Windward Dr., Padre Island • (361) 949-8041, (888) 949-8041

The Holiday Inn is the only full-service hotel directly on the Gulf of Mexico. Step into the lobby and you'll know you're near the Gulf: The walls have been painted with vistas of undersea life (complete with dolphins, sharks, and other sea creatures), and marine aquariums encircle the front desk.

Amenities include a fully equipped exercise room including a sauna, two swimming pools, a hot tub, playgrounds, shuffleboard, and golf

and tennis at the nearby Padre Isles Country Club. Meeting rooms can accommodate as many as 200 people.

Each room comes with a microwave, refrigerator, coffeemaker, in-room safe, hair dryer and fax/modem capabilities. The nautical motif is evident here, too, in the starfish that decorate bedspreads and window accents.

Kingsville Area

Days Inn Suites
$$ • 715 S. U.S. Hwy. 77, Bishop • (361) 584-4444, (800) 329-7466

The Days Inn in Bishop, a few miles north of Kingsville, offers 40 suites on two floors. Located on U.S. Highway 77 (the main thoroughfare through town), this Spartan pink-and-blue motel features single rooms, each of which has one king-size bed, or double rooms, each with two queen-size beds. All rooms have refrigerators and microwaves. Suites come with a separate living area and small desks. Jacuzzi suites also are available. Amenities at the Days Inn include a swimming pool, hot tub, and free continental breakfast.

Holiday Inn Kingsville
$$ • 3430 U.S. Hwy. 77 S., Kingsville • (361) 595-5753, (800) 465-4329

You won't forget you're in South Texas if you stay at the Holiday Inn Kingsville. Its red-tile roof and Spanish-mission look invites you to contemplate the strong influence of Mexican culture on the region. Amenities include a swimming pool, lounge and—for those of you driving an 18-wheeler—adjacent convenience store and truck stop.

Each room comes with one king-size bed or two queen-size beds. A large meeting room can hold as many as 70 people; a smaller room can accommodate as many as 20.

Best Western Kingsville Inn
$$ • 2402 E. King Ave., Kingsville
• (361) 595-5656, (800) 528-1234

The Best Western's peach walls and teal trim lend a definite tropical flavor to this 50-room motel at the intersection of King Avenue and U.S. Highway 77. You'll also find a few palm trees and brightly colored flowers decorating the grounds of this highly regarded lodging. Each room comes with one king-size bed or two queen-size and cable television with HBO. Amenities include a swimming pool with hot tub and a free continental breakfast.

Quality Inn
$$ • 221 U.S. Hwy. 77 S., Kingsville
• (361) 592-5251, (800) 424-4777

This beige-and-forest-green, two-story motel is at the intersection of U.S. Highway 77 and King Avenue, a five-minute drive from downtown Kingsville. The Quality Inn offers newly remodeled rooms, each of which has one king-size bed or two queen-size beds. Some rooms come with microwaves and refrigerators. Other amenities include cable television with HBO, a free continental breakfast, and complimentary evening cocktails.

Comfort Inn
$$ • 505 N. U.S. Hwy. 77, Kingsville
• (361) 516-1120, (800) 228-5150

You can tell the Comfort Inn is the newest addition to Kingsville's accommodations offerings, and not just because the paint looks fresh and the landscaping is brand new. No, the Comfort Inn also features amenities you won't find in many older motels, such as in-room hot tubs and a business center. This 47-room hotel located on the north side of town opened its doors in March 1998. It offers rooms with one king-size bed or two queens, hot tub rooms with king-size beds and two-room suites.

In-room amenities include coffeemakers, microwave ovens, refrigerators, and hairdryers. Other amenities include a swimming pool, exercise room, laundry facility and free continental breakfast of bagels, bread, fruit, cereal, juice, and coffee.

For added security, visitors and guests of this beige 3-story motel must travel through the lobby to reach the rooms.

Bed and Breakfast Inns

From a graceful antique-filled guest room to a woodsy primitive cottage, visitors to the Corpus Christi area will discover a wide-ranging assortment of bed and breakfast inns.

In this longtime resort region along the Gulf coast, the bed and breakfast inn is a relatively new phenomenon that caters to a select but growing population, according to Pat Hirsbrunner, owner of Sand Dollar Hospitality, a company that handles reservations for more than a dozen of the facilities in the area.

Hirsbrunner's company began handling reservations for bed and breakfasts in 1983, and she has since marveled at the robust health of the local industry. One of the first facilities was Anthony's which had its start in Corpus Christi and is today doing business in the nearby town of Rockport.

"I'm pleased to say there are more midweek guests than ever before. Business people are discovering the charm of bed and breakfasts," she said.

Today an estimated 500 to 1,000 Corpus Christi area visitors a year choose to stay in local bed and breakfast inns. Some may be corporate

LOOK FOR:
• North Bay
• Corpus Christi
• Port Aransas to Padre Island
• Kingsville Area

Price Code

As elsewhere in this book, we've created a price structure intended to provide a general overview of the cost of staying here. The prices listed are for one night, double occupancy; tax is not included in our price estimate.

$	Less than $75
$$	$76 to $95
$$$	$96 to $125
$$$$	More than $126

At Padre Island's Fortuna Bay Bed & Breakfast, guests have a great view of the area's canals.

Photo: courtesy of Fortuna Bay Bed & Breakfast

executives who remain in town for months, while others are weekend travelers.

During our journeys around the region, we've been charmed by the assortment and beauty of the area's bed and breakfast inns.

Finding these little jewels—each unique and attractive in a distinctive way—is like exploring for hidden treasure. With a good set of directions, you too will be able to discover these gems—tucked behind a grove of oak trees, hidden inside a 100-year-old mansion or ensconced on a restful island cove.

Some bed and breakfasts, especially those in the towns surrounding Corpus Christi, offer special-interest features such as birding information or hunting trips. Others simply offer the combination of intimacy and luxury that many travelers have come to expect from this type of accommodation.

Some inns have a two-night minimum and require a deposit; if you cancel, make sure to do so at least 48 hours in advance to get a refund on your deposit.

Rates at Corpus Christi area bed and breakfasts range from $65 to $200 per night. You can expect to see a 12 to 13 percent hotel-motel tax added to the price tag.

In general, most of the bed and breakfast inns listed below do not allow small children or pets. As a rule, then, we'll only make a note if youngsters or pets *are* permitted. However, you should always check with the innkeepers before you make reservations.

North Bay

Anthony's by the Sea
$-$$ • 732 Pearl St., Rockport
• (361) 729-6100, (361) 853-1222,
(800) 460-2557

With a tree-shaded front lawn that opens onto a small city park, this longtime bed and breakfast inn has unique and unpretentious charm. Managers Sharon Smith and Beth Burgess offer hospitality and informality in this home with fascinating and eclectic furnishings, including some real finds from local antique dealers. Our personal favorites are the ironwork chandeliers (bought for $20 apiece) that hang on the covered patio and an 1848 bedspread (a gift from a guest).

Breakfast is just as varied and accommodating—your choice could include poached eggs on toast, eggs Benedict, or Grand Marnier strawberry French toast.

There are three rooms in the main house,

including a honeymoon suite complete with velvet furniture and a wet bar, and two smaller rooms with a shared bath. A guest house across the patio has two double beds, a sleeper sofa, and a kitchen. The inn also offers the Spanish room with stone floors, a living suite, and old family photos along the wall.

Children and pets are allowed and the owners' resident schnauzer, Miho, keeps an eye on visitors—an estimated 6,500 during the past five years. An outdoor pool, covered patio, and hot tub (as well as an abundance of hummingbirds) are among the outdoor attractions.

Blue Heron Inn
$$-$$$ • 801 Patton St., Rockport
• (361) 729-7526, (361) 853-1222,
(800) 528-7782

This 100-year-old yellow-brick house has been a bed and breakfast since 1994, offering guests a view of Aransas Bay and access to Rockport beaches. The Federal-style house was built in 1890 by an Oklahoma developer. It was sold and renovated in the early 1900s, and it withstood the hurricane of 1919 but suffered much damage.

The Blue Heron's antiques, crystal chandeliers, and picturesque waterfront views provide gracious accommodations for visitors. The four rooms are decorated in inviting pastel colors. The two upstairs share a bath. Breakfast includes coffee, juice, fresh fruit, a meat or egg dish, muffins, and toast.

With its bricked patio and large tree-shaded yard, this inn has been the setting for many weddings and parties. The grounds are well tended, accented with bougainvillea blooms and palm trees. The inn will happily provide picnic lunches, bicycles, beach towels, and information about area daytrips.

Cayman House
$$, no credit cards
• 5030 Texas Hwy. 35 N., Rockport
• (361) 790-8884, • (888) 660-BIRD

Billed as "the birder's bed and breakfast," this graceful wooded inn features a main house with two guest rooms, a guest cottage with two full beds, a hummingbird garden and sea kayaks or bicycles for rent.

Owners Donna Knox and Michael Marsden are lifelong birders who moved to the Coastal Bend from the Cayman Islands—hence the name. Their inn is in a wooded corridor that's frequented by migratory birds coming through the area. Eighteen species of warblers were sighted here one October weekend in 1996. In addition, Cayman House is headquarters for Coastal Bend Birders, which offers full- and half-day birding tours of the area. Marsden, a guide himself, provides assistance in locating and identifying rare birds, as well as an extensive collection of field guides, videos, and sound recordings. See our Birding chapter for more about Marsden's tours.

Breakfast includes a fresh fruit plate, juices, homemade nut breads, muffins and homemade jams, and a hot entree of an egg dish, waffles, or buttermilk pancakes, and a choice of tea or coffee. Complimentary sack lunches are available for those birders heading out for a day in the field.

Cygnet
$$, no credit cards
• **1450 Weeping Willow St., Rockport**
• **(361) 729-7009, (361) 790-7992, (800) 528-7782**

Owners Analisa and Steven Kennedy have created a country-style cottage in a secluded area that's sure to enchant those looking to escape life's stresses. The cottage features American primitive decor and is on 17 acres near Rockport. It offers visitors a double bed, a queen-size sleeper sofa, kitchenette and—perhaps most unusual of all—an outdoor hot tub in an old cattle tank. Birders have been particularly attracted to this quaint bed and breakfast, which is surrounded by plenty of vegetation that draws flocks of migratory birds. The cottage is also included on the Rockport-Fulton Hummingbird Festival home tour each September.

The Kennedys provision the cottage with fixings for breakfast, including farm-fresh eggs, a loaf of homemade bread, cereal, milk, juice, fresh fruit, and whatever else the season inspires them to include.

The Habitat
$-$$ • **170 Fourth St., Lamar, Rockport**
• **(361) 729-2362, (361) 853-1222, (800) 528-7782**

Four rustic log cabins on a seven-acre lake setting offer a relaxing back-to-nature experience at this friendly bed and breakfast, owned by Wayne Nugent. The cozy cabins—which are decorated with colorful paintings by Nugent's late grandmother—sleep from four to eight, depending on the size, and each features its own bath with shower, kitchen, screened porch, and other amenities, plus an outdoor barbecue pit and picnic table.

There are plenty of graceful live oak trees, a pond that reportedly serves as home to an alli-gator, lots of hiking paths, plenty of space for birders to check out their favorite species or a grazing deer, and the whole place is located a mere quarter-mile from Goose Island State Park.

Nugent's wife supplies breakfast goodies in each cabin that include homemade banana pecan and dewberry pecan muffins, grapefruit, coffee, milk, orange juice, and cold cereal—plus tortilla chips and homemade salsa for afternoon snacking. Children are welcome.

Hoopes' House
$$$ • **417 N. Broadway St., Rockport**
• **(361) 729-8424, (361) 853-1222, (800) 924-1008**

Built in the 1890s, this graceful yellow mansion is listed in both the Texas and National Register of Historic Places. Its history of serving guests dates back nearly a century as well: Carefully preserved historic documents indicate that Mrs. Jim Hoopes ran a boarding house here as early as 1906. Today, Hoopes' House is one of the more enchanting inns available, with polished hardwood floors, intricately carved fireplaces, and fine art decorations such as Audubon prints, antiques, and Oriental rugs.

Breakfast is likely to include fresh fruit, an egg casserole or French toast, or blueberry pancakes.

The main house contains four guest rooms with private baths, each furnished in a different theme and color. A newly added wing has four additional guest houses, including one with wheelchair access. The manicured grounds feature seasonal plants such as bright hibiscus flowers around a sparkling swimming pool, hot tub, and shady gazebo.

Knolle Farm and Ranch, Bed, Barn and Breakfast
$-$$$ • **F.M. Rd. 70, Sandia**
• **(361) 547-2546, (361) 853-1222, (800) 528-7782**

Many of the city's older residents remember school field trips to this longtime dairy operation among towering oak trees in the Nueces River Valley. The Knolle family have since swapped Jerseys for Texas beef cattle, and have turned part of their lovely ranch into a unique inn.

Billed as a "bed, barn and breakfast," the Knolles also offer accommodations for guests' horses: eight stalls in the barn, two riding arenas and acres of trails to ride. It costs an extra $20 per night to stable your horse here.

As for the more traditional bed and breakfast services, guests can choose from facilities ranging from a simple room and bath to a three-bedroom, three-bath guesthouse with all the amenities, all furnished in French country style with antiques and down comforters. The main quarters offer accommodations for six to eight, including a king-size bed, four twin beds, a foldout sofa, kitchen, and laundry room. A smaller hunting cabin has two twin beds, a foldout sofa, kitchen, and bathroom, while the smallest room—called "The Dog House"—has a double bed and private bath.

Nonriders are welcome, too—activities include fishing, canoeing, birding, and relaxing. A full breakfast is served and can include French toast casserole or maybe eggs Benedict, plus fresh fruit and beverages. In addition, guests can arrange picnic baskets (at an extra charge); gourmet dinners; private hunting for dove, duck and goose; riding instruction; and participation in a cattle roundup. Children are welcome.

Our Place on the Bay
$$ • 1233 Bayshore Dr., Ingleside-on-the-Bay
• (361) 776-6484, (361) 853-1222, (800) 528-7782

Owners Jane and Gary Irving have transformed this 9,950-square foot former restaurant into a rustic paradise, where visitors can watch dolphins frolic in the nearby ship channel or fish for flounder from the lighted pier. Within this long building, set in the middle of a huge parking lot on the water, are five cozy rooms with private baths, and two bunk rooms that can accommodate eight to 10 people. There is a community living area, dining room, and a large kitchen.

The Irvings provide a deluxe continental breakfast for their guests, including coffee, juices, muffins, bagels, pastries, croissants, eggs, assorted cereals, milk and fresh fruit including mangos, kiwis, grapes, apples, oranges, and bananas. Located on the McGloin Bluff, the facility has a panoramic view of the Corpus Christi Bay, the ship channel, nearby Naval Station Ingleside and an array of wildlife, including blue herons, cormorants, and pelicans.

In addition to a lighted pier, the facility features a boat launch, a harbor and decks on the south side and west side. This facility has hosted visitors from Scotland, England, Italy and Egypt, as well as prominent national and state politi-

cians. The Irvings also offer a 10 percent discount for senior citizens and military members, and can make special accommodations for children.

Corpus Christi

Colley House
$, no credit cards
• 211 Indiana Ave., Corpus Christi
• (361) 887-7514, (361) 853-1222, (800) 528-7782

This lovely older home sits a block from the bayfront and offers old-fashioned charm and easy hospitality. Owners Evelyn and Tom Bookout once ran a bed and breakfast in Newport, Rhode Island, and they've turned this home into a quaint and restful paradise.

Two rooms for guests include gleaming hardwood floors, crown molding, floral rugs, antique dressers, and old framed black-and-white photographs. The two bedrooms are separated by a charming living area that has double French doors, saltillo tile floors, sofa, television, VCR, and refrigerator. It opens onto a shady wooden deck and a peaceful garden—a popular place for guests to breakfast.

Evelyn, who teaches business technology at a local college, and Tom, a retired naval officer, make breakfast a creative culinary experience: Recent offerings have included spinach omelet and banana bread, oatmeal pancakes with Cointreau sauce, or migas (Mexican-style eggs scrambled with corn chips, onions and more) with cinnamon rolls.

George Blucher House Bed & Breakfast Inn
$$$–$$$$
• 211 N. Carrizo St., Corpus Christi
• (361) 884-4884, (361) 853-1222, (800) 528-7782

Built in 1904, this galleried Victorian two-story home near downtown has been furnished in the style of the city's earliest residents. Antiques, lace curtains, and traditional hospitality are offered by owner Tracey L. Smith. Nestled quietly beneath towering magnolia, elm, anachua, pecan and oak, the historic George Blucher home sits just across the street from Blucher Park, an internationally renowned bird sanctuary, and next door to two more stately Blucher homes owned by the Junior League of Corpus Christi.

In addition to birders and history lovers, this bed and breakfast has also proved popular with legal professionals, who can walk two blocks to the courthouse from here. There are six rooms, all with private baths, furnished with grace and comfort in mind.

Expect a real treat at breakfast time—a typical menu, served by candlelight with fresh linens and fine china, could include fresh-squeezed orange juice, freshly ground coffee, stuffed baked apple in puff pastry, homemade muffins and an omelet or eggs Benedict.

The Ginger Rose
$, no credit cards
- **Buckingham Estates, Corpus Christi**
- **(361) 992-0115, (361) 853-1222,
  (800) 528-7782**

The owners of this tasteful, art-filled residence on the city's south side have been hosting visitors for more than three years. The Braswells' love of all things French is clearly visible in many aspects of their elegant home, from its name to the furnishings and menu, which may include homemade French madeleines. A collection of dainty glass statues fills a china cabinet, while French paintings and framed posters hang on the walls. One of the guest rooms is painted a romantic pale pink and decorated with antiques, a double bed, a swag of French fabric over the headboard, and bouquets of fresh roses. The other room features a tapestry hanging on the wall, a queen-sized bed with antique iron headboard and crocheted lace bedspread, and a lovely stained glass window. There is a swimming pool, access to tennis courts and a wonderfully inviting library for visitors' use.

Breakfast is served in the formal dining room and can include such gourmet delicacies as iced or hot cappuccino, gingerbread pancakes with lemon sauce or individual ham-and-cheese soufflés served with raspberry mini-muffins.

Michelet's Bed and Breakfast
$$–$$$ • 141 Atlantic St., Corpus Christi
- **(361) 887-8808, (361) 853-1222,
  (800) 528-7782**

Four upstairs rooms overlooking Corpus Christi Bay make this a picturesque retreat, conveniently located two miles from downtown. Owner Donna Mickley has furnished her two-story home with plenty of beautiful antiques, turning it into a stunning retreat. She also provides for the needs of those who just can't seem to tear themselves away from the job—this home has a business center, complete with Pentium computer, fax machine, color printer, copy machine, scanner, and DSL Internet connection.

For those who want to get away from the stress of everyday life, check out the sparkling swimming pool or indulge in one of Donna's delicious breakfasts. A typical menu includes fresh fruit, muffins, French toast stuffed with nuts and brown sugar, two kinds of breakfast meat, and juice, coffee and tea. Fresh baked goods are available throughout the day as well. Children under 18 are not allowed because of the swimming pool.

Ocean House
$$$$ • 3275 Ocean Dr., Corpus Christi
- **(361) 882-9500, (361) 853-1222,
  (800) 528-7782**

This beautiful Spanish-style mansion and guest house, with stucco walls and red-tiled roof, offers serious luxury, seclusion, and elegance within the setting of a private and very well-furnished home. Located on the city's showcase oceanfront boulevard, the inn offers a surprisingly intimate and luxurious environment. There are five separate suites, each with its own private entrance, plush full bath, television with VCR, and incredible bayfront views. A beautiful swimming pool, well-tended garden, outdoor hot tub, private parking, and made-to-order breakfast are among the amenities. Other unique attributes of this bed and breakfast are the conference room available for meetings, fax and modem hookups in every suite, and full kitchens in two of the suites.

Celebrity guests who have stayed here include tennis stars Monica Seles and Lindsey Davenport, former education secretary William Bennett and a number of entertainers. The home sits on nearly an acre of prime oceanfront real estate—and has large enough grounds to accommodate special events such as weddings, family reunions, fundraising events, and corporate banquets. Owner Stan Shoemaker says he rented the grounds out for six weddings one year.

On the weekend, a chef will prepare whatever guests want for breakfast; during the week, when the rates drop, guests are offered an continental array of pastries, fresh fruit, cereal, coffee, juice, and tea.

Smith Place
$$ • Lamar Park, Corpus Christi
- **(361) 853-1222, (800) 528-7782**

Two cozy guest cottages are tucked inside

the glorious backyard of this home about four blocks from the bayfront in one of the city's loveliest neighborhoods. Cissy and Sid Smith opened their bed and breakfast two years ago, with admirable results. The cottages are small, but comfortable with a television, VCR, telephone, refrigerator, microwave, private bath, toaster, and coffeemaker. Cissy treats her guests like valued relatives—she'll bring you lemonade and snacks while you sit poolside; offers use of her huge pool, outdoor deck, spacious yard and even her son's basketball hoop and treehouse; and supplies you with beach towels, coolers, and beach chairs.

Breakfast is casual and Cissy says most of her guests prefer to eat by themselves, so she supplies bounteous fruit baskets, bagels and muffins, and she also stocks guests' fridges with soft drinks, yogurt, jams, and wine. She clears and washes the breakfast dishes and replaces them in the cabinet, restocking any food items that may be running low.

Children and pets are allowed but she says most of her guests are corporate visitors, who tend to stay for months and end up becoming friends with the Smiths. Corporate rates are available for long-term guests. This place keeps a low profile—it's homey, cozy, warm, and very welcoming.

Port Aransas to Padre Island

Coquina Bay
$$, no credit cards.
• **13906 Isla Colon, Corpus Christi**
• **(361) 853-1222, (800) 561-8180**

Brightly blooming bougainvilleas and hibiscus greet visitors at the front entrance of this white stucco home on Padre Island. Inside, the decor is nearly all white and very elegant—giving an atmosphere of cool sophistication. A blue-tiled swimming pool and hot tub sit outside, inviting guests to relax. Those with more energy may want to partake of owner Terry and Sonya Quiroga's charter boat service, renting a daylong trip or a moonlight cruise on the Quiroga's 34-foot sailboat.

There are two guest bedrooms here, each bedroom with its own private bathroom, king-size bed, and television. All of the rooms are spacious and light, with huge picture windows that overlook the canals that line the backyard. You can fish for trout, drum, or flounder off the back deck.

The breakfast menu includes old-fashioned favorites such as bacon, eggs, hash browns, pancakes, or toast. Pastry, fruit, and coffee are offered for early birds, including anglers who may want to get out of the house before sunup. In fact, the Quirogas will tailor their breakfast schedule to visitors' needs—one group of anglers arranged to have dinner instead of breakfast because they wanted an early start on the day's fishing.

Harbor View B&B
$$ • 340 W. Cotter Ave., Port Aransas
• **(361) 749-4294, (361) 853-1222,**
  (800) 561-8180

This three-story, Mediterranean-style townhouse contains three large bedrooms and two baths as well as a master suite. Located on one of the main streets in Port Aransas, the house is near the Port Aransas ferry landing.

A wooden deck behind the house features potted plants, deck chairs, and a pier. Overlooking the Port Aransas Municipal Harbor, guests have easy access to a nearby swimming pool, beach combing and boat charters. Guests can also moor their own boats but need to make reservations well in advance of arrival.

Owner Marlene Urban serves an elegant breakfast that includes seasonal fresh fruit, juices, blueberry muffins, pancakes or waffles, and egg-and-meat casseroles. A two-night minimum stay is required, and guests should make reservations at least a week in advance.

Fortuna Bay B&B
$$$, no credit cards
• **15405 Fortuna Bay Dr., Corpus Christi**
• **(361) 949-7554, (361) 853-1222,**
  (800) 561-8180.

You can fish for trout from the wooden deck of this condominium-turned-bed and breakfast, take a leisurely swim in the pool, or head out for a day at the beach. Owner John Fisher has turned three of the 10 condos on his three-story, red-tile roofed property into bed and breakfast places. Each has a living room with couch and chairs, television, kitchen with all the amenities, bedroom with queen-size bed, large bathroom and a washing machine and dryer (a real plus at the beach!)

As an added attraction, John provides guests with an hour-long boat tour of the area that usually includes sightings of pelicans, roseate spoonbills, and blue herons. Because John belongs to the nearby country club, guests also have golfing, swimming, and tennis privileges.

A continental breakfast is provided in each

condo; it includes coffee, juice, fresh grapefruit or cantaloupe, strawberries, bananas, homemade pigs-in-blankets and cinnamon rolls or apple fritters. He even has fishing rods available for guests' use. Children under 2 can stay here free, but no teenagers or pets are allowed.

Kingsville Area

B Bar B Ranch
**$–$$ • County Rd. 2215, Kingsville
• (361) 296-3331**

Originally part of the historic King Ranch, the B Bar B is an old ranch house that has been restored and turned into an inn by owners Patti and Luther Young.

There is a rustic, relaxed atmosphere at this inn, which is nestled beneath a mesquite grove, eight miles south of Kingsville. Surrounded by a 220-acre working ranch, the B Bar B is a favorite for hunters (for dove, quail, turkey or nilgai, an exotic antelope-like animal) and

people needing a weekend getaway. Furnishings are reminiscent of a luxury hunting lodge—a stone fireplace, high ceilings with wooden beams, mounted trophy heads, overstuffed furniture and old West artwork. There are six bedrooms with private baths, two hot tubs, a swimming pool, a gazebo, and a picnic area. In addition, the Youngs have a cottage by the pool with four additional beds.

Birders also have been coming to the ranch, which is listed on the Greater South Texas Birding Trail and is a pick-up site for the King Ranch Birding Tour. Some of the species sighted here are purple martin, ladder-backed woodpecker, curved-billed thrasher, great horned owl, and a variety of hawks.

The breakfast menu varies, but usually includes fresh fruit and an entree such as French pancakes, biscuits and gravy with nilgai sausage, or a breakfast taco buffet.

Pets are not allowed indoors, but there are 98 kennels for boarding. There is an additional cost for boarding your dog.

Weekly and Long-term Rentals

LOOK FOR:
- **North Bay Area**
- **Corpus Christi**
- **Port Aransas to Mustang Island**

Price Code

Prices indicated by the dollar-sign code are for high season, double occupancy per night for one-bedroom units or, when a one-bedroom is not offered, the smallest unit available. Some places offer a variety of rooms for two adults, and the range in prices is reflected in our listing.

$	Less than $50
$$	$51 to $75
$$$	$76 to $100
$$$$	$101 to $150
$$$$$$	More than $150

If you prefer staying somewhere that more closely resembles a vacation home than a hotel, then the accommodations listed in this chapter are for you. The lodgings listed here—most of which are condominiums—are designed with long-term renters in mind. Most, if not all, come with full kitchens, housewares, washers and dryers, and more space than your average hotel room or suite.

Most long-term rental properties in the area are near the beaches from Port Aransas to Padre Island and in the Rockport/Fulton area. This is not to imply that you cannot stay as long as you want at area hotels and motels (you can stay as long as your money holds out), or that brief stays are not allowed at the lodgings mentioned in this chapter. But the accommodations we include here generally deal with people planning to stay more than a couple of nights. You're more likely to run into vacationers or winter Texans in these types of places, whereas business travelers will more likely be found at the establishments listed in our Hotels and Motels chapter.

Many visitors to the Corpus Christi area stay a week, several weeks, or even months at a time. Summer is the high season (late May through early September), with some accommodations charging high-season rates in March, traditionally spring break time for colleges. Other seasons are the regular season (roughly September, October, early November, April and early May) and the winter season (mid-November to the end of March), with winter the least expensive. Winter rates can be less than half of summer rates, with regular-season rates somewhere in the middle. Expect to pay $10 to $30 more per night on weekends, holidays, and dates that coincide with special events.

The closer you are to the water, the more you will pay; and the better your view of the water, the higher your rates will be.

Discounts are available for active military, seniors, and groups and for extended stays. Daily, weekly, and monthly rates are available at many places, and most, if not all, accommodations are open year round.

Most properties mentioned here require a two-night minimum stay most of the time and three nights during major holidays. Reduced monthly rates are available at some places after the summer season is over.

Maximum occupancy rules are strictly enforced, including those for children of all ages. Vehicles must be registered at the front desk or risk being towed at owners' expense. Many properties require an advance deposit of one night's rent for all reservations, and some require you to pay the balance due upon check-in. The accommodations listed in this chapter accept major credit cards unless otherwise indicated. Most do not accept personal checks.

You can assume that all accommodations have televisions, telephones, and maid service unless otherwise mentioned. Pet policies vary. Some accept them, some don't. Others charge a fee (nonrefundable). Smoking and nonsmoking rooms are available in most places, as are handicapped-accessible rooms. Check before making reservations.

Our listings are divided into our four geographical areas: North Bay Area, Corpus Christi, Port Aransas to Padre Island, and Kingsville Area. The listings are arranged alphabetically in the Corpus Christi section and north to south by city in all other sections.

North Bay Area

Bayfront Cottages
$ • 309 Fulton Beach Rd., Rockport
• (361) 729-6693

These small, salmon-colored cottages next to the fully restored 19th-century Fulton Mansion run west from Aransas Bay on two acres of well-kept grounds. Each one- and two-room unit comes with a kitchenette, and most come with queen-size beds. The waterfront unit has a king-size bed and most two-room units come with sofa sleepers in the living room.

Amenities include a boat launch and docking facilities for vessels as long as 25 feet, cable television, picnic tables, barbecue pits, a lighted 660-foot fishing pier, swimming pool, guest laundry, shuffleboard, and banquet facilities.

Calm Harbor Rentals
$$$$–$$$$$ • 3805 Business Hwy. 35, Rockport
• (361) 729-1367

Calm Harbor Rentals handles vacation homes and condominiums on canals mostly in areas south of Rockport. The company handles both short- and long-term rentals for properties in City By The Sea, Bahia Bay, and Palm Harbor. A minimum two-night stay is required.

Key Allegro
Real Estate Company and Rentals
$$$$–$$$$$ • 1798 Bayshore Dr., Rockport
• (361) 729-2333, (800) 348-1627

Key Allegro Rentals handles more expensive rentals primarily in waterfront areas. Most locations are either right on the water or have a

view of it. Its rentals are concentrated in Key Allegro and the Rockport Country Club, with some in Copano Ridge, Lamar, and City By The Sea. Key Allegro requires a two-night minimum stay.

RE/MAX Security Real Estate Rentals
$$$$ • 2730 Business Hwy. 35 N., Rockport
• (361) 729-2256, (800) 221-5028

Security Real Estate handles mostly short-term and long-term condo rentals in the Rockport/Fulton area. It manages more than 100 properties in the medium price range. A minimum two-night stay is required.

Sun Harbour
$$ • 1141 N. Fulton Beach Rd., Fulton
• (361) 729-2073

These 13 small cottages on Fulton Beach Road lie nestled between twisting live oak trees and towering palms on a hill running west from Aransas Bay. Cottages are laid out on either side of a driveway divided by a small greenbelt. Hammocks hang from the many trees that dot the landscape. Amenities include laundry room, swimming pool, hot tub, 220-foot lighted pier, barbecue area, and picnic tables.

One-bedroom and studio cottages also are available. All cottages come with fully equipped kitchens. A two-bedroom cottage overlooking the bayfront has a screened-in porch and large private deck. A two-story townhouse comes with one full bath, two half-baths, and a balcony overlooking the swimming pool and bay.

Corpus Christi

Christy Estates
Executive Suites and Apartments
$$$–$$$$ • 3942 Holly Rd., Corpus Christi
• (361) 854-1091, (800) 678-4836

The executive suites at Christy Estates just might make staying several miles from the bay worth it. These 16 one- or two-bedroom suites, which the company refers to as mini-spas, feature freshwater, European-style, individually controlled Whirljet Spas. Apartments come with full-sized kitchens, dining areas, bedrooms, and living rooms. Bedrooms come with double, queen-, or king-size beds. All suites come with two televisions and some come with large-screen televisions. Suites range in size from 750 to 1000 square feet.

Christy Estates Suites provides maid service, housewares, and cable television with

HBO 1 and HBO 2. Outdoors you'll find two swimming pools and an Italian-tile in-ground hot tub. Themed spas, more elaborate spas with more jets and without a living room, also are available, along with sauna spas that come with a sauna in the spa area. These rent for $25 to $45 more per day.

Villa Del Sol
**$$$$ • 3938 Surfside Blvd., Corpus Christi
• (361) 883-9748, (800) 242-3291**

You won't find a better view than the one from a room facing southeast in this Corpus Christi Beach condominium project. Step out on the balcony and take in the view of Corpus Christi Bay and the Lexington Museum on the Bay set amid the backdrop of downtown Corpus Christi and the bayfront. If that's not pleasing enough to the eye, check out the villa's award-winning gardens replete with red and orange oleander and bougainvillea, palm trees, pastel lilies, and purple and pink petunias.

One-bedroom condominiums come with a small kitchen, radio, free cable TV with HBO and The Disney Channel, and a full bath. All rooms come with a queen-size bed, a sofa sleeper, and two bunks in the hallway that children find irresistible. Other amenities include laundry facilities, two swimming pools, three hot tub/spas, barbecue pits, meeting rooms, and a playground.

Port Aransas to Mustang Island

The Dunes
**$$$$$ • 1000 Lantana St., Port Aransas
• (361) 749-5155, (800) 288-3863**

At The Dunes condominiums you get the best of both worlds: a first-class condominium right on the beach and proximity to Port Aransas shops and restaurants. The Dunes is one of the few properties that isn't separated from the beach by sand dunes. The beach comes right up to the back door. It's also positioned in such a way that many guests have views of the beach, the Gulf of Mexico, and sunsets behind the Corpus Christi skyline.

The Dunes offers 85 furnished one-, two-, and three-bedroom suites with balconies mea-

suring more than 200 square feet. Linens are exchanged daily and maid service is offered every three days. Amenities include a fitness center with weight equipment, power treadmills and exercise bikes, a heated, heart-shaped swimming pool, and a hot tub ringed with tropical flora, tennis courts, and a lighted, concrete fishing pier.

Sand & Surf Condos
**$$$–$$$$ • 1423 S. 11th St., Port Aransas
• (361) 749-6001**

This may be the only vacation spot that brags about what it doesn't have. It doesn't have a swimming pool or tennis courts or a Jacuzzi or bocci ball courts. What it does have are 20 one-bedroom units a short walk from the water. Each unit has a separate living room area and fully equipped kitchen. Some come with two televisions and a washer and dryer. Daily and weekly rentals are on the second floor and have a beach view.

Sea Sands Condominiums
**$$$–$$$$ • 1421 S. 11th St., Port Aransas
• (361) 749-6246, (800) 221-1447**

The Sea Sands Condominiums are about two blocks from the Gulf of Mexico in Port Aransas proper. The buildings are white brick with red-tile roofs, and the layout resembles an apartment complex. Efficiency, one-, two- and three-bedroom units are available. Each comes with free basic cable TV. A swimming pool is on the complex.

Sandcastle
Fine Luxury Resort Condominium
**$$$$–$$$$$ • 800 Sandcastle Dr.,
Port Aransas
• (361) 749-6201, (800) 727-6201**

The name isn't a marketing gimmick. This place is nice—very nice. Begin with the fact that each of its 180 rooms overlooks the Gulf of Mexico, add an eye-pleasing and unusually shaped swimming pool (it looks sort of like a butterfly) and finish it off with attractive, wicker furniture. What you end up with is a well-planned, well-kept high-rise resort that's ideal for a beach vacation.

Efficiencies, one-, two-, and three-bedroom condominiums come with cable television, complete kitchens, and linens. Some balconies not only look out on the Gulf of Mexico, but over-

INSIDERS' TIP

Other than a few homes in Rockport's Key Allegro, the Corpus Christi area has fewer homes for rent than other beachfront destinations you may have visited.

look the swimming pool and sunbathing area as well. Among the many amenities you'll find here are tennis courts, a boardwalk to the beach, a fish-cleaning building, separate sun deck area and a protected beach area.

Executive Keys
$$$ • 820 Access Rd. 1-A, Port Aransas
• (361) 749-6272, (800) 556-6999
Comfort and function are the selling points at this condominium complex, not luxury and eye-popping decor. Amenities include a private balcony or patio, swimming pool, recreation room, laundry facilities, volleyball, shuffleboard, and picnic areas. Condominiums in this three-story complex are privately owned and leased to the public part of the year. Efficiency, two-bedroom, three-bedroom and two-story townhouses are available. The Executive Keys is on the beach.

Aransas Princess
$$$$$, no credit cards
• 720 Beach Access Rd. 1-A, Port Aransas
• (361) 749-5118, (800) 531-9225
Sand and saltwater get you down? Hang out around the swimming pool and enjoy the beach without all the mess. The Aransas Princess has the best poolside view: The swimming pool overlooks the Gulf of Mexico. Or, if the beach and waves beckon, take the short stroll down the boardwalk and you'll be ready to build sandcastles or go for a swim in the surf.

Amenities in this eight-story, beautifully landscaped complex include fully equipped kitchens with microwaves, trash compactors, and dish-washers, wet bars with built-in ice makers, full-size washers and dryers, large bathrooms and closets and private balconies facing the Gulf. A second swimming pool, shuffleboard, lighted tennis courts, heated out-door Jacuzzi and dry sauna with dressing rooms and showers are available. Two-bedroom, two-bedroom with den, and three-bedroom residences are available.

Although the Aransas Princess doesn't accept credit cards as payment, you'll need one to make reservations and at check-in time.

Port Royal Resort Condominiums
$$$$$ • 6317 Texas Hwy. 361,
Port Aransas
• (361) 749-5011, (800) 242-1034
They say everything is big in Texas, and

Port Royal proves it with its 500-foot-long, four-tiered swimming pool, heralded as the state's largest. With a swim-up bar and grill and a mountain slide, the swimming pool is the centerpiece of this U-shaped, 210-unit complex overlooking the Gulf of Mexico. Only a 30-minute drive from Corpus Christi International Airport, this gated community on Mustang Island is a world away from city life.

A five-minute stroll across a boardwalk takes you over rolling sand dunes to the sparsely populated beach, where you can hunt for seashells or swim in warm gulf waters.

Units come with one, two or three bedrooms, a complete kitchen with full-size appliances, dining area, living room with built-in stereo system, washer and dryer, cable television, wet bar and master suite with whirlpool tubs. Three-bedroom units have full gulf views and built-in spas on the balconies. Other amenities include 7,000 square feet of meeting space, water and sand volleyball, lighted tennis courts, and shuffleboard courts. The third-floor restaurant, The Atrium, serves seafood, hamburgers, and sandwiches and overlooks the swimming pool and gulf

Sandpiper Condominiums
$$$$$ • 6745 Texas Hwy. 361,
Port Aransas
• (361) 749-6251, (800) 789-2898
You'll find the 12-story Sandpiper Condominiums situated on the Mustang Island beach, 7 miles from Port Aransas and 17 miles from Corpus Christi. Each of its 107 units overlooks the beach and the Gulf of Mexico. Large balconies off the living areas of all condos offer great views and enough space for outdoor furniture. Condos come in one-bedroom, two-bedroom or two different three-bedroom floorplans. All come with full kitchens, living rooms, dining rooms, and two bathrooms. Amenities include a swimming pool with whirlpool spa, sun decks, tennis courts, and meeting and activity rooms.

The Sandpiper is particularly proud of its comfortable lobbies (they have two). The largest is the Gulf Front Lobby, where you'll always find a full pot of coffee. Guests can relax and talk in wicker chairs with plum-colored cushions. The Gulf Front Lobby's smaller neighbor, the Sunken Reading Lobby, beckons those looking for a cool and quiet place to curl up with a favorite book or chat with a close friend.

INSIDERS' TIP
An advance deposit of one or two nights' rent is sometimes required and cancellation policies vary.

Mayan Princess
**$$$$$ • 7537 Texas Hwy. 361,
Port Aransas**
• (361) 749-5183, (800) 662-8907

The oversized Jacuzzi hot tub in the master bedroom is one reason visitors return to the Mayan Princess year after year. Others include its three-lagoon swimming pool and hot tub, two tennis courts, its location on the Gulf of Mexico and its luxurious one-, two- and three-bedroom units. All condos come with complete kitchens, living areas, dining areas, washers and dryers, and basic cable. You can rent a VCR and movies in the lobby of this five-story complex. All rooms face the beach; guests on the second floor and higher have a view of the water.

El Constante
Beachfront Condominiums
**$$$$$ • 14802 Windward Dr., Padre Island
• (361) 949-7088**

You won't find many places to stay on Padre Island that are right on the beach, so El Constante has a leg up over many condominiums in the area by virtue of its location on North Padre Island, although not all units face the beach.

Condos here come with one or two bedrooms. One-bedroom units will sleep four people. Two-bedroom condos are two stories tall with two full bathrooms upstairs and a half-bath downstairs; they sleep six. Amenities include a swimming pool, heated Jacuzzi, and fully equipped kitchens.

The Gulfstream
**$$$$$ • 14810 Windward Dr., Padre Island
• (361) 949-8061, (800) 542-7368**

Next door to El Constante you'll find The Gulfstream, a six-story condominium project on North Padre Island's beach and seawall. Many of the Gulfstream's 131 units overlook the Gulf of Mexico and the beach between J.P. Luby Park and Bob Hall Pier. All units overlook a heated, fan-shaped swimming pool.

Amenities include cable television, all-electric kitchens including microwave and dishwasher, hot tub, shuffleboard, laundry facilities and a recreation, party and game room. All units come with two bedrooms, two baths and fully equipped kitchens with dining and living areas. Guests have access to nearby Padre Island Country Club, including golf, tennis, and club and bar facilities. Prices vary depending on whether you have a full ocean view or a partial ocean view.

Campgrounds and RV Parks

Each fall the population of the Corpus Christi area swells by the thousands as RV owners from the Midwest and other northern points head south for the winter. To accommodate them, RV parks have cropped up throughout Corpus Christi and surrounding cities, especially in the Rockport area, which boasts more than 20 RV parks in a city of 6,500 people.

You'll find an RV park in almost every town in the Corpus Christi area and at least one that's miles from the nearest town. Some are big, fancy professionally run facilities that resemble miniature cities, while others are mom-and-pop operations where solitude and peace are favored.

The area also has several campgrounds. As you might expect, they tend to be far from populated areas. Many allow RVs, and many RV parks allow tents. The best time for tent camping (unless your tent is air-conditioned) is between late November and early May when the temperature and humidity are relatively low. A word of warning: Hot, sticky conditions are possible year round, although these tropical spells are generally shorter and less severe than in the summer. The high season for RV camping is between October and March. You'll need to make reservations for that time period several months in advance.

Campsites and RV parks are listed together in this chapter. They're divided into four sections—North Bay Area, Corpus Christi, Port Aransas to Padre Island, and the Kingsville area—and are listed from north to south within each category. You may be surprised by the scarcity of RV parks in Corpus Christi. For several years, economic development proponents have lamented the lack of a major RV park in the city. Maybe that's because the neighboring communities have done such a good job of catering to the RV market, or perhaps because RVers prefer to settle in more remote areas.

Each listing gives you a general description of the site's location and appearance as well as a list of amenities. You can assume that each site is well maintained, has a good reputation and would be a good place to spend a week, a month or longer. Each listing includes daily rates for two adults, including sales tax where applicable. Utilities are included in the price unless otherwise noted, and all parks offer more economical weekly and monthly rates. In most parks, electricity is charged separately when you pay by the month. Major credit cards are accepted unless otherwise indicated.

Other miscellaneous tips:

• Some parks have cable television at every site; others have it at only a few sites. Some include the cost of cable in their daily rates; others charge extra for it.

• Propane gas can be purchased at all sites, either from the proprietor or from a delivery truck that visits regularly.

LOOK FOR:
• North Bay Area
• Corpus Christi
• Port Aransas to Padre Island
• Kingsville Area

•Discounts are available at most parks. They include discounts for stays of two days or longer, groups and Good Sam Club members, who receive a 10 percent discount from participating parks.

•Cancellation policies vary. Many parks require a 48-hour notice to receive a full refund.

•Generally there are no maximum or minimum stays. Stay a day or a lifetime.

•Wheelchair-accessible sites are available at some parks.

•Most parks allow pets and children.

•Public consumption of alcohol or the display of an open container in Texas state parks is prohibited.

•Overnight visitors pay a daily fee, and the number of occupants allowed at each site often is limited.

•Most campgrounds and RV parks observe a quiet time, which generally falls between 10 PM and 8 AM.

North Bay Area

Goose Island State Park
• **Park Road 13, off Texas Hwy. 35, Lamar**
• **(361) 729-2858**

You can camp in the woods or at the beach when you pitch your tent or park your RV at Goose Island State Park. This 314-acre facility overlooking Aransas Bay stretches inland for a mile to dense brush and abundant live oak and mesquite trees. This state-run facility is about 6 miles north of Rockport in an unincorporated area known as Lamar. From Texas Highway 35 head east for 1.4 miles down tree-lined Park Road 13. On your way, visit a Catholic shrine and the ancient Stella Maris Chapel. See our Attractions chapter for more information. When you come to a four-way stop, hang a right (you'll still be on Park Road 13) and drive south for 1.2 miles to the park entrance.

The park has 102 RV sites and 25 camping sites. All sites come with water; only the RV sites have electricity (30-amp electrical service). Reservations are accepted. Amenities include a recreation hall, dump station, toilets, showers, grills, a lighted (and extremely long) fishing pier, boat ramp, and playgrounds.

Rates for RV sites are $11 to $13 per night plus an entry fee of $2 per person per day for anyone age 13 and over. Camping sites are $8 per night plus entry fees. See our Parks chapter for more information.

Rockport 35 RV Park
No credit cards • 4851 Texas 35 N., Rockport
• **(361) 729-2307, (800) 392-2930**

White concrete streets and pads give this 178-site RV park that clean, well-maintained look that makes you want to stay awhile. It's like walking into a hotel room and finding the carpet has just been vacuumed. Shady sites are limited here, but the lack of development on the surrounding land and the park's proximity to Rockport and other local attractions make it an appealing spot to park your rig. Amenities abound at this 14-year-old RV park. They include showers, phone hookups, cable television, on-site resident managers, security, laundry facilities, enclosed hot tub, 4,000-square-foot recreation room, exercise room, horseshoes, picnic tables, portable barbecue pits, and a fish-cleaning table. Sites come with full hookups (30- and 50-amp electrical service).

Rates are between $18 and $20.50 a day depending on the size of your vehicle.

Bahia Vista RV Park
• **5801 F.M. 1781, Rockport**
• **(361) 729-1226, (800) 953-1226**

Bahia Vista sits on the site of one of the area's earliest settlements. This 80-site park sits amid Rockport's wind-swept liveoak trees overlooking Copano Bay.

Amenities include a 300-foot lighted fishing per, fish-cleaning station, swimming pool, recreation hall, game room, large shaded spaces, showers, laundry room, boat tie-ups, and campfires are allowed in some areas. Security lights and on-site owners and managers add a touch of security.

Full hookups and pull-through sites available. Rates are $17 a day.

Circle W RV Ranch
No credit cards • 1401 Smokehouse Rd., Rockport
• **(361) 729-1542, (877)-422-CIRW**

This 306-site park is at the end of Smokehouse Road a few miles south of Rockport and about a mile west of Aransas Bay. It's laid out around several small ponds (two stocked with fish), clubhouses and an indoor pool and hot tub. Amenities at this retirement-oriented RV ranch include restrooms, showers, paved streets, exercise room, mail room, pool room, barbecue shack, laundry facilities, pay phones, cable television, planned activities October through March, a library, and five recreation rooms. The manager lives on the ranch. Planned activities include exercise classes, dancing, bingo, potluck dinners, bridge, cribbage, horseshoes, crafts, and occasional live music.

Rates for sites, which have full hookups (30- and 50-amp electrical service), are $23 a day.

ICW RV Park
No credit cards • 427 E. Ransom Road, Aransas Pass
• **(361) 758-1044**

At first glance we didn't think much of this park. Located on an abandoned airfield, it's severely lacking any trees, grass, or anything else green. It's appeal, we soon learned, is its location on the Intracoastal Waterway and its 41 waterfront lots (134 total). Here you're sure to find enough sun and sea breezes to last you a lifetime.

Amenities include a 360-foot lighted fishing pier, three fish-cleaning tables, full hookups (20-, 30- and 50-amp electrical service), telephone and cable TV available, security lights, public telephones, bathhouse, Laundromat (with a pool table), game room, picnic area (with cabanas, tables, barbecue pits, and restrooms), and a coded security gate.

Rates are $16 a day for land sites with single pads, $17 a day for land sites with double pads and $21 a day for waterfront sites.

Sea Breeze RV Park
• **1026 Seabreeze Ln., Portland**
• **(361) 643-0744, (888) 212-7541**

Tucked away on the west end of Portland, this 138-site RV park provides a secluded spot overlooking Nueces Bay. This is a destination park with a creek running through tree-studded grounds. Only a few sites actually overlook the water, and most of those do not have trees. Spots farther inland are surrounded by shade trees. Sites come with complete hookups (30- and 50-amp electrical service) and phone hookups. Amenities include a fishing pier, clubhouse, showers, cable television, laundry facilities, picnic tables, barbecue pits, RV storage, dump station, and a spa with a swimming pool, hot tub,

and sun deck. Corpus Christi's major tourist attractions are a 10-minute drive away.

Rates are $20 a day.

Corpus Christi

Puerto del Sol RV Park
• **5100 Timon Blvd., Corpus Christi**
• **(361) 882-5373, (888) 353-5373**

Water lovers will adore this 53-site park perched on the northern tip of Corpus Christi Beach. Just a stone's throw from U.S. Highway 181, this small RV park overlooks Corpus Christi Bay. Two popular Corpus Christi tourist attractions are nearby: The Texas State Aquarium and the Lexington Museum on the Bay (a decommissioned aircraft carrier). See Attractions chapter for more about these sites. Downtown Corpus Christi and the scenic Corpus Christi bayfront are a five-minute drive away. Amenities include picnic tables, ice, RV supplies, laundry facilities, game room, recreation room, planned activities, full hookups (30- and 50-amp electrical service), showers, dump station, and eight sites with telephone hookups.

Rates range from $19 to $21 a day depending on how close you are to the water. Tent sites are not available.

Hatch RV Park
• **3101 Up River Rd., Corpus Christi**
• **(361) 883-9781, (800) 332-4509**

Hatch RV Park touts itself as the most "centrally located" RV park in Corpus Christi, and that much is true. It's also a fair distance from the water, which, for some, might rule it out as a vacation destination. But we've included it here because of its amenities and the overall clean appearance displayed during a recent visit.

This 130-site park, including 25 pull-throughs, has full hookups (20-, 30- and 50-amp electrical service), cable TV, a general store, hot showers, restrooms, on-site propane, game room, recreation room, and pay phones. Plans call for a pool and spa to be completed in late 2000. It's located two miles from many Corpus Christi attractions such as the Texas State Aquarium, the Corpus Christi Greyhound Race Track, and the Bayfront Arts and Science Park.

> ## INSIDERS' TIP
> **Camping at the Padre Island National Seashore can be a lesson in protecting endangered species. Each year, park biologists release endangered Kemp's ridley sea turtle hatchlings into the wild in an effort to establish a nesting spot on Padre Island.**

CAMPGROUNDS AND RV PARKS

Rates are $25 a day for back-in sites and $27 a day for pull-throughs.

Colonia del Rey
- **1717 Waldron Rd., Corpus Christi**
- **(361) 937-2435, (800) 580-2435**

Colonia del Rey is a perfect compromise for those who can't decide whether they would rather be close to the beach or to Corpus Christi's shopping and restaurants. This approximately 200-site RV park is in Flour Bluff, a Corpus Christi neighborhood on the city's south side. Padre Island is a 10-minute drive south, and Corpus Christi's main shopping and restaurant district is an equal distance in the opposite direction. You'll find Flour Bluff less crowded and more rural than most Corpus Christi neighborhoods. Folks here have their own school district, and many think of themselves as Flour Bluff residents first and Corpus Christi residents second.

Sites come with full hookups (30- and 50-amp electrical service). Amenities include a dump station, cable television and telephone hookups, restrooms, showers, laundry facilities, swimming pool, picnic tables, seasonal recreation hall, game room, planned activities, general store with RV supplies, and a pay phone.

Rates are $21 to $23 a day. Gravel sites are $21 and concrete sites are $23. Tent sites are available for the same price.

Port Aransas to Padre Island

Island RV Resort
- **700 Sixth St., Port Aransas**
- **(361) 749-5600**

This 199-site RV park made our list because of its reputation for good service. It's in the middle of Port Aransas, less than a mile from the beach and about the same distance from local restaurants and shopping. A few newer sites are paved, the rest are grass. Amenities include a dump station, vehicle wash area, ice, bathhouse, RV supplies, pool, spa, shower, public telephone, recreation hall, organized activities, laundry facilities, playground, patios, and cable television.

Rates are $20 a day. Electricity is extra for weekly and monthly stays. Tent sites are available at $20 a day.

Nueces County Park
No credit cards • East end of Cotter Ave., Port Aransas
- **(361) 749-6117**

Head east on Cotter Avenue from the ferry landing in Port Aransas. Wend your way through a residential area and continue past the University of Texas Marine Science Institute on your left. When you get to the beach, you've arrived at the Nueces County Park in Port Aransas, known by locals as Port Aransas Park. The park has 75 sites with electricity and water and allows primitive camping on the beach. Amenities include a dump station, flushing toilets, showers, bathhouse, picnic shelters, and the Horace Caldwell Pier, a 1,245-foot lighted pier. On the pier you'll find a snack bar/convenience store where you can buy ice and basic groceries and rent fishing tackle. Pier operators charge a $1 admission fee. Park rangers are on duty 24 hours a day.

Rates are $15 a night for sites with electricity and water. The fee for primitive camping is $6 a night. There is a 14-night limit on all stays. Cash and travelers checks only. See our Parks chapter for more information.

On The Beach RV Park
- **907 Beach Access Rd. 1A, Port Aransas**
- **(361) 749-4909,**
  (800) 932-6337 closed 12-2

The name sums up the major appeal of this 60-site RV park in Port Aransas. You'll be a short stroll from the Gulf of Mexico and a brief car ride from local restaurants and shops. On The Beach has full hookups (30- and 50-amp electrical service), a fish-cleaning station, restrooms, hot showers, laundry, recreation room, public telephone, and cable television.

Rates are $18 to $21 depending on whether you have a site on the park's perimeter or on the inside. Tent sites are not available.

Pioneer Beach Resort
- **120 Gulfwind Dr., Port Aransas**
- **(361) 749-6248, (888) 480-3246**

Pioneer RV Resort is a fairly recent addition

INSIDERS' TIP

Most RV parks in the Coastal Bend allow pets on a leash. But many prohibit certain breeds of dogs (such as Doberman Pinchers and Pit Bull Terriers), and others approve or reject pets on a case-by-case basis.

to the family of RV parks that populate the area. Pioneer is so new it almost sparkles compared with many of its older competitors. Concrete streets and pads gleam under the South Texas sun, and the grounds are freshly landscaped. This 110-acre park (60 are developed) on the beach side of Texas Highway 361 has 362 full hookup sites with 20-, 30- and 50-amp electrical service. It also features a recreation meeting hall with kitchen, two swimming pools, Jacuzzi, climate-controlled bathhouses, fish-cleaning station, laundry facilities, general store, dump station, cable television, telephone service, propane, and playground equipment. Guests may take part in organized activities—the resort has a seasonal activity director—and a manager is on-site.

Rates are $20.95 to $256.95 a day. Cable is an extra $1.50 per night. There are no tent sites.

Mustang Island State Park
• **Texas Hwy. 361, Port Aransas**
• **(361) 749-5246, (800) 792-1112**

The state of Texas runs this 48-site RV park and campground, and what it lacks in amenities it more than makes up for with good, solid service. You won't find a swimming pool or recreation center here, but the grounds are clean and well maintained and you'll feel safe knowing park rangers are keeping an eye on the place. Upon arriving you'll pay an entrance fee of $3 per person older than 12. The park is on the beach of Mustang Island, 14 miles south of Port Aransas. The park has 48 paved RV sites (also available for tent camping) with water and electricity. Hot showers are nearby. Primitive and freshwater tent sites are available along the beach. Amenities include restrooms, recycling bins, pay phones, picnic shelters, a dump station, and a Texas State Parks Store where you can buy ice and souvenirs.

Rates are $12 a day for paved sites and $7 a day for unpaved beach camping sites. See our Parks chapter for more information.

Nueces County Padre Balli Park
• **15820 Park Rd. 22**
• **(361) 949-8121**

You'll find this county park north of the Padre Island National Seashore, just south of the Corpus Christi city limit, and right on the beach. It has 66 RV sites and 12 tent sites with water and electricity (bring a 50-foot extension cord) and an unspecified number of primitive camping sites along the beach. Amenities include a dump station, restrooms, hot showers, concession stand, picnic shelters, laundry fa-

cilities, first-aid station, and a lighted fishing pier. Park rangers are on duty 24 hours a day. Each person will pay $1 to enter the pier and a $1 fee per fishing pole.

Camping rates are $15 a day for RV and tent sites with utilities and $6 a day for primitive camping. There is a 14-day limit for both RV and tent campers. See our Parks chapter for more information.

Padre Island National Seashore
• **9405 S. Padre Island Dr., Corpus Christi**
• **(361) 949-8068**

Whether camping in a tent or parking your RV, you won't find more primitive conditions than those at Padre Island National Seashore. The trade-off? Pristine beaches, an abundance of wildlife and a location far removed from civilization. The national park has slabs without hookups for more than 40 RVs and tents and unlimited primitive camping along the beaches. The first 5 miles of beach are accessible by two-wheel-drive vehicles; the next 55 miles are accessible via four-wheel-drive vehicles only. Your stay is limited to 14 days. The park has a dump station, toilets, cold showers at the visitors center, year-round interpretive programs, and nature trails.

The park charges a $10 entrance fee good for seven days; an annual pass is available for $20. An additional $5 fee is charged for anyone wishing to visit the popular windsurfing site known as Bird Island Basin or to launch a boat; an annual pass sells for $10. Sites with slabs go for $8 a night; camping on the beach is free. Discount passes for senior citizens and people in wheelchairs are available. See our Parks chapter for more information.

The park is open 24 hours a day. The visitors center is open every day from 8:30 AM to 4 PM except Christmas and New Year's Day and from 8:30 AM to 6 PM between Memorial Day and Labor Day.

Kingsville Area

Oasis RV and Mobile Home Park
No credit cards • 2415 E. Santa Gertrudis, Kingsville
• **(361) 592-0764**

This RV and mobile home park at the intersection of Santa Gertrudis and U.S. Highway 77 in Kingsville is an ideal spot for those who want to be close to local attractions. Naval Air Station Kingsville is 2 miles east, and downtown Kingsville and Texas A&M University-

CAMPGROUNDS AND RV PARKS

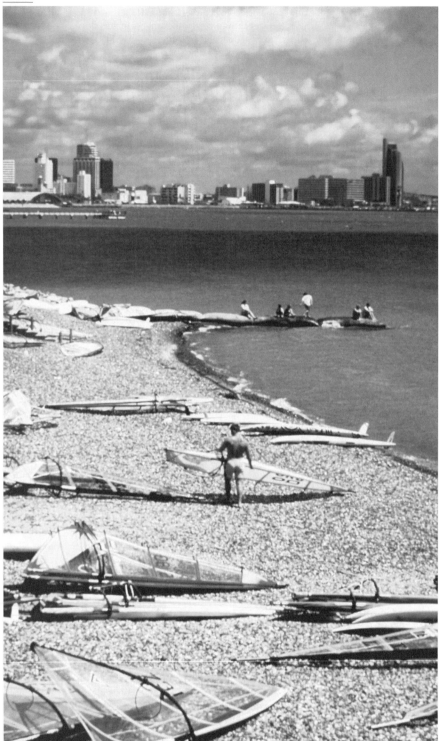

The national windsurfing championships are held each year along Corpus Christi's Bayfront.

Photo: courtesy of the Greater Corpus Christi Business Alliance

Kingsville are fewer than 2 miles to the west. Oasis is a 148-site park on 24 enclosed acres. Amenities include a playground, recreation hall, mail boxes, laundry facilities, showers, and a nearby driving range.

Rates are $15 a night.

Country Estates Mobile Ranch Inc.
No credit cards • F.M. Rd. 1717, Kingsville
• (361) 592-4659

Take a nice, scenic drive in the country past mesquite trees and farmland to Country Estates, a 125-site RV and mobile home park, just 1.5 miles south of Kingsville. Watch the Navy training jets take to the air as they practice takeoffs and landings at nearby Naval Air Station-Kingsville. Amenities of Country Estates include a recreation building, swimming pool, laundry facilities, showers, and restrooms. The park offers full hookups and 30- and 50-amp electrical service.

Rates are $18 a day.

SeaWind Resort
•F.M. Rd. 628, Loyola Beach
• (361) 297-5738

When developers announced plans to build a 134-site RV park east of Loyola Beach at the end of a country road way out in the middle of nowhere, more than a few people shook their heads and wondered how anyone could come up with such a crazy idea. But it turns out a lot of people like living far from civilization, espe-cially when they can do it in an RV park packed with amenities and situated on a beautiful South Texas waterway.

The SeaWind Resort overlooks the Cayo del Grullo, which leads to the popular fishing spots of Baffin Bay and the Laguna Madre, and is right next door to Kaufer-Hubert Memorial Park. See our Parks chapter for more information. Anglers and bird watchers will love this park laid out near two freshwater lakes. Amenities include a beach, group picnic shelters, single picnic tables with grills, restrooms, a two-story observation tower overlooking the bay, a 500-foot lighted fishing pier, and a four-lane boat ramp. You'll also find a parking area, birding overlook, 1-mile walking/jogging trail with 12-station senior fitness course, playground, horseshoe pits, soccer fields, and softball fields. The resort offers laundry facilities, a recreation center, post office boxes, restrooms, showers, a meeting room, and planned activities. Sites come with full hookups (30- and 50-amp electrical service), and telephone service is available.

Twenty-two overflow parking sites are available in the winter with 20-amp electrical service and water in most cases. Another 25 pull-through sites are planned for late 2000 or early 2001 with water and electrical service but no sewer hookups.

Rates are $16 a day. Tent sites are available at $10 a day.

INSIDERS' TIP

Generally speaking, the closer you are to the water the higher your rate will be.

Restaurants

Price Code

The dollar-sign code in each restaurant listing serves as a guide to give you an idea of the cost for an average dinner for two, excluding cocktails and wine, appetizers and desserts, tax and tip.

$	Less than $10
$$	$11 to $20
$$$	$21 to $40
$$$$	More than $40

South Texas's hospitality is never more evident as in the kitchen and dining room. There is a wide-ranging assortment of restaurants to visit throughout the region, from small-town family diners to national franchises.

The local restaurant selection has expanded greatly in recent years, particularly in Corpus Christi. It seems that every major national restaurant chain has arrived in this city, and residents of neighboring towns frequently drive to the big city of Corpus Christi to dine out. You can see these restaurants when you drive along S. Padre Island Drive, which has earned the nickname "Restaurant Row" among locals.

But please don't limit your culinary experimentation to those franchises while you're here. There are also a number of excellent locally owned restaurants that may offer you a more authentic taste of Corpus Christi. We've selected the best of the local hangouts for inclusion in this chapter, trying to lead you to some of South Texas's best eating. Because you already know what to expect from the chains, we're not going to include them in here.

We're also pleased to relate that there are definitely some restaurants worth visiting here—Beulah's in Port Aransas, the King's Inn near Kingsville, Joe Cotten's Barbecue in Robstown, Water Street Seafood and the Yardarm in Corpus Christi. All offer cuisine that would compare favorably in much larger metropolitan areas.

Be sure to try some of our regional specialties, which represent the culinary influences that converge in South Texas: Mexican, Texan, and coastal. Grilled fresh seafood is always a good choice, as is fried shrimp. The range of Tex-Mex fare, including enchiladas, tacos, chalupas, homemade tortillas, and chile rellenos, is very popular. Chicken fried steak is a Texas specialty that makes ordinary beef—in this case, tenderized round steak dredged in flour and fried in hot oil—into a dish that's tasty, filling and altogether delicious. And beef barbecue, that mainstay of Texans' midday meal, is also worth sampling—slow-cooked over glowing coals for hours until it's fork tender and sure to please anyone's palate.

A fairly recent food arrival is the paletera, or fruit restaurant. Mexican fruit cups—fresh chunks of tropical fruit doused with chile powder, fresh lime juice and salt—offer an authentic taste from south of the border. These tangy fruit cups and frozen, concentrated fruit bars (called paletas) are a wonderful and healthful snack. Many of these restaurants have only counter service. And take note: These fresh fruit cups are usually served with a generous sprinkling of salt, chile powder and lime juice, which provides a zesty flavor. Cucumber, more often found in vegetable salads than in fruit salads in the U.S., is an interesting addition.

As for dress, South Texas is a casual kind of place, particularly in the summertime. We don't know of any restaurants that require the men to wear ties to dinner. Men can usually get by with jeans or khakis—remember that for cowboys, a freshly pressed pair of jeans and a starched white shirt equals fancy dress. Women wear shorts, slacks, or sundresses to most of the restaurants, and sandals seem to be the favorite year-round footwear. Of course, there are always those special occasions when you're a little more gussied up than usual, and that's fine, too. But don't feel you have to dress to the nines for any of these restaurants.

As in other chapters, the restaurants are grouped by area, then listed alphabetically under the name of each city or town. The areas include North Bay, which encompasses the towns from the Aransas National Wildlife Refuge through Portland; Corpus Christi; Port Aransas to Padre Island; and the Kingsville area. So if you wanted to find a restaurant in Aransas Pass, you would look in the North Bay Area section then under the heading for Aransas Pass.

Prices can range widely, from incredibly inexpensive Mexican meals to pricier steak dinners. Unless otherwise noted, you can assume that the restaurants accept major credit cards.

So loosen your belt and enjoy!

North Bay Area

Aransas Pass

Julie's Backyard Bistro
$$–$$$, no credit cards
• **2212 A-1 Hill Rd., Aransas Pass**
• **(361) 758-7895**

Billed as "a gourmet haven in the middle of nowhere," this place certainly is as advertised. It takes a little doing to find it, tucked between Aransas Pass and Rockport off the Texas Highway 35 bypass. But the food is worth the trouble—elaborate seafood and steak dishes prepared lavishly and served in an elegant outdoor patio. You have to drive past bass boats and chain-link fences to get to this little bistro, and then cross a Japanese footbridge over a dancing brook.

Each night's innovative nouvelle cuisine is chalked on a board. Among the entrees we've sampled or heard praised by friends are snapper Florentine, in a crunchy breading topped with green chile sauce; crab cakes and adobe mayonnaise; and stuffed shrimp. Desserts can range from cappuccino bread pudding to truffle chocolate torte. Only open for dinner Wednesday through Saturday, it's best to make reservations because the dining area is rather small.

Mac's Pit Barbecue
$$ • **1933 W. Wheeler Ave., Aransas Pass**
• **(361) 758-0641**

For more than two decades, the Martinez family has been serving slow-cooked beef brisket, pork ribs, beef ribs, chicken, polish sausage, and ham to customers in the Corpus Christi area. This is the most recent arrival of three area restaurants run by the family; other locations are Texas Highway 35 in Gregory and

815 Market Street in Rockport. The restaurant also caters.

Fulton

The Boiling Pot
$$$ • **201 S. Fulton Beach Rd., Fulton**
• **(361) 729-6972**

Informal is the word for this restaurant. Wear your old clothes and prepare to get your hands messy feasting on the kind of Gulf Coast fare you'd be served at a typical Louisiana-style crab boil. The food is tossed into a big kettle and boiled with peppery spices, then literally dumped onto your butcher-paper covered table. Diners don bibs and take mallet in hand to crack open a steaming pile of boiled crabs. Also served with the crabs are shrimp, crawfish, spicy sausage, potato chunks, and corn on the cob.

Rockport

Back 40
$–$$ • **1101 Texas Hwy. 35 N., Rockport**
• **(361) 729-3478**

Stop here for a hearty breakfast before heading for the water. Known for its home-style cooking and the colorful wall murals, this restaurant offers a variety of family-pleasing meals for breakfast, lunch, and dinner. You can get eggs, bacon, and biscuits in the morning, or order steaks, chicken, and seafood at lunch and dinner.

The Big Fisherman
Seafood Restaurant
$–$$ • **519 Texas Hwy. 188, Rockport**
• **(361) 729-1997**

This longtime family-owned restaurant specializes in big appetites, offering an assortment of all-you-can-eat deals on steak, seafood, and chicken. The Texas Boil features two pounds of assorted crab legs, crab claws, and boiled shrimp for $21.95—enough to feed at least four. You'll also find great prices on lunch specials, including steak and fried shrimp with a baked potato, salad, or gumbo—all for $5.95. There's also an oyster bar and lounge.

Charlotte Plummer's
$$ • **202 N. Fulton Beach Rd., Fulton**
• **(361) 729-1185**

This is a longtime local favorite dining spot, serving fresh seafood and grilled steaks overlooking the peaceful waters of the Fulton Harbor. Try the whole stuffed flounder, or the chargrilled shrimp. You can also get seafood salads, steaks, homemade desserts and more. With its traditional seafood fare, pleasant atmosphere and variety, this is a good place to take a group or a large family.

Copano Provisioning Co.
**$–$$ • 6619 Texas Hwy. 35 N.,
Holiday Beach**
• (361) 729-1703

This Italian deli beside a gas station north of Rockport serves spaghetti, spicy muffalettas, and crunchy cannolis. We like the calzone stuffed with ham, salami, provolone and tomato, as well as the Italian salads. The food is served on paper plates, which seems incongruous with the fare—but the kitchen makes it all worthwhile.

Crab-N
**$$ • City by the Sea, Texas Hwy. 35 S.
• (361) 758-2371**

This casual, waterfront restaurant between Rockport and Aransas Pass specializes in fresh seafood and unique combinations—such as a pecan-crusted flounder with crab relish, or shrimp grilled with mango chile sauce. They offer chicken, heavy beef and blackened prime rib, too. You can also bring your own ready-to-cook catch and the kitchen will fix it how you like—blackened, sautéed, broiled, or fried. For dessert, try the homemade key lime pie.

Duck Inn
**$$ • 701 Broadway St., Rockport
• (361) 729-6663**

Established in 1946, this venerable restaurant specializes in breakfast specials, steaks, and fresh seafood. Try the homemade deviled crab, golden fried shrimp or baked flounder and crispy fried onion rings. Across from Rockport Beach Park, it also offers daily lunch specials, senior citizens' and children's menus. Stop on your way out for a day of fishing.

Palapa Restaurant
**$$$ • 39 Mazatlan at the Key Allegro
Marina, Rockport
• (361) 729-2630**

We love the outdoor deck in the back of this waterfront eatery, where you can sip your drink while waiting for a table. Ritzy food in a casual setting is this restaurant's byword. Order from a menu that includes lobster, oysters Rockefeller, rack of lamb and beef medallions with crab and shrimp buttercream—served up by waiters and waitresses in Hawaiian shirts and khaki shorts.

Valenari's Restaurant and Gallery
**$$$ • 105 N. Austin St., Rockport
• (361) 727-0717**

Live piano music, local artwork and gourmet cuisine make a visit to this downtown Italian restaurant an exquisite experience. This is a great place for a more formal or romantic dinner, with specialties such as gorgonzola-stuffed steak, fresh grilled seafood and a variety of creative pasta dishes. There is also an extensive wine list. It's open for dinner only Wednesday through Saturdays.

Portland

Elm Street Cafe
**$$ • 900 Elm St., Portland
• (361) 643-5350**

This cheery blue-and-white cafe serves home-style cooking of the sort you might find in your grandmother's kitchen. We've sampled a tasty beef stew here, thick with chunks of potato, carrots, and onion, and topped with two flaky biscuits. They also make an excellent chicken-fried steak.

Corpus Christi

Andy's Kitchen
**$ • 5802 S. Staples St., Corpus Christi
• (361) 992-0351**

Hearty, home-cooked breakfasts and traditional-style lunches draw crowds of regulars to this cozy, family-operated cafe. The model train that runs around the track placed near the ceiling is a special delight to youngsters. You can get old-fashioned favorites such as baked chicken, meatloaf, vegetable soup, and fresh biscuits here.

Bamboo Garden
**$$ • 1220 Airline Rd., Corpus Christi
• (361) 993-7993**

Sneak into this quiet, peaceful Chinese restaurant when you're tired of shopping at the nearby malls and strip centers. House specialties include a spicy beef in brown sauce with baby corn and mushrooms, fresh shrimp and scallops in a delicate garlic sauce, and Peking duck.

Bar B Q Man
**$$ • 4931 IH-37 S., Corpus Christi
• (361) 888-4248**

This barbecue restaurant has been catering to generations of professionals and laborers alike with its no-nonsense emphasis on tender beef brisket, pork ribs, sausage, chicken, and ham. You go through a cafeteria-style line and tell the servers what you want from the steaming platters, then take your heaping plate to a table in the large dining area. Plates come with barbecue sauce, beans, salad, and bread. As the menu says, "A sandwich here is a meal—plenty of meat." You can also get orders to go, meat by the pound, smoked whole hams or turkeys and quarts of side dishes.

Bayou Grill
$–$$ • 3741 S. Alameda St., Corpus Christi • (361) 854-8626

With fishing nets hanging from the walls and wooden signs, you get the feeling that you're inside a Louisiana camp house. And the food is just as authentic, from the hefty portions to the flavoring. We've had the catfish po'boy, and red beans and rice, served with a large and tasty sausage. On another visit, we had tender broiled Gulf snapper with bonne sauce (cream gravy with crawfish tails), accompanied by creamed spinach and French-fried corn on the cob (interesting). The Bayourita (a frozen Margarita boasting 14 percent alcohol) comes from an old family recipe.

INSIDERS' TIP

If you're going to barbecue your own meat while visiting here, check out Moody's Meat Market, (361) 992-6512, 4703 S. Alameda Street, for the city's best selection of steaks, ribs, roasts, chicken, and German-style sausage.

Bel-Aire Drugs
$ • 2741 S. Staples St., Corpus Christi • (361) 853-0396

We have friends who swear that this 1950s-style pharmacy lunch counter makes the best hamburgers in town. And they may be right—the burgers are grilled and juicy, with just the right amount of greasiness. If you're going to lunch here, be sure and arrive a little before noon because seating is limited. You may have to wait among the aisles, where you can browse the selection of shampoo and greeting cards.

B&J's Pizza
$$ • 6335 S. Padre Island Dr., Corpus Christi • (361) 992-6671

This place will spoil you forever for eating ordinary pizza. We should know—it's awfully difficult to settle for anything less now that we've come to know and love their version of the Italian dinner pie. All the ingredients are fresh, and the crust is thin and crispy and alto-

gether perfect. Plus, there are literally hundreds of beverage selections here: domestic and imported beers, non-alcoholic beers, soft drinks, iced tea, and more. Among favorite pizzas to try here are the Polynesian with Canadian bacon, pineapple, and mushrooms; Jack's Special with fresh garlic, onions, Italian sausage and pepperoni; and the vegetarian garden pizza, with fresh tomatoes, green peppers, broccoli, fresh garlic, and herbs. Sandwiches are served here, too. A game room/bar is adjacent.

Catfish Charlie's
$$ • 5830 McArdle Rd., Corpus Christi • (361) 993-0363

The name says it all—the best thing to get here is the fried catfish, which is crisp and buttery tasting, served with coleslaw, jalapeno-flecked hush puppies, Cajun red beans and thick fries. There are also frog legs, shrimp, chicken-fried steak, gumbo and SOB's (shrimp stuffed with oysters, wrapped in bacon and grilled). Rustic surroundings, friendly atmosphere, and quick service make this a good place to take the family.

Crystal's
$$ • 4119 S. Staples St., Corpus Christi • (361) 857-8081

An eclectic menu and a pleasant atmosphere make this a popular dining spot. You can get anything from Tex-Mex to baby-back ribs or dinner salads at this restaurant. We recommend the chicken-stuffed chile relleno, which is topped with pecans, raisins, and sour cream. Appetizers are also tasty—nachos, fried potato skins, and fried mozzarella cheese sticks.

Dentoni's Pizza
$$ • 415 William St., Corpus Christi • (361) 881-9886

With its sleek decor and late-night hours, this chic pizzeria caters to the club crowd and the hip business workers. There are 12 varieties of pre-made pizza, but the staff will also customize for you—and you can get a single slice or a whole pie. The crust is homemade and yeasty, the spicy tomato sauce is laced with oregano, and the toppings range from traditional to unusual. We like the white pizza (topped with olive oil, mozzarella cheese and oregano), the spinach Florentine (spinach, tomatoes, red onion, and mushrooms) and the Southwest ver-

RESTAURANTS

sion (pesto sauce, mozzarella cheese, and grilled chicken). Salads are good too, particularly an antipasto salad that features different types of greens, salami and pepperoni slices, black olives, green pepper, tomatoes, cucumbers, and anchovies.

Elva's
$, no credit cards • 3511 S. Staples St., Corpus Christi • (361) 851-9931

This unpretentious diner features some of the best Tex-Mex deals in town. For less than $5, you can get a Mexican platter of enchiladas swathed in beef gravy, a crispy beef taco, a bean and cheese chalupa, and fresh flour tortillas. Meals come with a basket of fresh fried tortilla chips, thin, salty, and slight greasy—just as they should be.

Executive Surf Club
$-$$ • 309 N. Water St., Corpus Christi • (361) 884-SURF

Surfboards jutting from the walls serve as tabletops at this casual eatery, which serves assorted burgers, batter-dipped french fries, nachos, gumbo, and salads. We recommend the surf burger—a hamburger topped with refried beans, corn chips, onions, cheese, and salsa. For lighter appetites, try the grilled chicken salad—tender slices of chicken atop lettuce, served with cheese, tomato, and the fabulous house creamy walnut dressing. There's also live music most nights. Order at the bar, then wait for your number to be called to pick up your food hot from the grill. You can eat indoors or outside on the patio, which makes it a great place to take restless children.

Frank's Spaghetti House
$$ • 2724 Leopard St., Corpus Christi • (361) 882-0075

As one restaurant reviewer put it, this Italian eatery was launched long before noodles became known as pasta. This renovated house is cozy and intimate, with red-checked tablecloths and traditional Italian favorites. Try the meaty lasagna, or the chicken piccata.

Golden Crown Chinese Restaurant
$$-$$$ • 6601 Everhart Rd., Corpus Christi • (361) 854-5506

Classy Cantonese-style fare is served in this elegant south side restaurant. Lunch is a good bet, with an assortment of daily specials such as chicken and asparagus. Garnishes include storks and cranes carved from sweet potatoes.

Hofbrau Steaks and Bar
$$ • 1214 N. Chaparral St., Corpus Christi • (361) 881-8722

Texas flags, neon beer signs and bargain lunch specials are the hallmarks of this rugged steakhouse. Regulars know that the Wednesday lunch special is chicken-fried steak, and they plan their day accordingly. We've also enjoyed a chopped sirloin topped with cheese and jalapeño sauce, served with thick steak fries and a salad.

Imperial Cafe
$ • 5702 S. Staples St., Suite A-4, Corpus Christi • (361) 980-1423

This unique and appealing little cafe has gained quite a popular following—it offers excellent Thai cuisine, Vietnamese food, Italian fare, and delicious baked goods. Decorated with gilded vases, tea canisters and even a trickling fountain, the atmosphere is as unusual as the menu. Try the delicious spring rolls, the green curry (chicken, mushrooms, bamboo shoots, and green beans in a curry and coconut stew), or any of the sumptuous vegetarian dishes. We also like the variety of herbal teas and coffees, as well as the rich desserts, from a white-and-dark chocolate cheesecake to the Ghiradelli chocolate almond bars.

Jeron's Tea Room
$-$$ • 517 Everhart Rd., Floor 2 (inside Sister Sue's Antiques), Corpus Christi • (361) 980-1939

This quaint tea room serves salads, sandwiches, quiches, and more in an antique shop. We recommend the house lasagna, which is rich and creamy and satisfying. We also love the cheesy broccoli quiche, with its flaky crust and generous portion (even a real man could fill up on this quiche!). The entrees come with generous green salads and miniature corn muffins that have a delightful hint of sweetness. For vegetarians, try the garden sandwich of fresh avocado, cucumber, and mushrooms on honeywheat bread. Lemon cake and apple crisp are

INSIDERS' TIP

Here's a Texas bumper sticker that pays homage to the state's love of red meat: "Support beef—run over a chicken."

RESTAURANTS

Whataburger

In the Lone Star State, the fast-food battlefield contains a uniquely Texan contender—and one that's headquartered in Corpus Christi.

Alongside the ubiquitous golden arches and burger monarchy found in all major—nay, even many minor—communities, you'll see something just as distinctive to South Texans and equally enticing. It's the orange-and-white striped roof of a Whataburger restaurant.

Whataburger (pronounced exactly the way it's spelled) is a burger joint with a Texan flavor. You can get jalapeños on those hearty quarter-pound hamburgers. Or you can order chicken fajitas for lunch or sausage-and-egg taquitos for breakfast.

And while it's classified as fast food, Whataburger's specialty is made-to-order burgers, so it's not quite as quick as the other Mc-chains. To some eaters, that's a disadvantage; to others, it's a plus. We figure it depends on your preference.

Harmon A. Dobson, a Corpus Christi entrepreneur whose dream was to "provide the public with the ultimate burger—the Whataburger," founded Whataburger in 1950. The chain's slogan was: "It's not just a hamburger—it's a Whataburger." And the philosophy was to allow the customer to dictate what would be on the burger, including fresh lettuce, tomatoes, pickles, onions, salad dressing, ketchup, or mustard.

Dobson's first restaurants served the signature Whataburger, cold drinks, and potato chips from large wooden boxes, 10-feet-by-23-feet.

The now-familiar structure of the restaurants was designed in 1961, featuring the orange-and-white striped roof on an A-frame building. Other additions since then have included drive-through facilities.

Dobson died in an airplane accident in 1967, and his wife, Grace, took over the corporation.

The company has expanded mightily. Whataburgers can now be found

(Continued on next page)

Whataburger restaurants have a distinctive orange-and-white striped roof and a South Texas flavor.

Photo: courtesy of Whataburger

RESTAURANTS

throughout the Sunbelt, in Texas, Alabama, Arizona, Florida, Louisiana, New Mexico, and Oklahoma. There are approximately 525 Whataburger restaurants in the southern United States and Mexico, with 80 percent of them in Texas.

Still, the basic foundation of the franchise remains the same: a grilled, quarter-pound 100-percent beef patty on a 5-inch bun with a sprinkling of lettuce, three slices of tomato, four slices of dill pickle, chopped onion, mustard, salad dressing, or ketchup. Whataburger added chicken sandwiches and chicken strips in 1988 and began accepting credit cards in 1989. The company opened its 500th site in 1995.

As for us, we like Whataburger's juicy burgers and fried chicken strips, crispy french fries, and fountain drinks. We find the fare fresher tasting and more flavorful than at the other fast-food restaurants.

On the other hand, we know of folks who can't stand Whataburger and would much prefer to pick up a burger at McDonald's or Burger King. Late-night debates sometimes focus on the pros and cons of Whataburger's offerings and speculation about whether there are some innate reasons why some people love 'em and others hate 'em. Could it be a regional thing? Are native Texans more likely to prefer the more full-bodied, home-cooked flavor of these burgers?

You'll have to open wide and let your taste buds decide for you.

RESTAURANTS

among the daily dessert offerings. Owner Bette Hoelscher also provides teas for special occasions and private receptions.

Jezebelles
$$ • 100 Shoreline Blvd., Corpus Christi • (361) 887-7403

Inventive sandwiches and salads are served in this soothing restaurant in the Art Center of Corpus Christi. You can browse the center's gift shops and art displays after you finish your meal, or you can get your art-gazing in while eating—paintings on the restaurant's walls are by local artists and are changed monthly. A wall of windows facing the bay provides patrons with a great view. As for the food, we like the chicken salad flavored with chopped grapes, walnuts and chutney, as well as the roast beef with melted Monterey Jack cheese, sautéed onions, and mushrooms. Desserts are also worth trying—the kitchen usually has several sinfully sweet offerings each day. This restaurant is open for lunch only and is closed on Sunday and Monday.

Kiko's
$–$$ • 5514 Everhart Rd., Corpus Christi • (361) 991-1211

A perennial favorite for standard Tex-Mex food, this restaurant serves massive portions of favorites. Fresh, hot tortillas accompany enchi-

ladas, tacos, tamales, and rice and beans. We also like the beef and chicken fajitas, served on a sizzling skillet and accompanied by Spanish rice, refried beans, guacamole, and fresh flour tortillas. Service is quick, and the food is good. It can be crowded so you may have to wait for a table on a weekend night. Breakfast is also a popular choice here, with taquitos, omelets, and more.

Kobe Japanese Steak House
$$ • 5134 Carroll Ln., Corpus Christi • (361) 851-2555

Watching the chef can be as much fun as eating the food at this Japanese restaurant. Dinner guests sit around a large table to observe as a knife-wielding, wisecracking cook deftly slices, dices, chops, seasons, grills, and sautés the orders on a sizzling hot stove right at the table. Teriyaki steak, shrimp, and chicken are Kobe specialties; other favorites are the fried rice, delicious vegetables, and fresh sushi. Kobe Japanese Steak House is open for dinner only. Reservations are recommended.

La Paletera
$ • 5021 Kostoryz Rd., Corpus Christi • (361) 857-2042

With beautiful fresh fruit platters and delicious fruit milkshakes, this is a refreshing culinary addition to the restaurant scene. There are four locations in Corpus Christi and this is the largest and maybe the most popular—we feel fortunate when we can find a parking spot in the tiny lot. Be sure to try the spicy seasoning—salt, chile powder and lime juice—atop your chunks of watermelon, strawberry, pineapple, grapes, apple, fresh coconut, and more.

La Bahia
$ • 224 N. Mesquite St., Corpus Christi
• (361) 888-6555

This is where locals come for breakfast and lunch, taking sustenance for their business day from the hearty fare served quickly and at extremely low prices. You can get a plate of huevos rancheros (eggs with salsa) and refried beans, tortillas, bacon, and coffee for under $5. However, we prefer to visit here at lunchtime to fill up on cheesy enchiladas, tacos, nachos, rice, and refried beans. This is near the police station, so you're sure to see plenty of cops inside. County and city officials also tend to frequent this amiable place.

Longhorn Steak and Ale
$$ • 4307 Avalon St., Corpus Christi
• (361) 992-7731

Steaks, seafood, chicken, and southwestern favorites are the specialty of this comfortable restaurant near a row of antique shops. You can get a rib eye, fried chicken, stuffed flounder, or a chicken-avocado salad here. There are also daily blackboard specials and a children's menu.

Luciano's Italian Restaurant
$$ • 1821 S. Alameda St., Corpus Christi
• (361) 882-3191

Long a staple of the Corpus Christi dining scene, this is a revived version of the original Luciano's. And the food seems every bit as tasty and traditional as the original. We like the shrimp Lancianese, which is named for the Luciano family's hometown in Italy—it features grilled shrimp in a cream sauce, served over spaghetti noodles. Also try the veal scaloppini and the delicious ciabatta (a light Italian bread).

Mac's Barbecue
$ • 4301 S. Alameda St., Corpus Christi
• (361) 993-2233

This small, yellow eatery is easy to miss. But it offers succulent beef brisket and delectable sausage sandwiches that are worth the trouble. The furnishings are basic, but everything is neat and clean. And don't expect a waiter—order from the counter and then go sit at one of the tables and wait for your name to be called.

Mamma Mia's
$$–$$$, no credit cards
• 128 N. Mesquite St., Corpus Christi
• (361) 883-3773

The atmosphere, from Italian arias in the background to the odor of fresh-baked bread and garlic, is great at this downtown restaurant. And the food is fabulous. Favorites include red snapper linguine in a cream sauce with capers and artichoke hearts to pasta pesto alla marino, which features basil, pine nuts and olive oil with broccoli and mushrooms. Owner Marino Delzotto, with pipe in mouth, goes from table to table, greeting customers and making sure all is well. Assorted slices of thick, warm homemade breads arrive rapidly on your table, for dipping in a plate of olive oil, balsamic vinegar, or both. If you order wine, they'll set the jug on your table and rely on you to count your own glasses. If you have room for dessert, try the zabaglione, strawberries in a sauce of marsala, egg, and sugar. This is one of the city's most popular Italian restaurants, so it can get a bit crowded. Its popularity is largely due to word of mouth because they don't advertise.

Mao Tai
$$ • 4601 S. Padre Island Dr.,
Corpus Christi
• (361) 852-8877

Easily one of the city's most established Asian restaurants, there are more than 80 items on the extensive menu. Among the favorites are spicy General Tso's chicken and the Hunan-style combination of beef, scallops, and shrimp.

Marbella's
$$–$$$ • 1002 Chaparral St.,
Corpus Christi
• (361) 883-8087

A sophisticated, eclectic menu is the hallmark of this downtown restaurant in a cavernous warehouse-like building. Patrons tend to be more enthusiastic about the dinner menu than the lunches. Among the recommendations are the pecan-crusted redfish, which is served with a cilantro beurre blanc sauce and surrounded by chunks of tomato and avocado.

Marco's
$$–$$$ • 3812 S. Alameda St.,
Corpus Christi
• (361) 853-2000

Great pasta and fresh seafood prepared by a

consummate Italian chef are worth the high price tag. During a recent visit, we began our meal with hot, homemade bread and a pureed tomato-and-basil spread. Next we had fettuccine Alfredo with chicken, which was creamy and rich, studded with morsels of tender chicken breast. A friend had the linguini alla vongole, fresh clams in the shell steamed with oil, garlic, white wine, and tomato sauce. We also like the red-pepper pasta stuffed with sausage and broccoli, served with walnuts, black olives, and a creamy tomato sauce. Dessert was a sinfully rich slice of dark chocolate cake flavored with amaretto, layered with marzipan and glazed with dark chocolate.

Marco's Bistro
$$–$$$ • 5630 McArdle Rd.,
Corpus Christi
• (361) 986-9332

From deep-dish pizza to homemade pasta, you should find something to tantalize your tastebuds at this charming little bistro, located in an upscale shopping center. The sophisticated cuisine, served in an atmosphere of informal elegance, includes everything from shrimp in Alfredo sauce and chicken Marsala to steaks, fish or salad. The chef has an especially deft hand with the desserts, including the creamy cheesecake.

Oasis Coffee House
$–$$ • 320 William St., Corpus Christi
• (361) 887-7662

Located in the Water Street Market, this café serves light sandwiches, cakes, cookies, muffins, and an energizing array of coffees and coffee-based drinks. Stop by for delicious cafe lattes, cappucinos, espressos, and cafe mochas here. This café also sells coffee beans by the half-pound and pound, with more than a dozen varieties in regular and decaf.

Old Mexico
$$ • 3329 Leopard St., Corpus Christi
• (361) 883-6461

For many longtime residents, a visit to this Mexican restaurant is a time-honored tradition. All the new culinary arrivals in town have thinned the crowds, but this place continues to serve dependable Tex-Mex fare. We particularly like the puffy tacos—fried to a delicate, air-filled fluffiness, then topped with cheese or guacamole. Enchiladas are good, rice is fluffy and the tortillas are freshly made and hot. A pecan praline or bowl of sherbet comes with each meal.

Origami
$$–$$$ • 1220 Airline Rd., Corpus Christi
• (361) 993-3966

If you like sushi, you'll like this neat Japanese eatery. There are more than 50 varieties with ingredients ranging from raw tuna and cucumber to cooked shrimp and smoked eel. Entrees include shrimp tempura and teriyaki chicken.

Price's Chef
$ • 1800 S. Alameda St., Corpus Christi
• (361) 883-2786

At this venerable and old-fashioned coffee shop, you can linger over a steaming cup of java and a plateful of scrambled eggs and toast, while reading the daily newspaper. Our favorite breakfast item is the pecan waffle, which is fluffy and thick and altogether a sweet wake-up call for your taste buds. Lunch is just as satisfying with home-style Southern culinary delights such as meatloaf, ham steak or chicken with dumplings. The entrees vary daily, and are served with vegetables and a dessert. Long a tradition with many locals, this coffee shop fills up quickly at lunchtime and after church on Sundays. Waitresses are friendly and easy-going, and they're likely to remember your preferences when you've been here several times.

Republic of Texas Bar and Grill
$$$–$$$$ • 900 N. Shoreline Blvd.,
Corpus Christi
• (361) 886-3515

On the 20th floor of the Corpus Christi Marriott Bayfront, this restaurant offers a spectacular view of the waterfront and equally spectacular food. Its lush, opulent surroundings harken to Texas's oil-boom era, and its unabashed emphasis on quality beef reflect a time when steak was the first choice of those dining out. The restaurant also typically serves wild game each evening, including exotics such as ostrich and wild boar. This is a great place for celebrating an anniversary or other special occasion, or for a romantic escape. Service is ex-

INSIDERS' TIP
The fiery pepper called the jalapeño is much beloved by South Texas cooks. It actually originated in Jalapa (or Xalapa), the capital of the Mexican state of Veracruz.

RESTAURANTS

cellent. Try to get here around sunset for a front-row seat at nature's nightly drama. It's also a good place for drinks and appetizers.

Rosita's
$–$$ • 2319 Morgan St., Corpus Christi
• (361) 883-8363
• 5253 S. Staples St.
• (361) 906-1007

Start your day with an order of breakfast taquitos—that's eggs and a filling such as potato, cheese, bacon or sausage, wrapped in a fresh flour tortilla—and you may have to skip lunch. For lunch try the enchilada platters, cheesy, chili-sauced enchiladas with refried beans and rice. Owners Johnny and Rosie Rodela have been offering their brand of traditional Mexican cooking to an appreciative clientele in their bustling westside restaurant and now to folks on the southside. Furnishings are basic Tex-Mex, from the posters featuring Tejano stars and the calendar with the picture of the Virgin of Guadalupe. Servers can be a bit brusque, but the food is great.

Rusty's
$–$$ • 1645 Airline Rd., Corpus Christi
• (361) 993-5000

Hamburgers, chicken sandwiches, rib-eye steak sandwiches, and Bohemian sausage are the purview of this unpretentious restaurant. Order your food at the front counter, where you can check out the thick, fresh hamburger patties. The bread is homemade, and there is a nice selection of domestic and imported beer and wine (by the glass).

Santa Fe Deli
$ • 1124 Ayers St., Corpus Christi
• (361) 882-3354

Sandwiches or daily hot entrees, including cabbage rolls and moussaka, are available at this unassuming deli. The menu includes traditional offerings such as pastrami, roast beef and ham and cheese, as well as more unusual items including the Power Veggie sandwich, with cream cheese, sprouts, white onion, tomato, avocado, and tabouli.

Small Planet Delicatessen and Bakery
$$ • 42 Lamar Park Ctr., Corpus Christi
• (361) 855-1892

We can't resist the crumbly, buttery scones (preferably washed down with a nice big cup of cafe mocha) at this supernaturally delicious deli. Its wide-ranging clientele, from the young and hip to the older and upscale, converge in the mornings and at lunchtime to partake of gigantic sweet rolls, cappuccino, fruit salad, vegetarian lasagna, pesto pizza, and the like. The cakes, pies, and tarts are displayed with artistic grace under glass. The food almost looks too good to eat. Almost, we said. Look for the blackboard specials on daily hot entrees or try one of the specialty sandwiches, such as the Mediterranean, which features spinach, onion, feta cheese, and fresh dill in flaky fillo pastry. The furnishings are equally celestial, and the staff is personable and attentive.

Snoopy's Pier
$$, no credit cards
• 13313 S. Padre Island Dr., Corpus Christi
• (361) 949-8815

This is our favorite of the eateries beneath the JFK Causeway. It features traditional fried shrimp, juicy hamburgers, and broiled fish. As befits a waterfront restaurant, the atmosphere is casual and rustic, with an outdoor deck that fills up quickly during warm spring and summer evenings. Order at the front of the restaurant, then come to pick up your food when your name is called. During the occasional cool days, the fireplace in the front room lends a cozy atmosphere.

Sonja's
$$ • 424 N. Chaparral St., Corpus Christi
• (361) 884-7774

With veal marsala and baked brie, this cafe-and-bakery brings a touch of European dining to downtown Corpus Christi. Try the French onion soup or the roasted pork loin in a cognac-apple glaze. And don't forget to leave room for some of the sumptuous homemade pastries for dessert.

Shoreline Grill
$$ • 6102 Ocean Dr., Corpus Christi
• (361) 992-3938

With an entire wall of windows, this restaurant provides a spectacular view of the bayfront. And the food is pretty good, too. Calamari, mesquite grilled shrimp, and baby back ribs are among the appetizer selections. Entrees range from grilled seafood to steaks.

Taqueria Acapulco
$–$$ • 1133 Airline Rd., Corpus Christi
• (361) 994-7274

You'll find good, hearty Tex-Mex food at bargain prices here. As an added bonus, the kitchen does some intriguing combinations that go a bit beyond ordinary Tex-Mex such as the

RESTAURANTS

aguacate gordita, a thick corn tortilla split open and stuffed with avocado, refried beans, and pico de gallo. Even the tacos are better than average, featuring finely cubed beef in a soft corn tortilla. The fresh fruit milkshakes, available in strawberry and banana, are also worth tasting.

Taqueria Jalisco
$–$$ • 902 S. Port Ave., Corpus Christi
• (361) 881-8739

With nine locations in Corpus Christi and surrounding towns, this locally owned restaurant chain is a longtime crowd pleaser. This is the original with an open view of the kitchen with the rich fragrance of chili, posole, and pepper. Expect traditional Mexican food, from breakfast taquitos to rich carne guisada.

Tien Tan
$–$$ • 5898 Everhart Rd., Corpus Christi
• (361) 980-0748

Sleek black and purple decor, ceiling fans, and sconces adorn this nifty Asian restaurant. We recommend the lunch buffet, where you can sample a range of dishes including crab rangoon—fried wonton stuffed with crabmeat and cream cheese—beef with broccoli, lo mein noodles, sesame chicken, and fresh green beans sautéed with pork.

Tokyo Den
$$ • 5625-B S. Padre Island Dr.,
Corpus Christi
• (361) 992-9611

Tucked into a strip center near the local Chuck-E-Cheese, this small Japanese restaurant is a soothing retreat from shopping stress and traffic jams. The menu includes Korean and Japanese specialties, and an array of sushi prepared by an expert chef. For a real treat, ask for bulgogi (beef) or Kaibi (short rib) to be grilled at your table.

The Torch
$$–$$$ • 4425 S. Alameda St.,
Corpus Christi
• (361) 992-7491

Steaks are the specialty at this family-owned Greek restaurant, which is reminiscent of the small, intimate restaurants that abounded in the 1950s and 1960s—before franchises took hold. The best night to visit is Wednesday, Greek night, when you can select from seven Greek entrees, including one that offers "a little bit of everything." The moussaka is a wonderful casserole of thinly sliced potatoes and eggplant with meat sauce and bechamel sauce atop.

While you're dining, you're likely to see owners Telly and Linda Gialouris circulating to chat with customers.

Town and Country Cafe
$–$$ • 4228 S. Alameda St., Corpus Christi
• (361) 992-0360

For down-home cooking like Mama used to make, head for this homey cafe. Regulars hit this place for coffee, omelets, and blueberry pancakes every morning. Others head over at noon to have the daily specials, which recently included beef tips and noodles, salmon patties, and liver and onions. The cooked vegetables (which can include anything from broccoli, carrots, fried okra, turnip greens to mashed potatoes) are excellent here, and you can get a plate with a choice of four vegetables plus cornbread—a healthy and satisfying meal.

Two George's
$$–$$$ • 5884 Everhart Rd.,
Corpus Christi
• (361) 993-8008

A bounty of seafood is served at this restaurant, where diners order fried shrimp, fried oysters, and broiled fish by the platterful. The family-style platters of food and other menu items, including several tasty avocado salads, were apparently modeled after those on the menu at the King's Inn, a famous and longtime seafood restaurant located near Kingsville (see below). The decor is nautical, with portholes for windows and trophy fish adorning the walls. Servings are large and the cost of a meal can depend on the market price for seafood.

Vietnam
$$ • 4501 S. Padre Island Dr.,
Corpus Christi
• (361) 853-2682

This family-owned restaurant offers the city's best Vietnamese fare, specializing in fresh, attractively presented food. Our favorite appetizers include deep-fried crab rolls and shrimp rolls wrapped in rice paper. We also recommend the Vietnamese crepe cake stuffed with shrimp, bean sprouts, and chicken. Chopsticks are optional as flatware is provided.

Wahoo's
$–$$ • 415 N. Water St., Corpus Christi
• (361) 888-8522
$–$$ • 5702 S. Staples St., Corpus Christi
• (361) 993-5111

Vibrant colors and bouncy zydeco music greet diners at these Cajun-style eateries, one located downtown and the other on the city's southside. The food is good and just as spicy as the atmosphere—check out the grilled seafood, peppery dirty rice, and blackened entrees, then wash it all down with a beer or soda.

Wallbangers
$$ • 4100 S. Staples St., Corpus Christi
• (361) 855-8007

Remember that old commercial where they keep asking, "Where's the beef?" Well, this is where the beef is—unabashed, monster servings of ground beef. With unfinished wood floors, neon beef signs, high-backed wooden booths and quick service, this caters mostly to families and young people. In addition to the half-pounder, the pounder, and the junior burger (a third of a pound of meat), you can also order something known as "The Big Banger," a three-pound burger and two pounds of french fries. It supposedly feeds six people. Diners place their orders at a counter, and wait for their names to be called. Chicken sandwiches and baked potatoes are also available.

Water Street Oyster Bar and Water Street Seafood Co.
$$–$$$ • 309 N. Water St., Corpus Christi
• (361) 881-9448, (361) 882-8684

These sister restaurants, with the same owner and same location, offer great fresh seafood in a classy atmosphere. This is the hands-down choice for locals who want to entertain out-of-town visitors. A nautical motif, complete with trophy fish hanging from the walls, adorns the Seafood Co., while an interesting rendition of Botticelli's *The Birth of Venus* is featured in the Oyster Bar. Our favorite entrees are the skewered, bacon-wrapped shrimp, and the grilled snapper in a crawfish Nueces sauce, but there is always an array of blackboard specials featuring fresh seafood. Although this restaurant serves a decent gumbo, the soup to get is the caldo xochitl (a fragrant chicken-and-rice soup served with slices of fresh avocado); and the house salad with creamy walnut-laced dressing.

Yardarm
$$$–$$$$
• 4310 Ocean Dr., Corpus Christi
• (361) 855-8157

Hidden inside this cheery yellow house on the bayfront is some of the area's best and most elegant cuisine. The atmosphere is straight out of Nantucket, complete with thick bowls of creamy chowder and a pierside view. The tables are cozy and close together, which lends an intimate and rather romantic feel to this restaurant. Start your meal with the oysters Rockefeller, which are hot and fragrant, bursting with flavor. The house salad, with red onion, black olives, lettuce and clove-marinated carrot coins, is wonderful. As for entrees, among those we've had and loved are pompano en papillote (cooked in a paper bag) and sole cooked in white wine, draped in spinach and topped with Hollandaise sauce. This is a great place for a romantic dinner or anniversary celebration. Expect a leisurely meal here—servers are attentive but this is fare meant to be savored, not gulped down.

Robstown

Cotten's Bar-B-Que
$$–$$$, no credit cards • U.S. Hwy. 77, Robstown
• (361) 767-9973

State governors and out-of-state dignitaries have been known to fly into this tiny community—even landing helicopters on the grassy median along the interstate—in order to partake of the beloved barbecue served in this wooden structure. Founder Joe Cotten, who died in 1992, established his reputation by slow-cooking corn-fed beef over mesquite wood all night. Family members who inherited the restaurant have continued his tradition. This place is simple, straightforward, and unpretentious. There is no menu—customers select sliced pork, beef brisket, ribs, or sausage. It arrives at the table on sheets of butcher paper. Served with it are the basic accompaniments of pinto beans in rich broth, sliced bread, tangy barbecue sauce,

The Yardarm is a favorite with locals for fresh seafood and a quaint atmosphere.

Photo: Daniel Fielder

RESTAURANTS

and thick slices of raw onion, radishes, pickle, and jalapeño. If you want seconds, summon the waiter to your table. Truly a South Texas tradition, many longtime customers eat here at least once a week, if not more often. And among the celebrities who have frequented Cotten's are Lyndon Johnson, Willie Nelson, Roger Staubach, and many of the Dallas Cowboys.

Port Aransas to Padre Island

Beulah's at Tarpon Inn
$$$ • 200 E. Cotter Ave., Port Aransas
• (361) 749-4888

Chef-owner Guy Carnathan's kitchen produces fabulous and creative dishes that entice locals and visitors to this graceful restaurant in the historic Tarpon Inn (see our Accommodations chapter). This is a place to go and make an evening out of the dining experience, so you can savor dishes like bacon-wrapped fresh tuna, roasted garlic mashed potatoes, a salad of greens in a dressing of toasted pecans, blue cheese, and soy balsamic vinaigrette. Patrons can sit indoors or on the breezy open veranda. The menu always includes fresh fish, steak, and rack of lamb. The restaurant is open for dinner Wednesday through Sunday and for Sunday brunch. Note: It closes from Thanksgiving until right after Christmas.

Crazy Cajun
$$ • 303 Beach St. at Station St., Port Aransas
• (361) 749-5069

This is a casual, down-home eatery that serves Cajun-style seafood. The boiled dinner of crab legs, shrimp, and crawfish comes to your butcher-paper-covered table for everyone to dig in. There's also live entertainment, including local bands.

Marcel's
$$$ • 905 Alister Rd., Port Aransas
• (361) 749-5577

A romantic dinner for two at this cozy gourmet restaurant might feature grilled salmon with crushed black peppercorns and garlic herb-butter sauce, or venison scallopini with shiitake mushroom sauce, cranberry-apple relish and homemade spaetzle (German egg noodles). Or what about sautéed flounder with Hollandaise sauce and capers, served with new potatoes. Chef Marcel Althauser pairs Gulf Coast sea-

food with hearty Germanic flavors for a winsome combination. There are always several daily specials on the blackboard, as well as the menu standbys of fresh seafood and fresh-cut steaks. It's open for dinner only.

Seafood and Spaghetti Works
$$ • Alister Rd. at Ave. G, Port Aransas
• (361) 749-5666

This funky geodesic dome seems an unlikely place to dine, but don't be put off by the odd-looking exterior. The kitchen has been producing a unique mixture of seafood, steaks, and Italian food for years. Be sure to check out the homemade desserts. It's open for dinner only.

Pelican's Landing
$$-$$$ • 337 N. Alister Rd., Port Aransas
• (361) 749-6405

Serving locally caught fish and aged beefsteaks, this restaurant offers quality dining in an island-inspired atmosphere. Decor includes palm trees in the front and an outdoor covered deck that's open for lunch and rustic furnishings. In business for more than two decades, it is known for the freshness of its seafood and its island specialties, including the popular shrimp Port Aransas (sautéed giant shrimp in a garlic butter sauce with mushrooms and tomatoes, served over fettuccine noodles.

Shell's Pasta Seafood Restaurant
$$ • Ave. G and 11th Sts., Port Aransas
• (361) 749-7621

A relative newcomer to the island restaurant scene, this bistro has rapidly gained a following with its pasta dishes, seafood entrees, and fresh baked breads. The luncheon blackboard specials on a recent winter day included: linguine with hickory smoked fennel sausage, baby corn, roasted peppers, and herbs; spinach fettuccine with apple-smoked bacon, diced tomatoes, and broccoli in a cream sauce; a fish sandwich on focaccia bread with baby mixed greens; capellini with seafood, roasted tomatoes, green onion, and cilantro; and a Caesar salad with marinated grilled chicken. All the breads and desserts are homemade.

Venetian Hot Plate
$$-$$$ • 232 Beach St., Port Aransas
• (361) 749-7617

Paintings of gondolas and Italian scenery set the tone at this cozy little restaurant. The entrees are delicious, from classics such as spaghetti carbonara to more creative items like a filet mignon with a gorgonzola sauce. Other offerings include pasta, veal, steak, and fresh croissants.

Kingsville Area

Black Diamond Oyster Bar
$–$$ • 503 E. Corral St., Kingsville
• (361) 592-6051

This restaurant is an institution for many longtime residents, serving fried shrimp and fish in an unpretentious setting.

El Jardin
$$ • 330 E. Henrietta Ave., Kingsville
• (361) 595-5955

Indulge in a hearty platter of grilled beef fajitas with fresh flour tortillas, seasoned pinto beans and Spanish rice at this family-owned cantina. Servings are generous, and the service is friendly and courteous.

Harrell's Kingsville Pharmacy
$ • 204 E. Kleberg Ave., Kingsville
• (361) 592-3355

Hop on a stool and order a double-meat home-style burger with a fountain cherry Coke. Nick Harrell III is the third-generation owner of this longtime drugstore and soda fountain. He has a keen sense of the business's place in local history. Service is friendly and warm. We also like browsing among the sundry items in the drugstore after our meal.

King's Inn
$$$ • F.M. Rd. 628, Riviera
• (361) 297-5265

This seafood restaurant that sits on the edge of Baffin Bay is one of the area's best—as attested to by the legion of loyal customers who routinely make the 90-mile trek from Corpus Christi to dine here. For decades, the Ware family has been dishing up golden fried shrimp in a beer-batter crust and crunchy fried oysters in cornmeal breading. Your meal comes with french fries, but don't waste time filling up on those—instead, try the thick, juicy sliced tomatoes in the house tartar sauce, which bears no resemblance whatsoever to the usual gooey mixture that comes in a jar. Its ingredients are a closely guarded secret. The sliced avocado salad and the Bombay salad—mashed avocados with a touch of curry—are heavenly. Food is served family-style, and it is plentiful. The atmosphere is waterfront casual, with linoleum floors, fake wood paneling and old family photos on the walls, offset by crisp white table linens and excellent service.

Wild Olive
$$ • Seller's Market, 205 E. Kleberg Ave., Kingsville
• (361) 595-4992

This tearoom attracts shoppers and visitors alike and you can browse among the handcrafted wares after you finish lunch. There are sandwiches, soups, quiche, and desserts available. It's open for lunch Wednesday through Friday.

Young's Pizza
$–$$, no credit cards
• 625 W. Santa Gertrudis Ave., Kingsville
• (361) 592-9179

A classic college-area hangout, this has an eclectic atmosphere and menu. The house specialty sandwiches and baked potatoes have monikers that are as creative as the ingredients. Patooties are Young's accompaniment-laden potatoes, such as the Aw Rootie, with avocado, cheddar and Parmesan cheeses, tomato, onion, salt, pepper, butter, and the mysterious Aw Rootie Sauce. Our hands-down favorite sandwich is the Texicali, which features tender sliced beef, sautéed onion and mushrooms, melted cheese, sliced jalapeños, and mayonnaise on a soft, fresh-baked bun. And even though we're willing to mention it here, we've not yet gathered up our nerve to taste the shrimp and sauerkraut pizzas.

RESTAURANTS

Nightlife

Since the first cowboys crooned to their cattle under the starry skies, there has always been night music in South Texas. The many-splendored styles of music favored by South Texans keep the mood lively at a variety of clubs throughout the region, from boot-stompin' country-and-western tunes to the mournful jazz and blues and the lively rhythms of rock 'n' roll.

Many clubs have decades of history in this region, while others are relative newcomers. Corpus Christi has experienced an explosion of new nightclubs, particularly in the downtown area, that cater to a varied and diverse clientele—from a luxurious cigar-and-martini lounge to a Tejano dance club.

Remember that the drinking age here is 21, and although 18- to-21-year-olds are allowed into some bars, they usually pay a higher cover charge and aren't permitted to drink alcohol.

If bars aren't your scene, you'll find plenty of other nighttime activities in the Coastal Bend including outdoor events as well as romantic waterfront cruises. Movie theaters abound, as do video stores for rental of films to watch at home or your hotel room. Some of our favorite haunts are the local bookstore-coffee bars, great places to meet folks, visit and even listen to live music. We would also urge you to spend at least one evening simply walking along the bayfront in the moonlight. Particularly in the summertime, when the cooling breezes temper the heat, it may be the best time of day to be outdoors.

Most of these clubs are open seven days a week unless otherwise indicated.

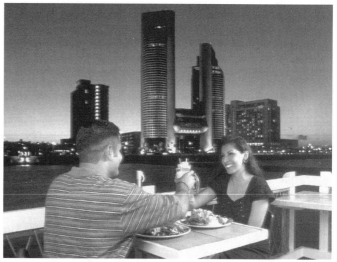

Diners can feast on scrumptious seafood while admiring the beautiful Corpus Christi bayfront.

Photo: courtesy of the Greater Corpus Christi Business Alliance

As in most of our other chapters, we've grouped our nightlife offerings into categories, then further broken them down by geographical area. So you can look for live music in Corpus Christi or Kingsville, or movie theaters in the North Bay area.

The geographic groupings begin at the northernmost tip of our coverage area and proceed southward along the coastline. Of course, the preponderance of nightlife is available in the larger cities, such as Corpus Christi and Kingsville, but you'll discover a few clubs worth visiting in the smaller towns as well. Check the Corpus Christi newspaper's "Weekend" section on Friday for a listing of all the live bands appearing over the weekend; the newspaper also lists weekend events and activities as well as those for the coming week.

Live Music

North Bay Area

Boiling Pot
Fulton Beach Rd., Rockport
• **(361) 729-6972**

This restaurant hosts a house band on select evenings; call first to see if there will be live music, which includes mostly blues and some country. For more information about the food served, see our Restaurants chapter.

Rudder's Bar and Grill
415 S. Austin St., Rockport
• **(361) 790-7245**

Rudders, a longtime restaurant and bar in downtown Rockport, features live blues and folk music on Tuesday nights, with an open mike jam session starting at 8 PM. There is no cover charge. The atmosphere is casual, and the food is eclectic, ranging from hamburgers and nachos to seafood and steaks.

Sandollar Pavilion
Fulton Beach Rd., Rockport
• **(361) 729-8909**

Steaks, seafood and live music on weekends, including everything from rock to country, make this a good nightspot to try. An outdoor bar offers a view of the bayfront and the boats, while pool tables and a large-screen television offer activities indoors.

Port Aransas to Padre Island

Ballyhoo Piano Bar
905 Alister St., Port Aransas
• **(361) 749-2600**

Piano music and blues can be heard live here all during the week, in this casual martini-and-cigar bar that's located near the beach.

Sharky's
2600 Highway 361, Port Aransas
• **(361) 749-4254**

You can hear classic rock to country-and-western tunes in this casual, beach-themed atmosphere. In addition to music and dancing, you'll find pool tables, pinball, foosball, darts, and other games.

Trout Street Bar and Grill
104 W. Cotter Ave., Port Aransas
• **(361) 749-7800**

Come to this harbor side seafood restaurant and bar to hear recorded reggae, Caribbean and Jimmy Buffet tunes. Or, if you prefer, you can catch sporting events on the big-screen television or pick up some tips from the how-to-fishing videos.

Corpus Christi

Blackbeard's On the Beach
3117 Surfside Blvd., Corpus Christi
• **(361) 884-1030**

A longtime fixture on North Beach, this restaurant and bar features live acoustic guitar music and plenty of munchies. There is no cover charge.

Buckets
227 N. Water St., Corpus Christi
• **(361) 883-7776**

This sports bar and grill offers munchies and drinks in an athletic-inspired atmosphere. It's a great place for watching the Monday night football game or televised boxing matches, as well as for shooting pool. A variety of live music is featured on the outdoor patio. The kitchen serves munchies including chicken strips, hamburgers, and salads.

Chelsea Street Pub and Grill
5858 S. Padre Island Dr., Corpus Christi
• **(361) 993-3322**

This eatery at Sunrise Mall features live music, usually rock 'n' roll, Monday through

NIGHTLIFE

Saturday. Cover charge is $1 on both Friday and Saturday.

La Playa
407 Schatzell St., Corpus Christi
• (361) 882-2664

This dance club offers recorded Tejano music, hip hop and dancing, with occasional live bands. It's open Wednesday through Sunday until 2 AM, and is open to those 18 years old and up. The cover charge varies depending on which day of the week you're there.

Liquid 2000
208 N. Water St., Corpus Christi
• (361) 888-8767

Offering dance and house music, this casual club attracts a wide range of clientele. It's open until 4 AM Friday and Saturday, and until 2 AM Wednesday and Thursday. Call for cover prices. There's also an outdoor patio.

Dr. Rockit's
709 N. Chaparral St., Corpus Christi
• (361) 884-7634

Open since the mid-1980s, Dr. Rockit's is one of the city's oldest venues for live music. It features an impressive lineup of noted musicians who play everything from reggae to blues and jazz, seven nights a week. All the standards from the Austin music scene play here, including the Killer Bees and Omar and the Howlers. Other performers have included Clarence Gatemouth Brown, Canned Heat, Charlie Musselwhite, Lou Ann Barton and Marcia Ball. The crowd here tends to be a bit older and more into the music than the social scene, unlike some of the other downtown haunts. The music is free Sunday through Thursday, and the cover charge on Friday and Saturday night can range from $3 to $10. The price depends on the featured musician.

Executive Surf Club
309 N. Water St., Corpus Christi
• (361) 884-7873

Owned by the same folks who operate the Water Street Seafood Co. restaurant next door, this perennially popular nightspot is a gathering place for the after-work crowd. Great munchies include nachos, batter-dipped fries, and burgers. And the outdoor patio makes for a fun place to listen to live music, which usually includes folk, country, or rock. Among performers who've been here recently are Robert Earl Keen and Johnny Lang. The mike is open for amateurs on Wednesdays, and you'll find 30 different beers on tap. There can be a cover charge, depending on the artist. For more information about the food served, see our Restaurants chapter.

Planet Luna
309 N. Chaparral St., Corpus Christi
• (361) 884-4229

This much anticipated nightclub—which was under construction for more than a year—opened in February 1999 to rave reviews. The 7,000-square-foot club spotlights salsa, merengue, and retro music in English and Spanish, and there is an occasional live band. It's an extravagantly decorated club, patterned after trendy nightclubs found on the East and West coasts, that is the brainchild of songwriter and recording artist A.B. Quintanilla III, the brother of slain Tejano singer Selena. Those willing to pay the $10 nightly cover charge will find plenty of upscale decor on two floors, including semi-private booths, polished wood dance floors, blue velvet trim on the walls and lots of chrome and curves. Platinum memberships are also available for those who want to pay $500 and breeze past the waiting crowds to get in.

This club is open 7 PM until 2 AM Wednesday and Thursday, and from 7 PM to 4 AM Friday and Saturday.

Santa Fe Cantina
1011 Santa Fe St., Corpus Christi
• (361) 888-8ROX (8769)

This longtime local bar offers live music, ranging from contemporary rock to pop or soul, in a casual atmosphere. The bands play on Wednesday through Saturday nights; on Tuesday, the bar offers free barbecue. Cover charge varies depending on the band, but usually is from $2 to $5 per person. The cantina is closed Sunday and Monday.

Tom Foolery's Chill and Grill
301 N. Chaparral St., Corpus Christi
• (361) 887-0029

The laid-back ambiance at this bar and restaurant attracts mostly a young crowd, with top-40 and alternative music. Refreshments include burgers and sandwiches, and the drink of

INSIDERS' TIP

Many communities publish weekly events in an independent newspaper that is free to the public. Look for one in your area for information on local entertainment.

NIGHTLIFE

choice is likely to be beer or kamikazes. Three wide-screen television sets, as well as 20 smaller TV screens, are ideal for the sports fanatic. Karaoke music is the big draw on Tuesdays, and live music, mostly rock, and dancing are featured on Friday and Saturday. Attire here is very casual—usually jeans or shorts and T-shirts. There is sometimes a cover charge here.

Zero's Hard Rock Club
6327 McArdle Rd., Corpus Christi
• **(361) 991-6042**
One of the only places in town to specialize in hard rock, this bar has very little in the way of décor but it does offer loud, head-banging music. Cover charge is $3.

Kingsville Area

Country Luau Saloon
115 University St. at W. King St., Kingsville
• **(361) 595-4331**
Welders and cowboys rub elbows at this casual saloon deep in the heart of South Texas. You can hear live country-and-western music on weekends. It's also especially popular with university students.

Flight Line
1210 S. 6th St., Kingsville
• **(361) 595-1991**
Live music, mostly rock 'n' roll, can be heard every Saturday night at this nightspot. The clientele includes Navy personnel from the nearby air station, college students, and a wide range of locals. There's a dance floor, three pool tables, two dart boards, pinball machine, and video games. Beer and wine coolers are served, as are set-ups for mixed drinks. The cover charge on Saturday night is $3 for singles, $5 per couple.

Gin Mill Saloon
1020 S. Sixth St., Kingsville
• **(361) 592-8835**
This large, informal facility is a casual place especially popular with the city's young professionals, who stop in after work to unwind. Karaoke music is featured on Tuesday, Thursday, and Saturday.

Texas Ranch Club
406 N. Sixth St., Kingsville
• **(361) 516-1045**
You'll hear plenty of Tejano and Western music at this casual club. A Friday-night buffet draws a good clientele, as does the dance floor.

Other Bars and Nightclubs

Port Aransas to Padre Island

Moby Dick's
517 S. Alister St., Port Aransas
• **(361) 749-7418**
This colorful nautical haunt offers a little bit of everything: pool tables, video games, a jukebox, burgers, fries, beer, and wine coolers.

Corpus Christi Area

B&J's Back Room
6331 S. Padre Island Dr., Corpus Christi
• **(361) 993-8773**
Pool tables, large-screen television sets, and great munchies make this a popular place to host going-away parties, reunions, and bachelor parties. The atmosphere is basic pool hall (dark, neon beer signs, etc.), but the adjoining pizza parlor has what many consider the area's best pizza, as well as an incredibly diverse array of foreign and domestic brews. See our Restaurants chapter for more information.

Stetson's
5831 Weber Rd., Corpus Christi
• **(361) 855-4886**
Put on your cowboy boots and hat when you head out to this country-and-western club, which has a disc jockey and dance floor. It draws a diverse range of ages and is open Wednesday through Sunday.

Vernon's
1030 Third St., Corpus Christi
• **(361) 882-0030**
A fixture on the local scene, this dark and unpretentious nightspot has been serving beers to blue collar workers as well as professionals for many years. Barbecue is served during the noon hour and free peanuts in the evenings.

Kingsville Area

Port O Call
1406 North 14th St., Kingsville
• **(361) 595-1238**
Mixed drinks, pool tables, and dart games

NIGHTLIFE

are the draw at this nightclub. It attracts mostly married couples, many of whom play in pool leagues or dart clubs.

Movie Theaters

North Bay Area

This area is served by Cinema 4 on Texas Highway 35 N. in Rockport, (361) 729-4448.

Corpus Christi

Corpus Christi's movie houses include the following: Cine 6, 4700 S. Staples Street, (361) 992-7821; Discount Cinemas, Sunrise Mall, 5858 S. Padre Island Drive, (361) 993-6965 or (361) 993-6966; Silver Cinemas, 4147 Five Points Road, (361) 242-9121; The Movies, Padre Staples Mall, 5488 S. Padre Island Drive, (361) 993-8500; and, finally, Tinseltown 16, S. Padre Island Drive at Greenwood Drive, (361) 814-3100.

Kingsville

In Kingsville, you can catch a flick at either of the following cinemas: Cine I and II, (361) 592-0641, 2001 Brahma Boulevard; and Rio VII Cinemas, (361) 516-1303, 1601 S. U.S. Highway 77.

Dinner Cruises

Corpus Christi Sailing Center Inc.
200 S. Shoreline Blvd., Corpus Christi
• **(361) 881-8503**
Sail aboard a yacht to Landry's Seafood House for a four-course dinner, then board again for a two-hour cruise into the setting sun. The cost is $55 for adults and teens, $25 for children ages 6 to 12 and $10 for children 5 and under.

Coffee Houses

Corpus Christi

Café Calypso
Inside Half-Price Books, Moore Plaza, Corpus Christi
• **(361) 993-5282**
Folk music, bluegrass, classic rock, and jazz are among the offerings at this coffee bar inside a bookstore. Coffee drinks and pastries are

served. Seating can be a bit tight, but tables are available outdoors too. Moore Plaza is at 5425 S. Padre Island Drive.

Barnes & Noble Cafe
5129 Blanche Moore St. at Moore Plaza, Corpus Christi
• **(361) 992-1339**
Students, scholars, and book lovers gather at this coffee shop in the middle of this massive bookstore, where they can read or chat while sipping Starbucks coffee, espressos, and specialty drinks. The cafe also serves soup, pastries, and cookies. Live music is featured several times a month, usually on a Saturday. The cafe is open daily until 11 PM.

Swing Street Cafe
5892 Everhart Rd., Corpus Christi
• **(361) 992-6611**
A range of contemporary music is offered at this trendy café and nightspot, ranging from blues and jazz to golden oldies and light rock. Guests relax on old sofas and armchairs in a space decorated with original artwork, while sipping cappuccino or soft drinks and snacking on sandwiches, salads, or pastries. There is no cover charge.

Planetariums and Observatories

King High School
5225 Gollihar Rd., Corpus Christi
• **(361) 994-6917**
View a program detailing the items of interest in the local night skies at this high school planetarium, which offers public shows on Tuesday evenings at 7 PM throughout the school year. The show changes with the seasons and costs $2 per person for adults and $1 for senior citizens and students. Very quiet pre-schoolers are admitted free. The doors open at 6:30 PM and no late seating is allowed.

Texas A&M University-Kingsville Observatory
Lon C. Hill Hall, 955 W. University St., Kingsville
• **(361) 593-2699**
Watch the starry skies of South Texas through the telescopes at this university observatory, which is used for astronomy classes taught by the physics department. The observatory is open to the public periodically for special events and is also available for group tours.

NIGHTLIFE

Shopping

Although the Corpus Christi area has its share of unique shops and buyers' enticements, let it be said from the start that shopping is not the primary reason most people visit this region. The Corpus Christi area has only a few malls, and they are more likely to contain typical department and specialty stores than to offer buyers a unique retail experience.

Let it also be said that strip centers have been booming, and those enormous, warehouse-like discount stores abound. You can find at least one Wal-Mart or Kmart in nearly every community—in Corpus Christi, the two sit side by side in at least one location. "Discount" is often the operative word here, because the low per capita income in South Texas probably tends to deter many of the nation's more upscale retailers from locating here. Weekend garage sales are especially popular; check the newspaper classified ads for locations and hours.

Nonetheless, the area offers attractions to shoppers. Several communities have renovated their downtown business districts to spotlight historical or unique attributes. And if you're looking for something fancy, you'll discover several posh shopping districts that specialize in designer clothing and jewelry, or artwork and antiques.

Keep in mind that the majority of stores and the greatest variety will be found in the area's largest city, Corpus Christi. The stores and malls in Corpus Christi tend to draw shoppers from the surrounding, more rural, communities as well as from over the border in Mexico.

On the plus side, friends from Houston and Dallas say they find better bargains here than in their own malls. Our out-of-town friends also like the less-crowded atmosphere at the shops and malls here. On the other hand, we can't deny that you'd find a wider selection of merchandise in more sophisticated and larger cities, including Dallas, Houston, and San Antonio.

As for food sales, it's worth noting that the primary grocery retailer in the Corpus Christi area is H.E.B. Foods Inc., headquartered in San Antonio. Corpus Christi has three Albertson's supermarkets (a big chain in Texas) and numerous smaller grocery stores. Diversity is sorely lacking here—we have but a smattering of health-food stores and none of the upscale gourmet markets that more metropolitan areas may have. The good news, though, is that groceries seem to be competitively priced, and fresh fruit and vegetables are particularly attractive year round.

Roadside vendors can also be a good source for fresh produce, particularly during peak growing seasons. You'll see pecans for sale in the fall and winter, ruby red grapefruit in the winter and assorted vegetables during the spring. We enjoy stopping and checking out the produce at these stands, and recommend it to visitors. The produce is often fresh from the field and bursting with flavor, and the prices are more than reasonable.

We'd be remiss if we failed to mention the shrimpers that sell their catch right off the boat. The T-heads in downtown Corpus Christi and Conn Brown Harbor in Aransas Pass are where the boats moor for the evening, and they definitely have the freshest shrimp around—those crustaceans were happily swimming in the water a few hours earlier. We've bought from them and find the prices reasonable, but some buyers are a little more wary of such independent vendors. As always, utilize

LOOK FOR:
• Malls and
  Shopping Centers
• Shopping Districts
• Antiques
• Farmers' Markets
• Bookstores
• Western Wear
• Variety Markets
• Beachwear and
  Souvenirs

common sense when purchasing seafood—it should look fresh, feel firm, and not have an overly pungent odor.

Here's a quick rundown of the area's largest retail centers and the more intriguing small venues. This is by no means an all-inclusive list, but we do want to provide visitors and newcomers with a good starting point to find what they need.

We'll start with the area's malls, including two in Corpus Christi and one in Kingsville, and large shopping centers. We'll then wend our way through the area's shopping districts, antiques, thrift and consignment stores, farmer's markets, bookstores, music stores and Western wear and souvenir shops.

Malls and Shopping Centers

Corpus Christi

Moore Plaza Shopping Center
5425 S. Padre Island Dr., Corpus Christi
• (361) 993-4100

The newest, fastest-growing retail center in the city, this strip center opened in 1989. Its major tenants include H.E.B. Food Stores, Target, PetsMart, Old Navy Store, Barnes and Noble Booksellers, and Pier 1. The choices of stores here provide everything from dining to coffee bars, and home furnishings to beauty supplies and clothing.

Among the restaurants at this center and nearby are EZ's, which specializes in burgers and pizza; Blimpie's sandwiches; Sirloin Stockade for steaks; and Taiwan Restaurant. A number of other restaurants, many affiliated with national chains, line the expressway that leads to this strip center.

For the bargain-minded, there's a Half-Price Books, which contains a nice cappuccino bar and live music on weekends (see our Nightlife chapter); and Once Upon A Child, a resale shop specializing in children's items.

Look here also for dry cleaners, auto parts, tuxedo rentals, haircuts, beauty supplies, electronics, video stores, and office supplies.

INSIDERS' TIP

Local shoppers love a bargain but you can avoid the crowds if you hit the stores early in the morning or later in the evening. Extended hours during peak seasons are also helpful.

Padre Staples Mall
5488 S. Padre Island Dr. at S. Staples St.,
Corpus Christi
• (361) 991-5718

This 28-year-old, two-story mall is anchored by major department stores including Dillard's, JCPenney, Foley's, Bealls, and Palais Royal. With more than 100 tenants, this mall has everything from shops to restaurants and a movie theater. Popular clothing chains include The Limited, The Gap, Gapkids, Benjamin's, Express, and Victoria's Secret. Among the more regional offerings are Smith's Guns, Reflections of Texas, and Trader Rick's Gems and Gold, selling just what their names imply.

At the center of the mall is a beautiful merry-go-round, with old-fashioned brightly painted horses on two revolving levels. This is a favorite for kids of all ages, and it can provide a fun break from shopping.

To quench your post-buying thirst and appetite, the mall has a food court near the movie theater entrance with such tenants as Bourbon Street Candy Company, Chao Praya (Chinese fare), Dairy Queen, Famous Corn Dog, the Original Cookie Company, Texas Hot Dog, Tropical Treats, and Villa Pizza. Other restaurants in the mall include Casa Olé, Chick-Fil-A, Harvest House Restaurant, and Luby's Cafeteria. A number of restaurants are also on the outskirts of the mall, including the Olive Garden, Chili's, and McDonald's.

The mall also has covered parking, stroller rentals, and wheelchairs (free with a refundable deposit).

Sunrise Mall
5858 S. Padre Island Dr. at Airline Rd.
• (361) 993-2900

Just a block away from Corpus Christi's other mall (why do they all congregate in the same area?) is Sunrise Mall, which contains more than 100 shops, restaurants, and business offices. The anchor tenants at this two-story mall are Mervyn's, Sears, Montgomery Ward, Stein Mart, and Burlington Coat Factory. This complex seems to cater to a slightly more youthful shopper, with shops such as Camelot Music, Collectible Treasures, which offers Beanie Babies and Pokemon collectibles, Payless Shoes, Rock 'n Roll Plus, and Melrose, which specializes in youth-oriented fashions. There are also athletic stores such as

FootAction, Foot Locker, Lady Foot Locker, and Oshman's Supersports USA.

A food court includes restaurants such as Chick-Fil-A, Corn Dog 7, Famous Corn Dog, Gyros and Kabobs, Great American Cookie Company, Las Palmas Express, Orange Julius, Oriental Express, Sbarro's-The Italian Eatery, and Wendy's. For a sit-down meal, try Chelsea Street Pub.

In addition, a military recruiting center and a hospital program for senior citizens is housed here, as is a branch of the Corpus Christi Police Department.

As at the city's other mall, you can rent strollers, borrow wheelchairs, and take advantage of a free escort to your car.

Kingsville Area

Kingsville Mall
1724 S. Brahma Blvd., Kingsville
• (361) 595-5741

A half-mile north of Southgate Mall (see next entry) is this shopping center anchored by Sears Roebuck Co., which is also the only retail outlet here. This mall contains mostly professional services, including Coastal Bend College, La Paloma Adult Day Care, and a home-healthcare service and rehabilitation center for nearby Spohn Hospital. There is also a restau-

rant, Casey's Deli, which specializes in sandwiches and salads, and Rentsmart, where you can rent furniture and appliances.

Southgate Mall
2331 S. Brahma Blvd., Kingsville
• (361) 595-5741

This is the larger, more established of two small malls in this town. The anchor store is Bealls (a department store). Other tenants include a video arcade, barber shop, Radio Shack, On-Cue Music and Books, Texas State Optical, Payless Shoe Source, and Regis Hair Stylists. Young people may want to check out the trendy clothing at Melrose or the fashion and accessories from Claire's. If you get hungry, you can stop at Southgate Café for a hamburger, or El Taquito for Mexican fare.

Shopping Districts

North Bay Area

Austin Street
Downtown Rockport

This downtown shopping district in the middle of Rockport offers a nice grouping of

Craftsmen at the King Ranch Saddle Shop make saddles and other high-quality leather products such as boots and purses.

SHOPPING

local and specialty shops, all within walking distance and near the waterfront.

In the Austin Street General Store, 502 S. Austin Street, you'll find fragrances, collectibles, linens, and seaside sculptures.

Belles & Bows, 203 S. Austin Street, offers gifts, collectibles, fresh country-style fudge, and decorative accessories that range from antiques and teddy bears to music tapes and CDs.

Bent Tree Gallery, 504 S. Austin Street, sells 18th- and 19th-century antiques such as furniture, silver, crystal, pocket watches, and Oriental rugs.

At Connections, 209 S. Austin Street, the merchandise includes unique jewelry, clothes, candles, CDs, and tapes.

Dojiggers Crafts and Gifts, 211 S. Austin Street, sells handmade crafts and gifts including Rockport T-shirts and country signs.

There's also the Estelle Stair Gallery, 406 S. Austin Street, with art, sculpture, furniture, jewelry, and tables made from cypress taken from an offshore oil rig buried since 1910. Also located at the gallery is Hippoccino's, which serves delicious espresso and specialty drinks.

Quilters will be in heaven at Golden Needles and Quilts, 701 N. Allen Place, which has fabric, patterns, supplies, books, kits, and—of course—needles. Instruction is available, and machine quilting services are provided.

Hidden Treasures, 207 N. Austin Street, has casual resort wear and a collection of Brighton purses, belts, and wallets.

Moby Dan's, 415 S. Austin Street, is for sailors and dreamers, with World War I British-issue sextants and compasses, an 1850 telescope, brass divers' helmets, lighthouses, carved coastal bird statues, T-shirts, and educational toys.

On the weekends, check out Rockport Pirate's Cove, 414 S. Austin Street, where vendors set up booths to sell a variety of items including arts and crafts, silver jewelry, paintings, and homemade chocolate.

Seaside Brass and Wood, 508 S. Austin Street, features art and gifts from around the world. Victoria's Gold and Gems, 401 S. Austin Street, sells jewelry with a nautical theme, from sterling silver to diamonds. This store also has an on-site jeweler for repairs, appraisals, and custom design.

Kailin's Closet, 410 S. Austin Street, is billed as "Grandma's favorite place to shop." And we can see why, with its selection of lovely christening gowns, toys, books, and children's clothing. There are also consignments, kites, and baby gifts.

For fine art, photography, and gifts, stop at Crystal Art Glass, 111 N. Austin Street.

Bird lovers should be sure to visit 4 The Birds, 92 S. Austin Street, which sells everything a birder could want—windsocks, flags, birdhouses, feeders, T-shirts, kites, books, videos, maps, art, computer software for birders, and hand-carved decorative birds. You can also get information about bird sightings, tours, and trips in the area.

The Niche Glass Art Gallery, 415 S. Austin Street, is a working studio and gallery that showcases stained glass, antiques, and hanging redfish and shorebirds.

Crazy Horse, 207 N. Austin Street, offers furniture, antiques, and accessories—many with a nautical or whimsical flair.

Comforts of Home, 103 S. Austin Street, features handmade, painted pine furniture by Texas artist David Marsh, as well as gift items, accessories, sterling silver jewelry, and casual furnishings.

INSIDERS' TIP

Many of the malls stay open late during the Christmas season, and the stores are often less crowded during those evening hours.

Corpus Christi

Crossroads Shopping Village
Airline at McArdle, Corpus Christi

Unique gifts in a quaint atmosphere is the hallmark of this tidy little shopping village. Among the retailers and restaurants here are Gruene Outfitters, where you can find a large assortment of outdoor gear from kayaks and fly-fishing rods to Birkenstocks and Patagonia outdoor wear; Salon Salon, which provides hair care, massage, facials, pedicures, and manicures; Cutie Pa-Tootie, for children's resale items; and Benjamin's, a youth-oriented clothing store that deals in Southern California-style fashions. you get hungry, you can stop at Gesundheit for European-style cuisine or Catfish Charlie's for fried fish and shrimp.

You'll also find Roosevelt Baker, for cameras and photo finishing; Phillip Randolph Jewelers, which offers designer jewelry from watches to rings, pearls to platinum; Nature's Bird Center, with a nice supply of items for birders and bird-lovers; and Disc Go Round for music needs.

Across the street is The Promenade shopping center, anchored by the perennially popular Toys R Us. Other stores and eateries in this center include Cavender's Boot City, for Western wear; Bamboo Garden Oriental Restaurant, and Origami Japanese Cuisine; Arrow Parcel and Post; Payless Shoe Source; Tobacco World for cigars, pipes, and tobacco; One-Hour Photo; and several other businesses.

Lamar Park
Doddridge St. at Alameda St.,
Corpus Christi
• (361) 854-8885

This little shopping village just three blocks from the bayfront is full of interesting and pricey stores. You can dine at several restaurants within this complex, and more shops and services are nearby, including a post office branch.

One of the most fun stores to visit here is Pilar's, 32 Lamar Park Center, which carries unusual items that fall into the category of colorful, creative, or folk art. The selection includes carved candlesticks and furniture, Mexican-style crucifixes and wooden toys, exotic jewelry and one-of-a-kind clothing. We also like the bags, belts, and artwork.

Nearby is Small Planet Deli, 42 Lamar Park Center, which serves food that is as artistic as it is delicious. Stop by for a mocha cappuccino or slice of three-layer carrot cake. Italian-food fans can also check out Marco's Restaurant, 3812 S. Alameda Street, which serves great pasta for lunch and dinner.

Madeline's Before and After, 11 Lamar Park Center, offers beautiful maternity clothes and exquisite infant and children's items, from lace gowns to fun animal-print toddler clothes.

Talbots, 3812 S. Alameda Street, carries high-quality, classic women's clothing.

At Gift and Gourmet Co., 3812 S. Alameda Street, you can find just about anything you want for your kitchen, from pasta makers to imported chocolates and gourmet coffees.

Three upscale shops, specializing in women's clothing—Franceska's at 3844 S. Alameda Street, Margaret's at 3842 S. Alameda Street, and Julian Gold Inc., 3840 S. Alameda Street—stand side-by-side here. And you can stop at Goldsmith's Jewelers for the crowning touch to your new outfit.

The Castor Collection, 38 Lamar Park Center, carries handsome and high-quality furnishings for the home.

Enter a little flower-filled courtyard to shop at Leslie's, 28 Lamar Park Center, where you can find fun and casual fashions and jewelry. Attached to the same shop is Marlene Alvarado, which specializes in art, furnishings, and other beautiful items for your home.

There is also Raymond Gray Photography, 21 Lamar Park Center, and Francisco's Salon, 29 Lamar Park Center, located here.

The Village Shopping Center
Doddridge St. at Alameda St.

This little shopping center, located across the street from Lamar Park Shopping Center, has a number of upscale shops and services.

A favorite among locals is Marie Colson Unique Custom Jewelry, 3815 S. Alameda Street. For lovely decorative and household items, try Jene Marie gift shop, 3835 S. Alameda Street, which sells fine china, glass art objects, kitchenware, and Crabtree and Evelyn products. High-quality shoes for women are featured at William's Fashion Shoes, 3849 S. Alameda Street, while Berry's & Still's Jewelers, 3855 S. Alameda Street, offers jewelry as well as watch and jewelry repair.

For high-quality artwork, visit Oliver's Gallery of Fine Art, 3847 S. Alameda Street.

In this same little shopping center are two beauty salons, Linda's Hair and Nails, 3841 S. Alameda Street, and Adolfo's Salon, 3843 S. Alameda Street; Sanborn's Travel, 3823 S. Alameda Street; and His and Hers Alterations, 3827 S. Alameda Street.

Taylor Center
3636 S. Alameda Street

Some of the area's most prestigious shopping names are located in this center, which is anchored by Taylor Brothers Jewelry, a popular jewelry store that recently partnered with Marie Colson Jewelry.

Among the stores located here are Elizabeth Ann's, which features designer clothing, Brighton leather handbags and belts, and formal fashions for women; Jack English, with high-quality menswear; Garrett & Co. Salon, where you can have your hair styled and your nails manicured; The Nail Quorum; The Piano Gallery; and CC Art Connection.

Other businesses in this center include All Aboard Travel, Layton Bros. Optical, Mail Center USA, and CC Outpatient Surgery.

Nearby is Gatherings, 3744 S. Alameda

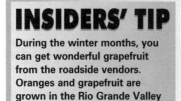

INSIDERS' TIP

During the winter months, you can get wonderful grapefruit from the roadside vendors. Oranges and grapefruit are grown in the Rio Grande Valley in far South Texas.

Street, a delightful gift shop that specializes in antiques, candles, clothing, jewelry, and toys. There's also an excellent children's bookstore, Rainbow Books and Learning Center, housed with this shop.

Water Street Market
309 N. Water St., Corpus Christi
• (361) 881-9322

About a dozen specialty shops and restaurants surround a courtyard downtown that draws residents and visitors alike. The anchors are the Water Street Seafood and Water Street Oyster Bar restaurants, as well as the more casual Executive Surf Club (see our Restaurants chapter). But you can also buy souvenirs and other items at an array of shops.

For all things from the Lone Star State, make a stop at Totally Texas, which offers T-shirts, gourmet foods, gift baskets, and other items.

Water Street Beach Company is a great place to pick up beachwear, towels, sand buckets, and souvenirs.

Gifts by the Sea has all the souvenir items you might want.

The Cat House is a store for feline fanciers, with cat cards, clothing, books, and even gifts for your own pet cat.

You can look for interesting items at Antiquity, which offers antiques including furniture, dolls, jewelry, and Oriental rugs.

The Gold Bug specializes in jewelry, including antique pieces.

CMR Gallery and Frame Shop showcases the work of local artists and artisans and offers framing services. It also carries jewelry and beads and offers instruction in jewelry making.

Doohicki's is a beauty salon.

And you can stop for cappuccino, sandwiches, or ice cream at the Oasis Coffee House.

Kingsville

Historic Downtown Kingsville

Start your shopping in this renovated downtown area with a visit to the King Ranch Saddle Shop, 201 E. Kleberg Avenue. This luxury shop contains leather goods, of course, including saddles, as well as women's and men's clothing, gifts, and luggage. It's a bit pricey, but you might be able to spring for a top-grain leather

wallet embossed with the King Ranch's distinctive cattle brand.

For vintage items, check out Josiebelle's Antiques and Gifts, 225-227 E. Kleberg Avenue, which carries richly hand-painted furniture with an antique flair.

La Potpourri of Gifts and Things, 219 E. Kleberg Avenue, offers a sampling of South Texas such as jellies, salsas, pottery, and picture frames. Upstairs in the same building (which housed the city's first newspaper and first City Hall) is Glenda's Attic, full of antiques, collectibles, and Christmas decorations.

The Pineapple Shop at Allen Furniture, Sixth and King streets, is a complete gift and bridal store, offering crystal, pottery, wood, and pewter items.

Roy's Hobbies and Electronics, 217 E. Kleberg Avenue, has art and crafts supplies, cellular phones and pagers, model trains, and coins.

Seller's Market, 205 E. Kleberg Avenue, is a creative marketplace where a variety of vendors sell handmade crafts, paintings, and jewelry. The historic building that houses this art center has been renovated as part of a downtown revitalization. Items for sale often include quilts, homemade desserts, paintings, jewelry, clothing, and notecards.

For unique gifts and Texas-style items, stop in at Horse Feathers Gift Shop, 210 E. Kleberg Avenue. Here you can find Christmas ornaments with Texas flair, candles, picture frames, and baskets made from used lariats.

The Cottage, 216 E. Kleberg Avenue, offers upscale gifts and clothing.

Book lovers will want to peruse the used volumes at Books n' Such, 214 E. Kleberg Avenue.

Gloria's Wedding Décor, 238 E. Kleberg Avenue, features everything you might need to plan your wedding or quinceanera, a traditional 15th birthday celebration for young Hispanic women.

At Totes & Things, 400 E. Kleberg Avenue, you'll find personalized leather goods and handbags.

Other notable shops here include Kingsville Jewelry and Watch Repair, 601 E. Kleberg Avenue, which specializes in custom jewelry, and Oliver's Distinctive Jewelry, 220 E. Kleberg Avenue, with a large selection of fine jewelry and gifts.

SHOPPING

The best place to satisfy your appetite from shopping is at Harrel's Kingsville Pharmacy, 204 E. Kleberg Avenue, which has an ample selection of cards and gifts and an old-fashioned soda fountain that serves up memorable milkshakes and burgers.

Another place to eat is the Wild Olive, a tea room in the Seller's Market, which serves great sandwiches and desserts.

Upper House Antiques, 211 E. Kleberg Avenue, offers high-quality furniture and collectibles from bygone eras.

Antiques

Here's a list devoted to some of the best antique shops in the Coastal Bend. Don't miss the ones we've already mentioned in the previous Shopping Districts section, though.

North Bay Area

Bent Tree Galleries
504 Austin St., Rockport
• **(361) 729-4822**

Named for the area's windswept oak trees, this gallery is set in a historic downtown building where you can find crystal, china, silver, and furniture from decades past.

Harcrow's Bluebonnet Mall
Hwy. 188, between Rockport and Aransas Pass, one half-mile from Texas Hwy. 35 S.
• **(361) 729-1724**

Furniture, jewelry, gifts, memorabilia, glassware, and fishing gear can be found in the 20 booths that fill this shopping area. This place is for the serious bargain hunter or the adventurous shopper.

Mary Ann's Antiques
1005 Main St., Rockport
• **(361) 729-1945**

From porcelain dolls to handmade quilts, this shop features unique items from yesteryear. Furniture, pottery, jewelry, collectibles, and Steiff animals comprise its inventory.

Moore Than Feed
902 W. Market St., Rockport
• **(361) 729-4909**

Yes, you can get tack, feed, and animal healthcare products in this old-fashioned country store. The shop also offers frontier antiques and a great selection of salt and pepper shakers.

Corpus Christi

Antiquity Ltd.
318 N. Chaparral St., Corpus Christi
• **(361) 882-2424**

You can find furniture, dolls, jewelry, and Oriental rugs here.

Betty's Trash to Treasures
3301 Ayers St., Corpus Christi
• **(361) 882-9144**
4315 S. Alameda St., Corpus Christi
• **(361) 882-9144**

Antiques, collectibles, primitives, household items, and used furniture are among the collections of a variety of dealers here. Expect to spend some time browsing—the variety can be overwhelming.

Country Pardners
4227 S. Alameda St., Corpus Christi
• **(361) 993-7327**

Check out the American antiques, gifts, and furniture at this shop located in the midst of several antique stores.

Country Peddlers
317 N. Chaparral St., Corpus Christi
• **(361) 887-6618**

A splendid selection of antiques and gifts is on display at this shop, situated in the central part of the city's "Antique Lane," Alameda Street.

Edlin's Auction
210 N. Alameda St., Corpus Christi
• **(361) 882-7253**

Antiques and other items can be had—sometimes for a song—at the twice-weekly auctions held here. The auctions begin at 7 PM every Friday and Saturday, with estate items and consignments that come from as far away as England and France.

Emma's Arbor
4209 S. Alameda St., Corpus Christi
• **(361) 985-8309**

What they call "gently used" furniture is offered at this pleasant shop, which also sells glassware, vintage jewelry, and collectibles.

Expressions of Love
2613 Airline Rd., Suite J10, Corpus Christi
• **(361) 992-2707**

You'll discover handmade items, porcelain dolls and antique furniture in this cozy store.

Gene's Antiques
4331 S. Alameda St.,
Corpus Christi
• (361) 994-0440

This dealer offers the best of American and European antiques and furniture, as well as matches sterling silver pieces.

Home Sweet Home
4333 S. Alameda St.,
Corpus Christi
• (361) 991-4001

Furniture, jewelry, glassware, and books are displayed through this store. The owners also do refinishing and repair of antiques.

The King Ranch Saddle Shop in Kingsville is a mecca for cowboy-loving tourists who want to take home a touch of South Texas.

Photo: courtesy of the Kingsville Convention and Visitors Bureau

Remarkable Consignments
525 Everhart Rd., Corpus Christi
• (361) 992-2283

This shop specializes in previously owned fine furniture and accessories, so you can find many exquisite items here. Prices can be high because this store specializes in luxury items.

Second-Hand Rose Antiques
4343 S. Alameda St., Corpus Christi
• (361) 993-9626

In addition to antique furniture, you can pick up collectible dolls and teddy bears here.

Sister Sue's Antique Market
517 Everhart Rd., Corpus Christi
• (361) 992-5300

Everything in here has been restored to its original luster, and the quality is excellent. Lovely antique furniture, delicate lacework, clothes, and gifts can be found here. And when you tire of antiquing, you can stop for coffee, desserts, or sandwiches at Jeron's café, located inside this tasteful store.

Kingsville Area

Glenda's Attic
219 E. Kleberg Ave., Kingsville
• (361) 592-7035

Antique furniture, collectibles, and Christmas decorations are for sale in this upstairs shop, located downtown in a historic building.

Josiebelle's Antiques and Gifts
225 E. Kleberg Ave., Kingsville
• (361) 592-3701

Look for hand-painted furniture, antique items, and other gifts here.

Opera House Antiques and Collectibles
211 E. Kleberg Ave., Kingsville
• (361) 595-7676

You can find antique furniture, china, glassware, and jewelry in this downtown collectibles shop.

Farmers' Markets

North Bay Area

Jimmy Woods Produce
Texas Hwy. 35 N., Fulton
• (361) 729-6856

Open-air bins are filled with seasonal fresh produce, including juicy oranges and grapefruit, squash, avocados, melons, sweet potatoes, grapes, lettuce, apples, and more. The enticing arrangement of fruits and vegetables makes it almost impossible to pass this place by. You can also purchase hot sauces and local honey here.

Bookstores

North Bay Area

The Bookshelf
1005 Concho St., Rockport
• (361) 729-9801

The Bookshelf sells used paperbacks for every age and taste, from thriller and mysteries to self-help books and science fiction. You can buy or barter (trade your own books for something else) at this store.

The Western Warehouse
3801 Hwy. 35 N., Rockport
• **(361) 729-0437**

This self-described "ugly yellow building" is home to thousands of used paperbacks, all for sale or trade. You can also purchase new Western wear here, from jeans to boots.

The Bookworm
3014 Hwy. 35 N., Ste. B, Rockport
• **(361) 790-8399**

Buy new or used books, get books appraised or locate hard-to-find volumes here.

Pat's Place
415 S. Austin St., Rockport
• **(361) 729-8453**

Pick up a copy of the latest bestseller or delve into a bit of Texana in this neat little shop. You can also place special orders, buy greeting cards or stationery, keep the kids amused with puzzles and games, or explore local history. A good selection of birding books can be found here.

Corpus Christi

Barnes & Noble Booksellers
5129 Blanche Moore St., Corpus Christi
• **(361) 992-1339**

This massive and tastefully appointed bookstore often seems almost like a library, with its comfortable reading chairs, hushed atmosphere and wide selection of literary material. Bring the kids to storytime or let them explore the book selection in the children's section while you browse through the many aisles. You can pick up soup, sandwiches or sweets, and gourmet coffee at the little cafe on the store's center island.

Books Plus
2211 Ayers St., Corpus Christi
• **(361) 884-0797**

This shop deals in used books, records, and tapes. You can even swap your just-finished paperback for one you haven't yet read. There is also a large supply of old magazines.

Half-Price Books, Records and Magazines
5425 S. Padre Island Dr., Corpus Christi
• **(361) 991-4494**

Buy, sell, or trade your used reading material at this friendly store. New and used books are for sale here, as are albums, tapes, and magazines. There's also a good selection of calendars and a coffee bar with live music.

Rainbow Books and Learning Center
3744 S. Alameda St., Corpus Christi
• **(361) 992-0590**

This store, tucked inside Gatherings gift shop, is the best place in town to buy children's books. Not only is the selection great, but the employees are knowledgeable about children's authors and tastes. Gifts and educational materials are also available.

Waldenbooks
Padre Staples Mall, Corpus Christi
• **(361) 991-8034**

When you get tired of looking for that perfect outfit, stop here to refresh your mind with something a little more intellectual. You'll find a large selection of the latest bestsellers, and there's always a sale rack near the front for browsing.

Kingsville

Books n' Such
214 E. Kleberg Ave., Kingsville
• **(361) 516-1164**

This downtown store specializes in used books.

On-Cue Music, Books and Movies
Southgate Mall, Kingsville
• **(361) 516-1210**

This store sells new books, cassette tapes, videotapes and CDs, and it also buys used CDs. Both adult and children's literature are featured.

Western Wear

North Bay Area

The Western Warehouse
Texas Hwy. 35 N., Rockport
• **(361) 729-0437**

Pick up a pair of jeans, a shirt, or some boots at this store—and then grab some reading material. In addition to selling new clothing, this store carries an inventory of 80,000 used books.

Corpus Christi

Boots-n-Britches Western Wear
5420 McArdle Rd., Corpus Christi
• **(361) 992-3501**

Whether you're an urban cowboy or a real cowboy, you'll find plenty of variety at this

SHOPPING

store. Dress boots, work boots, jeans, fashion accessories, belts, and buckles are available.

Cain's Western Wear
10709 Leopard St., Corpus Christi
• **(361) 241-2191**

You're bound to find what you need in this 6,000-square foot store, which carries clothing, boots, hats, and accessories. They also carry several exclusive name brands, including Brighton, which makes high-priced beautiful leather handbags and belts, and Red Wing workboots.

Cavender's Boot City
1220 Airline Rd., Corpus Christi
• **(361) 992-9225**

Name-brand Western wear and boots can be found in this huge store. Staff people are friendly and ready to explain the differences in types of boots. They will also help you find the right fit. Cavender's also sells jewelry and other accessories.

Kingsville Area

King Ranch Saddle Shop
201 E. Kleberg Ave., Kingsville
• **(361) 595-5761**

Here's a truly authentic Western store, where the King Ranch saddles are made—and tourists can buy quality leather goods that range from purses to belts. Clothing, hats, and other souvenirs, many embossed with the ranch's famous brand, are also available.

Adam Garcia Leather Shop
1304 Sixth St., Kingsville
• **(361) 516-0773**

This store offers Western wear, leather goods, accessories and a variety of unique gift items made from cowboy-style paraphernalia—how about a clock made from a spur?

Variety Markets

Corpus Christi

Corpus Christi Trade Center
2833 S. Padre Island Dr., Corpus Christi
• **(361) 854-4943**

There are more than 150 different merchants here selling their wares in 70,000 square feet of space. Items include everything from Mexican dresses and ponchos to electronics and

toys. Prices are generally reasonable, and most buyers are looking for a bargain. The trade center is open Friday, Saturday, and Sunday.

Beachwear and Souvenirs

North Bay Area

Maritime Museum Store
Texas Maritime Museum,
1202 Navigation Cir., Rockport
• **(361) 729-1271**

This shop in the museum lobby carries seafaring gifts that include reproductions of maritime artifacts, brass ship's bells, bosun's whistles, postcards, and educational toys.

Sea Shell Shoppe
120 N. Austin St., Rockport
• **(361) 729-6325**

You won't even have to go the beach to find seashells if you stop at this store, which is plentifully laden with a wide variety of beautiful shells, as well as beach-related souvenirs and gifts.

Port Aransas to Padre Island

Absolutely Everything Gifts
314 Ave. G, Port Aransas
• **(361) 749-4738**

You can eat a hamburger, buy T-shirts or shorts, or play a round of miniature golf at this interesting little gift shop. It's a great place to visit when you're tired of the surf and sun.

Cool Breeze Gift Shop
319 Church St., Port Aransas
• **(361) 749-6609**

This quaint and fun shop sells T-shirts, swimsuits, inflatable rafts, seashells, and sunglasses. You can also rent, buy, or sell surfboards. Easily recognized by the large toothy shark that hangs over the front door, the old fishing nets, and other nautical items.

Fly It!
Ave. G and 10th St., Port Aransas
• **(361) 749-4190**

A splendid selection of windsocks, colorful

kites, gifts, and toys make this a fun place to visit. This kite shop offers great opportunities for recreation or nice souvenirs.

Islander
Alister Rd. at Ave. G, Port Aransas
• **(361) 749-5408**

A wide assortment of beach paraphernalia can be found here, including hats, beach chairs, inflatable rafts, suntan lotion, windsocks, umbrellas, and beach towels.

Moby Dick's
317 S. Alister Rd., Port Aransas
• **(361) 749-5769**

Local color abounds here, from the big blue marlin in the front window to the risqué signs that play on this shop's name. You can rent surfboards or buy T-shirts, shells, jewelry, and sunglasses—or pick up a burger at the adjoining snack bar.

Pat Magee's
101 Ave. G, Port Aransas
• **(361) 749-4177**

Bathing suits, shorts, T-shirts, and sandals can be found at this popular beachwear shop. Open since 1969, it's one of the more well known places to buy surfing gear.

Silver Fox Trading Co.
221 Beach St., Port Aransas
• **(361) 749-4899**

Owner Pat Stone offers a large collection of hand-crafted jewelry, including Indian jewelry, ethnic and silver beads, crosses, and charms. The store also carries clothing and accessories.

Souvenir City
100 E. White St., Port Aransas
• **(361) 749-5564**

Pick up your T-shirts, seashells, picture frames, magnets, mugs, and beach goods at this well-stocked little shop.

Corpus Christi

Island Sports
S. Padre Island Dr. at Park Road 22, Corpus Christi
• **(361) 949-7443**
115 E. Ave. G, Port Aransas
• **(361) 749-5369**

Each Island Sports location is marked by a gigantic pink octopus—one of those whimsical beachfront landmarks that kids just love. You can get swimsuits and more here.

Ocean Treasures and Gifts
14049 S. Padre Island Dr., Corpus Christi
• **(361) 949-7558**

A giant conch shell marks the front entrance to this beachwear shop on the road to Padre Island National Seashore. You'll find plenty of swimsuits, sandals, T-shirts, shells, and inflatable rafts.

Sea Treasures
2902 Surfside Blvd., Corpus Christi
• **(361) 882-5160**
10513 S. Padre Island Dr., Corpus Christi
• **(361) 937-6341**

Swimwear, T-shirts, floats, and seashells are available at this store. You can also rent Boogie Boards for the beach.

Treasures on the Beach
2818 Surfside Blvd., Corpus Christi
• **(361) 881-9883**

T-shirts, toys, shells, and other items are available at this shop near the Texas State Aquarium and the aircraft carrier-turned-museum, Lexington Museum on the Bay.

SHOPPING

Attractions

You may be surprised upon reading this chapter to find several wildlife preserves listed among Corpus Christi-area attractions. But residents and frequent visitors will tell you that wildlife is one of the main reasons to visit the area. While there is no shortage of more traditional tourist attractions here, it's the abundant wildlife and access to it that sets the Corpus Christi area apart.

Talk to any avid bird-watcher and chances are they've either visited or wanted to visit Corpus Christi to see the large variety of migratory and resident birds here. Corpus Christi is situated along the Central Flyway, the route many birds take on their annual north-south migration. The most-watched bird to inhabit the area is undoubtedly the endangered whooping crane, which spends its winters at the Aransas National Wildlife Refuge. For more information on this and other birds, see our Birding chapter.

You'll find several wildlife preserves and nature tours listed in this chapter. But you'll also find museums, the state's largest aquarium, a decommissioned aircraft carrier, and smaller attractions, too. This chapter doesn't mention two of the most popular attractions in the area: beaches and fishing. That's because they've been given chapters of their own. See our Beaches and Watersports and Fishing and Hunting chapters for more information.

We've divided attractions into our four geographical areas: North Bay Area, Corpus Christi, Port Aransas to Padre Island, and the Kingsville area. Attractions in the North Bay Area are listed north to south. Those in the other areas are listed alphabetically.

The Harbor Bridge offers a stunning backdrop for the Water Gardens at the Corpus Christi Arts and Sciences.

Photo: courtesy of the Greater Corpus Christi Business Alliance

North Bay Area

Aransas National Wildlife Refuge
- **F.M. Rd. 2040, Austwell**
- **(361) 286-3559**

This 115,000-acre wildlife refuge 35 miles north of Rockport is the winter home of the endangered whooping crane, which, in the past 50 years or so, has made a comeback from the verge of extinction. The federal government created the refuge in 1937 to protect the whooping crane and other threatened coastal wildlife. Several boat tours to view the cranes are available (see our Birding chapter). The refuge also is home to alligators, deer, javelina, coyote, bobcat, raccoon, and feral hogs.

Thousands of migratory birds are attracted to the refuge on their journey between North America and Central America. As many as 392 species of birds have been spotted here.

The refuge is open between sunrise and sunset. Public facilities include a 16-mile paved tour road, Wildlife Interpretive Center, 40-foot observation tower, several miles of walking trails, and a picnic area. The Wildlife Interpretive Center is open daily from 8:30 AM to 4:30 PM. There's an entrance fee of $5 per carload or $3 if you're visiting the refuge alone. For more information see our Parks chapter. The refuge is seven miles south of Austwell.

The Big Tree of Lamar
- **2 mi. west of Park Rd. 13, Lamar**
- **(361) 729-2858**

This giant live oak is a charter member of the Live Oak Society of America and a former subject of one of *Ripley's Believe It or Not* cartoons. It stands 44 feet tall, measures 35 feet around and has a crown 89 feet in circumference. The Texas Forest Service estimates its age at more than 1,000 years. This state-champion live oak is said to have been a council tree for the Karankawa Indians and for the white men who came after them. To get there take Texas Highway 35 N. out of Rockport across the Copano Bay Causeway. Turn right on Park Road 13 a half-mile north of the causeway bridge. Drive two miles until you come to a four-way stop. Turn left on Palmetto Street and follow the signs to Big Tree.

Lamar Cemetery
- **Bois D'Arc St., Lamar**
- **(361) 729-9952, (800) 242-0071**

The Lamar Cemetery lies on a 1-acre tract in the Lamar Community, 10 miles north of Rockport near Goose Island State Park. The cemetery was established in 1838 when James W. Byrne and associates bought a league of land on Lookout Point and laid out the Lamar townsite, named after Mirabeau B. Lamar, president of the Republic of Texas.

The oldest grave marker is that of Patrick O'Connor (1822-1854), the New Orleans bookkeeper employed by James Byrne who married Byrne's niece, Jane Gregory. O'Connor had traveled west in the hopes of improving his poor health, but died a few hours after arriving in Lamar. The earliest known soldier buried here is John Fagan (1820-1860), a survivor of the battles of Lipantitlan and Goliad (see our History chapter). He and his 16-year-old daughter, Mary, both died of pneumonia in May 1860. Four sea captains are buried here, along with other prominent figures in Lamar's and Aransas County's history.

When the railroad passed Lamar by and the post office closed in 1915, the town dwindled and almost died. Vegetation overtook the cemetery, which became known as "Lost Lamar Cemetery." Few knew its location. An association formed in the 1940s raised money to clear and restore the cemetery. In 1968 the Lamar Women's Club sponsored the reorganization of the Lamar Cemetery Association and obtained a historical marker for the site. In May 1986 the oldest structure in Aransas County—Stella Maris (Star of the Sea) Chapel—was moved to a spot across from the cemetery.

The history of Lamar Cemetery and biographies of the people buried here are available at the Aransas County Library in Rockport, 701 E. Mimosa Street, (361) 790-0153. To get to the cemetery, take Texas Highway 35 N. from Rockport, cross the Copano Bay Causeway and turn right on Park Road 13. Take a left on Bois D'Arc Street. Lamar Cemetery is at the end of the street.

Stella Maris Chapel
- **Bois D'Arc St., Lamar**
- **(361) 729-6445**

Stella Maris (Our Lady of the Sea) Chapel in Lamar is reported to be the first church and oldest building in Aransas County. A French architect with the last name of D'Alsure, who also supervised construction of several homes in Lamar, designed the Catholic church. It was built by Moses Ballou in 1858, with the townspeople (and their slaves) making shellcrete bricks used in the construction.

The chapel survived two shellings during the Civil War. But a hurricane that hit the area in 1919 almost destroyed it, and it was nailed shut and abandoned. In 1931 Bishop Ledvinna of the Diocese of Corpus Christi rebuilt the structure, adding sleeping quarters and a porch. He, other priests, and seminarians used the church as a vacation and recreation center until the Sisters of Schoenstatt acquired it. After the sisters built a chapel of their own, they allowed Lamar residents to use the old church as a non-denominational church until another one was built in the area. Without a congregation, the church soon began to deteriorate. In 1972, Rockport resident Dennis O'Connor, who in 1920 had visited the church with his mother, Kathryn, sent a $10,000 donation from the Kathryn O'Connor Foundation to repair and maintain Our Lady of the Sea Chapel. In 1986 the chapel was moved to its present location near Lamar Cemetery, and the Aransas County Historical Society raised $50,000 to restore and preserve it.

The interior and its contents are virtually unchanged since the early 1930s. Today the Knights of Columbus, a Catholic fraternal organization, operates Stella Maris Chapel and maintains it through donations. It is available for special services of any denomination, and arrangements may be made for tour groups. Admission is free. To get there, take Texas Highway 35 N. from Rockport, cross the Copano Bay Causeway and turn right on Park Road 13. Take a left on Bois D'Arc Street. The chapel is at the end of the street.

Schoenstatt Lamar
• **100 Front St., Lamar**
• **(361) 729-2019, (361) 729-2771**

This small Catholic shrine is an exact replica of the original shrine in Schoenstatt, Germany, which is the center and "power station" of a Catholic religious movement of renewal known as the Schoenstatt Sisters of Mary. The Schoenstatt Movement, which is rooted in the shrine and strives to continue the mission of Mary, was founded by Father Joseph Kentenich (1885-1968), who believed an oncoming crisis in the church and world was imminent. In 1958 the Schoenstatt Sisters of Mary acquired the former Diocese of Corpus Christi property on which to build their motherhouse and shrine.

The small shrine, on a tree-shrouded hill overlooking Copano Bay, offers pilgrims a quiet spot in which to pray, meditate, and reflect. In the Schoenstatt Movement Center—built in 1974 to meet the needs of the growing Schoenstatt Movement—you can visit the Founder Memorial Room, which bears a similarity to the Founder Chapel in Schoenstatt,

Germany, where Father Kentenich was laid to rest in a sarcophagus. The shrine and Movement Center are open from 6 AM to 8:45 PM. Admission is free.

Copano Bay State Fishing Pier
• **Rockport**
• **(361) 729-8519 (north side), (361) 729-7762 (south side)**

This fishing pier began as a causeway across Copano Bay, but when a wider, stronger causeway was built the old one was closed to traffic and turned into a pier. Because taller boats are able to pass under the new causeway, the middle section of the old one was removed. That left two sections, one of which stretches 6,190 feet from the north side, while the other extends 2,500 feet from the south side. You can't miss this pier. Just head north on Texas Highway 35 from Rockport. When you get to the Copano Bay Causeway look to your left. The pier runs alongside it. Anglers can catch redfish, flounder, speckled trout, drum, sheepshead, and other species.

Open year round, this lighted pier has a public boat ramp on the south side and fish cleaning tables, concessions, and restrooms on both sides. Admission is $2 per fishing pole. Hours are 7 AM to 11 PM every day during the colder part of the year (October or November through February). Warm-weather hours are 6:30 AM to midnight Sunday through Thursday and 24 hours Friday and Saturday.

Fennessey Ranch
• **F.M. Rd. 2678 10 mi. north of Bayside**
• **(361) 529-6600**

In recent years the 170-year-old Fennessey Ranch opened its doors to tourism for the first time, offering birding trips, hay rides, wildlife photography workshops, wetland educational tours, hiking, and trips along the Mission River. In September and October, the ranch sponsors hummingbird and hawk expeditions along the river as thousands of birds rest in the trees on their way south. In the spring you can partake in wildflower and spring migration tours. All tours are guided by naturalists.

The ranch is part of a 750,000-acre Spanish land grant bestowed upon Irish immigrant Tom O'Conner in 1834. It covers several thousand acres adjacent to the Mission River, 40 miles northwest of Corpus Christi. Habitats on the ranch include wetlands, natural lakes, meadows, woodlands, miles of river and associated uplands. An environmental management plan calls for enlargement and enhancement of existing wetlands along with a wildlife management and rotational grazing program designed to maximize the diversity of species found there. Birders have spotted more than 400 species here, including green jays, woodstorks, and masked ducks. Sixteen plant communities exist here, along with 50 species of amphibians and reptiles and 70 types of moths and butterflies.

Admission fees per person are as follows: a half-day birding expedition, $18.50; a full-day nature tour, including lunch, $44; a one-day wildlife photography workshop, $75; and a two-day wildlife photography workshop, $150. Reservations are required for all events.

To get to the Fennessey Ranch from Corpus Christi, take U.S. Highway 181 across the Harbor Bridge. Drive through Portland and take Texas Highway 35 N. when you reach Gregory. Turn left on Farm-to-Market Road 136 and follow it for 13 miles until you reach Bayside. In Bayside the road becomes Farm-to-Market Road 2678. Follow it for 10 miles until you reach the Fennessey Ranch entrance on the west side of the road.

Paws and Taws Convention Center
• 402 Fulton Beach Rd., Fulton
• (361) 729-2388

A trip to this rustic building overlooking Aransas Bay is worth it just so you can gaze at the gleaming hardwood floor where square dancers face off from 8 to 10 PM every Wednesday night. Rockport-Fulton residents' love of square dancing led to construction of this building in 1965. Along with the regular Wednesday night dances, it hosts square dancing on weekends several times a year and line dancing from 10 AM to noon Monday, Wednesday, and Friday. The local chapter of AARP uses it to play bridge from 1 to 4 PM each Thursday. They also have dances each Thursday from 7 to 10 PM. The "Paws and Taws" name comes from square dancing terms: Male dancers are called "Paws," and females are their "Taws." Along with square and line dancing, the center hosts many community activities and private functions.

The center's office is open 9 AM to noon and 1 to 4 PM Monday through Friday. Drop by and take a look inside. The office is closed weekends, but the center is usually open for community or private functions. There's no charge just to look around.

Fulton Mansion State Historical Park
• 317 Fulton Beach Rd., Fulton
• (361) 729-0386

George and Harriet Fulton spared no expense when they built their Victorian mansion in 1874. With its ornate trimwork and Victorian-era furnishings, this stately mansion dwarfed its nearest neighbors. Along with the eye-pleasing flourishes evident to passersby, this 6,200-square-foot home was built with all the modern conveniences, including running water, flush toilets, central heat, a gas lighting system, a water-cooling system to preserve perishable food and a simple clothes dryer. Detailed finishing touches included walnut and cypress woodwork as well as chandeliers, fine rugs, and ornate furniture.

Fulton came to Texas in 1837 to fight in the war for Texas's independence, but he arrived too late to participate. After working at several jobs, Fulton took over his wife's inheritance when her father died, and used it to establish an extensive cattle-ranching business. Business was good, and in 1874 the Fultons began constructing their home. Most materials and construction equipment were shipped in from New Orleans and the East Coast at considerable expense.

This three-story, French Second Empire-style home is on a 2.3-acre lot overlooking Aransas Bay at the corner of Fulton Beach Road and Henderson Street. Guided tours are held year round Wednesday through Sunday at 9, 10, and 11 AM and 1, 2, and 3 PM. Admission is $4 for adults and teens and $2 for children 7 and older. Children 6 and younger get in free. Wear soft-soled shoes to protect the mansion's floors and rugs. Picnicking is allowed on the mansion's grounds.

The mansion is the setting for special events throughout the year, including "Christmas at Mansion," a two-day event every December that celebrates a traditional 1880s Christmas; "All Hallow Even," a one-day event held each October to celebrate Halloween and to explore the mansion's alleged history of hauntings; and Mayfest, a family event with Victorian games for children.

Connie Hagar Cottage Sanctuary
• Church and First Sts., Rockport
• (361) 729-9952, (800) 242-0071

Rockport provides a viewing platform and trails that lead to areas where you may spot resident and neotropical migrant birds. The sanctuary is open sunrise to sunset. Admission is free. For more information about Connie Hagar, see our Birding chapter.

The Texas Maritime Museum
• 1202 Navigation Cir., Rockport
• (361) 729-1271, (361) 729-6644

Inside the modern-looking Texas Maritime Museum next to Rockport Harbor you'll find exhibits and artifacts dedicated to the museum's mission to preserve and interpret the rich maritime heritage of Texas. Exhibits cover everything from the early days of French and Spanish exploration to the modern search for offshore oil and gas.

Exterior exhibits include a lifeboat from an offshore oil platform and a full-scale replica of a scow sloop. Inside you'll find interactive exhibits, family activities and an extensive maritime library that includes books, photographs, and videos.

The museum hosts several annual events including the Rockport Festival of Wines, the free Brown Bag Lunch Lecture Series, and the Music of the Sea Festival. While you're there, check out the museum store for gifts and collectibles. You'll find books, caps, T-shirts, jewelry, model boats, note cards, and toys, all with a nautical theme.

Museum hours are 10 AM to 4 PM Tuesday through Saturday and 1 to 4 PM Sunday. Admission is $4 for adults and teens and $2 for children ages 5 to 12. Children 4 and younger get in free.

Rockport Center for the Arts
• 902 Navigation Cir., Rockport
• (361) 729-5519

The Rockport Art Association calls this Victorian-style building at Rockport Harbor its home. Inside you'll find artwork by local, regional, and other artists. The house contains 5,800 square feet of gallery, classroom, lecture, and library space. The center's gallery presents work by local artists on a rotating basis, and hosts art classes and workshops for adults and children. A recently added sculpture garden features a 13-foot-by-20-foot whooping crane sculpture by Corpus Christi artist Kent Ullberg entitled "Rites of Spring." The garden features permanent and traveling sculptures. The center is open from 10 AM to 4 PM Tuesday through Saturday and 1 to 4 PM Sunday. Admission is free. For more information see our Arts chapter.

INSIDERS' TIP
Hours at many Coastal Bend attractions change from season to season, so we recommend you call ahead.

Conn Brown Harbor
• From Commercial Street (Texas 35 N.) take Staff Blvd. east, Aransas Pass

Visit Conn Brown Harbor and take a look at the Gulf and bay shrimping boats that catch and deliver millions of pounds of shrimp to processing plants along the shore. Look for the Seamen's Memorial Tower, dedicated to local fishermen who have lost their lives at sea. Harbor Park is behind the tower. Here you'll find public boat ramps and public fishing piers.

Rob and Bessie Welder Wildlife Foundation
• U.S. Hwy. 77, Sinton
• (361) 364-2643

Robert H. Welder founded this wildlife refuge through a device in his will. It occupies 7,800 acres, a small portion of a large ranch that has been in the Welder family for more than 150 years, having come to them through a land grant from the king of Spain. The refuge, which opened in April 1961, is dedicated to wildlife research and education and is funded through private means, having no official connection with state or federal agencies. The foundation provides fellowships for graduate students in wildlife ecology and management and related subjects. The foundation also publishes scientific papers and offers lectures to scientific, civic, and conservation groups.

The refuge, which lies 7.4 miles northeast of Sinton, operates as a working cattle ranch and oil field. Sixteen plant communities exist on the refuge, including about 1,400 species of native plants. More than 380 species of birds, 55 species of mammals, and 55 species of reptiles and amphibians have been recorded on the refuge. About 1,000 deer live on the refuge along with javelinas, Río Grande wild turkeys, Northern bobwhites, and several species of ducks and geese.

Free guided tours are given at 3 PM every Thursday except on holidays. The gates are locked at all other times. Tours take about two hours and include a visit to the Wildlife Foundation headquarters and museum in addition to a 10-mile bus tour of the refuge. While you're on the tour you'll learn about foundation objectives and current research.

Organizations wishing to schedule tours at times other than Thursday afternoon should contact Conservation Education, Welder Wildlife Foundation, P.O. Box 1400, Sinton, Texas 78387. Special tour groups are limited to a minimum of 15 and a maximum of 50 people. Tours will not be booked on Sundays. Cameras are allowed; pets are not. Water fountains and restrooms are available; food and other beverages are not. Picnicking and camping are not allowed. Admission is free.

Naval Station Ingleside
- 1455 Ticonderoga St., Ingleside
- (361) 776-1119

On the northern side of Corpus Christi Bay, Naval Station Ingleside is home to the Navy's mine warfare fleet, which amounts to 23 ships. The USS *Inchon*, the Navy's first command-and-control ship, is included in that figure, along with 10 Avenger-class mine countermeasures ships and 12 Osprey-class coastal mine hunters. The base features a 4,600-foot waterfront, with a 1,100-foot double-deck pier.

At one time the base was open to the public and free tours were given every week. But the threat of terrorist activities has forced the Navy to tighten security. Pre-arranged tours, including ship tours, are available for groups. Call several days in advance. For more information see our Military chapter.

Dolphin Connection
- Ingleside
- (361) 882-4126, (361) 776-2887

Since 1985, Erv and Sonja Strong have made it their business to befriend dolphins living in Corpus Christi Bay. Sonja Strong says she knows 65 dolphins by name and recognizes about 200 others by their dorsal fins. On your one-hour Dolphin Connection boat trip you will meet several pods of dolphins swimming just out of reach and occasionally coming close enough to touch. Tickets are $17 for adults and teens and $12 for children 12 and younger. Reservations are required. You'll receive directions to the launch site when you book your trip.

Corpus Christi

Captain Clark's Flagship
- Peoples Street T-Head, Corpus Christi
- (361) 884-1693, (361) 884-8306

Set sail for a narrated tour of the Corpus Christi bayfront and the Port of Corpus Christi aboard an air-conditioned, 400-passenger paddlewheeler or aboard the 250-passenger *Gulf Clipper*. Board the *Captain Clark* on the Peoples Street T-Head and sit inside or out. Your port tour will take you past the *Lexington* Museum on the Bay, the Texas State Aquarium, and the South Texas Institute for the Arts. Captain Clark's also offers sunset cruises into Corpus Christi Bay.

Four types of tours are available between Memorial Day weekend and Labor Day. A daytrip—a one-hour tour of the port leaving at 11 AM and 1 and 3 PM daily—costs $7 for adults and teens, $4 for children ages 4 to 11 and free

for children 3 and younger. A sunset cruise, a 90-minute tour of the port and bay, leaves at 7:30 PM Sunday through Friday; tickets are $8 for adults and teens, $4.50 for children ages 4 to 11 and free for children 3 and younger. If you prefer a livelier outing, take the sunset cruise with entertainment, a 90-minute harbor and bay tour leaving at 7:30 PM Saturday; tickets are $9 for adults and teens, $5 for children ages 4 to 11 and free for children 3 and younger. The party cruise with entertainment is a two-hour bay tour leaving at 9:30 PM Saturday; tickets are $10 for adults and teens, $5 for children ages 4 to 11 and free for children 3 and younger.

At all other times of the year, one-hour tours begin daily at 3 PM during the week and at 1 and 3 PM Saturday and Sunday . A 90-minute tour also leaves at 7:30 PM Saturday. There are no tours on Tuesday.

Corpus Christi Botanical Gardens
- 8545 S. Staples St., Corpus Christi
- (361) 852-2100

You'll find more than a thousand native plants at the 180-acre Corpus Christi Botanical Gardens, on the southern end of the city near new residential neighborhoods and the Kings Crossing Golf & Country Club. Nature trails wend their way along Oso Creek. You'll find mesquite trees, wetlands, and plenty of flowers. The Orchid House is home to the Larkin Orchid Collection, one of the largest collections in the Southwest with some 2,600 varieties. In the exhibit house you'll see bromeliads, cactus, cycads, fern, and plumeria surrounding a center courtyard and fountain. The shaded bird and butterfly trail will lead you to the birding tower overlooking Gator Lake (the 'gator for which it's named has been removed). There you're likely to spot roseate spoonbills, egrets, white pelicans, and ducks.

The visitor center hosts a rotating gallery of exhibits and a gift shop, where you can purchase botanical mementos made by volunteers. The gardens are open 9 AM to 5 PM Tuesday through Sunday. They're closed on Monday. Admission is $3 for adults and teens, $2.50 for seniors 65 and older, $1.50 for children ages 5 to 12 and free for children younger than 5.

Corpus Christi Cathedral
- 505 N. Upper Broadway, Corpus Christi
- (361) 883-4213

The Corpus Christi Cathedral may be the most architecturally impressive building in the Corpus Christi area. Built in the 1940s at a cost of $425,000, the cathedral was designed to meet the demands of the city's growing Catholic

Selena Quintanilla-Perez

Raised on Corpus Christi's Westide, Selena Quintanilla-Perez quickly rose to the top of the Tejano music scene with her spirited style and melodic voice. But on March 31, 1995, her starry life came to an end when her fan club president gunned her down at a Corpus Christi motel.

Her death at age 23 inspired a Hollywood movie in 1997 starring Jennifer Lopez and Edward James Olmos. Her killer, Yolanda Saldivar, was convicted of murder and is serving a life sentence in a Texas prison.

Even in death, Selena has continued to draw fans to Corpus Christi, where they can visit several landmarks of her life and tragic death. While brochures and highlighted maps aren't provided for visitors, local cab drivers and tourist officials know the route for the tour of Selena sites.

Stops include her house on Bloomington Street, her clothing boutique on Everhart Road, her recording studio on Leopard Street, and her grave at Seaside Memorial Park. Fans also go to the Days Inn, 901 Navigation Boulevard, where Selena was shot. The motel has discouraged fans from visiting by putting new room numbers on every door. The number of the room where Selena was shot is not displayed, but fans continue to try to seek out the room and take photographs where they think the crime occurred.

The city also has paid homage to Selena by naming a public auditorium

Selena Quintanilla-Perez, who grew up in Corpus Christi, rose to the top of the Tejano music scene before the president of her fan club shot her to death at a Corpus Christi hotel.

Photo: George Gongora

after her. More picturesque and photogenic is the Mirador de la Flor, a $600,000 pavilion in honor of the late singer. The pavilion, at the entrance of the Peoples Street T-Head on the city's bayfront, features a bronze statue of Selena facing the water.

The memorial was developed and funded by the Devary Durril Foundation and individual contributions. The sculpture was designed and made by local sculptor H.W. "Buddy" Tatum.

In addition to the memorial, there are a number of wooden boards where fans can inscribe messages. Adjacent to the pavilion is the Paseo de la Flor, or Walk of the Flower, a tile mural along the bayfront walkway below and behind the Mirador de la Flor. More than 500 children from South Texas towns created the mural featuring white roses.

Next to the sculpture of Selena is a single white, sculpted rose with an inscription that reads: "Her stage is now silent. Yet, her persona enriched the lives of those she touched and her music lives on."

population. It sits on a bluff overlooking downtown Corpus Christi and Corpus Christi Bay, and although much taller buildings have been added to the city's skyline, none stands taller in the hearts of the city's Catholic community.

The cathedral's architecture is described as late Spanish Colonial revival, with glazed terra cotta-roofed domes, rosette wrought-iron grillwork, spiral-turned stone columns, copper doors, stone urns on dome bases, a red-clay tile roof and two open belltowers. Builders used beige bricks common in many area buildings in the period. The taller of the two towers contains a 32-bell carillon and a clock on each of the four walls; the shorter tower holds the three original bells, which hung in the former cathedral building. On the front of the cathedral are two rondels that encircle the episcopal crests of Bishop Emmanuel B. Ledvina and Coadjutor Bishop Mariano S. Garriga, who oversaw the Cathedral's construction.

The pipe organs, which originally had 38 ranks, were renovated between 1978 and 1984 to bring the number of ranks to 97. It is one of the largest pipe organs in South Texas and the largest of any Catholic church in the state. The cathedral houses the Emmanuel Chapel (in the basement on the south side of the building), which includes a crypt for the burial of as many as 24 bishops of Corpus Christi. Four are buried there now. On the west side of the cathedral is the chancery of the Diocese of Corpus Christi, and to the north is the building housing parish offices and religious education.

Daily masses are held in Emmanuel Chapel at 7 AM on Tuesday and Thursday and 12:05 PM on Monday, Wednesday, and Friday. A communion service also is held at 12:05 PM on Thursday and masses are held twice on Saturday at 12:05 PM and 5:30 PM. Sunday masses are held in the cathedral at 7:30 AM, 9:30 AM, and noon.

You can visit the cathedral complex at any time. The cathedral itself is open from 8:30 AM to 4:45 PM Monday through Friday, 8:30 AM to 7 PM Saturday, and from 7:30 AM to noon Sunday. If you plan to visit the cathedral when a mass is not being held, enter through the courtyard door.

Corpus Christi Greyhound Racetrack
• **5302 Leopard St., Corpus Christi**
• **(361) 289-9333, (800) 580-7223**

Open at 11 AM year round seven days a week, the Corpus Christi Greyhound Racetrack offers live greyhound racing and wagering, along with simulcast greyhound and horse racing via live satellite. Races from Dallas, Houston, San Antonio, Arizona, Arkansas, Florida, Kentucky, and Massachusetts are broadcast seven nights a week and every afternoon. You can see live greyhound racing Wednesday through Saturday nights beginning at 7:30 PM, and Wednesday, Friday, Saturday, and Sunday afternoons beginning at 1:30 PM. Grandstand seating is completely enclosed and air-conditioned. The track has a food court.

Grandstand admission is $1, clubhouse admission (with monitors at your table) is $2, and parking is free. Senior citizens get in free at all matinees.

Corpus Christi Museum of Science and History
• **1900 N. Chaparral St., Corpus Christi**
• **(361) 883-2862**

Inside this museum near the Harbor Bridge you can learn about Columbus's voyages and their impact on the New World in "Seeds of

Change," a Smithsonian Institute exhibit on permanent display. The museum also houses artifacts from three Spanish galleons that wrecked on Padre Island in 1554.

The kids will enjoy the Children's Wharf, designed for ages three to seven. The Children's Wharf has hands-on activities for small children, including a kid-size shrimp boat, playhouse, and magnet tables. The museum also has a rather large gift shop with treats for both adults and children.

The museum, which is closed on Monday, is open from 10 AM to 5 PM Tuesday through Saturday and noon to 5 PM on Sunday. Admission is $5 for adults, $4 for seniors and military with identification, $3 for children 5 to 12 and free to children 4 and younger. On Saturday, children up to age 12 are admitted free from 10 AM to noon.

H.R. Brunner
Telephone Pioneer Museum
• **406 N. Carancahua, Corpus Christi**
• **(361) 884-1067**

This museum inside a Southwestern Bell office building chronicles the technological changes that have occurred in telephony during the past century. Exhibits include phones from before the turn of the century, a working cordboard that allows visitors to patch calls to and from phones in the museum, a coin-operated telephone from 1896, several hand-crank telephones, a display on the advent of dial telephones and displays of different types of cable used throughout the years.

The museum is open from 10 AM to noon every Thursday or by appointment. Admission is free.

Heritage Park
• **1581 N. Chaparral St., Corpus Christi**
• **(361) 883-0639**

Tour several beautifully restored homes representative of the Corpus Christi area's diverse heritage at this unusual park on the city's northern end. Several nonprofit organizations in Corpus Christi had nine historic local homes brought to this area along N. Chaparral Street between Fitzgerald and Hughes streets. Each organization has restored one home for historical and educational purposes.

The Galvan House, the large yellow house

INSIDERS' TIP

The bayfront seawall offers a great location for viewing seasonal fireworks displays, such as those scheduled for New Year's Eve and the Fourth of July. Be sure to arrive early to get a good spot.

---

in the center of the park, serves as the Multicultural Center, and features dynamic art exhibits depicting the city's heritage. It's open from 10 AM to 5 PM Monday through Thursday and 10 AM to 2 PM on Friday.

Guided tours of the park as well as six of the nine houses are offered at 10:30 AM on Thursday and Friday. Tours are $3 for adults and teens, $2 for seniors 55 and older and $1 for children. You can also take a self-guided tour by picking up information in the Galvan House. Bring a picnic and lunch on the park's beautiful grounds, or check the Merriman-Bobys House to see if they're serving lunch or dinner.

Port of Corpus Christi and Harbor Bridge
• **1305 N. Shoreline Blvd., Corpus Christi**
• **(361) 882-2080**

One of the most spectacular sights you'll see during your visit to Corpus Christi is a mammoth oil tanker cruising into port. With tiny and powerful tugboats leading the way, these enormous ships pass a few feet away from your vantage point beneath the Harbor Bridge, which arches 235 feet above the water. As one of the nation's busiest ports, Corpus Christi is visited by ships from nearly every country in the world, moving grain, farm products, oil, and chemicals. Viewing spots are available near the Harbormaster's office.

While you're there check out the convention and meeting facilities. Or drive across the Harbor Bridge and watch from the three-story observation tower. A pedestrian walkway on the bridge offers a great view of the port and city. To find out when ships will be arriving at or departing from the port, check the *Corpus Christi Caller-Times* business section. This is a free attraction.

South Texas Institute for the Arts
• **1902 N. Shoreline Blvd., Corpus Christi**
• **(361) 980-3500**

Designed by renowned architect Philip Johnson, the institute for the arts, formerly known as the Art Museum of South Texas, overlooks the bay and the Corpus Christi Ship Channel. Inside you'll find traveling exhibits of painting, sculpture, and photography. The permanent collection of photographs includes works by Ansel Adams and Victoria Livingston. The museum also has a children's area and gift shop.

The museum is open 10 AM to 5 PM Tuesday through Saturday and 1 to 5 PM on Sunday. Hours on the first Thursday of each month are 10 AM to 9 PM, and the museum is closed on Monday. Admission is $3 for adults, $2 for seniors, military, and students, and children 12 and under get in free.

Texas State Aquarium
- **2710 N. Shoreline Blvd., Corpus Christi**
- **(361) 881-1200, (800) 477-4853**

The Texas State Aquarium looks right at home perched on the tip of Corpus Christi Beach on the city's north end. The blue-and-white, four-story building overlooks Corpus Christi Bay, the city's bayfront and the entrance to the Port of Corpus Christi, the sixth-largest port in the United States.

The aquarium, dedicated to the study of plants and animals native to the Gulf of Mexico, opened in 1990, more than two decades after it was first proposed. The $31.6 million facility (funded entirely by private donations) opened to more than 100,000 visitors in its first month. Each year, between 400,000 and 500,000 people visit the aquarium, the first large public facility to focus exclusively on the Gulf of Mexico. Exhibits feature sand and nurse sharks, moray eels, barracudas, tarpons, and tropical fish.

The facility also boasts a seabirds and shorebirds exhibit and a touch tank where visitors can hold hermit crabs and other harmless sea creatures. Tourists stroll by dozens of small tanks in addition to a 132,000-gallon aquarium featuring a reproduction of an offshore oil rig and a smaller, although more colorful, tank with a coral reef similar to one found in the Gulf of Mexico. Other attractions include a 2,250-square-foot sea-turtle exhibit, a pool where visitors are allowed to pet a shark or a stingray, North American river otters, and The Octopus' Garden, a kid-friendly playground with a giant purple octopus as its centerpiece.

In addition to its many fish and other sea creatures, the aquarium offers a full day of educational programs at no extra charge. Visitors can get a close look at animals like baby alligators or birds of prey and watch scuba divers feed fish by hand.

Summer hours (from Memorial Day to Labor Day) are 9 AM to 6 PM Monday through Saturday, 10 AM to 6 PM on Sundays, and extended hours to 8 PM on Tuesdays. Hours the rest of the year are 9 AM to 5 PM Monday through Saturday and 10 AM to 5 PM on Sundays. The aquarium is closed Christmas Day.

Admission is $8.75 for adults, $6.75 for senior citizens, active-duty military and for ages 12 to 17, $5 for children ages 4 to 11 and free for children 3 and younger. Parking is $3. Strollers can be rented for $3.

Lexington Museum on the Bay
- **2914 N. Shoreline Blvd. Corpus Christi**
- **(361) 888-4873, (800) 523-9539**

You can tour World War II's most decorated aircraft carrier without having to worry about being shelled by enemy planes. The former USS *Lexington*, now decommissioned and converted into a floating museum, sits in shallow water off Corpus Christi Beach, a short distance from the Texas State Aquarium and downtown Corpus Christi.

Commissioned in 1943, the USS *Lexington* CV-16 served longer and set more records than any carrier in the history of the U.S. Navy. During World War II Tokyo Rose dubbed her the "Blue Ghost" after repeatedly defying reports that she had been sunk. The ship was the first U.S. carrier to enter Tokyo Bay after the treaty was signed with Japan in 1945.

Several historic planes are on display on the ship's flight deck, including a jet flown by the Blue Angels and an F-14, the Navy's premier fighter plane. Visit the flight deck, hangar deck, captain's quarters, admiral's quarters, navigation and flag bridge, sick bay, and the engine room. The ship also has a gift shop and cafe on board.

While you're here, see what it's like to fly a jet fighter in the *Lexington's* flight simulator.

The *Lexington* is open 9 AM to 5 PM every day except Christmas. Admission is $9 for adults and teens, $7 for seniors 60 and older and active or retired military, $4 for children ages 4 to 12 and free for children younger than 4. All tours are self-guided and require climbing steep stairs. Comfortable clothing and shoes with non-skid soles are recommended.

Port Aransas to Padre Island

Birding Center
- **Ross Ave. off Cut-Off Rd., Port Aransas**
- **(361) 749-5919**

Local and migratory birds find the Port Aransas wetlands an irresistible spot in which to inhabit or visit. The birding center provides seasoned bird-watchers and novices with plenty to look at. Vegetation is designed to attract hummingbirds as they migrate in the spring and fall. You may also catch a glimpse of a 6-foot alligator that lives here.

A boardwalk takes you over the wetlands to an observation tower, where you can look out over the Corpus Christi Ship Channel. The birding center is open 24 hours a day, and there is no admission fee.

Dolphin Watch
• **136 W. Cotter Ave., Port Aransas**
• **(361) 749-5252**

Hop aboard the 48-foot *Duke* for a two-hour tour of Port Aransas waters. Search for bottlenosed dolphin and watch them play in their natural environment. Then watch as the crew pulls a plankton net through the water and empties the contents into a jar for you to view through a small microscope. From the bird world, look for egrets, herons, spoonbills, gulls, pelicans, curlews, and other species.

You'll also get a chance to examine the contents of a shrimp trawl net pulled through the water and dumped into a sampling bin. The catch is often filled with crabs, shrimp, and fish.

Tickets are $15 for adults, $10 for children 5 to 12 and free to children 4 and younger. The *Duke* leaves Woody's Sport Center at various times depending on the season. Call ahead for reservations.

The Jetty Boat
• **136 W. Cotter Ave., Port Aransas**
• **(361) 749-5252**

Ride the jetty boat to San José Island north of Port Aransas and see what life is like on a privately owned island. Reachable only by boat, San José Island offers beachcombing, shelling, surfing, and swimming. Bring your own fishing equipment and fish from the north jetty. You also can go surf fishing, crabbing on the bay side, and seining.

The ferry leaves Port Aransas as early as 6:30 AM and as late as 6 PM depending on the season. The island has no restrooms or other public facilities. Tickets are $9.95 for adults and teens, $4.95 for children ages 2 to 12 and children younger than 2 ride for free.

Tarpon Inn
• **200 E. Cotter Ave., Port Aransas**
• **(361) 749-5555, (800) 365-6784**

The Tarpon Inn's history is the reason we've included it in this chapter as well as in the Hotels and Motels chapter, where you can read our Close-up on the inn. It is one of two accommodations in the Corpus Christi area to be listed on the National Register of Historic Places (the Hoopes' House Bed and Breakfast is the

Children of all ages enjoy watching the playful otters at the Texas State Aquarium.

Photo: courtesy of the Greater Corpus Christi Business Alliance

other). Inside its lobby you'll find a tarpon scale autographed by the late President Franklin D. Roosevelt. The scale is among more than 7,000 others caught by guests (Roosevelt wasn't one of them) and displayed on the walls of the hotel's lobby. The inn offers 24 small rooms filled with antiques.

The lobby is open from 9 AM to 10 PM every day. Admission is free.

University of Texas Marine Science Institute
- **750 Channel View Dr., Port Aransas**
- **(361) 749-6711**

Learn about Gulf marine life, plants and oceanography at this laboratory and research facility on the northern tip of Mustang Island. The institute is the center for the study of Texas's bays, the Gulf of Mexico and the world's oceans. Through audio/visual technology, faculty can share their expertise with students far from the coast. The institute offers undergraduate courses and provides master's and doctoral students immediate access to a variety of local marine habitats.

The visitor center is open from 8 AM to 5 PM weekdays. Inside you'll find several aquariums featuring sea creatures common to the Gulf of Mexico. Call ahead to find out whether a movie is planned for that day. Additional displays in the main building highlight current and past research projects.

Admission is free. From the ferry go straight down Cotter Avenue and follow the signs. You'll go past a traffic signal and one stop sign. The institute is at the end of the road right before you get to the beach.

Treasure Island Golf & Games
- **14041 S. Padre Island Drive, Corpus Christi**
- **(361) 949-1769**

These wind-swept courses on Padre Island are wrapped around an enormous waterfall that beckons adventure-seekers driving by on South Padre Island Drive. Treasure Island has two 18-hole courses, bumper boats, a game room, and an ice cream parlor. It also serves yogurt, soft drinks, hot dogs, pizza, and pickles.

The courses feature bridges, caves, and a miniature lighthouse. The easier of the two courses, known as the Adventure Course, costs $5 a round. The more difficult Challenge course is $6. Seniors older than 55 play for $4 a round, while children younger than 12 play for $3.50. A seven-minute bumper boat ride costs $5 per person. You must be at least 44 inches tall to ride alone, or 40 inches tall to ride with an adult.

Kingsville Area

John E. Conner Museum
- **905 W Santa Gertrudis, Texas A&M University-Kingsville, Kingsville**
- **(361) 593-2819**

The John E. Conner Museum is designed to preserve the social, political, and natural history of the Kingsville area and to interpret the bicultural heritage of the borderlands. Exhibits inside the Caesar Kleberg Hall of Natural History explore the ecosystems of the South Texas and Northern Mexico biospheres. Lifelike dioramas, nature's sounds, slide shows, and an award-winning video will give you a good idea of what the region is like.

The museum's ranching area features a chuck wagon, branding irons, saddles, barbed wire, and small ranching equipment. It also has on display 264 trophy mounts of North American game, including elk, moose, antelope, bighorn sheep, mountain goats, grizzlies, and whitetail deer. Exhibits change every four to six weeks. Two per year come from the museum's collections, while others are science exhibits from various sources. Each Monday from November until April, informal lunchtime lectures feature area citizens with interesting jobs.

The museum is open from 9 AM to 5 PM Monday through Saturday. Admission is free.

King Ranch Museum
- **405 N. Sixth St., Kingsville**
- **(361) 595-1881**

This museum set in a restored icehouse is

INSIDERS' TIP

The best place to find brochures on area attractions are at the three visitor centers operated by the Corpus Christi Convention and Visitors Bureau. They can be found at: Nueces River Visitors Information Center, 241-1464, 143 U.S. Hwy 37 S.; Padre Island Visitors Information Center, 949-8743, 14252 S. Padre Island Drive; and the Corpus Christi Visitors Center, 561-2000, 1823 N. Chaparral St.

home to custom-made automobiles, saddles, and other memorabilia. Experience life on the King Ranch in the early 1940s through the award-winning photographs of Toni Frissell. See a collection of saddles from around the world, various guns, including a King Ranch commemorative issue Colt Python .357 Magnum pistol. Also on display are antique carriages and vintage cars, including a custom-designed Buick Eight hunting car built in 1949 by General Motors.

The museum is open from 10 AM to 4 PM Monday through Saturday and from 1 to 5 PM Sunday. Admission is $4 for adults and teens, $2.50 for children ages 5 to 12 and free for children younger than 5.

King Ranch
• **Texas Hwy. 141 W., Kingsville**
• **(361) 592-8055**

At 825,000 acres the King Ranch is larger than Rhode Island and is one of the largest ranches in the world. It's also home to more than 60,000 cattle. Capt. Richard King founded the ranch in 1853. The Santa Gertrudis and King Ranch Santa Cruz breeds of cattle were developed there, along with the first registered American Quarter Horse.

Guided historical and agricultural tours are available daily. All tours leave from the King Ranch Visitors Center. During the winter season (roughly November through March), tours leave the visitors center on the hour between 10 AM and 3 PM and 1 to 4 PM Sunday. During summer hours, tours run at 10 AM, noon, and 2 PM Monday through Friday, on the hour from

INSIDERS' TIP
Students, senior citizens, and active and retired military often receive discounts at local attractions.

10 AM to 3 PM on Saturday and on the hour from 1 to 4 PM on Sunday. Tickets, including tax, are $7.47 for adults, $2.50 for children 5 to 12 and free to children 4 and younger. Tickets are sold on a first-come, first-served basis. Get there 45 minutes early to make sure you get a ticket.

Tours last 90 minutes and cover a 12-mile loop in which you will visit historical buildings and learn about horses and cattle. The following nature tours also are available at various times throughout the year (costs are quoted without tax included):

• Wildlife—This half-day, 26-mile loop through the Santa Gertrudis division of King Ranch introduces participants to common native wildlife. The cost is $17.50 per person.

• Bird-watching Day Tour—Designed for the avid bird-watcher, this nine- to 10-hour excursion covers areas of the Norias division of King Ranch. The cost of $99 includes lunch and transportation. Tours are held on specific dates throughout the year. Call for availability.

• Photography Tours—Photography blinds for waterbirds and songbirds can be reserved for $50 per person for half a day. A private, guided tour can be reserved for $50 a half day or $100 for the entire day, including lunch. Guided tours must have at least two people.

• Private Customized Wildlife and Bird-Watching Tour—This tour caters to your special interests, whether it's native wildlife or birds. Tours visit the Santa Gertrudis and Laureles divisions of the ranch. The cost is $50 for a half day or $100 for a full day, including lunch. There must be at least two people per tour. Reservations are required.

Kidstuff

We've turned to the ABCs for help in guiding you to the kid-oriented activities in the Corpus Christi area. Commercial, organized activities for the little ones are few and far between in this area, but don't let that discourage you. With the nearby beaches and year-round mild weather, Corpus Christi provides one of the state's best natural playgrounds.

In this chapter we've abandoned our usual geographic divisions in favor of an alphabetical listing of things to see and do throughout the area. Some letters have more than one activity listed under them, and many are mentioned in greater detail in our Attractions chapter. We're sure that once you've visited the area, you'll soon be adding your own favorites to the list.

LOOK FOR:
• A to Z Activities

A is for . . .

aquarium. At the Texas State Aquarium in Corpus Christi you'll see all sorts of creatures that make their homes in the Gulf of Mexico. Stare eye-to-eye with an alligator (from behind a thick pane of glass) or watch a stingray glide silently through the water. Let a hermit crab walk across your hand or reach in and pull out another harmless sea creature on display in the aquarium's touch tank. Marvel at the 132,000-gallon tank that recreates the habitat around an offshore drilling platform and gaze at the beautiful Flower Gardens coral reef exhibit. Downstairs you'll laugh at the antics of the frolicsome Texas river otters and squeal as you pet a bamboo shark. Outside you'll find pelicans and great blue herons living in their natural habitat. You'll also find sea turtles, birds of prey, and a playground. Children three and younger are admitted free. See our Attractions chapter for more information or call (361) 881-1200.

B is for . . .

boats that you can watch or rent along the Corpus Christi bayfront. Every Wednesday local sailors get together to race on Corpus Christi Bay. They gather inside the jetty that forms a semicircle around the two T-heads and one L-head (land extensions) protruding from the seawall. Take a seat on the Lawrence Street T-head and watch the boats cross in front of you while they await the starting horn. If you'd rather captain a boat yourself, check out the Peoples Street T-head for paddleboats you can rent. This seasonal activity is often available during warm-weather months only. You'll sail your boat in calm seas in an area free of large boat traffic. There's no number to call, just drop by the T-heads. In Rockport visit the Rockport Beach Park in downtown Rockport. You can also call (361) 729-9392.

For more information on sailing, see our Beaches and Watersports chapter.

C is for . . .

Children's Wharf at the Corpus Christi Museum of Science and History, (361) 883-2862, 1900 N. Chaparral Street. The Children's Wharf is in a large, open room that looks out on a circular fountain. Start with the life-size replica of a bay shrimping boat complete with life jackets and a bridge from which to captain the boat. Grab a fishing pole and troll for colorful plastic sharks, shrimp and starfish, or finish building a house with toy bricks. Play with magnets or a miniature car fitted with a sail and propelled by electric fans. Laugh at your reflection in funhouse mirrors or spell your name in giant letters on the museum wall. See our Attractions chapter for more information.

Guess what else C stands for: Chuck E Cheese's, (361) 993-8824, 5118 S. Staples Street, Corpus Christi. Chuck E Cheese's is loads of fun. This kid-oriented pizzeria is packed with video games and other games of skill. Win tickets and cash them in for prizes.

D is for . . .

dolphins that swim in the sea. Get up early and visit wild dolphins. You can't feed them, but if they're feeling friendly you might get to pet one. Since 1985 the proprietors of the Dolphin Connection, (361) 882-4126, have met and named more than 65 dolphins. Pay attention and you might just learn something. The proprietors are walking encyclopedias of information. Dolphin Connection tours leave from Ingleside. See our Attractions chapter for more information.

INSIDERS' TIP

A good place to take the kids for a picnic is Heritage Park in Corpus Christi. Several turn-of-the-century homes dot this beautifully landscaped park that on weekdays is sparsely populated. Call (512) 883-0639.

E is for . . .

exploring for seashells at local beaches. The best place to find them is on the Gulf of Mexico beaches, especially on the unpopulated San Jose Island north of Port Aransas. A boat takes visitors to and from the island several times a day. Another good place to search is Padre Island National Seashore. The farther you get from the visitor center, the greater your chance of finding a seashell or sand dollar. Keep your eyes peeled for hamburger sea beans, too. These marble-size wonders look like miniature hamburgers. Remember, the earlier bird gets the seashell. For information on boats to San José Island you can check out our Attractions chapter or call (361) 749-5252.

F is for . . .

feeding sea gulls. You can do this anywhere sea gulls congregate, although it should be noted that many restaurants and other commercial establishments discourage the practice. Buy a cheap loaf of bread—sea gulls are not picky eaters—and head for the water. In Corpus Christi the T-heads and Cole Park are good places to find hungry sea gulls. The gulls at Cole Park are especially aggressive. Bring a camera and snap a picture with 20 or 30 sea gulls suspended in the air above you. Brave souls should try this: hold a piece of bread (a large one is preferable) high in the air and wait for a gull to snatch it from your fingers. Don't worry, sea gulls are incredibly accurate. They rarely snatch a finger by mistake.

F also stands for fishing. You can fish all over the Corpus Christi area, but one good spot for kids is Indian Point Park and Pier, (361) 643-8555, on U.S. Highway 181 in Portland. The fishing is good, and the accommodations are nice. Fish from a 720-foot pier with a 280-foot T-head. For more information see our Fishing and Hunting chapter.

G is for . . .

golf—miniature and disc. You'll find two miniature golf courses at Treasure Island Golf and Games, 14041 S. Padre Island Drive. These courses feature ponds, waterfalls, caves, and a pirate theme. The facility also has bumper boats, video games, and ice cream. Call 949-1769.

The Corpus Christi area has three disc golf courses. Disc golf is played with a flying disc rather than clubs and a ball. It doesn't cost much to get started, and anyone can play. An 18-hole course is located in Live Oak Park on Sherry Street, Ingleside. For more information see our Parks chapter or call (361) 776-2517. An 18-hole course is located in Corpus Christi's West Guth Park on Up River Road north of Rand Morgan Road. A nine-hole course is located in Lamar Park, at the corner of Santa Fe Street and Barracuda Place.

H is for . . .

horses. You can ride carousel horses at Padre Staples Mall, (361) 991-5718, on S. Padre Island Drive in Corpus Christi or real horses at various riding stables throughout the area. Try Corpus Christi Riding Center, (361) 939-9494, 1901 Caribbean Drive, in Corpus Christi. Want to ride on the beach? Then visit Mustang Island Riding Stables, (361) 991-7433, on Texas Highway 361 south of Port Aransas. For more information, see our Recreation chapter.

I is for . . .

ice cream. In Corpus Christi try either of the two locations of the Marble Slab Creamery, (361) 851-1236, 3133 S. Alameda Street, and 5521 Saratoga Boulevard, (361) 993-2202. They both serve a wide variety of homemade ice cream with all sorts of candy and other yummy treats that can be mixed in.

J is for . . .

jumping on a giant trampoline floating on Corpus Christi Bay. The folks at the Holiday Inn-Emerald Beach, (361) 883-5731, 1102 S. Shoreline Boulevard, will let you jump to your heart's content as long as you pay the cabana boy (the cost is $5 per person per day) for the pleasure. During the summer months you'll find the trampoline floating in the shallow water right outside the Holiday Inn's back door.

K is for . . .

kites. You can fly them, study them, or both. The Corpus Christi area is a great place to fly a kite provided you launch your rig near the shore where you can take advantage of the strong gulf wind. Corpus Christi's Cole Park and the Rockport Beach Park in Rockport are among the best places to fly kites.

L is for . . .

libraries. Corpus Christi has several. Aransas Pass, Ingleside, Kingsville, Port Aransas, Portland, and Rockport have one each. At Corpus Christi libraries, toddlers and preschoolers enjoy weekly storytime sessions performed by the local children's librarian. Each brief session is filled with age-appropriate stories and songs designed to interest children in books. Call the Corpus Christi Central Library, (361) 880-7000, 805 Comanche Street, for more information. Although not a library, Barnes & Noble Booksellers, (361) 992-1339, 5129 Blanche Moore Street, does have its own storytime sessions every Saturday.

M is for . . .

McDonald's. Really. In the middle of the long hot summer you won't find a better place to run wild than the indoor play area at either the Flour Bluff McDonald's Restaurant, (361) 939-7907, 1229 Waldron Road, the Southside restaurant, (361) 855-0876, 4031 Saratoga Blvd., or the Westside restaurant, (361) 225-0511, 1610 S. Padre Island Drive. Sometimes it's too hot outside—even for kids—and who wants to melt in the sun when you can sip on a cold beverage in air-conditioned comfort?

M also stands for museums and marine science. In the Kingsville area check out the John E. Conner Museum, (361) 593-2819, on the Texas A&M University-Kingsville campus and the King Ranch Museum, (361) 595-1881, 405 N. Sixth Street. For more information on marine science in the area, grab the gang and head for the visitors center at the Univer-

KidsPlace in Cole Park is a mega-jungle gym that was built by the Junior League of Corpus Christi.

Photo: courtesy of the Greater Corpus Christi Business Alliance

KIDSTUFF

sity of Texas Marine Science Institute, (361) 749-6711, in Port Aransas. See our Attractions chapter.

N is for . . .

nature. The Hans Suter Wildlife Area is a great nature retreat for children. It's located on Oso Bay in Corpus Christi, and features short hiking trails through native habitat as well as a boardwalk over wetlands and an observation point to watch birds.

O is for . . .

octopus, as in Octopus' Garden, a playground at the Texas State Aquarium, (361) 881-1200, featuring a giant purple octopus figure as its centerpiece. Local children came up with the idea for the giant purple octopus, and a local architect turned their imaginings into reality. The playground has equipment for both toddlers and older kids. Swings, monkey bars, slides and a fountain are among its main attractions. Kids will love climbing inside the octopus and looking out on the playground below. For more information see our Attractions chapter.

P is for . . .

playground. Corpus Christi's Cole Park on the bayfront has one of the largest and best playgrounds anywhere. The main attraction is KidsPlace, an 18,000-square-foot wooden play area featuring castle turrets, drawbridges, cubbyholes, crawl spaces, and conventional playground equipment such as swings and slides. KidsPlace has areas for big and small kids and benches for weary parents. For more information see our Parks chapter.

Q is for . . .

quick cars at the C.C. Speedway, (361) 289-8847, 241 Flato Road, Corpus Christi. The speedway holds stock car races every Saturday night between April and August around a quarter-mile asphalt track. We recommend ear plugs, especially for the kids. Children 12 and younger get in free with a paying adult. Admission for adults is $8. For more information see our Spectator Sports chapter.

R is for . . .

roller-skating at Cityskates, (361) 993-7456, 8051 S. Padre Island Drive, Corpus Christi. This old-fashioned skating rink has a 14,000-square-foot hardwood (maple) skating area, snack bar, and video games. Friday night is teen dance night. Admission and skate rental costs $5.75.

S is for . . .

surreys. During warm months you can rent one of these four-wheeled, pedal-powered carriages along the Corpus Christi bayfront. They hold as many as four people. It's a great way to tour the bayfront while giving mom and dad some badly needed exercise. Take our advice: you'll enjoy it more in the spring and fall when the heat isn't as bad. Look for them along the seawall between the Peoples Street and Lawrence Street T-heads. They rent for about $10 per half-hour.

T is for . . .

taxi. No, not the four-wheeled kind. We're talking about the water taxi that travels between the barge dock on the north end of the bayfront to the Texas State Aquarium on the other side of the Corpus Christi Ship Channel. The water taxi runs between Memorial Day and Labor Day. For more information see our Getting Here, Getting Around chapter or call (361) 289-2600.

U is for . . .

the former USS *Lexington*. This decommissioned aircraft carrier-turned-museum, Lexington

Museum on the Bay, is on Corpus Christi Beach. What kid wouldn't like visiting this World War II-era warship? Commissioned in 1943, the USS *Lexington* served longer and set more records than any carrier in the history of the U.S. Navy. It now serves as a floating museum stocked with aircraft, exhibits and displays. For more information see our Attractions chapter or call (361) 888-4873 or (800) LADY LEX.

V is for . . .

video games. One of the best places to play is Tilt, (361) 991-0333, on the upper level at Corpus Christi's Padre Staples Mall. You'll find dozens of video and arcade games for all skill levels and interests. The city's other mall, Sunrise Mall, is home to another good video game arcade. Alladin's Castle, (361) 991-7478, is located next to the food court on the second level.

INSIDERS' TIP

Kids (and adults) can surf the Internet, play computer games, or read books at the Texas State Aquarium's small library. The library is located near the elevators on the aquarium's main floor.

W is for . . .

welcoming ships into the Port of Corpus Christi. Check for a schedule of incoming and outgoing ships in the *Corpus Christi Caller-Times* business section then take Chaparral Street past the Corpus Christi Museum of Science and History and park under the Harbor Bridge. Another good place to watch is from an observation tower on the opposite side of the ship channel near the Texas State Aquarium. Cargo ships and oil tankers are common sights.

W also stands for whooping cranes and windsurfing. Take a narrated tour by boat of the whooping cranes' winter habitat. For more information on birdwatching, see our Birding chapter or call (361) 729-9952 or (800) 242-0071. To learn to windsurf or to rent equipment, head out to Bird Island Basin at the Padre Island National Seashore. For more information see our Beaches and Watersports chapter or call (361) 937-2621 or (800) 793-7471.

X is for . . .

xeriscaping. The Corpus Christi Museum of Science and History, (361) 883-2862, 1900 N. Chaparral Street, has a xeriscape exhibit on the west side of the building featuring plants native to the Corpus Christi area. Xeriscaping is a method of landscaping using native plants that thrive under dry conditions. You'll get a good look at the area's flora without having to trek all over the area to find them.

Y is for . . .

YMCA and YWCA. Both facilities have exercise equipment, gymnasiums, swimming pools, and programs for children. The YMCA, (361) 882-1741, 417 S. Upper Broadway, has racquetball/handball courts. The YWCA, (361) 857-5661, 4601 Corona Street, provides free childcare for members. A one-day visitor's pass costs $10 to the YMCA and $6 to the YWCA.

Z is for . . .

zipping down the seawall on in-line skates. This is Corpus Christi's favorite place for in-line skating. Adults and children alike will enjoy the view and the wide-open expanse of the seawall. You can rent skates at M D Surf & Skate, (361) 854-7873, 4016 Weber Road, in Corpus Christi. They're also available at Odie's, (361) 882-7554, 403 N. Shoreline Boulevard on the Corpus Christi bayfront. In-line skates rent for about $15 a day for both children and adults, pads included.

Annual Events and Festivals

LOOK FOR:
• Month-to-Month
  Listings

Maybe it's the proximity of sand and surf, maybe it's the unquenchable sunshine—all we know is that South Texans love celebrations. Many of these celebrations seem to have been inspired by residents' devotion to the coastal elements. There are festivals devoted to oysters, shrimp, fishing, piracy, and the bay itself.

On the other hand, there are also a variety of more offbeat events: a cactus celebration, a hummingbird festival, and a bull-riders challenge. It seems that almost any topic can find itself the focus of a celebration—from art and music to ranching and history—and serve as a reason to break out the music and refreshments, and have some fun!

The events we've listed occur across the spectrum of Corpus Christi area communities and celebrate everything from the area's coastal industries to the presence of the U.S. Navy.

Besides the annual events listed in this chapter, you'll want to mark your calendars for monthly happenings at a wide-ranging list of locations. Some examples:

• A children's treasure hunt at the Corpus Christi Museum of Science and History is held every Saturday at 1:30 PM, and live animals are the focus of a program every Saturday at 11 AM. For more information call (361) 883-2862.

• Dive shows and fish feedings attract lots of visitors to the Texas State Aquarium in Corpus Christi. The shows are 10:30 AM and 2:30 PM daily in the Island of Steel Gallery, and 3:30 PM daily in the Outdoor Marsh Exhibit. For more information call (361) 881-1200.

• A waterfront art market in Corpus Christi is open to all artists and crafters, and is held 10 AM to 5 PM the first and third Monday of each month from March through December. Call (361) 880-3461 for further information.

• In the summer, free Sunday evening pops concerts and Thursday evening "Bay Jammin' Concerts" take place at Cole Park, along Ocean Drive in Corpus Christi. Call (361) 880-3100 for more information.

• Sailors and spectators can check out the Wednesday evening sailboat races at the Corpus Christi Marina. The races start at 5:30 PM and are visible from the T-head and L-heads along the bayfront.

• Monthly guided tours of the mine hunting vessels stationed at Naval Station Ingleside are available; check the local newspaper for times and dates. The base also offers a driving tour at 1:30 PM every Tuesday. For more information call (361) 776-4204.

• Over in Port Aransas, check out the shelling walks held at 9 AM on the fourth Friday of each month throughout the year. Or you can go on a guided bird tour, held at 9 AM every Wednesday at the Port Aransas Birding Center. For more information call (800) 45-COAST.

• In nearby Kingsville, you can take a tour of the city's beautiful and historic downtown buildings, including the beautiful Flato Opera House. Call (361) 592-6438 or (800) 333-5032 for more information.

Check the Friday "Weekend" section of the *Corpus Christi Caller-Times* for entertainment information about the upcoming weekend. Also, don't forget to review our Attractions chapter for information about other interesting sights to see.

There are always plenty of happenings at local bookstores, playhouses, and museums. Please check our Arts and Culture chapter for more information about these places and how to find out about ongoing or traveling exhibits, plays, or book readings.

We've listed admission fees when available and tried to give an approximate time of the month for each event. However, please check with organizers for the specifics on these events.

January

Sixth Annual Shallow Water Roundup and Seafood Bash
Port Aransas Civic Center and
Deep Sea Headquarters, Port Aransas
• **(361) 749-6339**

Hosted by the Port Aransas Boatmen, this two-day event includes a seafood dinner and a fishing tournament. The event, usually held in the middle of January, raises money for local youth scholarships. In the fishing tournament, there are prizes for biggest fish, smallest legal fish, mystery fish, and more. Registration is $35 for the fishing tournament, which includes admission to the dinner, and $15 for the dinner by itself.

Port Aransas Garden Club Tour
Various locations in Port Aransas
• **(361) 749-5919, (800) 452-6278**

Since 1994, this tour has allowed visitors and residents the opportunity to see the interiors of some of the grander homes in this island community. Usually held the last weekend in January or the first weekend in February, visitors can tour five homes that range from contemporary luxury to historic and traditional. Admission is $5 per person. Visitors can either

take an hour-and-a-half bus tour or drive themselves along the tour route. Proceeds are used for beautification projects in Port Aransas.

February

Stage Door Canteen
Lexington Museum on the Bay,
2914 N. Shoreline Blvd., Corpus Christi
• **(361) 888-4873, (800) LADY LEX**

This musical revue is modeled after the USO shows performed during World War II and now presented aboard this decommissioned aircraft carrier, which has been converted into a museum. The show, held in early February, includes plenty of Big Band-era music, dancing, and variety acts. Call for reservations and ticket prices.

A Celebration of Whooping Cranes and Other Birds
710 West Ave. A,
Port Aransas Civic Center, Port Aransas
• **(361) 749-5919, (800) 45-COAST**

Three days of workshops, seminars, birding tours, nature tours, and bird-related vendors honor the annual visit of a flock of whooping cranes to this coastal community. These elegant, endangered birds travel 2,500 miles to spend their winters on the Texas Coast. They arrive each October and stay through February or March. A record 159 birds wintered at the Aransas National Wildlife Refuge in 1996, and officials hope to see their numbers continue to increase each year. Naturalists and bird lovers from around the world come to study and monitor the population of these cranes, which are the largest birds native to North America.

The celebration is held during the latter part of February through the beginning of March. Admission to the exhibits is free; tours are $5 per person and seminars are $10.

See our Birding chapter for more about whooping cranes.

South Texas Ranching and Heritage Festival
Conner Museum, various sites at
Texas A&M University-Kingsville
• **(361) 592-8516, (800) 333-5032**

Ranch craftsmen, artisans, and storytellers demonstrate their skills during this three-day event held in honor of the city's ranching heritage. It's usually held at the end of February and is as educational as it is entertaining. Watch cowboys create leather goods for their ranch work, listen to ranchers recite poetry and enjoy a guitar serenade under the mesquite trees. There are booths, crafts, artwork, a chuck wagon cook-off, and even a ranch rodeo. Admission is free.

March

Fulton Oysterfest
Fulton Harbor on Fulton Beach Rd.,
Fulton Navigation Park, Fulton
• **(361) 729-2388, (800) 242-0071**

They say it was a brave person who ate the first raw oyster. Well, this festival is for those who pay homage to that courageous soul—an estimated 200,000 raw oysters will be consumed during this three-day salute to the delectable bivalve.

Sponsored by the Fulton Volunteer Fire Department, the event is held the first weekend in March and attracts an estimated 30,000 oyster lovers. Expect outdoor fun, games, entertainment, and activities that include oyster-shucking and oyster-eating contests. Last year's winners downed more than 200 raw oysters in five minutes!

There's also a carnival for kids and lots of arts and crafts booths that feature the talents of local artisans. Admission is $2.

Czech Heritage Festival
Bayfront Plaza Convention Center,
1901 N. Shoreline Blvd., Corpus Christi
• **(361) 882-9226, (361) 387-4391**

Investigate this area's Czech roots at this festival, which features arts and crafts, a country store, and lots of good Czech food.

San Patricio World Championship Rattlesnake Races
County fairground, Old San Patricio
• **(361) 547-6112**

At this annual event, snakehandlers are available to help the inexperienced with the racing rattlers. If that's not your speed, however, you can still enjoy the carnival, live music, and a taste of rattlesnake meat. Old San Patricio is located just about 30 miles northwest of Corpus Christi.

April

Buccaneer Days and Rodeo
Various locations in Corpus Christi
• **(361) 882-3242**

Celebrating the 1519 discovery of Corpus

Christi Bay, this festival begins each year with a group of "pirate queens" capturing the city's mayor and making him or her walk the plank. That good-humored dunking of the mayor in the bay waters represents the city's surrender to pirate rule for 11 days of entertainment and gaiety. A rodeo is held the week before Buc Days begins.

Other activities include an illuminated night parade through downtown to the bayfront, fireworks, music, sports events, an arts and crafts show, and a carnival. The festivities also include tournaments for tennis, golf, racquetball and archery, a bike ride, an airshow for radio-controlled craft, and a shoebox parade for youngsters (they build miniature floats out of shoeboxes). A music competition brings 5,000 to 6,000 students from high school bands and choirs to the city.

All the festivities are usually held the last week of April and the first week of May. Admission varies for the different events.

Folklife Festival
Multicultural Center,
1581 N. Chaparral St., Corpus Christi
• **(361) 883-0639**

Listen to music that has been passed from generation to generation, while enjoying traditional foods and viewing old-style arts and crafts. Admission is free.

Sand Sculptures
Port Aransas Beach, Port Aransas
• **(361) 749-4097, (800) 45-COAST**

This annual beach art event attracts sand sculptors from all over the world, who create their incredibly complex sculptures out of ordinary beach sand. Usually held on Easter weekend, this two-day event is free to the public. These sand artists also usually offer workshops to share their skills.

Rockport Homes Tour
Various locations in Rockport
• **(361) 729-5519**

Here's your opportunity to view the interior of four or five unique, fashionable, and lovely homes in the historic Rockport community. The tour, a fundraiser for the Rockport Center for the Arts, is held each spring. Admission is $10 per person.

Texas Cactus Festival
Various locations in Kingsville
• **(361) 592-8516, (800) 333-5032**

Taste the "prickly pear" (also known as cactus) in a variety of dishes that range from

Whooping Cranes

Avian visitors are always welcome in the Corpus Christi area, but few arrivals are more eagerly awaited than the flock of whooping cranes that has wintered here for decades.

These tall, elegant cranes are an endangered species. And the cranes that fly to the Aransas National Wildlife Refuge each fall are the world's only naturally occurring wild flock. That means that they reproduce in the wild, not in captivity, and it makes them objects of immense interest to scientists as well as birders.

With their cottony white plumage, black-tipped wings and red foreheads, whooping cranes are striking waterfowl. They are North America's largest birds, with adults standing at 5 feet tall with a wingspan of 7½ feet.

In 1996, a flock of 159 birds came from their nesting grounds in Canada to the Corpus Christi area—a flight of 2,500 miles and about 50 days. Officials estimate that there are only about 330 of the birds alive today, with half of them in captivity. The world's population of migrating whooping cranes fell to 14 or 16 in the 1940s. The whoopers that winter at Aransas National Wildlife Refuge, which was established in 1937, are the descendants of that flock.

For many in this coastal region, the arrival of the whoopers is one of the area's more thrilling fall rites. Rangers at the refuge count more than 80,000 registered visitors between November and March, from as far away as Canada and other foreign countries. Visitors can also see the cranes on boat tours that leave from Rockport, Fulton, and Port Aransas. Tours generally begin November 1 and continue through March. See our Birding chapter for phone numbers and prices.

In Port Aransas, officials celebrate the bird with a four-day festival that includes seminars, workshops, nature trips, demonstrations and food and crafts booths. It's held annually in late February and early March. See our Annual Events and Festivals chapter for more information.

(Continued on next page)

The endangered whopping cranes spend their winters at the Aransas National Wildlife Refuge north of Rockport.

Photo: courtesy of the Greater Corpus Christi Business Alliance

In Rockport, officials estimate that crane-seeking visitors spend approximately $5 million here each year.

The cranes are known for their size and also their trumpeting call, a distinctive and loud bugle-like sound that can be heard up to two miles away. And like all other cranes, the whooping crane symbolizes long life, fidelity, and happiness in many cultures.

One reason visitors so enjoy seeing the cranes is, of course, because the birds are so rare. They can also put on quite a show for their guests. The birds mate for life, and their life span is approximately 25 years in the wild or 40 years in captivity. They perform elaborate dances, bouncing up and down, flapping their wings, and bobbing their heads, to attract and keep their mates.

They dine on blue crabs while in Aransas and spend their winters on the marshlands at the refuge. They usually raise one chick per year, which has made their population growth painstakingly slow.

Humans have been the cause of the whooping cranes' demise. Development has meant the loss of breeding grounds and made the birds nearly extinct. In addition, the elusive birds and their eggs were prized by hunters.

Many experts believe that knowledge gained from the efforts to save the whoopers has benefited other endangered creatures, including six other species of cranes found around the world. Worldwide, there are 15 species of cranes, but only two are found in the United States: the endangered whooping cranes and the abundant sandhill crane, a smaller, gray crane.

Scientists who've been working to increase the cranes' numbers hope they can be downgraded from their current endangered status to the less-serious threatened status. To be put on the threatened list, there must be at least three self-sustaining wild flocks, with at least 40 nesting pairs in the Texas flock and 25 pairs in the non-migrating Florida flock, as well as an additional 25 pairs in a third flock expected to be started around the year 2000.

To help, officials have collected eggs from wild nests, raised the young in captivity to be released in new flocks and even led cranes on their cross-country migration in aircraft. But the greatest success in helping the cranes population grow has been in protecting the birds' natural habitat—such as the refuge along the Texas coastline.

entrees to beverages. Sponsored in mid-April by the King Ranch, the Kingsville Downtown Business Association, and the Texas Prickly Pear Council, this event sets its sights on promoting and informing folks about the lowly cactus and its many uses. Symposiums, cooking demonstrations, information about the medicinal properties of cactus, and research into cactus are scheduled.

Also, there is an annual wild-game luncheon that includes a trail ride, hay wagon ride, musical entertainment and activities for children. Arts and craft booths, games, and shopping are also offered.

Windfest
Various locations in Portland
• **(361) 643-2475**

Formerly known as Pioneer Days, this event celebrates the wind-tossed ambience of the coastal town of Portland. There is a carnival, arts and crafts, beauty pageant, 5K and 10K races, chili cook-off, and a jalapeno eating contest. The town of Portland is located just across the Corpus Christi Bay, about a 15-minute drive from Corpus Christi.

May

Ingleside Navy Days
Various locations in Ingleside
• **(361) 776-2906**

Ingleside Navy Days pays homage to the U.S. military presence that has revitalized this small town. Events include a beauty pageant, carnival, dance, entertainment, parade, 1-mile run, car show, games, and refreshments. Admission is free. The festival is usually held in mid-May.

Beach to Bay Relay Marathon
From Padre Island to
downtown Corpus Christi
• (361) 225-3338

Held on the third Saturday in May (Armed Forces Day), this popular relay marathon has gained a loyal and wide-ranging audience. Since its inception with two dozen teams in 1976, it has grown to include a field of thousands of runners from all over the state, nation, and Mexico. Each team of six runners must complete a marathon-length course (26.2 miles), with each of the six runners logging approximately 4.4 miles.

A total of 1,000 teams (or 6,000 runners) compete in the race each year. The course begins on Padre Island Beach at Nueces County Park and winds over the causeway, through the Naval Air Station and down Ocean Drive to Cole Park on Corpus Christi Bay. It concludes with a huge party at the park, where runners eat pizza and fruit, and drink soft drinks and beer while listening to live bands. Early registration is $120 per team.

U.S. Open Windsurfing Regatta, Corpus Christi
Oleander Point at South Cole Park on
Ocean Dr., Corpus Christi
• (361) 985-1555

Windsurfers and enthusiasts from around the world converge on the city for this annual event, usually held over the Memorial Day weekend. The four-day event, which was started in 1987, attracts windsurfers of national renown as well as spectators and amateurs. The city's bayfront location, with consistent southeast winds of 18 to 20 mph, has made it a premiere site for windsurfers. Winners can receive up to $70,000 worth of prizes during the weeklong competition. Other events include parties, music, and kite-flying.

Rockport Festival of Wines
Texas Maritime Museum,
1202 Navigation Cir., Rockport
• (361) 729-1271

Ten major Texas wineries participate in this festival launched in 1997. The affair offers samples of wine and specialty foods, plus participation by local restaurants and celebrity chefs. Local bands provide live entertainment. Proceeds benefit the Maritime Museum. Admission is $15 per person, and that includes a commemorative wine glass plus several tickets for wine tasting. You can purchase additional tickets separately.

Cinco de Mayo
Heritage Park, Corpus Christi
• (361) 883-0639

Cinco de Mayo marks the 1862 battle for Mexican independence and it is—obviously—a national holiday south of the border. But it's also a holiday dear to the hearts of many South Texans. In Corpus Christi, residents mark the

Each year, Corpus Christi hosts the Texas Jazz Festival—the only jazz festival in the nation still free to the public.

Photo: courtesy of the Greater Corpus Christi Business Alliance

event with mariachi music, ballet folklorico dancing, and plenty to eat and drink.

June

C-101 C-Sculptures
J.P. Luby Surf Park, Old Park Rd. 53, Mustang Island
• (361) 289-1000

Held annually on the second Saturday in June, this event is sponsored by local radio station KNCN-FM and was launched in 1977. It pays homage to the artistry, humor, and endurance needed to create massive sculptures out of beach sand.

As many as 110,000 people come to watch individuals and teams carve their impressive creations. These are nothing like the sandcastles you built as a kid: they can be as large as 20 square feet and require many hours of painstaking labor. Some entrants begin their work at midnight Friday, contest start time, and continue until judging time at 2 PM Saturday. One amazing recent entry was a beautifully detailed chameleon with its tongue stuck out to catch an unsuspecting fly.

Entry fees are $20 for the solo division and $25 per team. First-place winners get $1,000 for their efforts. The fun also includes live music, a volleyball contest, bikini contest, and bodybuilding contest. Proceeds benefit Texas Special Olympics.

July

Rockport Art Festival
Festival Grounds, Rockport Harbor, Rockport
• (361) 729-5519

This weekend around the Fourth of July is devoted to the display of beautiful, juried fine arts such as pottery, watercolor, acrylics, oils, woodcarving, and more. More than 100 booths set up in a colorful tent village on the festival grounds allow artists from throughout the Southwest to display and sell their works. The two-day event, sponsored by the Rockport Art Association, also offers food and music. Admission is $2. The festival grounds are on Texas Highway 35 Business.

INSIDERS' TIP

For an up-to-the-minute listing of monthly happenings through the Corpus Christi area, log on to the websites for the city's chambers of commerce or visitor's bureaus:
www.corpuschristi-tx-crb.org
www.portaransas.org
www. aransaspass.org
www.rockport-fulton.org
www.kingsville.org

Rockport Air Show
Rockport Beach Park, Rockport
• (361) 729-5519, (800) 242-0071

Aviation enthusiasts can spend the day at this annual event held on the Fourth of July. In the morning, there are static displays of aircraft ranging from modern planes to military jets to vintage aircraft. In the afternoon, there's a two-hour air show featuring aerial stunts, aerobatics, and military flyovers. There's no admission for the show, but there's a $3 parking fee to get on the beach. The park is on Texas Highway 35 Business.

Stars and Stripes
2914 N. Shoreline Blvd., Lexington Museum on the Bay, Corpus Christi
• (361) 888-4873

This Fourth of July event is held on the flight deck of this aircraft carrier-turned-museum and features a live performance by the Corpus Christi Symphony Orchestra. Musical selections include both popular and traditional patriotic music, and celebrated soprano Flicka Rahn performs as guest artist—a real treat. Dinner is served buffet style, and the evening ends with a fireworks display over the bayfront, choreographed to the symphony's music.

This is the museum's major annual fundraiser, and the ticket prices accurately reflect that. In previous years, admission has been $75 per couple, $45 per individual and $25 for ages 17 and younger. You can also purchase a table for 10 for $750. For current ticket prices, call the Lexington.

Deep Sea Roundup and Boat Show
Roberts Point Park and Civic Center, 710 W. Ave. A, Port Aransas
• (361) 749-6339

This fishing tournament, hosted by the Port Aransas Boatmen Association, lays claim as the oldest on the Texas coast. First held in 1932 as the Tarpon Rodeo, organizers changed the name when the tarpon ran out years later. Usually held the second weekend in July, champions receive substantial cash prizes and trophies for the largest fish caught in a number of categories.

The weekend's activities begin with registration and a cocktail party Thursday, fishing and a dinner Friday followed by more fishing, a

ANNUAL EVENTS AND FESTIVALS

dinner, and a dance Saturday. The event closes with a fish fry and awards ceremony on Sunday. Call for current entry fees.

August

The Miss Corpus Christi Area USA Pageant
Richardson Auditorium, Del Mar College, Baldwin and Ayers Sts., Corpus Christi
• (361) 985-1555

Teens and young women throughout the area vie to be crowned Miss Corpus Christi Area Teen USA and Miss Corpus Christi Area USA during this annual competition. Entrants participate in three categories—personal interview, swimsuit, and evening gown—for the chance to win up to $6,000 in cash and prizes. Winners represent the area in the Miss Texas Teen USA and the Miss Texas USA pageants. Tickets are $10 in advance and $12 at the door.

September

La Feria de las Flores
Downtown, Corpus Christi
• (361) 992-4209

Since 1959, La Feria de las Flores has celebrated the beauty and diversity of Hispanic traditions and crowned the community's young women with college scholarships in a spectacular pageant. Participants wear elaborate traditional costumes and perform regional Mexican dances that are breathtaking to watch. The young women also raise money by selling ads for the festival, providing additional scholarship funds for college-bound students. Since 1959, the council has awarded more than $817,000 in scholarship funding. Sponsored by the League of United Latin American Citizens Council No. 1, it is held the second Saturday in August. Admission is generally $5 to $10 per person.

Fiesta En La Playa
Rockport Festival Grounds, Rockport Beach, Rockport
• (361) 729-2063, (800) 242-0071

The Spanish name of this event translates literally to Festival on the Beach—and that suits

this event that celebrates the community's Hispanic heritage. Held on Labor Day weekend, this fiesta features folklorico dancers, mariachi bands, and piñata contests. If you dare, you can participate in the jalapeño-eating contest, the tamale-eating contest and the macho legs contest. Live music features local Tejano bands and country western music. Admission is $2.

Hummer/Bird Celebration
Various locations, Rockport
• (361) 729-6445, (800) 242-0071

Thousands of hummingbirds travel through this town during their fall migration, and this festival focuses on the vagaries and beauty of this fascinating bird. During the three-day festival, there are lectures, workshops, bus and boat field trips, and other programs, often presented by nationally renowned birding experts.

Although the hummingbird is the centerpiece here, there are also programs and trips to see many of the more than 500 other species of birds that can be found here including the whooping crane. It's held the second full weekend after Labor Day. Admission is $1.

Aransas Pass Shrimporee
Highway 361 at Johnson Ave., Aransas Pass Community Park, Aransas Pass
• (361) 758-2750, (800) 633-3028

Touted as "the biggest shrimp celebration in Texas," this event held in mid-September pays tribute to the small, succulent crustacean that this town's economy is based on. There are arts and crafts booths, a shrimp-eating competition, a men's sexy legs contest, a parade, a children's area, a carnival, and the Great Outhouse Race (which is exactly what it sounds like). And of course, there's lots of not-to-be-missed seafood—the full culinary range of shrimp—fried shrimp, shrimp gumbo, shrimp Creole, boiled shrimp, Cajun-style shrimp, etc., as well as standard festival fare of cotton candy, candy apples, and funnel cakes. Live entertainment usually includes Tejano music, country-and-western and even some rock 'n' roll. Other performers have included jugglers, comedians, and acrobats. Admission is $3 for adults, $1 for children and free for youngsters younger than six.

INSIDERS' TIP
While attending a festival, be sure to sample some of the South Texas taste treats offered—including funnel cakes, fried strips of dough sprinkled with powdered sugar—and chalupas, which are flat crisp corn tortillas heaped with refried beans, cheese, chopped tomato and lettuce, and jalapeño slices.

Bayfest
Shoreline Blvd. and the Bayfront
Arts and Sciences Park, Corpus Christi
• **(361) 887-0868**

This fall festival is aimed at families, offering every form of entertainment from carnival rides to arts and craft booths, fireworks, a parade, and a veritable smorgasbord of foods. Begun as a bicentennial celebration, this has become one of the major festivals in the area. And it's a boon for the local nonprofit groups, hundreds of which set up booths on the grounds and earn profits from the sale of everything from lemonade and ice cream to turkey legs and tacos. The children's area is especially worth visiting: it's got entertainment and hands-on creative games for the youngsters. Admission is $5.

Kleberg County Airshow
Kleberg County Airport, Texas Hwy. 141, Kingsville
• **(361) 595-8540, (800) 333-5032**

This festival, held every other year on a Saturday at the end of September, features a spectacular all-day air show with music, food, a carnival, dynamic air performances, and the "world's longest line dance" on the runway of the airport. Stunt pilots, naval aviators, vintage airplanes, and international performers are usually on hand. There's also a carnival, food booths, and refreshments. The day concludes with live music and dancing. The next one is scheduled for 1999. Admission is $7 per carload. The airport is west of Kingsville.

October

Rockport Seafair
Downtown and Rockport Harbor, Rockport
• **(361) 729-3312, (800) 242-0071**

Crab races, a seafood gumbo cookoff, a sailing regatta, and a children's fishing tournament are part of this annual Columbus Day festival's homage to the sea. One of the more fun events to watch is the "Anything that Floats But a Boat Race." The semi-seaworthy entries in this wacky race seem to pay homage as much to the creators' senses of humor as to their love of the water. We once saw something that looked like a floating outhouse make its way across the bay!

Expect an abundance of fresh seafood for sampling, including fresh shrimp and oysters. Other highlights include 5- and 10-kilometer runs, live entertainment, dancing, a parade, and a carnival. Admission is $2.

Violet Oktoberfest
Old St. Anthony's
Catholic Church and Museum,
U.S. Hwy. 44, Violet
• **(361) 387-4434**

The legacy of German settlers is recognized during this annual event, held the third Sunday in October at Old St. Anthony's Catholic Church and museum. Come see the classic cars on display and enjoy a barbecue beef dinner with beans, potato salad, coffee or tea, and dessert. For browsing, there's a country store that sells handcrafted arts and trinkets.

However, the real attraction for most visitors is a tour through the quaint old museum, which contains vintage farm equipment, cooking implements, and a display of turn-of-the-century priest's robes. The church, 5 miles west of Corpus Christi, dates back to 1910. There's no admission charge, but donations are requested. The barbecue dinner costs $6.

Texas Jazz Festival
Corpus Christi Bayfront, Corpus Christi
• **(361) 883-4500**

The longest running free festival in the country, this celebration of jazz was first held in 1958. Performers and fans from nationwide come to hear their favorite musicians play the sultry and glorious music of the jazz world. Audiences also are treated to blues, salsa, gospel, gunk, reggae, fusion, and swing music.

There's also an outdoor jazz Mass held on Sunday morning, informal cutting competitions held each evening, and a two-hour jazz cruise along the bayfront. Admission to the festival, concerts, and Mass is free, but there is a $15 charge for the cruise. This festival is usually held the fourth weekend in October.

> **INSIDERS' TIP**
> Buccaneer Days originated from a celebration first begun in 1917, known as Splash Days, which consisted of a bathing-beauty contest on the beach to signify the start of summer. The event was expanded and modified when residents felt the beauty contest lacked the necessary glamour for the growing city of Corpus Christi.

November

King Ranch Hand Breakfast
**King Ranch, Texas Hwy. 141 W.,
Kingsville**
• **(361) 592-3250**

Come see real cowboys lasso steers and pound horseshoes onto the hooves of their steeds during this widely attended event held in early November. This is a rare glimpse into the operation of the King Ranch, which is one of the world's largest working ranches. For the price of breakfast, you get served by a crew of cowboys and volunteers who ladle out scrambled eggs, biscuits, sausage, tortillas, refried beans, coffee, and orange juice. The event is outdoors, and visitors eat standing up or sitting on bales of hay around the show arena. Wear your cowboy boots and bring a hearty appetite. Admission is $5.

La Posada de Kingsville
Various locations downtown, Kingsville
• **(361) 592-3250, (361) 592-8516,
(800) 333-5032**

A series of events conducted from late November through mid-December commemorate the community's celebration of Christmas. A reenactment of *la posada*—the trip Mary and Joseph took as they searched for lodging on Christmas Eve in Bethlehem—is a high point of the celebration. Other events include a downtown lighting ceremony, caroling, breakfast with Santa Claus, a Jingle Bell Walk/Run, a tour of homes, and a parade. Admission is free.

Zachary Taylor Days
**730 S. Pearl St., Zachary Taylor Park,
Rockport**
• **(361) 729-6100, (800) 242-0071**

Sponsored by the Aransas County History Project and the Rockport-Fulton Area Chamber of Commerce, this three-day weekend focuses on Gen. Zachary Taylor's visit here more than 150 years ago during the war between the United States and Mexico.

Events scheduled include a reenactment of Taylor's arrival and his placement of the first American flag on Texas soil, a flyover of Navy planes, and recognition of local POW/MIAs. On a lighter note, residents wear period costumes and conduct other historical re-enactments, including an old-fashioned street fair with an auction of picnic baskets, a general store, pony rides, food booths, face painting, and children's games. Live music, a hand-cranked ice-cream contest, a beard and mustache contest and a pecan-pie bakeoff are other features. Admission is $1, and children younger than 12 are admitted free.

December

Sights and Sounds of the Season
**South Texas Institute for the Arts
1902 N. Shoreline Blvd., Corpus Christi**
• **(361) 980-3500**

During December, the museum hosts a delightful celebration of the holiday season that includes a nativity scene, a collection of art-inspired trees, and a 20-foot tree similar to the one in the Metropolitan Museum of Art. There are also special ornament and wreath displays, art workshops for children, and various choir performances. Suggested donation is $1 for adults, $.25 for children.

Harbor Lights Festival and Boat Parade
**Bayfront and various locations in
Corpus Christi**
• **(361) 985-1555**

The official lighting of the city's 75-foot-tall Christmas tree is the centerpiece of this annual yule celebration. Santa Claus arrives by boat, of course, and the boats along Shoreline Boulevard sport colorful lights for the occasion. In fact, the entire downtown area, from office buildings to the Harbor Bridge, wears Christmas lights, which gives the city a beautifully festive appearance for the season. Other activities include a children's parade down Shoreline, live entertainment, arts and crafts for the children, an illuminated boat parade through the bay waters, and fireworks. Admission is free.

The Arts

Artists have always drawn inspiration from nature, be they painters, sculptors or dancers. And in a coastal region, where climate and conviviality converge, artists have often found both a source of creativity and a welcome haven.

That's certainly true in the Corpus Christi area, which has a flourishing and diverse arts community that draws, paints, and shares its vision and creativity at dozens of area galleries and studios. And although your best bet for viewing the work of local artists is at the museums and art centers, you can also find plenty of illustration in your everyday travel through the region—from the bayfront sculptures along the waterfront in Corpus Christi to displays at area restaurants.

Corpus Christi is one of several major Texas cities to fund a public art program. Since its inception in 1987, 23 pieces of art have been installed in various locations throughout the city. Forms include pink granite sculptures, bronze sculptures, ceramic tile murals and oil paintings, depicting subjects that range from wildlife to history. The program commissions two to four pieces a year, paying $8,000 to $10,000 per piece. For information or locations of public art in Corpus Christi, call Pamela Gooby at the city's Park & Recreation Department, (361) 880-3461.

Our area boasts many renowned artists. Kent Ullberg is a sculptor whose larger-than-life statue of Jesus Christ adorns the entrance to the First United Methodist Church on Shoreline Boulevard. Jesus Bautista Moroles, a native Corpus Christi sculptor, is known for his work with large-scale granite figures. William Wilhelmi is a studio potter known worldwide. His work is featured in the Smithsonian Institution.

The Rockport region has attracted more than its share of fine artists, and the area has a healthy and active community of artists and studios.

The South Texas Institute for the Arts, which was designed by renowned architect Philip Johnson, presents a rotating schedule of diverse exhibitions and showcases works by local regional artists.

Photo: Daniel Fielder

Newcomers are welcome, and many studios offer lessons and classes for adults as well as children.

Theater productions and music, too, are available in the Coastal Bend. There is a fine symphony, as well as several university theaters and local playhouses. Increasingly, national productions have made their way down south to Corpus Christi—a welcome and long-awaited development for drama lovers. The Selena Auditorium often hosts traveling exhibits, including Broadway-based theater performances of *Joseph and the Amazing Technicolor Dreamcoat* and *Grease*.

To find out what's playing at local theaters or about upcoming exhibits, your best source is the *Corpus Christi Caller-Times*'s "Weekend" section in the Friday newspaper. The section provides up-to-date information about what's going on in the local and area community in the coming week, as well as later in the month. It also usually lists admission fees and telephone numbers to call for reservations.

Galleries

North Bay Area

Rockport

Little Gallery
• **Cactus and Fourth Sts., Fulton**
• **(361) 729-0246**

Artist and owner Chris Ely's gallery has been in this tree-shaded location for 23 years. She displays and sells her sketches and watercolors of local scenes and birds as well as other artists' sketches, paintings, and note cards. The gallery is open 1 to 4 PM daily except Wednesday.

Moroles Inc.
• **408 W. Sixth St., Rockport**
• **(361) 729-6747**

Nationally known sculptor Jesus Moroles works at a studio in Rockport, as well as at his newer exhibition center in New Mexico, to produce granite sculptures that adorn places as diverse as Houston and Albuquerque. Among his best-known pieces are: *Lapstrake,* a 64-ton, 22-foot sculpture for the E.F. Hutton, at CBS Plaza in New York City, across the street from the Museum of Modern Art; a 22-foot sculpture fountain for the Albuquerque Museum of Art in New Mexico; his largest single work, the

Houston Police Officers Memorial; and a sculpture plaza created for the Edwin A. Ulrich Museum in Wichita, Kansas.

Born in Corpus Christi, Moroles lives in Rockport. His studio is not open to the public. However, groups can arrange for tours by appointment. In 1996, Moroles also opened his Cerrillos Cultural Center, an exhibition, performance, and studio space in Cerrillos, New Mexico. His work has been featured in more than 200 publications, and Moroles lectures regularly about his work and the issue of public sculpture.

Estelle Stair Gallery
• **406 S. Austin St., Rockport**
• **(361) 729-2478**

This gallery, in a century-old downtown building, features oils, watercolor, and sculpture focused on the coast. Displays include carvings, exotic furniture, fountains, and jewelry. Art classes and workshops are available. The building itself has an old-fashioned, graceful feel, with high ceilings, wood floors and etched brick walls, as well as a garden in the back. It's open Tuesday through Sunday.

Po Po's Art Studio Inc.
• **1114 Main St., Rockport**
• **(361) 790-5104, (361) 790-3736**

This gallery and studio showcases the work of local artist Charles "Po Po" Cosby, as well as work by other artists. The collection of coastal and sporting artwork features shorebirds, lighthouses, hunting, fishing, and boating scenes. Classes are taught here, too. It's open 8 AM to 5 PM daily.

Simon Michael School and Gallery of Fine Art
• **510 E. King St., Rockport**
• **(361) 729-6233**

This was the first art gallery in the area when it was established in the 1950s. Longtime artist Simon Michael works in all media, including oils, acrylics, and watercolors, and features scenes and figure work from his worldwide travels. You can also view Remington and Russell bronzes (part of the artist's private collection) at this downtown gallery, which is open 9 AM to 4 PM daily.

Rockport Center for the Arts
• **902 Navigation Cir., Rockport**
• **(361) 729-5519**

The Rockport Art Association is housed in the 1890s Bruhl-O'Connor House, a blue and

THE ARTS

white Victorian-style building on the harbor. Created in 1967, the association was organized to promote work by local and regional artists, both professional and amateur. The building that houses the center was donated in 1983 and moved to the current site on the harbor. The center contains 5,000 square feet of gallery, classroom, lecture, and library space and counts more than 15,000 annual attendees at its events. Local artists' work is hung in the gallery on a rotating basis, and classes for adults and children are available.

The Rockport Art Association, which operates this center, sponsors an annual Art Festival each July (see our Annual Events chapter). The center provides tours, classes, and in-school workshops for more than 800 Coastal Bend children each year.

Among the better-known professional members of the association are Al Barnes, Herb Booth, John P. Cowan, Jesus Bautista Moroles, Harold Phenix, Steven Russell, E.M. "Buck" Schiwetz and Kent Ullberg.

Admission is free. The center is closed on Monday.

Portland

Dinah Bowman Studio and Gallery
• 312 Fifth Ave., Portland
• (361) 643-4922

Local artist Dinah Bowman is best known for her fish prints, which are meticulous prints of fishes on canvas as well as on T-shirts. She's also an expert at capturing the beauty and detail of other aspects of maritime life. Her gallery also displays work by other artists, mostly with coastal and marine life themes. You can also have framing done here. It's open 9:30 AM to 5:30 PM Monday through Friday, and 9 AM to 3 PM Saturday.

Ingleside

Golden Triangle
Art Association and Gallery
• Texas Hwy. 361, Ingleside
• (361) 776-7583

This art gallery was established in early 1997 and is housed in a historic city building deco-

rated with the official city bird, the blue heron. A nonprofit association, the Golden Triangle offers exhibits and lessons. It's open 10 AM to 4 PM Tuesday through Saturday and features the work of local artists in a variety of media, including oil, acrylic and pottery.

Corpus Christi

Art Center of Corpus Christi
• 100 Shoreline Blvd., Corpus Christi
• (361) 884-6406

In this lemon-ice colored building, on the median of Shoreline Boulevard, you will find exhibits that change monthly and a delightful tearoom, Jezebelles (see our Restaurants chapter). Chartered in 1972, the Art Center is committed to the promotion of local and area art and art education. Its membership includes approximately 600 working artists of all ages and skill levels, as well as a number of art patrons. Exhibit and work space for members is available for members, and free exhibits allow the community to view and enjoy the artwork.

The rotating exhibits display the work of individuals as well as 11 member groups from throughout the area. More than 5,000 visitors signed the guest register during 1997. The center also has classes, workshops, demonstrations, and gift shops. It's open Tuesday through Sunday.

Corpus Christi Art Connection
• 3636 S. Alameda Ave., Taylor Center, Corpus Christi
• (361) 854-1057

This gallery features works from local as well as national and international artists. You'll find original artwork and limited-edition prints by varied artists such as Kent Ullberg, Herb Booth, Doug Dawson, Guy Harvey, Lars Johnson, Mike Stidham, Tina Close, John Dearman, Lee Holt, Robert Moore, and Nico van de Linde. The gallery is open weekdays and by appointment on weekends.

Earth Works Pottery
• 15851 F.M. Rd. 624, Robstown
• (361) 387-6462

John and Barbara Wisnewski have been pot-

INSIDERS' TIP

Outdoor productions at the Port Aransas Community Theater are fun to attend, but remember that it can be quite warm—even after dark—in the summertime. Dress accordingly.

THE ARTS

ters since 1967, creating distinctive pieces with clean lines and soft pastel glazes. In addition to pottery, their showroom features original work by other artists, including paintings, handmade dolls, cutting boards, jewelry, and weavings. The 10,000-square-foot studio and gallery, west of Corpus Christi, is open Monday through Saturday or by appointment.

Guy Morrow Art Studio
- **817 Airline Rd., Corpus Christi**
- **(361) 992-2204**

Artist Guy Morrow, best known for his work in egg tempera, showcases his own works at this studio. Morrow, who grew up in Corpus Christi, specializes in private commissions. Art enthusiasts in the United States, Mexico, and Austria collect his works. His studio is open Monday through Friday.

Joseph A. Cain Memorial Art Gallery
- **Del Mar College Fine Arts Center, Baldwin and Ayers Sts., Corpus Christi**
- **(361) 886-1216**

This college gallery hosts visits from major artists such as Jesus Bautista Moroles, James Surles, Peter Selz, Ivan Karp, Luis Jimenez, Fritz Scholder, Marisol, Peter Saul, and Melisa Miller. In spring, the gallery holds an annual National Drawing and Small Sculpture Show and hosts a Tri-Group Exhibition by the South Texas Art League. In summer, selections from the Del Mar College Art Department permanent collection are on display.

Oliver's Village Gallery
- **3847 S. Alameda St., Corpus Christi**
- **(361) 855-0911**

Opened in 1977, this family-owned gallery features paintings and graphics from international and national artists and from prominent galleries such as Meredith Long Gallery in Houston; Gallerie De Tours in Carmel, California; and Wally Findlay Galleries in New York, Paris, Chicago, Los Angeles, and Palm Beach. The gallery specializes in stone lithographs, serigraphs, mezzotints, aquatints, etchings, limited-edition prints, woodcarvings, art glass, and bronze sculptures.

Ullberg Studios Inc.
- **3636 S. Alameda St., Corpus Christi**
- **(361) 851-1600**

World-renowned wildlife sculptor Kent Ullberg, a native of Sweden, works here in Corpus Christi. Ullberg is perhaps best known for the more than two dozen large-scale works he has done for museums and municipalities from Washington, D.C., to South Africa. A recent project was the largest bronze casting ever attempted, 36 feet high and 120 feet long, that captures the stages of a sailfish leaping from the water.

Ullberg has received numerous awards, and his work can be found in the private collection of H.R.H. Prince Berhard of the Netherlands as well as in countless museums and corporations worldwide.

In Corpus Christi, his "It is I" statue of Jesus

THE ARTS

Corpus Christi's Bayfront Arts and Sciences Park includes the South Texas Institute for the Arts, Selena Auditorium, Bayfront Convention Center, and Harbor Playhouse.

Photo: courtesy of the Greater Corpus Christi Business Alliance

Christ with arms outstretched toward the bayfront adorns the front entrance of the First United Methodist Church on Shoreline Boulevard (see our Close-up in the Worship chapter).

Weil Gallery
• Center for the Arts,
Texas A&M University Corpus Christi,
6300 Ocean Dr., Corpus Christi
• (361) 994-2314

This university gallery features traveling exhibits of paintings, drawings, and pottery. Weil Gallery is open daily when the university is in session.

Wilhelmi-Holland Gallery
• 300 S. Chaparral St., Corpus Christi
• (361) 882-3523

This gallery showcases the work of well-known Corpus Christi potter William Wilhelmi, who is known for his intricate and ornate pottery. It also features artwork and ceramics by a variety of local artists. Ben Holland is gallery director for this downtown studio. Wilhelmi, who came to Corpus Christi in 1969, is known for his landscapes of eucalyptus trees, sunsets, cows and cacti, calla lilies, and geometric designs on stoneware. Also popular are his so-called "little monsters," eccentric clay creatures that reflect a baroque style and offbeat wit. Wilhelmi's now-famous porcelain cowboy boots are permanently housed at the Renwick Gallery of the National Museum of Art of the Smithsonian Institution in Washington, D.C.

Port Aransas to Padre Island

Gary Osborne Fine Art
• 345 N. Alister St., Port Aransas
• (361) 749-6982

This studio offers a wide-ranging collection

Mexican-American culture—dance, music, and art—plays a large role in the social climate of South Texas.

Photo: courtesy of the Greater Corpus Christi Business Alliance

THE ARTS

of art including original works by nationally known artists such as Kent Ullberg, Dalhart Windberg, Raul Gutierrez, Joe Russell, Arlene Morgan, Stephanie Wooley and Sherridan M. "Sam" Smith. In addition to featuring original artwork, this gallery also offers framing services and sells handpainted furniture.

Art Center for the Islands
- **309 N. Alister St., Port Aransas**
- **(361) 749-7334**

This nonprofit art center for Mustang and Padre Islands is under the auspices of the Island Art Association, created to promote art activities and education. The center, which is staffed by volunteers, features exhibits by Coastal Bend artists as well as guest artists and students. It also houses a working studio and classroom, workspace and a gathering area for artists and students. Classes offered include painting, pottery, sculpture, writing, and music. The center, in the city's old pharmacy building near Pelican's Landing restaurant, is open daily.

Kingsville Area

Ben Bailey Art Gallery
- **Texas A&M University-Kingsville, University Blvd., Kingsville**
- **(361) 593-2619**

This university art gallery is open daily when the university is in session and features traveling exhibits as well as student art. The exhibits change regularly and admission is free.

Seller's Market
- **205 E. Kleberg Ave., Kingsville**
- **(361) 595-4992**

This downtown art center features paintings, crafts, jewelry, home-baked goods, quilts, prints, and clothing. Housed in a renovated century-old building, Seller's Market is open Tuesday through Saturday.

Museums

North Bay Area

Texas Maritime Museum
- **Rockport Harbor, Rockport**
- **(361) 729-1271**

Devoted to maritime objects, lore and artwork, this museum is worth a visit for all those who enjoy the sea. Recently, a spectacular traveling exhibit featured a collection of maritime

art from the Cigna Museum and Art Collection of Philadelphia, including paintings and other artwork of shipwrecks, epic storms, and flames at sea. The museum is open Tuesday through Sunday. Admission is $4 for adults and teens and $2 for children ages 5 to 12. Children ages 4 and younger get in free.

Corpus Christi

Asian Cultures Museum & Educational Center
- **1809 N. Chaparral St., Corpus Christi**
- **(361) 882-2641**

This fine museum contains a comprehensive collection of Japanese and other Oriental art, collectibles, and dioramas. Exhibits rotate periodically. The center is open 10 AM to 5 PM Tuesday through Saturday. There is no admission, but donations are welcome.

South Texas Institute for the Arts
- **1902 N. Shoreline Blvd., Corpus Christi**
- **(361) 980-3500**

Even though the building is a work of art, by renowned New York architect Philip Johnson. Its lean lines blend gracefully with the coastal landscape. Inside you'll find traveling exhibits of painting, sculpture, photography, and folkart. The permanent collection of photographs includes works by Ansel Adams and Victoria Livingston.

The South Texas Institute for the Arts, formerly the Art Museum of South Texas, is open Tuesday, Wednesday, Friday, and Saturday from 10 AM to 5 PM, Thursday from 10 AM to 9 PM, and Sunday from 1 to 5 PM. The museum is closed on Monday. There is no admission, but donations are welcome.

Kingsville

John E. Conner Museum
- **Texas A&M University-Kingsville, 700 University Blvd., Kingsville**
- **(361) 595-2819**

The exhibits in this museum, established in 1925, are designed to preserve the social and natural history of the area. Displays include those about the ecosystem and geosciences and lifelike dioramas. The collection spans eras from pre-Columbian through the 1980s, featuring artifacts from machinery and art to arrowheads and deer antlers. One of the more intriguing exhibits is that of a Colombian woolly mammoth approximately 13,000 years old that was

THE ARTS

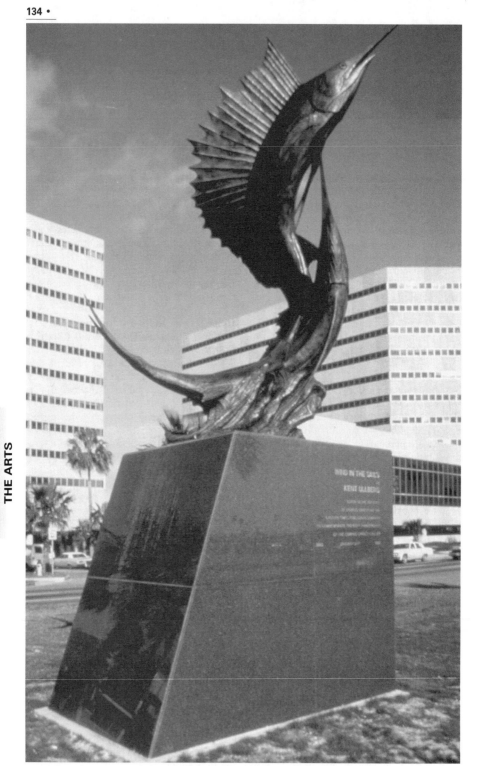

Stunning works by sculptor Kent Ulberg line Shoreline Drive in downtown Corpus Christi.

Photo: courtesy of the Greater Corpus Christi Business Alliance

excavated a mere 40 miles from the university campus. The museum is open weekday afternoons and by appointment. Admission is free.

King Ranch Museum
- **405 N. Sixth St., Kingsville**
- **(361) 595-1881**

This cowboy-themed museum near downtown contains a permanent exhibit of ranching and cattle-related items from the archives of the massive King Ranch, which is considered the birthplace of the American ranching tradition. The museum also hosts traveling exhibits such as a recent collection of photographs of Texas cowboys by David Stoecklein. It's open 10 AM to 4 PM Monday through Saturday, and 1 to 5 PM Sunday. Admission is $4 for adults; $2.50 for children ages 5 to 12; and free for children younger than 12.

Music

Corpus Christi Symphony Orchestra
- **1901 N. Shoreline Blvd., Corpus Christi**
- **(361) 882-4091,**
  (361) 883-6683 for tickets

World-class conductor Cornelius Eberhardt directs this symphony, a select group of almost 100 musicians. Its concert selections range from classics by Mozart, Haydn, and Beethoven, to modern masterpieces by Ibert, Stravinsky, and Prokofiev. During its 52-year history, internationally renowned guest artists such as Felipe Entremont, Van Cliburn, Helen Donath, Itzhak Perlman, and Leonard Rose have performed with the symphony. Other guest appearances have featured The Canadian Brass, The Romeros, Danny Wright, and the national tour production of Gilbert and Sullivan's *The Mikado*.

The symphony performs at annual events such as Bayfest and the Fourth of July celebration aboard the Lexington Museum on the Bay (see our Annual Events chapter).

Recent performances have included The Smothers Brothers, Prokofiev's *Alexander Nevsky*, *Bugs Bunny on Broadway*, the Corpus Christi Youth Symphony and the Side By Side Symphonic Spectacular featuring winners of the Corpus Christi and Kingsville International Young Artists Competition.

Cathedral Concert Series
- **Corpus Christi Cathedral,**
  505 N. Upper Broadway, Corpus Christi
- **(361) 888-6520**

With a half-dozen performances a year, this series is designed to offer high-quality cultural presentations for Coastal Bend residents at no charge. Since 1984, the series has featured diverse ensembles including the Vienna Boys Choir, the Roger Wagner Chorale, the King Singers, The Romeros, and the Academy of St. Martin-in-the-Fields Chamber Ensemble. Most of the performances are in the historic Cathedral, on the bluff in the heart of downtown Corpus Christi—a church with a wonderful acoustic temperament.

Funding for the performances is provided through corporate and private donations. More than 72,000 people have attended the series during the past decade. Recent performances have featured diverse artists such as Crystal Gayle, the Tommy Dorsey Orchestra, the London Brass and the Texas Boys Choir.

The Fryderyk Chopin Society of Texas
- **4610 Abner Dr., Corpus Christi**
- **(361) 853-6771**

Organized in 1989, this organization consists of people who love the music of Chopin and other keyboard composers. It sponsors annual performances by guest artists such as the Russian trio, Jazz de Moscou; Calogero De Liberto of Italy; and Tadashi Imai of Japan.

Wolfe Recital Hall
- **Del Mar College, Baldwin and Ayers Sts.,**
  Corpus Christi
- **(361) 886-1214**

The college's orchestra, concert choir, chamber music society, and theater singers use this college recital hall. It also is the setting for programs by guest artists. The college performances are free and guest artist performances cost $1.

Theater

Port Aransas to Padre Island

Port Aransas Community Theater
- **(361) 749-6036, (361) 749-5340**

Established in 1990, this theater group produces a variety of shows. Recent productions include *Sylvia* and *A Night at the Theatre*. The outdoor stage, at the corner of Alister and White streets, begins its season with a spring cabaret show and continues with productions through August. During the winter, the productions are held indoors at various restaurants and community centers. Productions have included *The Taming of the Shrew*, *Peter Pan*, *Greater Tuna*, *On*

THE ARTS

Golden Pond, Mousetrap, Little Shop of Horrors, The Gin Game, The Lion in Winter, Nunsense, and *The Odd Couple.* The group also hosts a Halloween haunted house and a summer children's play.

Corpus Christi

Neil Tribble Bartlett Theatre
• **Del Mar College, Baldwin and Ayers Sts., Corpus Christi**
• **(361) 886-1509**

In the college's Fine Arts Center, this theater has an annual Shakespeare festival in the summer and a Mime Plus One-Acts each spring. Recent productions included *Macbeth, The Musical Comedy Murders of 1940, Reckless,* and *Sophomore Showcase.* Tickets are $4 for general admission; $3 for senior citizens, faculty and staff; and $1 for students. The Shakespeare Fest tickets are $5.

Harbor Playhouse
• **1 Bayfront Park, Corpus Christi**
• **(361) 888-7469 box office,**
  (361) 882-5900 business office

Harbor Playhouse is the oldest and most popular venue for theater in Corpus Christi, hosting a variety of plays that range from adult to children's fare. The playhouse traces its history back to February 12, 1925, when a group recruited by a newspaper ad did a single performance of Booth Tarkington's *Seventeen* at the old high school on Carancahua Street. Calling itself the Corpus Christi Players, the group averaged four plays a year until the Great Depression; it incorporated as Little Theatre Corpus Christi in 1948 and opened a building on Alameda Street. In 1972, the current theater was built by the city at Bayfront Plaza, near the city's museums, convention center, and auditorium. The organization has a mailing list of 12,000 patrons. More than 40,000 subscribers, individual ticket buyers, and tourists see productions each year.

The playhouse has a main stage season of six productions, including three musicals and a variety of both modern and classic comedies and dramas. There is also a summer musical, a one-month miniseason of summer melodramas, and a Young People's Theatre program for children ages 5 to 18.

Tickets are $14 for main stage musicals and

$8 for non-musicals. Reservations are recommended.

Richardson Auditorium
• **Del Mar College, Baldwin and Ayers Sts., Corpus Christi**
• **(361) 886-1355**

This college auditorium is used for a number of community events, including the Buccaneer Classics Music Festival each April and the Corpus Christi Concert Ballet's production of *The Nutcracker* each December. In addition, the college hosts the Driscoll Foundation/Dr. McIver Furman Del Mar Lectureship in the Health Sciences in February, the International Corpus Christi Young Artists' Competition in February, and the Del Mar Jazz Band Concert in the spring.

Recent performances included a reading by novelist and poet Ana Castillo, and a one-act show, *The Witty World of Will Rogers,* a theatrical performance by Gene McFall.

Warren Theater
• **Texas A&M University-Corpus Christi, 6300 Ocean Dr., Corpus Christi**
• **(361) 994-5800 box office**

You can see drama, opera, musicians, and musicals at this university theater. In recent years, featured performers during the Distinguished Visitors in the Arts Series have included pianist Gayle Martin Henry, the Haydn Trio Vienna, cello and piano duo Joanne Kong and James Wilson, and pianist Berenice Lipson-Gruzen.

Productions are also presented at the Wilson Studio Theatre. In 1997, the university produced *Jesus Christ Superstar* and *The Passionate Puccini* as well as Neil Simon's *Rumors.*

Kingsville

Jones Auditorium and Little Theatre
• **Texas A&M University-Kingsville, 700 University Blvd., Kingsville**
• **(361) 593-3401**

The university's theater arts and communications department regularly presents productions that range from Shakespearean drama to modern farces. Recent productions have included *The Lady from Havana, Sorority Sisters from Hell, King Henry IV, The Dream of Don Juan*

> **INSIDERS' TIP**
>
> The Asian Cultures Museum in Corpus Christi is one of only five Asian culture museums in the United States.

Gaspar, Aladdin, Day of Absence, Confessions of Women from East L.A., and *Charley's Aunt.* Admission is $3 per person.

Dance

Corpus Christi

Ballet Nacional
- **4411 Gollihar Rd., Corpus Christi**
- **(361) 854-6528**

Founded in 1983, this dance company's goal is to promote and preserve the Latin cultural heritage through music and dance. Under the guidance of artistic director Ricardo Villa, the company of 45 men and women stage two annual productions, including an elaborate and formal show known as *Noche de Gala* each winter, and a more lighthearted show in the summer called *Summer Salsa*.

The winter show in 1998, held in February at the Selena Auditorium, ran the musical gamut from Beethoven's Fifth Symphony to a scene from the Broadway hit *Miss Saigon,* and included Ravel's *Bolero* and a Tejano rendition of *Charanga.* Guest artists were Efrain Guerrero and mariachi vocalist Mari McLean. Tickets are priced from $6 to $12. The dance group celebrated its 15th anniversary in 1998.

Corpus Christi Ballet
- **5610 Everhart Rd., Corpus Christi**
- **(361) 991-8521**

Founded in 1974, the Corpus Christi Ballet's first season included *Peter and the Wolf* and *The Nutcracker.* It continues to perform *The Nutcracker* as an annual Christmas production, in addition to numerous other works.

In 1991, Mikhail Baryshnikov's White Oak Project came to Corpus Christi. Other guests companies that have performed here include the Fort Worth Ballet, Stars of the American Ballet, Ballet Stars of Moscow, the Jose Limon Dance Company and the Houston Ballet.

The 1997 season featured performances by the St. Petersburg Ballet, four performances of *The Nutcracker* and two performances of *Cinderella*.

The ballet has also played host to international stars including Damian Woetzel of the New York City Ballet; Paloma Herrera, Guillaume Graffin and Julie Kent of the American Ballet Theatre; and Carlos Acosta and Tiekka Scoffield from the Houston Ballet. The ballet also has an educational outreach program that includes special performances for young children and lectures/demonstrations on school campuses.

Corpus Christi Concert Ballet
- **3441 S. Alameda St., Corpus Christi**
- **(361) 854-7969**

This 20-member ballet company, under the direction of Nancy Sulik, performs several productions a year. In a recent season, its classical and contemporary ballet productions included *The Nutcracker, Tales of Hans Christian Anderson* and *Tea and Tales*.

As a member group of the Student Performing Arts Series, the company also produces the dance segment each year for 8,000 area students, who attend the educational ballet matinees of *The Nutcracker* and a selected spring gala, both of which feature professional artists.

Shows are designed to stimulate student interest in the performing arts and different styles of dance, performed by company members. The ballet company is supported by the Concert Ballet Guild, a volunteer organization that promotes and publicizes the company's activities

THE ARTS

Parks

Residents of the Corpus Christi area are fortunate to have two national natural areas within reasonable driving distance. The Padre Island National Seashore is a few miles south of Corpus Christi, while the Aransas National Wildlife Refuge—winter home to the endangered whooping crane—lies 35 miles north of Rockport. Both parks give visitors a good look at what coastal Texas looked like before Spanish and American settlers began pouring into the area, and the variety of birds and plant life is unique to this part of the country.

The Corpus Christi area, known officially as the Texas Coastal Bend, also is home to several state, county, and municipal parks. The following is a list of many of the better parks in the area.

North Bay Area

Aransas
National Wildlife Refuge
F.M. Rd. 2040, Austwell
- **(361) 286-3559**

The endangered whooping crane is the star of this 115,000-acre wildlife refuge 35 miles north of Rockport. These shy birds, which make the refuge's saltwater marshes their winter feeding grounds, have made a comeback since their numbers dwindled to as few as 15 in 1941. Much of that success is due to the creation of the refuge in 1937 to protect the vanishing wildlife of coastal Texas. For more information about the whooping cranes, see our Birding chapter.

But there's more to the refuge than whooping cranes. This remote refuge on Blackjack Peninsula (named for its blackjack oaks) also is home to alligator, deer, javelina, coyote, bobcat, raccoon, and feral hogs (see The Natural World chapter for more about these creatures). Grasslands made up of bluestem and other prairie grasses, live oaks, and redbay thickets cover deep sandy soils ringed by tidal marshes and broken by long, narrow ponds.

Thousands of migratory birds are attracted to the refuge's brackish tidal marshes on their journey between North America and Central America. Birders have spotted as many as 392 species at the refuge, including pelicans, herons, egrets, spoonbills, shorebirds, ducks, and geese. Warblers are abundant from mid-April to early May (see our Birding chapter). Freshwater ponds farther inland are home to alligators, turtles, frogs, snakes, and birds.

The refuge is open between sunrise and sunset; public camping is not allowed. All visitors must register daily. Public facilities include a 16-mile paved tour road, Wildlife Interpretive Center, 40-foot observation tower, several miles of walking trails and a picnic area.

Food and fuel are not available on the refuge. Bring mosquito repellent, watch for poisonous snakes and keep an eye out for wildlife on the roads. Pets must be on a leash at all times.

The Wildlife Interpretive Center is open daily from 8:30 AM to 4:30 PM. The entrance fee is $5 per carload or $3 if you're visiting the refuge alone. The refuge is 7 miles south of Austwell.

Goose Island State Park
Texas Hwy. 361,
off Texas Hwy. 35, Lamar
- **(361) 729-2858**

This 314-acre state park is at the conjunction of the Aransas,

Copano, and St. Charles Bays about 10 miles north of Rockport. It's a pleasing mix of shoreline and woodlands with camping facilities (127 sites) available in both areas (see our Campgrounds and RV Parks chapter). The park stretches inland from the bayfront to thickets made up of brush and live oak and mesquite trees.

The park is known for "Big Tree," the largest coastal live oak tree in the state (see our Attractions chapter). Anglers will love the fishing opportunities. Cast for speckled trout, redfish, drum, flounder, and sheepshead from your boat or from the park's 1,620-foot fishing pier. The park also is a good site for crabbing and oystering.

Water birds, waterfowl, shore birds, and passerines (birds that perch) are common at the park.

Campsites have picnic tables, barbecue grills, and water. Most sites come with electricity, except for 25 sites on the mainland. Park amenities include group facilities, a recreation hall, youth group area, a short, paved hike-and-bike path, two playgrounds, and a two-lane boat ramp with loading dock.

Bring insect repellent and firewood. Canvas shoes are recommended for bayfront activities. Reservations are recommended and can be made as much as one year in advance. Expect to pay an entry fee of $2 per person per day for anyone 13 or older.

The park office is open from 8 AM to 5 PM every day. The gate leading into the park is open from 6 AM to 10 PM.

Rockport Beach Park
210 Seabreeze Dr., Rockport
• (361) 729-9392

The 61-acre Rockport Beach Park near the city's downtown came into being in the 1950s when the Aransas County Navigation District No. 1 dredged the adjacent Little Bay (now a bird sanctuary) and placed the material on a sandbar jutting out into Aransas Bay.

In 1988 the city developed the park for day use and began charging an entrance fee. Facilities include two pavilions with upstairs verandas, restrooms and party rooms, playground equipment for both older and younger children, a band shell, an 800-foot fishing pier, a lighted fishing jetty (open 24 hours a day), and a walking trail. The park has a four-lane boat ramp, a separate launch for sailboats and catamarans, and watersport rentals (see our Beaches and Watersports chapter). Other amenities include a saltwater pool with concrete bulkhead, 75 picnic tables with covered cabanas, barbecue

pits, volleyball courts, and handicapped-accessible picnic cabanas and water fountains.

The park's mile-long beach is a great place for children to swim. There are no undertows, high tides, or rough waves, and the water is shallow for about a quarter-mile from shore.

The park is open from 5 AM to 11 PM Sunday through Thursday and 5 AM to midnight on Friday and Saturday. Admission is $3 per vehicle per day after 12:30 p.m. or $7 for a one-year pass.

Aransas Pass Community Park
Johnson Avenue,
two blocks east of Texas Hwy. 361,
Aransas Pass
• (361) 758-3111, (361) 758-2750

This park, established in 1993, serves as the site for Aransas Pass's annual Shrimporee Festival to celebrate the city's ties to the shrimping industry (see our Annual Events and Festivals chapter). It's also home to the Aransas Pass Little League and hosts softball tournaments and soccer matches.

Located near two saltwater ponds, the park features a pavilion, covered picnic tables, barbecue grills, restrooms, playground equipment for both little tykes and older children, and playports with stairs, slides, and tunnels. Concession stands are open when Little League teams are playing or when a softball tournament is under way.

Located on The Great Texas Coastal Birding Trail, the park also is home to 450 feet of recently constructed boardwalk, two observation platforms overlooking ponds and 260 feet of paved walkway.

Admission is free. The park is open from 8 AM to 9 PM every day.

Live Oak Park
East of F.M. Rd. 1069, Ingleside
• (361) 776-2517

This park's major claims to fame are the live oak trees for which the park is named and the 18-hole disc golf course, one of only two in the Corpus Christi area. (The other course is in West Guth Park in Corpus Christi.) Disc golfers use flying discs instead of golf balls and aim at baskets instead of holes. Locals enjoy the park's picnic tables, barbecue pits, playground equipment, three tennis courts, basketball court, baseball field and small lake with a hike-and-bike trail around it. Plans are under way to add a sand volleyball court.

Live Oak Park, which became an official city park in 1995, is included on The Great Texas Coastal Birding Trail (see our Birding chapter).

PARKS

Admission is free. The park is open 24 hours a day. Portions of the park can be reserved. Alcohol is allowed by permit only. Farm-to-Market Road 1069 is just 2 miles south of Texas Highway 361.

Portland Municipal Park
Lane Rd. and Memorial Pkwy., Portland
• (361) 777-3301

Locals refer to this park as "13-acre park" even though it now covers more than 21 acres on Portland's north side. You'll find wide-open spaces at this community park, with a mostly flat landscape and mesquite trees throughout.

Facilities include an amphitheater, three sets of restrooms, two lighted tennis courts, a basketball court, two baseball fields, playground equipment, and a group pavilion with electricity and a barbecue pit that's available for rent.

The park is open from 6 AM to 11 PM Sunday through Thursday and from 6 AM to midnight on Friday and Saturday. Admission is free.

Corpus Christi

Cole Park
1500 block of Ocean Dr., Corpus Christi
• (361) 880-3461

You can't beat the view from this 43-acre park on the Corpus Christi bayfront. Developed in 1969, this park sits at the bottom of a steep hill sloping down from the city's scenic thoroughfare known as Ocean Drive. Look east and you're confronted with the beauty and grandeur of Corpus Christi Bay; turn west and admire the beautiful homes. Look north and you'll see the city skyline, the Harbor Bridge, and the Nueces Bay Causeway in the distance.

Cole Park is a popular attraction for people from all over the city. No other city park comes close to matching this one for beauty and fun activities for children. The main attraction for the little ones is KidsPlace, an 18,000-square-foot wooden play area (see our Kidstuff chapter). Cole Park also is a great place to fly a kite or hold a barbecue.

The Cole Park Amphitheater is the site of the city's annual Thursday Night Concert Series. The music offered is an eclectic mix ranging from jazz, reggae and rock, to blues and Texas folk and country.

The southern portion of the park, known by many locals as Oleander Point, is the site of the annual U.S. Open Sailboarding Regatta (see our Annual Events and Festivals chapter and the Spectator Sports chapter).

Admission is free. The park is open from sunrise to sunset.

West Guth Park
On Up River Rd.,
north of Rand Morgan Rd., Corpus Christi
• (361) 880-3461

This 80-acre park on the city's northwest side has two things you won't find in most other parks: hills and a disc golf course. The Corpus Christi area is mostly flat, so when you find a hilly spot it's a nice change of pace.

West Guth also is home to an 18-hole disc golf course. Disc golfers use flying discs instead of golf balls and aim at baskets instead of holes.

West Guth also has a swimming pool, senior center, duck pond, jogging trail, group pavilion, playground equipment, and restrooms. Turkey Creek runs through the property. Admission is free. The park is open from sunrise to sunset.

To get here take Interstate Highway 37 north to the Rand Morgan Exit. Turn left, go under the interstate and turn right on Up River Road. The park will be on your left.

Hazel Bazemore County Park
F.M. Rd. 624, Corpus Christi
• (361) 949-8122

This 77-acre park just outside the Corpus Christi city limit is a haven for bird watchers, especially hawk watchers (see our Birding chapter). Every year thousands of hawks roost in the park's abundant trees to rest on their long migration. This 28-year-old park, named after a longtime bird watcher, has two nature trails, including one that leads to a blind overlooking a marsh.

Facilities include picnic tables, a shelter with barbecue pit, playground equipment, restrooms, observation tower, and public boat ramp. You can fish or swim in the Nueces River. The park is open 24 hours a day. The park lies a mile west of U.S. Highway 77.

Port Aransas to Padre Island

Roberts Point Park
East of south ferry landing, Port Aransas
• (361) 749-4158

You can't get any closer to the water than Roberts Point Park in Port Aransas. This 50-acre park dedicated in 1991 sits on a peninsula overlooking the Corpus Christi Ship Channel, where cargo ships, pleasure boats, and dolphins are common sights. The park was named after longtime residents Elda May and George E. "Florida" Roberts, who built a driftwood house there in 1931.

The park is due east of the ferry landing adjacent to the city marina. Facilities include a fishing pier, fish-cleaning station, observation tower, picnic pavilion, amphitheater, boat slips, soccer field and playground equipment for toddlers and older children. The park has restrooms, sand volleyball, horseshoe pits, basketball court, shuffleboard, and a fishing ramp for the handicapped.

A small wildlife interpretive center has been added to the park near the ferry landing. It includes flowers, trees and a small pond with a waterfall. Plans call for enlarging the site and adding signs with information on birds, migration and xeriscape gardening.

Admission is free. The park is open 24 hours a day.

Port Aransas Park
End of Cotter Ave., Port Aransas
• **(361) 749-6117**

The great thing about this park is that you can enjoy the beach and still be less than a mile from your favorite restaurants. It's on the beach at the end of Cotter Avenue, southeast of the ferry landing past the University of Texas Marine Science Institute.

The park has camping and RV sites (see our Campgrounds and RV Parks chapter), flushing toilets, showers, bathhouse, picnic shelters and the lighted 1,245-foot Horace Caldwell Pier. The snack bar/convenience store on the pier sells fast food, ice and basic groceries. You can also rent fishing tackle there. You'll pay a $1 entrance fee to get on the pier. Entry to the park is free, and it's open 24 hours a day.

Mustang Island State Park
Texas Hwy. 361,
14 miles south of Port Aransas
• **(361) 749-5246, (800) 792-1112**

This 3,703-acre park on the southern end of Mustang Island has been owned and operated by the state of Texas since the land was purchased from private owners in 1972. Its primary draw is the relatively unpopulated beaches that stretch 5.5 miles along the Gulf of Mexico. Most of this park 14 miles south of Port Aransas is undeveloped. The bulk of activity occurs along a short section of beach near the park headquarters and a 48-site RV park and campground (see our Campgrounds and RV Parks chapter).

Recreational activities include swimming, sunbathing, camping, picnicking, and fishing. Facilities include parking, restrooms, dressing rooms, hot and cold showers, shade shelters, picnic tables, pay phones, and a Texas State Parks Store, where you get get your hands on such items as ice and souvenirs.

Visitors can tour numerous historic homes in Heritage Park.

Photo: courtesy of the Greater Corpus Christi Business Alliance

The park is open from 8 AM to 10 PM. Office hours are 8 AM to 5 PM. The park charges an entrance fee of $3 per person for those 12 and older.

Nueces County Padre Balli Park
15820 Park Rd. 22
• (361) 949-8121

This 374.5-acre park is just outside the Corpus Christi city limit and a few miles north of the Padre Island National Seashore. Padre Balli (pronounced bay-YEE, although most locals use the English pronunciation) is operated by Nueces County and is popular among anglers, surfers and sunbathers.

Anglers are drawn to the lighted, 1,240-foot Bob Hall Pier, dedicated by the county in the fall of 1983 after Hurricane Allen destroyed its predecessor three years earlier. Surfers also find the pier to their liking. Waves breaking near the structure are considered especially nice among the waxed-board set.

INSIDERS' TIP

The Hilltop Community Center, 11426 Leopard St., is a great place to view native brush habitat. The center trails are open during daylight hours.

Facilities include RV and tent sites (see our Campgrounds and RV Parks chapter), restrooms, hot showers, concession stand, picnic shelters, laundry facilities, and first-aid station. Park rangers are on duty 24 hours a day.

Padre Balli is open 24 hours a day year-round. Park admission is free, but the charge is $1 per person to enter the pier. An addition $1 is required for a fishing pole.

Padre Island National Seashore
9405 S. Padre Island Dr., Corpus Christi
• (361) 949-8068

Padre Island National Seashore was founded in 1968, six years after President John F. Kennedy signed a bill authorizing the purchase of 80.5 miles of Padre Island for a national seashore. Padre Island is one of a chain of islands that stretches along the Atlantic and Gulf coasts of the United States from Maine to Texas.

The national seashore is undeveloped other than facilities to accommodate visitors on its northern edge. It's one of the longest stretches of primitive, undeveloped ocean beach in the United States. You'll see white sand-and-shell beaches, picturesque dunes, grassland, and tidal flats. See our Beaches and Watersports chapter for more information.

You can swim or fish in the Gulf of Mexico or the Laguna Madre, the area between the island and the mainland. Gulls, herons, ducks,

sandpipers, terns, and egrets are among the 350 species of birds that inhabit the island. Inland you'll find killdeer, meadowlarks and sandhill cranes. Animals that make the island their home include coyotes, blacktailed jackrabbits, lizards, and Western diamondback rattlesnakes.

Facilities include RV and camping sites (see our Campgrounds and RV Parks chapter), toilets, cold showers, picnic tables, The Grassland Nature Trail (a three-quarter-mile wheelchair accessible trail), year-round interpretive programs, a boat launch, and a visitors center.

The first 5 miles of beach are accessible by two-wheel-drive vehicles; the next 55 miles are accessible via four-wheel-drive only.

The park charges a $10 entrance fee good for seven days; an annual pass is available for $20. An additional $5 fee is charged for anyone wishing to visit the popular windsurfing site known as Bird Island Basin or to launch a boat; an annual pass sells for $10. Ask about discount passes for the handicapped and senior citizens.

The park is open 24 hours a day. The visitors center is open every day in the off-season from 8:30 AM to 4 PM except Christmas and New Year's Day; it's open from 8:30 AM to 6 PM between Memorial Day and Labor Day.

Kingsville Area

Dick Kleberg Park
U.S. Hwy. 77 at Escondido Rd., Kingsville
• (361) 595-8591

This park named after a member of the King Ranch family is on the south side of Kingsville between U.S. Highway 77 bypass and Business U.S. 77. The park has plenty of wide-open spaces and is home to the J.K. Northway Exposition Center. Inside the park you'll find six soccer and eight softball fields, five baseball fields, a sand volleyball court, a basketball court, and two tennis courts. Other facilities include picnic tables, a 1-mile hike-and-bike trail along Escondido Creek, a large playground and two smaller playgrounds, a recreation hall, a pier, and barbecue equipment. Escondido Creek is listed on The Great Texas Coastal Birding Trail (see our Birding chapter).

The park is open from 7:30 AM to 11 PM from March through October. The rest of the year, the park closes at 9 PM. Admission is free.

Kaufer-Hubert Memorial Park
F.M. Rd. 628, Loyola Beach
• (361) 297-5738

This waterside park east of Loyola Beach in Kleberg County is a long drive from just about anywhere—but don't let that stop you. Anglers and nature lovers will love this facility, which is part of a 134-site RV park known as SeaWind RV Resort (see our Campgrounds and RV Parks chapter). The drive from Corpus Christi will take about an hour.

Kaufer-Hubert overlooks the Cayo del Grullo, which feeds into the popular fishing sites of Baffin Bay and the Laguna Madre. Facilities include campgrounds, group picnic shelters, single picnic tables with grills, two freshwater lakes, restrooms and a two-story observation tower overlooking the bay. Other facilities include a 500-foot lighted fishing pier, four-lane boatramp/parking, sand beach with shower, birding overlook, a walking/jogging trail with 12-station senior fitness course, playground, horseshoe pits, and soccer/softball fields.

The park is close to the renowned Kings Inn Restaurant (see our Restaurants chapter) and is open from 7:30 AM to 11 PM. Admission is free.

PARKS

Birding

Birds have been wintering in South Texas for many years, so it should be no surprise that birders—that binocular-toting population of folks who follow, track, chart, and simply enjoy birds—have followed suit.

And the Corpus Christi area known as Texas' Coastal Bend, with its nearly year-round subtropical climate and tremendous variety of birds, is rapidly becoming known as a birder's paradise.

Of the nearly 800 species of birds that live in North America, almost 500 are present at some time during the year in the Coastal Bend. Some of the birds that people travel great distances to see here are the least grebe, white-tipped dove, Couch's kingbird, green jay, pyrrhuloxia, great kiskadee, tropical parula, and ferruginous pygmy owl. And that's not even mentioning the hummingbirds and the whooping cranes, both of which are the focus of entire celebrations and seminars because of their annual visits here. (See our Close-up on whooping cranes in the Annual Events and Festivals chapter.)

What makes the Texas Coastal Bend so popular with birds? Well, several elements combine to attract such large numbers and varieties of birds, according to the avian experts. Geography plays a large role in enticing a wide variety of birds to either settle or winter here: Because we're on the coast, we have seabirds, shorebirds, and marsh waders, as well as songbirds, game birds, and raptors.

In addition, South Texas draws thousands of migrant birds along what is known as the Central Flyway—kind of a flight plan for avian travelers. Other birds traveling the Mississippi Flyway choose to circle around the coast rather than risk the Gulf crossing, and still others are diverted eastward from the Rocky Mountain Flyway. Tropical species from Mexico also frequently cross the Rio Grande into our region.

Climate and weather contribute to the situation. In the summertime, birds from Central and South America that come to nest here join resident species. In the winter, birds from northern breeding grounds—some as far away as the Arctic—come to spend the mild winter months with us. And the spring and fall migrations are spectacular, making the region a premier destination for birders around the country.

It's easy enough to spot these birds. There are city parks and hot spots, state and county parks, a national seashore, a national wildlife refuge, bird sanctuaries and more. The most grueling part of your visit may be deciding where to go and how long to stay!

Although birds have long been visiting South Texas, the business of courting birders and other nature-loving travelers has only begun to take flight in the past decade. Cities and counties now recognize the value of promoting and protecting their natural resources, including birds and other wildlife, as an economic safeguard. The community of Kingsville has even adopted its own "city bird"—the emerald-colored green jay.

All of which is good news to birders. It means that birds and their homes will be better cared for. And that means there will be more birds to see.

If you're new to the birding game, have no fear. There are many maps and guidebooks to acquaint you with the resident and visiting species.

You can also take a birding tour with a local nature group, such as the

Audubon Outdoor Club of Corpus Christi, which celebrates the spring migration with bird walks in Blucher Park every Saturday and Sunday morning (except Easter) in April and May.

The privately operated Rob and Bessie Welder Wildlife Foundation Refuge offers free tours on Thursday afternoons. A 12-mile loop on the Santa Gertrudis Division of the King Ranch is open to the public daily, with free maps available at the ranch entrance on Texas Highway 141 at Kingsville.

There are also paid tours, on land and on the water, to help you locate specific species. Among the more popular are boating trips to see the whooping cranes and other birds, available in winter from Rockport and Port Aransas. Other tours by local birding experts are additional options, and these usually offer half-day or full-day trips into the wilderness to find some of the more elusive species. We've included a listing of guided tours, with prices when available, at the end of this chapter.

A recommended birding guide for this area is *A Birder's Guide to the Texas Coast* by Harold Holt, published by the American Birding Association. To order a copy, call (800) 634-7736.

In this chapter we also try to acquaint you with some of the most popular birding sites in the Corpus Christi area, including information about which birds can be seen there. Admission is free at city parks; however, state and county parks generally charge a small fee.

This is not an all-encompassing list of birding sites in the area. We've tried to hit some of the highlights, but the many places where you can bird in the Corpus Christi area are simply too numerous to mention. More detailed guides are available from local chambers of commerce, as well as in many of the books about birding on the Texas coast. In addition, the state has published one of the more comprehensive and easy-to-use maps of the Coastal Bend's birding hot spots in literature about the Great Texas Coastal Birding Trail (Central Texas Coast). Texas officials created this 500-mile birding trail, the first of its kind in the United States, to guide birders through the Texas coast and its diverse bird population. This map represents Texas officials' recognition of the importance and growing interest in Texas birding—said to be among the nation's best.

INSIDERS' TIP

The late birder and researcher Roger Tory Peterson published 34 birding guidebooks, but the only state with such birding diversity that it merited its own book was Texas. Peterson's *Field Guide to the Birds of Texas* was first published in 1963 and contains a wealth of useful information.

For information about statewide birds and maps, contact the Texas Parks and Wildlife Department at (800) 792-1112 or the Texas Department of Transportation at (800) 452-9292. Local chambers of commerce also have copies of the map.

Dozens of Corpus Christi area sites are included on the state map. Each site is marked with a trail number and a logo, and some sites are enhanced with observation platforms, boardwalks and kiosks. In addition, local chambers of commerce also publish birding lists and maps to help visitors find the birds that visit their city or town.

Sponsored by the Houston Audubon Society, the statewide Rare Bird Alert hotline, (713) 964-5867, and the Houston hotline, (713) 922-2757, are good sources for the most recent information about unusual birds seen along the coast. For more information about birding in the Coastal Bend, call the Coastal Bend Birding Hotline, at (361) 883-7410; the Audobon Outdoor Club of Corpus Christi; Coastal Bend Audubon Society, (361) 882-7232; Kingsville Bird and Wildlife Club, (361) 592-7558; and the Convention and Visitors Department of the Greater Corpus Christi Business Alliance, (361) 881-1888 or (800) 766-BEACH.

Birding Sites and Resources

North Bay Area

Aransas National Wildlife Refuge
• F.M. Rd. 2040, Austwell
• (361) 286-3559

This is the winter home of the whooping crane, which attract thousands of birders annually. But it's also known among birders for its exceptional variety of resident and transient birds, including roseate spoonbill, reddish egret, white and white-faced ibis, and a variety of ducks, grebes, and shorebirds. Look for hummingbirds from late spring through the fall.

A variety of other wildlife, including wading birds, alligators, crested caracara, javelina, and armadillos, is active in early morning and late evening. You can pick up a map and bird checklist from the wildlife interpretive center, near the refuge's entrance; the center is open from 8:30 AM to 4:30 PM. The refuge itself is open daily from sunrise to sunset. It is seven miles south of Austwell. See our Parks chapter for more information.

Connie Hagar Cottage Sanctuary
• **E. First and Church Sts., Rockport**
• **(361) 729-6445, (800) 242-0071**

A 6½-acre sanctuary managed by the Friends of Connie Hagar, this site pays homage to a longtime birder who essentially put the Coastal Bend on the birding map. (See our Close-up on Connie in this chapter.)

Hagar, born in 1886, moved with her husband to Rockport in 1934 and soon began birding. Her reports of birds sighted in the Coastal Bend were the first that alerted the national birding world to the tremendous variety and wealth of birds in the Coastal Bend, particularly during the migratory season. This site is where Hagar and her husband Jack owned and operated a small hotel, Rockport Cottages, for birders in the 1930s. Although the sanctuary is small, it contains a wide variety of birds. Vireos, warblers, grosbeaks, and flycatchers can fill the woods, and the grassy fields have dickcissels, sparrows, and buntings. A daily bird list in the kiosk identifies what others have seen there.

4 The Birds
• **92 S. Austin St., Rockport**
• **(361) 790-9700**

A birding headquarters for visitors and locals, 4 The Birds offers custom-blended and bulk birdseed, birdhouses and feeders; CD-ROM programs to help you identify birds; books and identifying guides; updated information about tours and trips; and a selection of candles, T-shirts, kites, windsocks, art, and photography.

Goose Island State Park
• **Off Texas Hwy. 35, Lamar**
• **(361) 729-2858**

This live oak-draped state park serves as a migratory stop for many land birds, while a variety of waterfowl (loons, grebes, common goldeneye, red-breasted merganser, and red-head) make appearances along the shores. Don't forget to visit Big Tree, the nation's largest live

oak with an estimated 1,000 years under its bark. Rails, gallinules, common yellowthroat, and marsh wrens frequent this area along the marshes.

Campsites are available, and the park has a nature trail. The park is 2.6 miles east of Park Road, 13 miles from Texas Highway 35. See our Parks chapter for more information.

Live Oak Park
• **East of F.M. Rd. 1069, Ingleside**

Within the city of Ingleside is this community park that offers outdoor recreation and a nature trail. Live Oak Park is a remnant of the extensive oak forest that once bordered Redfish Bay. Birds encountered here are thrushes, thrashers and ground-dwelling warblers such as worm-eating, hooded and Swainson's. Farm-to-Market Road 1069 is 2 miles south of Texas Highway 361. See our Parks chapter for more information.

INSIDERS' TIP

Take plenty of insect repellent with you while birding, since you may encounter mosquitoes or chiggers.

Rockport Demo Bird Garden and Wetlands Pond
• **Intersection of Texas Hwy. 35 and F.M. Rd. 3036, Rockport**

This hummingbird garden is jointly maintained by the Texas Department of Transportation and the community of Rockport. It serves as a stopping point for thousands of mostly ruby-throated hummingbirds in early September and October. The garden also features educational information about the hummingbird and a boardwalk that extends into a huge patch of trumpet creeper plants, a favorite of hummingbirds.

Rob and Bessie Welder Park
• **U.S. Hwy. 181 N., 2.5 mi. north of Sinton**
• **(361) 364-2381**

The City of Sinton recently dedicated these 45 acres—within this 300-acre multi-use park named for the Welders—as a natural preserve. The area contains open grasslands, scattered trees, and an observation platform that overlooks a pond. Birds you may see here include common yellowthroat, marsh wren, and migrant land birds.

Rob and Bessie Welder Wildlife Foundation Refuge
• **U.S. Hwy. 77, 7.5 mi. north of Sinton**
• **(361) 364-2381**

This privately owned wildlife refuge occupies 7,800 acres, a small portion of a large ranch that has been in the Welder family for more than 150 years. The refuge, which opened in April 1961, is dedicated to wildlife research and education. It operates as a working cattle ranch and oil field.

Sixteen plant communities exist on the refuge, including about 1,400 species of native plants. More than 380 species of birds, 55 species of mammals, and 55 species of reptiles and amphibians have been recorded on the refuge. About 1,000 deer live on the refuge along with javelinas, Río Grande wild turkeys, Northern bobwhites, and several species of ducks and geese.

Visitors can take a free public tour at 3 PM Thursdays that includes a walk through the compound of buildings, then a driving tour of the refuge. No reservations are required. The refuge also hosts an annual Bird and Field Day, usually at the end of February or early March, that attracts many birders and nature lovers.

Welder Park
• 700 N. Rachal Ave., Sinton

Tucked away in a remote corner of Sinton, this park (not to be confused with the Rob and Bessie Welder Park listed above) is closed to vehicular traffic. Park at the entrance and walk in to find migrating land birds, water thrushes (prothonotary warbler and common yellowthroat), warblers, and a number of species along the fence, such as the blue-gray gnatcatcher and Bewick's wren.

Corpus Christi

Blucher Park
• 100 block of Carrizo St., Corpus Christi

This little park adjacent to Corpus Christi Central Library is filled with dense woods and a small creek that attracts plenty of migrating land birds, including flycatchers, thrushes, vireos, and warblers. Some of the city's original

The tiny, speedy hummingbird is honored each September in Rockport at the annual Hummer/Bird Celebration.

Photo: courtesy of the Rockport-Fulton Area Chamber of Commerce

BIRDING

Connie Hagar: Spotlight on Birds

She was "a wren of a woman"—97 pounds—and given to wearing dresses even in the field. Her first reports of the birding abundance on the Texas coast met with overwhelming skepticism, but when the experts arrived to question her numbers, she calmly led them to see the birds she had described—and quelled all doubts.

Connie Hagar devoted her life to birds in the tiny community of Rockport, where today a sanctuary is named after her. And after 35 years of daily record-keeping on hundreds of birds, she is now recognized as one of the state's first and premier birders. The first book about her, *The Life History of a Texas Birdwatcher*, was written by Karen Harden McCracken and published in 1986. It is remarkable in its detail and in the sheer force of its subject's personality.

As McCracken herself writes in the preface, "Hers was the most phenomenal memory I have ever encountered. I was constantly amazed by her vivid recollections of events, people, details, even dialogue—she could remember what was said and who said it."

McCracken, who knew Hagar, based her book on hours of interviews and Hagar's own daily note taking, letters, and photographs. Another book about Hagar is in the works as well, according to the Friends of Connie Hagar, a Rockport-based group dedicated to preserving Hagar's history and contribu-

This is a copy of a photograph taken by Alfred Eisenstadt that appeared in Life magazine on September 10, 1958. The photographer wanted Connie Hagar to wear pants—but she insisted on wearing a dress, her normal birding attire.

Photo: Alfed Eisenstadt

tions—and to furthering public awareness and appreciation of the birds in Texas.

Noted ornithologists have also given widespread recognition to Hagar's research. The late Roger Tory Peterson, the highly respected author of birding field guides, called her "the wonder-woman of Rockport." Ornithologist Harold Holt wrote that Hagar "opened the eyes of the growing numbers of birdwatchers to the fact that Rockport is one of the most productive areas on the entire Texas coast. The diminutive Connie Hagar put Rockport on the birding map, and by the time she died, in 1973, the place had become a magnet for birders as well as for birds."

Born in the north Texas town of Corsicana in 1886, Martha Conger Hagar moved to Rockport in 1934 after spending a month there with her sister. Her husband Jack bought the Rockport Cottages, a motel complex, which soon became a coveted vacation spot for the nation's birders.

Hagar's love of nature came from her father, who introduced her early to the beauty of the birds and plant life. As an adult, she and her sister formed a nature study group that was intended as a memorial to their beloved father. In 1928, she began to make daily observations of her birding expeditions in what she called the "Nature Calendar," a practice she continued for 35 years. Those notes, written on pages in blank ledgers, became a source of scientific record for future ornithologists. She wrote about wildflowers, her daily life and always of the birds—the painted buntings, hummingbirds, cactus wrens and bluebirds, that she so loved.

Hagar was a sweet and intelligent woman who dedicated herself to the study of nature, particularly birds. She mentored many young birders, and she readily deferred to the scholars—even when they were skeptical about her ability. Her solution was always to show them what she had seen, and she turned all her doubters into fans and defenders by her simple, straightforward manner and her dedication.

As a Rockport resident, she and her husband soon became intimately involved in the community's life. The locals grew accustomed to seeing Connie Hagar and her dog, Fuzzy, looking for birds. They were probably quite a pair—Hagar in her dresses and with the snake stick she used to fend off rattlers and other reptiles, and the dog, who alerted his beloved mistress to the presence of snakes and other dangers.

As for Hagar's attire, she apparently once tried wearing jeans in the field but felt too uncomfortable, due to her genteel upbringing—and a photo taken by her brother meant to poke fun at the pants only confirmed her dislike of the outfit. She wore dresses from then on, much to the dismay of famed *Life* photographer Alfred Eisenstadt, who came to Rockport to photograph her for a spread in the magazine in 1956.

Hagar was also notable for her willingness not only to learn about birds, but also to share what she knew. For decades, she volunteered to speak at social gatherings, schools, and other public forums as part of her fervent desire to acquaint people with the natural world and its avian inhabitants on the Texas coast. She also worked to band birds for years, and often wrote articles and columns about her research for newspapers and magazines.

Despite her active schedule, Hagar was not always in good health. She courageously battled blindness during much of her adult life.

When she died, at age 86, in 1973, family, friends, and birders throughout the nation mourned her. The extraordinary national and even international recognition she received during her lifetime led the Texas State Historical

(Continued on next page)

Commission to dedicate a state marker in her honor—waiving the customary requirement that the designee be deceased no less that 20 years.

A citation from the National Audubon Society summed up her life's contributions with eloquence: "You opened our eyes to that great miracle of the natural world, the migration of birds. You enriched our knowledge by patient, open-minded and courageous observation and reporting of the facts—so many of them unbelievable. In your selfless devotion to the truths of nature, you have literally discovered the link between heaven and earth."

Visitors to Rockport can see the Connie Hagar Cottage Sanctuary, the site of the Rockport Cottages she and her husband managed. It now consists of a 6½-acre nature preserve, maintained by the Friends of Connie Hagar. There is also the Connie Hagar Wildlife Sanctuary, designated in December 1943 and managed by the Texas Parks and Wildlife Department.

In addition, you can view a state marker, the graves of Connie and Jack Hagar and a demonstration hummingbird and butterfly garden in Rockport, which is maintained by the Friends of Connie Hagar. For more information about any of these sites, call the Rockport Chamber of Commerce, (361) 729-6445 or (800) 242-0071.

families lived along this street, and several of its homes have been restored, including one that's been turned into an environmental education center.

The Audubon Outdoor Club of Corpus Christi conducts birding tours through this park at 7:30 AM every Saturday and Sunday in April. One caveat on this park: It seems to also attract a number of vagrants, so we recommend that predawn birders bring a buddy for security.

Corpus Christi Botanical Gardens
• 9545 S. Staples St., Corpus Christi
• (361) 852-2100

An assortment of native habitats, including a wildflower field, nature trail through mesquite woods, an alligator lake, and a bird and butterfly trail, attracts birds and birders. You'll be able to see species such as groove-billed ani, long-billed thrasher, curve-billed thrasher, pyrrhuloxia, and olive sparrow, as well as water birds such as least grebe and Couch's kingbird. See our Attractions chapter for more information.

Fred Jones Nature Sanctuary
• Moore Ave. (F.M. Rd. 893) and
County Rd. 69, Portland

This nature sanctuary is an oasis of vegetation in the middle of an agricultural region. Privately maintained by the Audubon Outdoor Club of Corpus Christi, it's worth a visit during migration, particularly for vireos and warblers. Donations are requested. This is also a great place to view spring wildflowers.

Hans A. Suter Wildlife Area
• Ennis Joslin Rd. at Oso Bay

A boardwalk provides access to the lagoon, where you can spot dozens of shorebirds as well as land birds in migration. Shorebirds can be seen here all year, including white pelicans, spoonbills, egrets, herons, gulls, and terns. Migratory birds also arrive in winter. Check the newspaper for the tide tables, as these birds are best seen as the tide is falling.

Hazel Bazemore County Park
• F.M. Rd. 624 at Nueces River,
half-mile west of U.S. Hwy. 77

Hawk migration in September and October brings tens of thousands of hawks through this brushy park—and attracts birders worldwide. The hawks tend to migrate on the season's first cold fronts, often in September or October. Also look for bluebirds in the winter time, as well as owls, paraques, warblers, hummingbirds, and shorebirds. The park has a nature trail and restrooms. Ask for a map and bird checklist. It is open 7 AM to 10 PM daily. See our Parks chapter for more information.

Nature's Bird Center
• 5830 McArdle Rd. at Airline Rd.,
Corpus Christi
• (361) 992-2473

This store specializes in items intended for birds and birders, including guidebooks, binoculars, feeders, baths, seed, houses, and T-shirts with—what else?—birds on them. Owner Vicki Simon also offers an array of gift items, such as

BIRDING

wind chimes, and provides information about birding sites, bird sightings, and tours.

Pollywog Pond
• **Upriver Rd. at Sharpsburg Rd.,**
Corpus Christi

A collection of lakes and pools creates a habitat for numerous water birds, songbirds and migrants. These old Water Department settling ponds can attract black-bellied whistling ducks, least grebe, least bitterns, white-winged doves, great kiskadee and groove-billed anis. Walking can be rough in some places.

Port Aransas to Padre Island

Aransas Pass Wetlands
• **Conn Brown Harbor, Texas Hwy. 361**
between Aransas Pass and Port Aransas

Best in the winter, Conn Brown Harbor attracts shorebirds such as loons, grebes, diving ducks, and pelicans. The stretch of state highway between the two towns is bordered by Redfish Bay and lots of tidal flats and sandy spots, where you can find waterfowl, shorebirds, and species such as loons, grebes, American oystercatcher, snowy plover, and sooty tern.

Port Aransas Birding Center
• **Ross Ave., Port Aransas**
• **(361) 749-5919, (800) 45-COAST**

This facility includes a boardwalk that extends into a freshwater marsh that attracts waterfowl such as black-bellied whistling ducks, cinnamon teal, grebes, heron, and egrets, cormorants and shorebirds such as black-necked stilt and roseate spoonbill.

Mustang Island State Park
• **Texas Hwy. 361,**
14 mi. south of Port Aransas
• **(361) 749-5246**

Look for gulls, terns, and shorebirds along this beach where the birds you're likely to see include lesser black-backed gull, glaucous gull, piping, and snowy plovers, red knots and Wilson's plover. Camping facilities are available at this state park (see our Parks chapter for more information).

Padre Island National Seashore
• **Park Rd. 22, Corpus Christi**
• **(361) 949-8068**

The nation's longest barrier island, this 133,000-acre national park extends from Cor-

pus Christi to Port Isabel, 80 miles to the south. Most of the beach is accessible only in a four-wheel-drive vehicle, but you can see plenty of birds along the entrance road and the visitors center. Expect to see peregrine falcons, migrant land birds, gulls, terns, and shorebirds and a variety of raptors, including white-tailed kite, white-tailed hawk, and ferruginous hawk. Primitive and developed camping facilities are available. For more information about this park, see our Parks chapter.

Kingsville Area

Dick Kleberg Park
• **U.S. Hwy. 77 and Escondido St.,**
Kingsville

A trail along the lake provides a perfect vantage point to see vermilion flycatcher, waterfowl, and nesting sparrows. Resident species include golden-fronted and ladder-backed woodpeckers, green jay, great kiskadee, and curve-billed and long-billed thrashers. You can also see both pipits, although the Sprague's is rare. See our Parks chapter for more information.

Drum Point (Baffin Bay)
• **F.M. Rd. 772 and County Rd. 1132**

Follow this unpaved road to look for herons, egrets, pelicans, waterfowl, and shorebirds. Especially of interest is the white form of the reddish egret, a type of heron which favors saltwater. In April and September migrations, you can see millions of swallows and martins along the bluff here. This is a good fishing spot, too.

Hawk Alley
• **Texas Hwy. 285**
between Kingsville and Falfurrias

This stretch of road is so named by local birders for the multitudes of raptors spotted here. Resident species include white-tailed hawk, Harris' Hawk, crested caracara, red-tailed hawk, and ferruginous hawk, while migratory species include Mississippi kite, broad winged hawk, and Swainson's hawk.

Kaufer-Hubert Memorial County Park
• **F.M. Rd. 628, Loyola Beach**

Look for herons, egrets, and shorebirds in the wetlands and mudflats at the mouth of Vattman Creek in this county park. Also, you can find waterfowl such as greater scaup, black scoter and surf scoter at the ponds, and ground-dove, green jays, and olive sparrows in the brush. Camping facilities are available. Also, you can fish from the lighted pier.

BIRDING

King Ranch
• King Ranch Visitors Center,
Texas Hwy. 141 W., Kingsville
• (361) 592-8055

This is one of the largest working ranches in the world, specializing in longhorn cattle and quarter horses. Its 825,000 acres also attract thousands of birds, including some of the more rare species. A number of South Texas specialties, which you're unlikely to see elsewhere in the United States, are commonly seen here. You can take one of the hourly bus tours along the loop road in the ranch and find anhinga, kingfisher, black-bellied whistling ducks, cactus wrens, curve-billed thrashers, green jays (the city's official bird), and great kiskadees. Private birding tours into the exterior of the ranch will bring you more variety (see our listing of guided tours below).

Louise Trant Bird Sanctuary
• U.S. Hwy. 77 near Riviera

This is a marsh maintained by the Audubon Outdoor Club of Corpus Christi. You can find soras wintering here, and yellow-headed blackbirds make their appearance in the cattails in spring. Rare species sighted here are the red-billed pigeon and masked duck.

Santa Gertrudis Creek Bird Sanctuary
• U.S. Hwy. 77 at F.M. Rd. 1717,
Kingsville

This is an extensive marsh inhabited by species including least grebe, black-bellied whistling duck, purple gallinule, marsh and sedge wrens, and a variety of herons and egrets. Also

Roseate Spoonbills are year-round residents along the Coastal Bend.

Photo: courtesy of the Greater Kingsville Economic Development Council

look for great kiskadee and green jay in the surrounding mesquite woodlands, as well as cave swallows nesting in the culverts during the summer.

Birding Tours

Even the most experienced birders often choose to have a tour guide during their birding adventures so they can more quickly locate a particular species. Tours are also helpful when the area you want to bird is closed to the public. And last, but not least, there are the boat tours that allow birders access to remote areas and rare species.

We've described some of the more popular tours in the Coastal Bend and provided telephone numbers for more information or reservations. Please call ahead for reservations to make sure that there is a place for you on these trips.

Capt. John Howell's *Pisces*
• 1015 N. Allen St., #B;
Rockport Harbor; Rockport
• (800) 245-9324

The *Pisces* offers two daily tours, from 8 AM to noon and 1 to 5 PM, to Aransas National Wildlife Refuge. The tours are conducted November through April. The 58-foot boat holds 49 passengers. There is a limited supply of binoculars for rent on board, so it's probably wise to bring your own pair. You'll be able to see brown pelicans, roseate spoonbills, great blue herons, and, of course, whooping cranes. Hot and cold beverages and snacks are sold on the boat. The cost is $25 per adult and teen ($2 discount on the adult fare for seniors) and $17 for children younger than 12.

Capt. Ted's
Whooping Crane Tours
• Sandollar Pavilion,
Fulton Beach Rd., Fulton
• (361) 729-9589, (800) 338-4551

For more than 20 years, Capt. Ted Appell has been guiding tourists through the Coastal Bend wetlands to see endangered whooping cranes and nesting areas of other birds. His boat, the *M.V. Skimmer*, operates the whooping crane tours from November 1 through April 30 and tours of the rookery islands in April and May. During the three-hour trip through wetlands and bays, Capt. Ted provides an entertaining narrative about the Coastal Bend birds and their habits. Continental breakfast is also provided. These tours are for adults only, and begin at 6:45 AM. Reservations are required. Price is $33 per person.

Coastal Bend Birders
- **5030 N. Texas Hwy. 35, Fulton**
- **(361) 790-8884**

Full and half-day guided tours of the Coastal Bend are led by longtime guide Michael Marsden. Michael and his wife, Donna, also run Cayman House, a bed-and-breakfast inn for birders in Rockport (see the Bed and Breakfast Inns chapter). These tours are suitable for everyone from beginners to advanced birders. Transportation is in a seven-seat minivan equipped with telescopes, binoculars, and identification guides. A half-day tour for one person is $50; the cost is $100 for a full-day tour. The rates go down with the size of your group—for example, it costs $25 per person for a group of six to take a half-day tour, and $50 per person for a group of six to take the full-day tour. A lunch is provided with the full-day tour.

INSIDERS' TIP

Two rare birds seen on the King Ranch include the jabiru (a South American stork photographed on the ranch) and the only North American record of the double-striped thick-knee, a chicken-sized tropical bird that resembles some sandpipers and plovers.

Fennessey Ranch Nature Tours
- **F.M. Rd. 2678, 10 mi. north of Bayside**
- **(361) 529-6600**

This private ranch is open for tours by reservation only. The ranch, east of Refugio, offers birders an array of wildlife including black-bellied whistling duck, mottled duck, masked duck, least bittern, purple gallinule, common moorhen, and marsh wren in the marshes; sparrows in the grasslands; hummingbirds in migration; and sandhill cranes, geese, and other waterfowl. For more information see our Attractions chapter.

King Ranch Nature Tours
- **King Ranch Visitor Center,
Texas Hwy. 141 W., Kingsville**
- **(361) 592-8055**

This 825,000-acre private ranch has only recently ventured into the ecotourism business,

offering nature and birding tours that range from half-day to four-day retreats. The half-day wildlife tour is 3½ hours long and takes visitors through a variety of habitats on the ranch. Offered October through March, it costs $17.50 per person plus tax.

The full-day birding tour (nine to 10 hours) takes you from one end of the ranch to the other, where you'll see ferruginous pygmy owls, tropical parula, Audubon's oriole, and northern beardless tyrannulet. Lunch is provided. It costs $99 per person plus tax.

For those who want total immersion in South Texas life and nature, try the four-day retreat package. Participants stay at cottages on the ranch, and meals and transportation are included. The cost is $589 per person plus tax.

There are also private tours that can cost up to $100 per person. These tours are customized and offer glimpses of specific birds, such as the ferruginous pygmy owl, white-tailed hawk, or LeConte's sparrow.

Reservations are required for all of the tours, and the number of people allowed per trip is limited. Some tours are seasonal so please call in advance to avoid disappointment. See our Attractions chapter for more information.

Lucky Day Charters, Rockport
- **Rockport Harbor, Rockport**
- **(361) 729-GULL, (800) 782-BIRD**

The 75-foot catamaran *M.V. Wharf Cat* departs daily from both Rockport and Port Aransas on whooping crane tours November through March. From Rockport, the tour begins at 10 AM and lasts until 2 PM Wednesday through Sunday, taking birders through Aransas Bay to the Aransas National Wildlife Refuge, while the captain provides a narrative. The trip from Port Aransas is slightly longer, starting at 10 AM and ending at 3:30 PM, Mondays and Tuesdays. Binoculars and spotting scopes are on board, as well as a snack bar with refreshments. The *Wharf Cat* is a twin-hulled boat with covered lower deck and an outdoor observation deck. The cost is $25 for adults and teens and $17 for children 12 and younger.

Fishing and Hunting

For fishing and hunting enthusiasts, the Corpus Christi area offers a veritable bounty on sea and land. Anglers have long known about the abundant marine life found in the waters off the Texas coast, traveling here for deep-sea excursions as well as excellent bay fishing. Among the most prominent of visitors were President Franklin D. Roosevelt, who fished for tarpon here during his vacations from the White House, and President George Bush, who shot quail here during presidential getaways.

The good news for anglers is that the area's populations of redfish, speckled trout, and black drum are at record highs—the best since the 1970s—thanks to strict regulations and catch limits that have helped increase the species' numbers. In addition, the state has been restocking the bays and the results have been spectacular.

The area offers several types of fishing. You can go offshore fishing in the Gulf of Mexico or bay fishing in the nearby, shallower waters. In addition, anglers can try their hand at surf fishing, fly fishing, and fishing from piers or jetties. Serious anglers will want to head over to Port Aransas, one of the state's premier headquarters for offshore fishing. With more than a dozen fishing tournaments and countless fishing guides and charter services, you can easily fish all year in Port Aransas.

If you're lucky enough to have your own boat, then all you need is to find a public launch site and some bait, and you're set to go. Other visitors may want to avail themselves of a guide service, a charter boat, or a party boat. A party boat generally takes 25 to 80 people out for a half-day or daylong trip; the per-person rate can range from $22 to $75, depending on if you go into the bay or the Gulf of Mexico. The boat operator furnishes all your tackle and other equipment. A charter boat outing is more expensive. You arrange with a boat captain for a private, guided group trip of four to six people. It can cost $350 to $700 a day.

An abundance of wildlife, particularly waterfowl, makes the Corpus Christi area popular as well with duck, dove, and quail hunters. Many locals have private leases on some of the sprawling ranches that extend across South Texas; others will opt to sign on with a guided tour or take their chances on public lands that are overseen by the Texas Parks and Wildlife Department. There are also several hunting lodges in the Corpus Christi area that offer packaged hunts for those interested in duck, dove, quail, feral hogs, or deer. At a cost of several hundred dollars per day, a hunter will receive a guided hunt, meals and lodging at a quality resort in the great outdoors.

Obviously, you will need a fishing or hunting license from the Texas Parks and Wildlife Department to participate in any of these activities. Licenses are available from marinas, sports stores, and other sites throughout the Coastal Bend. In addition, you can obtain current information about season, size, bag, and possession limits on saltwater fish, freshwater fish, waterfowl, and other animals. A resident combination hunting and fishing license for Texans is $32, and you'll pay additional fees for saltwater stamps, tarpon tags, and red drum tags. Nonresidents can get a license for $30, or a temporary (five-day) license for $20. For more information about fishing and hunting licenses or to purchase licenses by credit card, contact the state at (800) 895-4248 or (800)TX LIC 4 U.

A good place to keep abreast of the latest in hunting and fishing news is to check out newspaper columnist David Sikes, who writes about the South Texas outdoors for the *Corpus Christi Caller-Times*. His column is published on Thursday and Sunday.

Fishing

For each of our four geographic areas in the Texas Coastal Bend, we include a summary of the fishing scene and offer recommendations for businesses you can contact if you are planning to ply area waters for that trophy catch—or some salty sea yarns about the one that got away.

North Bay Area

Aransas Pass

Aransas Pass offers countless bait and tackle shops that supply all your angling needs, including rental equipment. From shore, wharves, piers and jetties, anglers can expect to catch redfish, speckled and sand trout, sheepshead, flounder, croaker, skipjack, and drum.

Group boats provide bay and deep-sea fishing for half or full days, while charter cruisers are available for offshore sport. Species caught from group or charter boats may include tarpon, sailfish, marlin, kingfish, mackerel, ling, pompano, bonito, red snapper, warsaw, and many others.

As for fishing from piers, check out the Conn Brown Harbor piers in Aransas Pass at the Harbor Park.

Guides and Equipment

Hampton's Landing
430 Ransom Rd., Aransas Pass
• **(361) 758-1562**
Hampton's Landing is the main fishing dock in the area. Here you'll find launch sites, ice,

bait and some of the city's best fishing guides. The boats from here go into Aransas Bay and Redfish Bay.

The Crabman
Marina and Seafood Market
Texas Hwy. 361 E.,
Port Aransas Causeway, Aransas Pass
• **(361) 758-0294**
This marina offers the equipment to get your own fresh catch—and it even sells fresh shrimp and oysters if you come back empty-handed. Among the services it offers are a free boat ramp, charter boats, live bait and tackle, guide services, boat rentals, and personal watercraft rentals (during the summer).

Fin & Feathers Marina and RV Park
Texas Hwy. 361, Aransas Pass
• **(361) 758-7414**
You can pitch your tent at the water's edge, hook up your recreational vehicle, take a hot shower, have a picnic, or launch your boat from Fin & Feathers Marina. Other amenities include a 600-foot lighted fishing pier and boat slips. You can also buy fresh shrimp for eating, live and dead bait, tackle, beer, ice, soft drinks, and snacks.

South Bay Bait and Charters
Redfish Bay Marina
1950 Texas Hwy. 361 E.,
Port Aransas Causeway, Aransas Pass
• **(361) 758-2632**
You can get rental boats, charter deep-sea and bay fishing trips, use the free boat ramp and buy bait, sodas, beer, ice. About a dozen charter companies work from here. There's also an RV park here.

Rockport

You would be hard-pressed to find more fishing guides than there are in Rockport, considered one of the best bay fishing sites along the Texas coast. From here, you can fish in Aransas Bay, Redfish Bay, Copano Bay, Mesquite Bay, and San Antonio Bay. Guide boats operate from Goose Island State Park, Rockport Beach Park, and Cole Harbor.

The jetty sheltering Rockport Yacht Basin is a popular spot for bay fishing; dawn hours generally are the most productive. Many hotels and motels on the bayfront maintain private fishing piers for guests. Depending upon the season and proverbial luck, catches may include redfish, sand and speckled trout, catfish, croaker, sheepshead, flounder, and drum.

Group-boat bay fishing is also available at the yacht basin. Offshore species may include tarpon, sailfish, marlin, ling, wahoo, king mackerel, bonito, pompano, red snapper, warsaw, and others.

Public fishing piers are the Fulton Harbor Pier on Fulton Beach Road and the piers at the north and south ends of Rockport Beach Park. Another popular fishing pier is Copano Bay State Fishing Pier, (361) 729-8519 or 729-7762, a lighted facility with a public boat ramp, concessions, and restrooms. Copano Bay State Fishing Pier is open 24 hours a day, seven days a week. Admission is $2 per fishing pole. For more information, see our Attractions chapter.

Guides

The best place to start looking for a guide is the Rockport-Fulton Area Chamber of Commerce, (361) 729-6445 or (800) 242-0071, which offers a regularly updated list of the city's fishing guide services. In addition to bay fishing, Rockport guides also offer fly fishing—a relatively new phenomenon on the Gulf Coast, but one that is increasingly popular among anglers

who like the challenge of laying a lure atop an unsuspecting fish.

Redfish Lodge on Copano Bay
901 Rattlesnake Point Rd., Rockport
• (361) 729-8100

For a packaged fishing experience, check out the Redfish Lodge on Copano Bay. This is where anglers can get the full and deluxe treatment: all meals, transportation to and from the airport, lodging and guided fishing trips for redfish and trout in nearby Copano Bay. The 14-person lodge caters mostly to corporate groups, and the cost is $425 per day per person. The lodge also offers duck hunting packages.

Port Aransas to Padre Island

Port Aransas bills itself as a fishing capital, and there's plenty of evidence to support that claim. The height of the offshore fishing season extends from Memorial Day to Labor Day, when drift fishing and troll fishing for king mackerel is popular, as is blue-water fishing for dolphin, marlin, and sailfish.

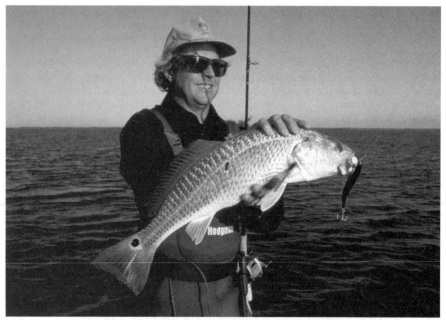

*Fishermen flood the waters of the Coastal Bend year-round to reel
in varieties like flounder, redfish, and trout.*

Photo: Larry Bozka

However, offshore fishing is also popular during the fall and winter months. In the fall and spring, you can catch tuna, amberjack, or red snapper, and in the winter, red snapper is the primary attraction. If you're fishing in the bay, you can expect to catch trout and redfish most of the year, although spring and summer are the best times.

Surf fishing is also a popular activity, particularly in the summertime. Some of the best places to try surf fishing are Horace Caldwell Pier in Port Aransas Park on Mustang Island, and Mustang Island State Park, south of Port Aransas. Anglers will find trout and redfish during the right conditions, when the surf is clear and calm.

Other popular fishing sites include Redfish Bay Pier on Texas Highway 361, east of Port Aransas, and the rock jetties, which extend a mile into the Gulf of Mexico and form the entrance to the Corpus Christi Ship Channel.

Over on Padre Island at Nueces County Padre Balli Park, fishing is particularly popular at Bob Hall Pier, especially at night during the summer months. The area is also good for surf fishing.

Head over to Malaquite Beach at Padre Island National Seashore for surf fishing. There is a 60-mile stretch of beach that's accessible only by four-wheel drive vehicle and is excellent for surf fishing of sharks, Spanish mackerel, redfish, trout, and tarpon.

The area's one and only professional surf fishing guide on the national seashore is Billy Sandifer, (361) 937-8446. Sandifer offers anglers guided tours as well as nature tours of the pristine and rugged beach area along the national seashore. The daylong nature tours, which can include birding, beach combing or whatever the customer wants, cost $150 for two people, and $25 additional for every other person with a maximum of five. The fishing tours, which include everything except food and drinks, often last more than 12 hours, Sandifer says. He charges $350 for two people, $75 for a third and $50 each for a fourth and fifth person. Sandifer knows the surf: he says 64 species of fish have been caught there, and one of his customers once caught an 820-pound shark.

Charters and Party Boats

If you're interested in either a party boat or charter boat from Port Aransas, we offer you several choices for locating guides or other services. We also include choices that specialize in inshore and bay fishing.

Dolphin Dock and Barracuda Inc.
300 W. Cotter Ave., Port Aransas
• **(361) 749-6624, (800) EYE-FISH**

A good spot for party boats and charters, Dolphin Docks attracts the more salty fishermen with a wide variety of bait, weights, and other equipment.

Deep Sea Headquarters
416 W. Cotter Ave., Port Aransas
• **(361) 749-5597, (800) 705-3474**

Party boats are the main attraction here, but Deep Sea Headquarters also has some charters. Plenty of boats are available, from the largest to the smaller ones.

Fisherman's Wharf
900 N. Tarpon St., Port Aransas
• **(361) 749-5448, (800) 605-5448**

Fisherman's Wharf offers both party boats and charter boats. Some of the largest boats, 80-foot-long, 3-foot-wide catamarans, operate out of this popular marina, and it attracts a lot of tourists.

Island Queen
Woody's Sports Center,
136 W. Cotter Ave., Port Aransas
• **(361) 749-5252**

Among the boats that operate from here is the *Island Queen*, a bay-fishing party boat that is an old, converted ferry. You can climb aboard for a four-hour fishing trip at the rate of $23.95 per adult, $11.98 for children ages 5 to 12, and free for 4 and younger. The price includes rod, reel, bait, and tackle.

Woody's Sports Center
136 W. Cotter Ave., Port Aransas
• **(361) 749-5252**

For those interested in inshore or bay fishing, Woody's Sports Center is the place to go for equipment, boat charters, and guided tours. For 30 years Woody's has been a sports lover's headquarters. This store also offers amenities including rental slips, a seafood market, fuel, T-shirts, hats, and other fishing accessories.

Corpus Christi

The headquarters for fishing in the Laguna Madre is the John F. Kennedy Causeway, which is lined with piers, opportunities for bank fishing and marinas. There are about a dozen good guides who work along the Laguna Madre. In the following listings, we describe several of the major marinas for launching a boat, buying bait and finding a guide.

Conventional bait fishing and fly fishing are available here. Longtime guide Don Hand of the Coastal Bend Guides Association can recommend some reputable fishing guides. Call (361) 993-2024.

Fly fishing has been growing in popularity here, with many anglers trying their luck at catching a redfish in the shallow surf waters along the Laguna Madre and Redfish Bay. Several recently established businesses cater to this growing trend.

If you don't have a boat, you can still go fishing at some of the rock jetties and piers in the area. During the spring and summer, it's common to see young kids walking down the street in the bayfront area, toting their fishing rods and sometimes the catch of the day.

Fishing Piers and Jetties

Corpus Christi Municipal Marina
Lawrence Street T-Head, Corpus Christi
• **(361) 882-7333**

Folks can fish for free at many spots along this marina area: in the little park at the waterfront-end of Peoples Street, along the seawall, on the rock jetty that extends from the Memorial Coliseum area and at the wooden fishing pier on Powers Street at Shoreline Drive.

The Coliseum area jetty, 520 S. Shoreline Boulevard, (361) 881-9122, also is the site of a Wienerschnitzel, a fast-food chain that features mostly hot dogs. This jetty also has public restrooms and showers.

Cole Park Pier
1500 block of Ocean Dr., Corpus Christi
• **(361) 880-3461 city,**
  (361) 884-7275 amphitheater

This wooden pier is a favorite free fishing spot for many local residents. And if the kids get bored with fishing, they can always play on the playground—called KidsPlace—at the park. The pier area has restrooms and a concession stand, but the concession stand's hours are unpredictable (city officials say they open it if weather permits).

Indian Point Park and Pier
U.S. Hwy. 181,
between Corpus Christi and Portland
• **(361) 643-8555**

On Corpus Christi Bay, this pier is a favorite fishing site for local anglers as well as visitors. You can catch drum, redfish and gafftop

here, depending on the season. The park and pier are owned by the city of Portland and include a 720-foot fishing pier with a 280-foot T-head, restrooms and a concession stand that sells bait, tackle, snacks, and drinks. Birdwatching jetties are near the pier for when you tire of fishing.

The pier fee is $1 per person and $1 per fishing pole, but you can get an annual pass for $100, or $50 for senior citizens. Children ages 3 and younger get in free when accompanied by an adult. The park and pier are open 24 hours a day.

Charter and Party Boats

Captain Clark
Peoples Street T-Head, Corpus Christi
• **(361) 855-7089**

This 65-foot boat carries large groups, usually about 65 people, into Corpus Christi Bay to catch sand trout, whiting, gafftop, drum, and small sharks. The *Captain Clark* regularly goes out on two or three four-hour trips per day, but the schedule can vary by season. It's best to call ahead to get the week's schedule. The cost is $15 per adult and $10 for children ages 4 to 11, with an additional $4 fee to rent tackle, or you can bring your own. There is a snack bar on board the boat, and bait is provided. The *Captain Clark* is also available for private charters.

Marinas

Copeland's Marina
4041 S. Padre Island Dr., Corpus Christi
• **(361) 854-1135, (361) 749-7464**

You can sign up for a chartered deep-sea fishing or scuba diving trip at this shop. The fishing trips, which include all your equipment, bait, tackle, and lunch, range in price from $40 per person for a five-hour trip and $60 per person for a nine-hour trip to $75 for a 12-hour trip. Also offered is an overnight trip for $149 per person, which includes a bunk and three meals. The excursions are on board *Adventurer*, an 85-foot boat that sleeps 33, has air-conditioning and heating, and a full galley, and departs from Port Aransas. The shop also sells scuba diving and snow skiing equipment.

Marker 37 Marina
13317 S. Padre Island Dr., Corpus Christi
• **(361) 949-8037**

This full-service marina, on the upper Laguna Madre, has been in business since 1988, offering fuel, bait, tackle, a guide service, boat launching, and fish cleaning. You can sign up for a half-day charter fishing trip at a cost of $250 for two people, or a full day for $350 (the price includes everything except your lunch and drinks). Anglers catch trout, redfish, flounder, drum, and sheepshead.

Land and Sea Marina
13246 S. Padre Island Dr., Corpus Christi
• (361) 939-9296

Fifteen fishing guides operate out of this full-service marina on the Laguna Madre. Established in 1982, the marina offers a lighted fishing pier, fishing licenses, fish cleaning, RV hookups, boat slips, and a boat ramp, and it sells bait, tackle, sandwiches, and drinks. The fishing guides will take you into the Laguna Madre and Baffin Bay at a rate of $350 for two people all day, or $250 for a half-day. All equipment is furnished, but customers do have to bring their own food and drinks.

Outfitters

Gruene Outfitters
1233 Airline Rd., Corpus Christi
• (361) 994-8361

You can buy fishing gear, outdoor clothing, Wilderness Systems kayaks and more at this fly-fishing specialty shop. The store concentrates on saltwater fly fishing, but also has gear for freshwater fly fishing. While you're here, you can test out a new rod in the outdoor casting pond, pick up some tips on fly fishing and grab a list of guides for this area. The staff also offer casting seminars, fly-tying classes and kayak demonstrations, as well as information about where to go for wade fishing (for those who don't have a boat).

Kingsville Area

For fishing in the Kingsville area, your best bet is Baffin Bay, which is renowned for its large trout. The Riviera area, south of Kingsville on U.S. Highway 77, is where you'll find guides, lodges, and a good fishing pier.

Baffin Bay, in contrast to Port Aransas and Rockport, offers a quieter fishing environment and tends to draw serious anglers who want to devote their entire time to fishing. On the one hand, there aren't as many distractions and the fishing areas are less likely to be crowded. On the other hand, if you're with family members who aren't into fishing, they won't find quite

as many activities such as shopping, museums or recreation as in the area's more bustling communities.

Try the Kaufer-Hubert Memorial Park for a launch ramp to fish on Baffin Bay.

The area is home to one really fine restaurant, King's Inn, which draws customers from wide and far for its delectable fried seafood and avocado salads. For more information see our Restaurants chapter.

Fishing Pier

Kaufer-Hubert Memorial Park
East on F.M. Rd. 628, Loyola Beach
• (361) 297-5738

This waterfront park overlooks the Cayo del Grullo, which feeds into Baffin Bay and the Laguna Madre, and offers some of the best fishing in this area. The facility is part of a 137-site RV park known as SeaWind Resort (see our Campgrounds and RV Parks chapter). You'll find a 500-foot lighted fishing pier as well as campgrounds, restrooms, picnic tables, and a boat ramp.

Fishing Lodges and Guides

Bailey's on Baffin Bay
Riviera
• (361) 595-4666

This three-bedroom lodge is situated on Baffin Bay, which is home of Texas's speckled-trout record. Located just 20 miles south of Kingsville, this rural lodge has a living area with fireplace and bar, television, stereo, telephone, fax machine, screened porch, private beachfront and a private, lighted fishing pier. With accommodations for up to six people, it is a great place for anglers, hunters, or family vacations. You can bring your own boat or hire a professional fishing or hunting guide. The Lodge charges $75 per person per night including breakfast only, or $125 per person per night for all meals. Free airport shuttle service is available from Corpus Christi International Airport, Klebert County Airport, and Brooks County Airport.

B Bar B Ranch Inn
County Rd. 2217 off U.S. Hwy. 77,
8 mi. south of Kingsville
• (361) 296-3331

Guide Luther Young offers hunting and fishing tours as well as a stay at a restored old ranch house. The B Bar B Ranch Inn was originally part of the nearby historic King Ranch, and it still retains a rustic and isolated feel. An all-day guided fishing trip in Baffin Bay is $300 per person, with a minimum of two people, and the price includes room and board (see our Bed and Breakfast Inns chapter).

Wild Horse Lodge
Riviera
• (361) 584-3098

The Wild Horse Lodge consists of three water-front houses at Baffin Bay with accommodations for hunting and fishing parties. You can rent a house and fish on your own for $125 per night for one or two people ($25 for each additional person) in the Lodge or Bird's Nest, $30 for each additional person in the Ranch House. In addition, there is a Bunk House that costs $75 per night for two people and $25 for each additional person. Tax is not included in the prices quoted above.

You can also arrange a chartered day of fishing (which includes a guide, tackle, artificial bait and cleaning of your catch) for $400 for two per day, and $50 for each additional person in the boat. The fishing trips are in Baffin Bay and Laguna Madre. Reservations are required.

INSIDERS' TIP

Salwater fly fishing was first popularized in Florida and has moved over to the Texas coast, where an increasing number of anglers are trying their hand at the sport.

a weekend at a ranch that offers a packaged hunt.

Under a program launched recently by the state, public lands are now set aside for hunting. A list and map of these lands is available to anyone who purchases a $40 public hunting permit from the Texas Parks and Wildlife Department. Call (800) 895-4248. South Texas has 20 public dove hunting sites within an 80-mile radius of Corpus Christi. If you choose to use these public lands, you'll fare best if you visit the prospective site before your hunt to check out the availability of your quarry.

Under Texas regulations, youngsters (16 and younger) can hunt for free with a licensed adult.

For a guided tour, check out the following guide services, lodges, and ranches.

North Bay Area

Waterfowl hunting is particularly popular in Aransas Pass and Rockport. In Rockport, you can hunt in the bay or in the marshes.

Guides

Guides are available in addition to the company described below, including Tommy Ramzinsky, (361) 729-4493, and Brad Smythe with Web Foot Guide Services, (361) 790-8354. You can also acquire a list of local guides from the Rockport-Fulton Area Chamber of Commerce, (800) 826-6441.

South Bay
Hunting Club and Guide Service
Aransas Pass
• (361) 758-1432

Hunters who want basic ferry service to an already prepared blind or guide services can call Gordon Spears of the South Bay Hunting Club. Spears heads up a family-owned business that consists of guides who use air boats to ferry hunters to duck blinds already set up in the South Bay, which is between Aransas Pass and Port Aransas.

Longtime guide Spears has been operating this service since 1963, and much of his business is from repeat customers who've been coming to them for decades. The company has five air boats and 35 duck blinds that are fully de-

Hunting

Dove and quail are the most popular birds for hunters in South Texas, although duck and other waterfowl are also abundant. Turkey, deer, feral hog, and nilgai (an exotic antelope) are also sought after by hunters, but they can be more expensive to shoot when you take into account the cost of deer leases and guided tours running in the thousands of dollars.

As for deer hunting, the brush country of South Texas produces most of the state's trophy bucks and also offers some of the most expensive hunting in the state. Locating a place to hunt can be the most arduous part of the experience, particularly for hunters coming from states with large tracts of public land that are open to all comers. Since some 97 percent of Texas's land is privately owned, you generally have to find private land on which to hunt. Leasing hunting rights is a firmly established practice in which many folks share in a seasonal hunting lease on a specified pasture or area. Others do day leasing or pay a fee to the owner for each day of hunting; still others opt for a package lease, paying for a guided hunt or coyed. The cost is $65 per person per hunt, either in the morning or evening, and hunters can expect to get teal, widgin, pintails, and redheads. Additional guide services are available for those who can't identify the birds in flight.

Spears is a fishing guide from March through October and a hunting guide from October through January. His fishing trips, in his 23-foot Haynie boat, cost $350 for the first two people and $50 for each additional person (up to four). He furnishes the bait and tackle.

Corpus Christi Area

Dos Vaqueros Lodge
P.O. Box 1035, Refugio
• (361) 543-4905

This deluxe lodge is located on a working cattle ranch (with approximately 1,500 head of cattle) that is one of the area's most historic. Dos Vaqueros is located on one of the great old cattle ranches in South Texas. Founded in 1834, with land grants from both Mexico and the Republic of Texas, the sprawling Rooke Ranch has been owned by descendants of Daniel and Catherine O'Driscoll for over six generations.

The owners now lease out 12,000 acres for the hunting season, and have opened a cowboy-themed guest ranch during the rest of the year. Accommodations are luxurious and spacious, furnished in southwestern-style decor.

You can hunt for white-tailed deer, turkey, dove, quail, and feral hogs here. For $3,500,

hunters get a three-day stay and the opportunity to bag a buck, a doe, or a hog. There is also a nine-hole golf course, swimming pool, wetlands, birding area, a lit roping arena, a park with campfire, grills, and picnic benches, and a private airfield with two paved 4,500-foot runways.

Fennessey Ranch
F.M. Rd. 2678, 10 mi. north of Bayside
• (361) 529-6600

The Fennessey Ranch offers a wide array of recreational opportunities, including hunting, birding, and nature viewing. The ranch is part of a legendary 750,000-acre land empire that has been in the same family for 165 years. Today it consists of 4,000 acres of wetlands, meadows, natural lakes, and Mission River frontage. It's in Refugio County, about 45 minutes north of Corpus Christi.

You can hunt for 15 species of ducks, including gadwalls, canvasbacks, teals, wood ducks, pintails, northern shovelers, and fulvous tree ducks. You can also hunt a Russian boar from an African-style duck blind or bag a trophy white-tailed deer. The cost of a one-day wild-boar safari is $185; a one-day duck hunt is $135. And a guided, white-tailed trophy deer hunt (a four-day excursion) costs $3,100.

Knolle Ranch
F.M. Rd. 70, Sandia
• (361) 547-2546

The Knolle Ranch offers private dove, duck

Bird hunting draws enthusiasts from all over the world to South Texas.

Photo: courtesy of the Greater Corpus Christi Business Alliance

and goose hunting during the season. This ranch, which also operates a bed and breakfast inn (see our Bed and Breakfast Inns chapter), is 35 miles west of Corpus Christi in the Nueces River Valley. Long a dairy farm, the owners transformed it into an English country-style inn that caters to horse owners, hunters, and other visitors.

The rates per gun, per day, are $35 for dove, $75 for duck, $110 for geese and $145 for a duck and goose combination. Hunters bring their own shotguns and gear, while field work is done by the guides. Staff clean the gear and guns as well as process the birds after the hunt.

Knolle Ranch also offers cross-country riding, lodging for horses, riding instruction, birding, canoeing, skeet shooting, and gourmet meals.

Kingsville Area

B Bar B Ranch Inn
County Rd. 2215 off U.S. Hwy. 77,
8 mi. south of Kingsville
• (361) 296-3331

The inn is a restored ranch house that doubles as a bed and breakfast (see our Bed and Breakfast Inns chapter). Owner and guide Luther Young offers a two-day, two-night dove hunt for $350 per person and quail hunts for $850 per person per day that includes the use of his professionally trained bird dogs. Also available are a two-day, two-night spring turkey hunt for $950 per person and a two-day, two-night nilgai bull (an exotic antelope found in South Texas) hunt for $1,500 per person.

Beaches and Watersports

LOOK FOR:
• **Area Beaches**
• **Equipment Rental and Sales**
• **Sailing**
• **Scuba Diving**
• **Surfing**
• **Windsurfing**

The Corpus Christi-area is a mecca for beach and watersports enthusiasts, who are drawn to the water, sand, and warm weather. There's no better place along the Texas coast to stroll the beach, sail across calm waters, or zip around on a personal watercraft.

Beaches are concentrated along the barrier islands that extend from north of Corpus Christi to the Padre Island National Seashore to the south. The North Bay area has one real beach, a 1-mile-long, man-made beach built with dredge material. The Kingsville area has no beaches; much of the Padre Island National Seashore is in the same county as Kingsville, but to approach them by road you have to go through Corpus Christi. Corpus Christi has three small beaches that pale in comparison to those found on Mustang and Padre Islands. Two of those beaches are mentioned below.

When you talk about beaches in the Corpus Christi area you're really talking about one beach stretching the length of Mustang and Padre Islands. The beaches look pretty much the same: white sand stretching 50 yards or so from the water's edge to sand dunes. What's different is the development that has sprung up around them. The northern end of Mustang Island is packed with high-rise condos and other tourist-oriented businesses, most in the city of Port Aransas. On the opposite side of the spectrum is the undeveloped Padre Island National Seashore, where development is limited to the visitor center on the northern tip.

Many visitors are surprised to learn that cars are allowed on most area beaches. The speed limit is 15 mph, and Texas motor vehicle laws are enforced. A beach parking sticker is required for all Nueces County and Port Aransas beaches. Proceeds from the sale of parking stickers fund beach improvements. The Nueces County Parks and Recreation Department issues 30-day permits for $5.39 and annual permits for $10.78. Both prices include tax. You can buy permits from convenience stores, county offices, beach vendors, park and recreation employees on the beach, and at the Nueces County Parks office, (361) 949-8122, 15820 Park Road 22. Beach parking permits also are required at most beaches within the Port Aransas city limits. The cost is $6 per calendar year. Beaches at the southern end of town do not require permits.

Lifeguards staff most area beaches between Memorial Day and Labor Day. You'll also find lifeguards on Nueces County beaches during spring break.

Watersports run the gamut from fishing and sailing to riding personal watercraft and paddleboats. Fishing is such a popular and diverse sport that we've devoted an entire chapter to fishing and hunting. The vast majority of watersports take place in Rockport, Aransas Pass, Port Aransas, and Corpus Christi. Watersports equipment can be rented at many beaches from vendors. You also can find equipment at the businesses and municipalities listed in this chapter. We've divided beaches and watersports equipment rentals into two sections. The prices listed should be considered approximations, as prices could change by the time this book is published. Call ahead to get the latest figures. Businesses that rent watersports equipment either close down in the winter or work reduced hours. In the winter they can be hard to reach. We've noted their months of operation and change in hours wherever possible.

The Corpus Christi Municipal Marina, a service of the City of Corpus Christi Park & Recreation Department, offers water-related activities for residents and nonresidents. Activities include fishing, sailboat races, and sailing classes. For information or to obtain registration forms, visit the Corpus Christi Municipal Marina office on the Lawrence Street T-Head or call (361) 882-7333.

Beaches

North Bay Area

Rockport Beach
210 Seabreeze Dr., Rockport
• (361) 729-9392

This man-made beach built on a spoil island is part of the 61-acre Rockport Beach Park near the city's downtown. Although in existence since the 1950s, it wasn't until 1988 that the city developed it for day use and began charging an entrance fee (see our Parks chapter). The 1-mile-long beach overlooking Aransas Bay is a great place to take the kids. The water is shallow for a quarter-mile into the bay, there are no undertows and high tides and rough waves are scarce.

Facilities include two pavilions with upstairs verandas, restrooms, and party rooms; playground equipment for older and younger children; a band shell; and an 800-foot lighted fishing pier. Other amenities include a lighted fishing jetty (open 24 hours a day); a walking trail; a four-lane boat ramp, and separate launch for sailboats and catamarans. You'll also find watersports rentals; a saltwater pool with a concrete bulkhead; 75 picnic tables with covered cabanas; barbecue pits, volleyball courts; and wheelchair-accessible picnic cabanas, and a water fountain.

The park is open from 5 AM to 11 PM Sunday through Thursday and 5 AM to midnight on Friday and Saturday. Admission is $3 per vehicle per day after 12:30 PM or $7 for a one-year pass. There are no lifeguards.

Corpus Christi

Corpus Christi Beach
North of the Harbor Bridge, Corpus Christi

This former residential neighborhood fell into decline over the years only to be revived when it was chosen as the site for the Texas State Aquarium. The Lexington Museum on the Bay (a decommissioned aircraft carrier) soon followed, and it wasn't long before other tourism-related businesses moved in. Several businesses have failed in recent years, though, and the area's future remains very much uncertain. Corpus Christi Beach (often referred to as North Beach by city old-timers) is on the north side of the Port of Corpus Christi across the towering Harbor Bridge. The beach isn't as large and the sand isn't as fine as those on Mustang and Padre Islands, but you don't have to drive far to get there. The sand is not native to this area. It was brought in after hurricane Celia destroyed the beach in 1970.

Attractions include restaurants, gift shops, hotels, motels, and condominiums (see our Attractions chapter). Lifeguards are on duty during summer months.

Emerald Beach
East side of Holiday Inn Emerald Beach, Corpus Christi
• (361) 883-5731

Don't let the location fool you—this is a public beach. It's right outside the back door of the Holiday Inn, which leads many to believe it's private property. It isn't. This may be the smallest beach you've ever seen; it runs the length of the Holiday Inn. The water is shallow and protected on the sides by jetties extending 50 yards or so into the bay, which helps keep it calm. Facilities include rinse showers, sun deck, bar, lounge chairs, beach umbrellas, banana rides (a giant inflatable banana pulled by a personal watercraft) and, in the summer months, an enormous trampoline in the bay. Jumping privileges cost $5 per person per day. Fees are: beach umbrellas, $8 a day, lounge chairs, $3 a day, inner tubes and Boogie Boards, $2 for two hours or $5 all day, and banana rides, $10 per person for a 15- to 20-minute ride.

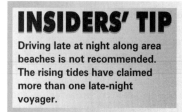

INSIDERS' TIP

Driving late at night along area beaches is not recommended. The rising tides have claimed more than one late-night voyager.

Port Aransas to Padre Island

Nueces County Park
End of Cotter Ave., Port Aransas
• (361) 749-6117

The beaches along Mustang Island are pretty much the same in terms of surf and sand. What makes this area different is the proximity to area condos and the restaurants and shops in Port Aransas. It's accessible from Port Aransas via Cotter and Beach streets or Avenue G off Alister Street. The park has camping and RV sites (see our Parks and Campgrounds and RV Parks chapters), toilets, showers, bathhouse, picnic shelters, and the lighted 1,245-foot Horace Caldwell Pier. The snack bar/convenience store on the pier sells fast food, ice, and basic groceries. You can also rent fishing tackle here. It costs $1 to get on the pier. Entry to the park is free; it's open 24 hours a day. Lifeguards are on duty during spring break and between Memorial Day and Labor Day.

Mustang Island State Park
Texas Hwy. 361,
14 miles south of Port Aransas
• (361) 749-5246, (800) 792-1112

The state of Texas owns and operates this 3,703-acre park on the southern end of Mustang Island. That means two things: They charge an entrance fee, which limits crowds, and they keep the beach in good shape, removing trash and sea waste and smoothing the sand with heavy machinery. The beach, which runs for 5.5 miles along the Gulf of Mexico, is popular with families because no cars are allowed.

Sites for tent and RV camping are nearby (see our Campgrounds and RV Parks chapter). Other facilities include restrooms, dressing rooms, hot and cold showers, shade shelters, picnic tables, pay phones, and a Texas State Parks Store, where you can buy ice and souvenirs. The park is open from 8 AM to 10 PM. Office hours are 8 AM to 5 PM. The park charges an entrance fee of $3 per person for those 12 and older. There are no lifeguards on duty.

J.P. Luby Park
Southern tip of Mustang Island,
Corpus Christi

This beach on the southern end of Mustang Island is a favorite among surfers, young people, and skimpy bathing suit fans. To get there from Corpus Christi, head north on Park Road 53

(also known as Texas Highway 361) and turn right at the first road. The beach is dead ahead. Facilities include portable toilets, covered picnic tables, showers, lights, and a covered pavilion. Lifeguards are on duty during spring break and between Memorial Day and Labor Day.

Rainbow-Beach Rentals has floats, inner tubes, chairs, umbrellas, shade structures, inflatable kayaks, Boogie Boards, dinghies, and bicycles for rent. Shade structures are made from PVC pipes and a 6-foot-by-8-foot section of tarp. Many rentals come in several sizes, which explains the range in prices. Prices are as follows: umbrellas, $5 to $20 a day; shade structures, $10 a day; chairs, $2 to $5 a day; inflatable kayaks, $6 an hour; child-sized inflatable kayaks, $3 an hour; inner tubes, $2 to $6 an hour; dinghies, $4 to $5 an hour; floats, $3 to $4 an hour; Boogie Boards, $2 to $4 an hour or $5 to $15 all day; bicycles, $6 an hour. Rainbow-Beach Rentals is open 9 AM to 6 PM from May through September.

INSIDERS' TIP

Campfires on Nueces County beaches can cover an area no larger than three feet and can be no higher than your knees.

Nueces County Padre Balli Park
15820 Park Rd. 22, Corpus Christi
• (361) 949-8121

This 374.5-acre park is just outside the Corpus Christi city limits and a few miles north of the Padre Island National Seashore. Padre Balli is especially popular among anglers and surfers. Anglers are drawn to the lighted, 1,240-foot Bob Hall Pier. Surfers are attracted to the waves that break near the pier, a situation that in the past has resulted in conflicts as surfers became entangled in fishing lines.

Facilities include RV and tent sites (see our Campgrounds and RV Parks chapter), restrooms, hot showers, concession stand, picnic shelters, laundry facilities, and first-aid station. Park rangers are on duty 24 hours a day.

Padre Balli is open 24 hours a day year round. Admission is free. There is a $1 charge per person to enter the pier and a $1 fee per fishing pole. Lifeguards are on duty during spring break and Memorial Day and Labor Day.

Padre Island National Seashore
9405 S. Padre Island Dr., Corpus Christi
• (361) 949-8068

"Secluded" best describes the Padre Island National Seashore. The barrier island south of Corpus Christi retains much of the unspoiled grandeur that prompted President John F. Kennedy to authorize its purchase in 1962. It's

Searching for Seashells by the Seashore

If you're tempted to search for hidden treasure while beachcombing, you've come to the right place. And we're not referring to the long-lost gold supposedly left in these waters by marauding pirate types. We're talking nature's bounty here—a veritable treasure trove of seashells. The tides are your best guide for finding these shells. High tide carries the shells onto the sand, and low tide leaves them in plain sight on the beach. Your best bet is to go seashell searching sometime in between—but the earlier the better. Someone else may beat you to the best shells if you wait too long.

When you search, bring a bucket and a digging tool. You may find a lettered olive, sand dollar, ark shell, star fish, sea whip, or crab shells. One of the best places to search is at Padre Island National Seashore, where you'll find miles of pristine shoreline for wandering. Winter is the best time to go, when storms called "northers" disturb the water and push more shells ashore.

A note of caution: Not all the items you find on the beach are treasures some are trash. You may find plastic, glass, and lumber along the shore, the discarded garbage of offshore vessels. Be wary of any drum that appears to have toxic materials-any such "find" should be reported immediately to the park rangers.

Here are some of the more commonly found seashells in this area:

Turkey Ark

Saw-toothed Pen Shell

Transverse Ark

Lettered Olive

Sundial

Atlantic Cockle

Lightning Whelk

Bay Scallop

Murex

Coquina Clams

Scotch Bonnet

Moon Snail

Iris Tellin

Disk Dosinia

Sand Dollar

one of the longest stretches of primitive, undeveloped ocean beach in the United States. You'll see white sand-and-shell beaches, picturesque dunes, grassland, and tidal flats.

Malaquite Beach is near the visitor center as you enter the park. Here you'll find umbrella rentals, toilets, cold showers, and shaded picnic tables. The first 5 miles of beach are accessible by two-wheel-drive vehicles; the next 55 miles are accessible via four-wheel-drive only.

The park charges a $10 entrance fee good for seven days; an annual pass is available for $20. An additional $5 fee is charged for anyone wishing to visit the popular windsurfing site known as Bird Island Basin or to launch a boat; an annual pass sells for $10. Discount passes for senior citizens and handicapped individuals are available. The park is open 24 hours a day. The visitor center is open every day except Christmas and New Year's Day from 8:30 AM to 6 PM between Memorial Day and Labor Day and 8:30 AM to 4 PM the rest of the year. There are no lifeguards on duty.

Whitecap Beach
The end of Whitecap Blvd., Corpus Christi

This area north of Nueces County Padre Balli Park is located on Padre Island and within the Corpus Christi city limit. It's located just south of area condominiums near the Holiday Inn Gulf Beach Resort. Locals often refer to the area as Whitecap Beach, although the city of Corpus Christi has not officially given it that name. The beach runs for about a quarter of a mile inside the city limits then falls under Nueces County's jurisdiction for another quarter mile before becoming Nueces County Padre Balli Park. The beach is well maintained here, less crowded than J.P. Luby Surf Park and less remote than the Padre Island National Seashore.

Rainbow-Beach Rentals has floats, inner tubes, chairs, umbrellas, shade structures, inflatable kayaks, Boogie Boards, dinghies, and bicycles for rent. Shade structures are made from PVC pipes and a 6-foot-by-8-foot section of tarp. Many rentals come in several sizes, which explains the range in prices. Prices are as follows: umbrellas, $5 to $20 a day; shade structures, $10 a day; chairs, $2 to $5 a day; inflatable kayaks, $6 an hour; child-sized inflatable kayaks, $3 an hour; inner tubes, $2 to $6 an hour; dinghies, $4 to $5 an hour; floats, $3 to $4 an hour; Boogie Boards, $2 to $4 an hour or $5 to

$15 all day; bicycles, $6 an hour. Rainbow-Beach Rentals is open from 9 AM to 6 PM from May through September.

Equipment Rental and Sales

Boat Rentals

AME Charters Sailing Center
97 S. Austin St., Rockport
• (361) 729-8225

AME Charters offers several sizes of sailboats for rent. Boats include Sunfish, 14-foot to 18-foot boats, catamarans, and 25-foot boats for longer excursions. There is a two-hour minimum on all rentals. Rates are: Sunfish, $10 an hour, $50 daily; 14-foot to 18-foot boats, $20 an hour, $75 daily; catamarans, $20 an hour, $75 daily; 25-footers, $150 a day, $200 for a weekend and $450 for the week.

Little Bay Marine
1838 Broadway, Rockport
• (361) 729-7409, (361) 729-7461

Little Bay Marine has eight boats available for rent, ranging from a 17-foot Hydra Sport to a 24-foot party barge. Prices for a five-hour, half-day range from $140 to $192 and from $175 to $240 for a full, 10-hour day. Boats come with a full tank of gasoline, instructions, compass, fishing chart, and life jackets. You'll be charged for fuel used. To reserve a boat, you'll be charged half the boat rental fee; the other half is due when you arrive to pick up your boat. No deposit required.

INSIDERS' TIP

Locals say meat tenderizer helps reduce the pain of jellyfish stings.

Crabman Marina & Seafood
Texas Hwy. 361
between Aransas Pass and Port Aransas
• (361) 758-0294

The Crabman has four 16-foot aluminum, flat-bottomed boats with 15-horsepower outboards available. The cost is $50 a half day, $80 a full day for two people and $10 extra per person for more than two people. No more than four people are allowed in a single boat. A $30 deposit is required per boat. Boats come equipped with lifejackets, anchor, oars, and a full gas tank.

South Bay Bait and Charters
Texas Hwy. 361,
between Aransas Pass and Port Aransas
• (361) 758-2632

South Bay has nine 16-foot Sea Ark aluminum boats with 15-horsepower Yamaha motors for rent. A five-hour half-day costs $50 for two people and $10 extra per person for more than two adults. A full day costs $75 for two people and $10 extra per person for more than two. The company furnishes gasoline, life jackets, paddles, and an anchor. There is a $25 deposit on each boat.

Personal Watercraft

North Bay Area

Watercraft Rentals
Rockport Beach Park
• (361) 729-9509

Watercraft Rentals has Jet Skis, Waverunners, and Sea Doo personal watercraft available for rent. The cost is $45 for a half-hour and $80 for an hour. The price covers gasoline and life jackets. No deposit is required. Watercraft Rentals operates from spring break through the Labor Day weekend.

Paradise Jet Ski Rentals Inc.
136 Cotter Ave., Port Aransas
• (361) 749-6904

Paradise Jet Ski Rentals is on the docks of Woody's Sports Center just east of the ferry landing. You can rent a Jet Ski for one to three people by the hour or by the half-hour. They go for about $45 a half-hour and $70 an hour. Gas and life jackets are furnished. You must leave an open credit card or personal check of $500 per machine as a safety deposit. Paradise is open from 9 AM to sunset every day between March 1 and October 31.

INSIDERS' TIP

Walking or driving on sand dunes is prohibited.

Corpus Christi

Island Watersports Center
1102 S. Shoreline Blvd., Corpus Christi
• (361) 880-8901

Generally open from spring break through the end of September, Island Watersports rents Yamaha Waverunners from its bayfront location on Emerald Beach outside the Holiday Inn. Island Watersports is open from 9 AM to dusk during the summer. Call ahead. Waverunners

rent for $20 for 15 minutes, $35 for 30 minutes and $60 for an hour. A life jacket and gasoline are included in the price. No deposit required.

Paddleboats

Rent a paddleboat at the Peoples Street T-Head along the Corpus Christi Bayfront. On most summer days the water is relatively calm in Corpus Christi Bay, and the T-Head and rock breakers ringing the Corpus Christi Marina make the water near the rentals even calmer. Drop by the T-Heads in warmer months to check on availability and prices. Paddleboats generally rent for about $10 a half hour. In Rockport visit the Rockport Beach Park in downtown Rockport or call (361) 729-9392. Paddleboats there also rent for about $10 per half hour.

Sailing

North Bay Area

AME Charters Sailing Center
97 S. Austin St., Rockport
• (361) 729-8225

Ame Charters has been in business going on three years. In addition to renting sailboats (see the listing under Boat Rentals), owner Early Hall offers sailing lessons for all levels. Boats include Sunfish, 14-foot to 18-foot sailboats, catamarans, and 25-foot boats. Lessons cost about $25 an hour.

Rockport Yacht Club
722 Navigation Cir., Rockport Harbor,
Rockport
• (361) 729-3115, (361) 729-5622

The Rockport Yacht Club is a fancy name for a bunch of folks who like boats. You don't have to have a fancy yacht to join—all you need is a boat, a love for the water, and a $150 initiation fee. Annual dues are $150 for individuals and $180 for families. Nonresident dues are $100 for singles and $120 for families. Both sailors and power boaters are welcome here.

The club meets at 6:30 PM on the third Thursday of each month at its clubhouse at Rockport Harbor. The club sponsors bay sailboat races every spring, summer, and fall, a race/cruise from Port Aransas to Port Mansfield on Labor Day Weekend, a race from Corpus

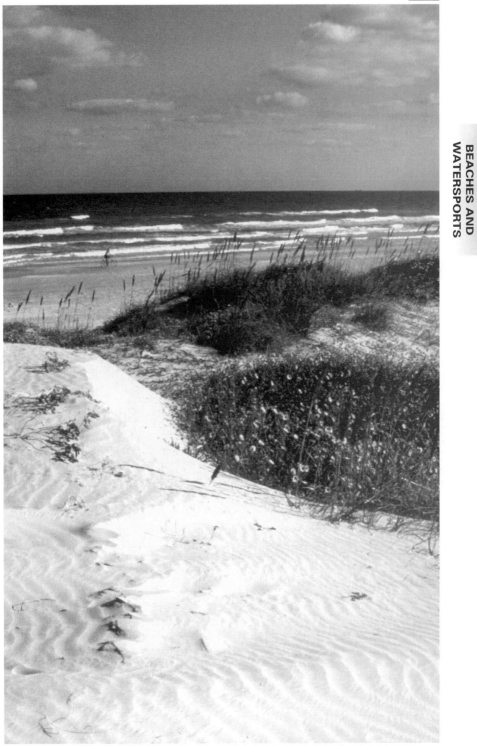

Tourists from all over the world travel to Corpus Christi each year to enjoy its pristine beaches.

Photo: courtesy of the Greater Corpus Christi Business Alliance

Christi to Rockport during the October Seafair (See our Annual Events and Festivals chapter), a Christmas Light Parade, and a Sunfish sailing instructional program.

Corpus Christi

Corpus Christi Sailing Center
200 S. Shoreline Blvd., Corpus Christi
• (361) 881-8503

Sail on vessels from 30 to 46 feet with captained charters or under your own guidance for four hours to a week. The sailing center also offers sunset supper cruises, Sunfish sailboat rentals, new boat and kayak sales, basic keelboat sailing instructions, and a Sunfish sailing school for adults. Sunset supper cruises include a four-course dinner at a seafood restaurant on a boat in Corpus Christi Bay, followed by a two-hour sailing trip on the bay. Tickets (including dinner) are $55 for adults and teens, $25 for children ages 6 to 12 and $10 for children younger than 6.

A basic keelboat sailing course is held from 9 AM to 5 PM on Saturday and Sunday. The cost is $190, including textbook. A three-day basic coastal sailing course takes you along the Texas coast as you learn to sail and live aboard the boat. The cost is $590, including food and textbook. The Sailing Center also offers a five-day, live-aboard course. The cost is $990, including food and textbook.

Wednesday Night Sailing Regatta
Lawrence Street T-Head, Corpus Christi

The Wednesday Night Sailing Regatta is held every Wednesday beginning at around 6 PM from the Lawrence Street T-Head. Races are held on varying courses on Corpus Christi Bay. While they await the signal to start, boats crisscross inside the rock breakers that form a semicircle around the Corpus Christi Marina. Registration takes place on the Lawrence Street T-Head 30 minutes before the race begins. There is no entry fee.

Scuba Diving

Ascuba Venture
6121 S. Padre Island Drive, Ste. A,
Corpus Christi
•(361) 985-1111

Ascuba Venture offers equipment sales and service along with classes from beginner on up to more technical classes such as cave diving, wreck diving, and stage decompression diving.

It also offers dive tours all over the world, venturing to such places as Fiji, the Grand Caymans, Costa Rica, and the Bahamas.

People come from all over the country to dive with Ascuba Venture. Visitors to Corpus Christi may be able to take part in a dive trip to the Port Aransas jetties or an offshore oil rig. Spearfishing and underwater photography classes also are available.

Copeland's Marine
4041 S. Padre Island Dr., Corpus Christi
• (361) 854-1135

Copeland's Marine offers scuba diving lessons, daytrips, and sleeper trips throughout most of the year. A new scuba diving class starts up about once a month throughout the year, while dive trips leave from Port Aransas each week except in December and January. *The Adventurer* takes divers to offshore oil rigs and the 7½-Fathom Reef, 80 miles south of Corpus Christi. Copeland's also offers trips to the Flower Garden Marine Sanctuary, 100 miles offshore, where fish gather in large numbers. The air-conditioned and heated 85-foot custom dive boat comes with a full galley and room to sleep 33. A daytrip costs about $99 per person. Sleeper trips range anywhere from $139 to $299 per person.

Surfing

The best places to surf in the Corpus Christi area are Bob Hall Pier at Nueces County's Padre Balli Park, Mustang Island State Park, and Horace Caldwell Pier in Port Aransas.

Port Aransas

Bo Jon's
220 E. Ave. G, Port Aransas
• (361) 749-3133, (361) 749-6478

Bo Jon's is really two stores in one. Situated side-by-side and offering much of the same merchandise, one store serves as a "half-off" store selling older merchandise while the other sells the latest styles at normal retail prices. Both sell sportswear, T-shirts, bathing suits, and suntan products. The "new" store also sells surfboards made by Spider, G&S, Blue Hawaii, Ocean Energy, Rusty, and others. They also rent Boogie Boards for $5.50 a day with a $30 deposit and beach chairs for $5 a day with a $25 deposit. At the "half-off" store, older Boogie Boards go for $4 a day with a $25 deposit. Hours are 9 AM to 9 PM.

Pat Magee's
101 Ave. G, Port Aransas
- **(361) 749-4177**

Pat Magee's has been in business here since 1969. His island shop offers swimwear, sportswear, T-shirts, and watersports equipment, including surf boards, Boogie Boards, and ocean kayaks. Rental prices are as follows: surf boards, $15 a day; Boogie Boards, $5 a day; and ocean kayaks, $35 a day for a single and $45 a day for a two-person kayak. You must have a valid driver's license to rent equipment.

Corpus Christi

Wind and Wave Water Sports
10721 S. Padre Island Dr., Corpus Christi
- **(361) 937-9283**

Wind and Wave rents all sorts of water toys, including surfboards, Boogie Boards, and kayaks. Surfboards rent for $20 a day, Boogie Boards go for $10 a day, and kayaks rent for $35 to $45 a day. The shop is open from 9 AM to 7 PM on weekends throughout the year and 9 AM to 7 PM Monday through Friday in the spring and summer. In the fall and winter, Wind and Wave is open 10 AM to 6:30 PM on weekdays.

Windsurfing

People come from all over the world to windsurf in the Corpus Christi area. Corpus Christi is one of the windiest cities in the nation. The annual U.S. Open Windsurfing Regatta is held at South Cole Park, known by longtime locals as Oleander Point, and attracts professional windsurfers from all over the world.

In addition to South Cole Park, popular windsurfing spots include the Laguna Madre and Bird Island Basin at the Padre Island National Seashore. South Cole Park, it should be noted, is not a place for beginners. You're better off learning in the Laguna Madre or Bird Island Basin, where the water is relatively shallow and calm.

Bird Island Basin is the area's favorite windsurfing spot. The water is flat and chest deep. Beginners feel safe knowing they can stand up if they fall in, while more experienced windsurfers like it because the calm water allows them to go faster.

Worldwinds Windsurfing
Bird Island Basin
- **(361) 949-7472, (800) 793-7471**

Worldwinds rents windsurfing equipment and gives lessons from March through November at Bird Island Basin, a popular windsurfing spot at the Padre Island National Seashore. A four-hour beginner class (including equipment) costs $55. Advanced lessons are available for $45 an hour. Equipment for beginners rents for $20 for two hours and regular equipment rents for $30. Regular equipment rents for $55 a day or $275 for a week. Worldwinds offers all new equipment each year. The shop is open from 10 AM until around 5 PM. They also have new and used equipment for sale.

To get to Bird Island Basin, you'll have to pay two entrance fees: one for the Padre Island National Seashore and another fee for Bird Island. The park charges a $10 entrance fee good for seven days; an annual pass is available for $20. It's an additional $5 to enter Bird Island Basin; an annual pass sells for $10.

Recreation

Maybe it's the year-round warm weather or perhaps it's being so close to nature, but whatever the reason, Corpus Christi-area residents participate in a wide variety of recreational activities throughout the year.

Hunting and fishing are such popular activities here that we've devoted an entire chapter to them. See our Fishing and Hunting chapter for details on fishing spots, guides and stores as well as favored hunting spots. And as you might imagine, watersports also are popular here, so we've set aside a chapter for those activities as well. For more information see our Beaches and Watersports chapter.

What's left? Plenty. The Corpus Christi area offers everything from archery to volleyball, along with youth leagues, little leagues and a vast selection of classes and leagues offered by local park and recreation departments. If you don't see your favorite activity listed in this chapter, call the park and recreation department of the city nearest you and ask about it.

Corpus Christi has the most to offer with leagues and classes throughout the city. The athletic/recreation office of the Corpus Christi Park & Recreation Department operates the Corpus Christi Gym and the Ben Garza Gym. Each offers a variety of athletic programs open to youth. Volleyball, basketball, weightlifting, and martial arts are offered throughout the year. The Corpus Christi Park & Recreation Department also offers adaptive programs for people with disabilities. For more information on these or other activities call the athletics office at (361) 880-3460.

There are other park and recreation departments in the area that also cater to the public's fun and fitness needs: Rockport, (361) 729-2213; Aransas Pass, (361) 758-5301; Portland, (361) 777-3301; Port Aransas, (361) 749-4111; Ingleside, (361) 776-2517; and Kingsville (Kleberg County), (361) 595-8591.

Recreational activities are listed in alphabetical order to make it easier to find an activity in which you are interested. Entries in each category are then divided into geographic regions under appropriate headers.

Archery

11 AM to 8 PM Monday through Friday, 10 AM to 4 PM on Saturdays.

Clyde's Archery Inc.
5564 Ayers St., Corpus Christi
- **(361) 855-3116**

Clyde's Archery Inc. has been in business since 1981 and is the third-oldest archery shop in Texas. Clyde's boasts 20 indoor ranges as well as a full-service repair shop. The shop carries major brand-name bows as well as other archery needs such as videos and camouflage clothing. You can also sign up to go bow hunting. The shop is open

Tejas Archery Club
5564 Ayers St., Corpus Christi
- **(361) 855-3116**

The Tejas Archery Club is the oldest archery club in Texas. Its charter dates back to the 1930s. Dues are $50 a year. Members participate in leagues and tournaments. The club has a 28-target course in northwest Corpus Christi featuring shots from 10 to 80 yards away. The club hosts a tournament once a month.

Baseball

South Texas Adult Baseball League
Corpus Christi
- **(361) 241-5949**

This men's league began its ninth year in March 2000 with 15 teams playing a 12-game season. Keep in mind that this is baseball—known by enthusiasts as "hardball"—and not the softer, slower softball. The league has two seasons: the spring season runs from March to May, while the fall season runs from August to October. Both seasons include playoffs and an all-star game. Players can participate in either the 18-and-older category or in the 30-and-older category.

All games are played at Equistar Park on McKenzie and Haven roads in northwest Corpus Christi. You can be matched with a team or organize your own. Teams hold tryouts to determine whether you're qualified to play. Fees are $75 per person to pay for umpires, use of the field, baseballs, and maintenance. Team managers participate for free, and player/managers are allowed.

Billiards

Clicks Billiards
4535 S. Padre Island Dr., Corpus Christi
- **(361) 851-2680**

Throw your pool cue in the back seat and head for Clicks, where chances are you won't have to wait for a table. Clicks, which you'll find along Corpus Christi's main shopping and dining district, has 18 Brunswick pool tables, including two 9-foot-long pool tables. At Clicks you rent a table by the hour. The cost is $6.50 at most times, although you can find cheaper rates.

Clicks also has a full-service bar, video games, two electronic dart boards, two foosball tables, a CD jukebox, electronic interactive trivia, 13 midsize televisions, and one big-screen TV. Clicks sponsors pool leagues and pool and darts tournaments. It's open from 11 AM to 2 AM Monday through Saturday and noon to 2 AM on Sunday.

Slick Willie's Family Pool Hall
5600 S. Padre Island Dr., Corpus Christi
- **(361) 906-0229**

Slick Willie's touts itself as a family pool hall. Kids are allowed during daytime hours. Step inside and you'll find a clean, pleasant at-mosphere where adults and kids can enjoy the sport of billiards. They even have sawed-off cue sticks for the little ones, although they'll still have to navigate the full-sized tables.

Slick Willie's has 23 tables in all, along with two TV sets, electronic dart boards, full-service bar, game room, and electronic games that can be played at the bar. They also serve sandwiches, pizza, popcorn, and chips.

They're open from 11 AM to 2 AM Monday through Saturday and noon to 2 AM on Sunday.

Bowling

You won't regret packing that 18-pound bowling ball when you visit the area. Bowling is a popular sport here, and bowlers have five bowling centers to choose from, including four in Corpus Christi. At least two bowling associations have formed for people who share a common interest in the game. You can reach the Corpus Christi Women's Bowling Association at (361) 992-5424 and the Corpus Christi Area Bowling Association Inc. at (361) 854-2624.

The Corpus Christi Park & Recreation Department offers bowling for adults with mobility difficulties. The program is designed for adults having problems with balance and mobility, including those using a wheelchair, walker or cane and anyone suffering stiffness from arthritis or recent surgery. Spouses, care providers, and assistants also may participate. The group meets at 1:30 PM Wednesday at Saratoga Lanes, 6116 Ayers Street.

North Bay Area

Sully's Bowling Lanes
2285 W. Wheeler Ave., Aransas Pass
- **(361) 758-3225**

Sully's, the only bowling center in the North Bay area, has 16 lanes, a video/game room and a snack bar. Rates are $2.75 a game and $1.85 to rent shoes. Sully's has league play Sunday through Thursday beginning at 7 PM. Call the bowling center to join. A few lanes usually are available for open play even on league nights.

Sully's is open Sunday through Thursday from noon until 10 PM and noon to midnight on Friday and Saturday. Senior and military discounts are available Monday through Thursday until 6 PM. Sully's offers a youth bowling league on Saturday from 11 AM to 1 PM and Glow-Bowl with music and disco lights from 9 PM to midnight on Friday and Saturday nights.

RECREATION

Corpus Christi

AMF Saratoga Lanes
6116 Ayers St., Corpus Christi
• (361) 857-2695

AMF owns two bowling centers in Corpus Christi, including the AMF Saratoga Lanes on the city's south side. Its 40 lanes are the most in the Corpus Christi area. The center also has a snack bar, lounge, video/game room, billiards, darts, and automatic computerized scoring. Rates are $2.50 a game weekdays before 5 PM and $3.50 a game thereafter. Rates are $3.50 a game before 10 PM on Saturdays and all day Sunday. Saratoga Lanes offers late-night bowling with black lights and a disco ball from 10 PM to 2 AM on Friday and Saturday. The cost is $4 a game. Shoe rental is $2.50 for adults and $2 for children. League play is held Monday through Friday beginning at 6 PM, and open lanes are available most nights. The center opens at 10 AM on Monday, Thursday, Friday, and Sunday and 9 AM on Tuesday, Wednesday, and Saturday. Closing time is around midnight except on Friday and Saturday nights when the lanes close at 2 AM.

AMF also operates AMF Hilltop Lanes, 12150 IH-37, (361) 241-2700, Corpus Christi. Prices, hours, and facilities are similar here.

Cycling

The Corpus Christi area could either be considered a great place for cycling or one of the worst, depending on whether you're headed into the wind or have it at your back. The relatively flat landscape makes cycling long distances a breeze (no pun intended), unless you find yourself battling against the ever present wind.

The Corpus Christi area has few biking lanes and established cycling paths. In Corpus Christi, you can cycle along the seawall or along the special bike path on Ocean Drive. The city is in the process of building a hike-and-bike trail connecting the seawall to bayfront parks. The path runs through both parkland and the Ocean Drive bike lane. Be careful. The speed limit along Ocean Drive is 40 miles per hour, and many motorists exceed that. Port Aransas is a great place to ride. The city itself is so small that a bicycle is a legitimate transportation option. And if you're into long-distance cycling, ride the 26-mile length of Mustang Island from Port Aransas to Padre Island. Again, be careful. Drivers along this stretch of Texas Highway 361 often reach speeds in excess of 70 miles per hour, and they've been know to pass on the shoulders where cyclists ride.

Port Aransas

Island Bikes
736 Tarpon St., Port Aransas
• (361) 749-6566

Island Bikes rents old-fashioned single-speed beach cruisers year round from its Port Aransas shop. The shop has 25 to 30 bikes available to rent for one hour to one month. It also sells bikes and accessories, rents bike trailers, and repairs bikes. Bikes rent for $5 an hour, $15 a day, and $45 a week. Monthly rentals vary. Island Bikes provides free pickup and delivery within the Port Aransas city limit for anyone who spends $25 or more. The shop is closed on Tuesdays and open noon to 6 PM on Sundays and 9 AM to 6 PM the rest of the week.

Corpus Christi

Corpus Christi Bicycle Club
• (361) 883-4517

Hop on your bike and join the Corpus Christi Bicycle Club for its weekend rides around town. Non members are welcome provided they supply their bikes and helmets. The group meets every Saturday at Jason's Deli, 5325 Saratoga Boulevard, to commune with fellow pedal pushers and pursue their passion for cycling. The club also participates in special events. The most notable is the annual Island Breeze, a 68-mile ride around Corpus Christi Bay held the last weekend in October. The club also promotes cycling safety and cycling education in local schools. Membership dues are $15 a year for individuals and $25 a year for families. Children are welcome, and helmets are required for all rides.

Odie's
403 N. Shoreline Blvd., Corpus Christi
• (361) 882-7554

Odie's is located across the street from the Corpus Christi seawall, a 2-mile-long concrete barrier built to protect the city from hurricanes. Cyclists, joggers, skateboarders, and in-line skaters take to the wide concrete surface to enjoy the beautiful water, the cool breeze, and the downtown scenery.

Odie's offers cruiser bikes for $7 a day. These big-wheeled, single gear bikes are great for folks who want to take a leisurely cruise around the area. Odie's also rents in-line skates for $15 a day and skateboards for $7 a day. They're open from 10 AM to 7 PM Monday through Saturday and 10 AM to 5 PM on Sundays.

Disc Golf

Bay Area Disc Golf Association
- **(361) 758-6466, (361) 851-8236, (361) 980-1961**

The 30 or so members of the Bay Area Disc Golf Association sponsor monthly tournaments open to players of all skill levels. Want to learn? Just show up at their monthly tournaments and someone will loan you a disc or two. Disc golf is played like regular golf using flying discs instead of a ball and club. It's cheap and easy to learn. You can make do with one $10 disc, although four is considered the minimum number required to play a good round.

The Corpus Christi area has three disc golf courses. Live Oak Park in Ingleside features an 18-hole course. The park is east of Farm-to-Market Road 1069 and two miles south of Texas Highway 361. A second 18-hole course is in Corpus Christi's West Guth Park on Up River Road north of Rand Morgan Road. A nine-hole course can be found at Lamar Park, at the corner of Santa Fe Street and Barracuda Place. (For more information see our Parks chapter.)

Call for tournament information. You can play anytime free of charge. An association membership is $25.

Golf

Year-round warm weather makes the Corpus Christi area a great place for golfers. Even in the middle of winter it's usually warm enough to play a round of golf at one of the area's several courses. You can even play in shorts on many winter days.

Want to hit a few practice shots before heading out to the course? Head to the driving range. Many courses have their own ranges. Stand-alone ranges include: Cimarron Golf Driving Range, (361) 993-8180, 3752 Cimarron Road, Corpus Christi; Pro 37 Sports, (361) 241-5553, IH-37 and Violet Road, Corpus Christi; Paradise Golf Center, (361) 939-9578, 9449 S. Padre Island Drive, Corpus Christi; and The Kingsville

RECREATION

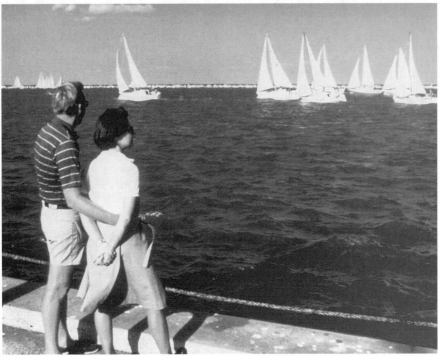

Sailing can be enjoyed year-round in windy, warm South Texas.

Photo: courtesy of the Greater Corpus Christi Business Alliance

Ballpark, (361) 592-2444, 2520 E. Santa Gertrudis Avenue, Kingsville. Following is a list of area courses.

North Bay Area

Rockport Country Club
101 Champions Dr., Rockport
• **(361) 729-4182**
This 18-hole, par 71 course is open to United States Golf Association country club members. Unlike many other South Texas courses, trees are abundant here. Most are of the live oak variety common to the North Bay Area. The course has a nice mix of short and long holes, big and small greens. Sand and water hazards are abundant.

Fees, which include cart rental, are $51 weekdays and $61 on weekends. Winter Texans can play unlimited golf for $235 a month for singles and $395 a month for couples. Cart fees for winter Texans are $10 per person per round.

Corpus Christi

Gabe Lozano Sr. Golf Center
4401 Old Brownsville Rd., Corpus Christi
• **(361) 883-3696**
Gabe Lozano Sr. Golf Center has both a regulation 18-hole course and a nine-hole executive course. It also has a pro shop, snack bar, and lighted driving range. The 6953-yard, par 72 course is open seven days a week. The course is long and flat with lots of water and a little sand. The greens are usually in excellent shape, and wind conditions are generally breezy. Greens fees for the 18-hole course are $12.25 weekdays and $14.50 on weekends. After 3 PM, fees are $10.25 weekdays and $10.75 on weekends. Senior citizens 60 and older pay $8.50 on weekdays at all times. Fees for the executive nine are $6.75 weekdays and $8.25 on weekends; rates are the same for seniors. Cart rentals are $15.50 for two people and $10.50 for singles. Walking the course is allowed.

Oso Beach Municipal Golf Course
5601 S. Alameda St., Corpus Christi
• **(361) 991-5351**
This municipal golf course on the city's southside has an 18-hole course, pro shop, and snack bar. It's open every day. This 6223-yard, par 70 course is flat with small greens, lots of water, and breezy conditions. Greens fees on weekdays are $12.25 ($10.25 after 3 PM). Weekend fees are $14.50. The rate for seniors 60 and older is $8.50 Monday through Friday. Carts rent for $15.50 for two people or $10.50 for singles.

Pharaohs Golf Club
7111 Pharaoh Dr., Corpus Christi
• **(361) 991-2477**
This golf club on the city's southside offers an 18-hole course, driving range, pro shop, and restaurant. The 6000-yard, par 70 course has water on 15 of 18 holes. It's mostly flat with lots of palm trees, narrow fairways, and mid-size greens. Public play is welcome. Fees are $14.25 on weekdays and $21.50 on weekends. Carts rent for $10.75 per rider.

Port Aransas to Padre Island

Padre Isles Country Club
14353 Commodore Dr., Corpus Christi
• **(361) 949-8056**
Padre Isles touts itself as "island golf with a touch of Scotland." That's because this windswept 18-hole course near the Gulf of Mexico has few trees to speak of along its 6150-yard, par 72 course. The state's only golf course located on a barrier island boasts tournament condition fairways, greens and tees, natural sand dunes covered with native vegetation and water on 15 holes.

This course is open to members of other United States Golf Association country clubs and visitors staying in one of several area condos with club privileges. The club has a full-service pro shop, cart and club rentals, driving range, practice green, tennis courts, swimming pool, and a clubhouse with bar and grill.

Greens fees, including cart rental, are $48 weekdays and $60 weekends. Call for winter Texan rates.

Kingsville Area

L.E. Ramey Golf Course
U.S. Hwy. 77 S. at F.M. Rd. 3320, Kingsville
• **(361) 592-1101**
This 18-hole municipal course is about a half-mile southeast of Kingsville near the naval air station. It includes a pro shop, driving range, and snack bar. It's open every day. Greens fees are $11 weekdays and $13 weekends for un-

limited golf. Cart fees are $6.50 per person for nine holes and $10 per person for 18. Monthly memberships are available for $70 for singles and $112 for families. This 7100-yard, par 72 course is flat and open with lots of trees.

Horseback Riding

Mustang Ranch Riding Stables
Texas Hwy. 361, Mustang Island
• (361) 991-7433, (361) 749-5055

Corpus Christi adds its own particular spin on this popular activity by offering horseback riding on the beach. For more than 10 years the Mustang Ranch Riding Stable has been offering horseback riding on the beach on Mustang Island. The ranch has horses to suit everyone from children on their first ride to experienced equestrians. It also offers hayrides, beach parties, catering, live music, and dancing. Mustang Ranch is open year round beginning at 9 AM and closing at around 5 or 6 PM. The cost is $25 an hour for adults, $20 an hour for children 12 and younger, and children 5 and younger can ride with an adult for no additional charge.

INSIDERS' TIP

You can rent pedal-powered surreys along the Corpus Christi Bayfront. Four people can fit in these four-wheeled, covered vehicles. They're a great way to see the sights.

To get there from Corpus Christi, take S. Padre Island Drive south across the John F. Kennedy Causeway to Padre Island. Turn left on Texas Highway 361 and drive 6.5 miles. The riding stables will be on your right.

Kayaking

Kayaking has become quite fashionable in the Corpus Christi area in recent years due to the abundance of water and the influx of lightweight kayaks that are generally much easier to carry and maneuver than a traditional canoe. Lots of open, flat water and windy conditions make canoeing more work than most people can stand. Favorite launch sites can be found along the Nueces River in West Guth Park, Oso Bay, Corpus Christi Bay, and the Laguna Madre.

Port Aransas recently inaugurated a kayak launch port and a kayak trail that allows adventurers to paddle their way along one of three routes depending on how far you want to go. Kayaks can be rented for $35 for a single and

$45 a day for a double from several places including Pat Magee's, (361) 749-4177, in Port Aransas; and Wind and Wave Water Sports, (361) 937-9283, 10721 S. Padre Island Dr., Corpus Christi. Inflatable kayaks for adults and children can be rented from Rainbow-Beach Rentals at J.P. Luby Surf Park and Whitecap Beach for $6 for adult-sized kayaks and $3 an hour for child-size kayaks.

Laser Games

Laser Station
4535 S. Padre Island Dr., Corpus Christi
• (361) 852-1077

Strap on your laser gun and step inside this darkened, high-tech arena for 25 minutes of Star Wars battle. Laser Station features black lights, mirrors, and laser guns that shoot a narrow beam of red light from one end of this former movie theater to the other. Laser Station players wear vests that record how many times they've been "shot" and how many times they've "shot" someone else. The one with the most hits wins.

Single-game price is $7; it costs $5.75 each for two or more games.

Laser Station is open 4 PM to 10 PM Monday through Thursday, 4 PM to midnight on Friday, 11 AM to midnight Saturday and 2 PM to 10 PM Sunday.

Martial Arts

North Bay Area

Master Lenny's Tae Kwon Do
2600 Lakeview Dr., Rockport
• (361) 790-9710, (361) 790-9710

Master Lenny strives to instill discipline, self-confidence, and self-control in his students through the Korean martial art of tae kwon do. This defensive art emphasizes kicking techniques designed to give the user an advantage over larger opponents. Students, who range in age from 5 to 75, participate in local tournaments for trophies and medals. Beginning and advanced classes are available for children and adults. Most classes are held in the evening.

Master Lenny also teaches classes in Portland. Call for locations and times.

Corpus Christi

Martial Arts America
4701 Ayers St., Ste. 301, Corpus Christi
• **(361) 852-4299**

Martial Arts America emphasizes the enhancement of life skills rather than kicking and punching. The school has a theme each month with a lesson plan and drills designed to emphasize that theme. It strives to teach children and adults to set and achieve goals for themselves. Adults can also improve their aerobic conditioning and learn self-defense. Classes are offered in the mornings and evenings in private or group settings.

Kim Soo Karate
Oso Recreation Center, 1111 Bernice Dr., Corpus Christi
• **(361) 937-2320, (361) 991-3700**

Kim Soo Karate combines Japanese, Chinese, and Korean arts into one system known as chy yon ruy. Chy yon ruy is designed to build internal and external power and to control anger. It is taught as a discipline rather than as a sport, stressing becoming a mentally and physically balanced and responsible person rather than

winning trophies and medals. Classes are offered for men, women, and children in the evening.

Paintball

Paintball Sports Field
Chapman Ranch Road
between Weber Road and Staples Street, Corpus Christi
• **(361) 814-3830**

Paintball Sports Field features nine fields with different characteristics such as trenches and hills. The cost is $19 per person for all the equipment you need. They're open from noon to 6 PM seven days a week.

Parachuting

Sky's the Limit
1508 W. F.M. Rd. 351, Beeville
• **(361) 358-9330**

Drop in for an adrenaline rush at Sky's the Limit in Beeville. Your first jump will be as a passenger secured to a jumpmaster. Fifteen minutes of instruction is all that's needed to experience the sport without having to worry about doing anything your first time out. The cost is $150.

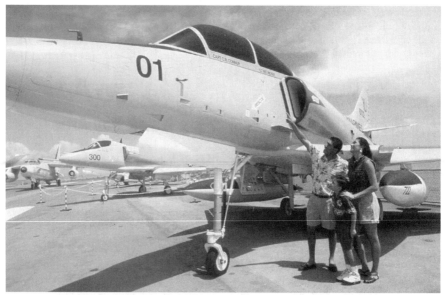

Naval Air Station Corpus Christi is a great place to see a Navy aircraft up close.

Photo: courtesy of the Naval Air Station-Corpus Christi

For those who want to become certified to skydive alone, Sky's the Limit offers an eight-hour program with seven levels of instruction and seven jumps for $1,000. The lessons and jumps can be paid for one at a time. The first lesson and jump is $200, the second and third are $150 each and the next four are $125 each. Post-certification jumps are $35 each if you use their equipment and $14 each if you provide your own. Jumps take place on weekends and holidays in a big field near Beeville. They're open from sunrise to sunset.

To get to Beeville from Corpus Christi, take U.S. Highway 181 north across the Harbor Bridge. The highway will take you northwest through Portland, Gregory, Taft, Sinton, and Skidmore before coming to Beeville, 60 miles away. Get on U.S. Business Highway 181, which takes you through Beeville. Take a left on F.M. Rd. 351 and drive 2.5 miles. Sky's the Limit is on your left.

Racquetball

YMCA
417 S. Upper Broadway, Corpus Christi
• (361) 882-1741

You don't have to be a member to play racquetball or handball on one of the Y's four courts. All you need is $10 or a Y card from anywhere in the world to gain access to courts, whirlpool, steam room, Nautilus machines, free weights, cardiovascular room, indoor pool, and fitness classes. The complex is open from 5:30 AM to 10 PM Monday through Friday, 8 AM to 6 PM Saturday and noon to 6 PM Sunday.

Roller Skating

Cityskates
8051 S. Padre Island Dr., Corpus Christi
• (361) 993-7456

This old-fashioned skating rink has a 14,000-square-foot hardwood maple skating area, snack bar, and video games. It offers free beginning skating lessons, ladies night, private company and school parties, birthday parties, tiny tots skating, teen night, and aggressive skating using ramps, rails, and quarter-pipes.

Running/Walking

Popular running/walking areas in Corpus Christi are along the two-mile-long seawall on Shoreline Boulevard and Ocean Drive, which runs along the bayfront. The beach is popular, too, as is the two-mile-long West Guth Park running trail. West Guth Park is on Up River Road north of Rand Morgan Road.

Corpus Christi Roadrunners
• (361) 881-6166

This nonprofit club of 300 organizes several local races each year and donates the proceeds to charity. Races include 5K runs, half-marathons, and the increasingly popular Beach-to-Bay Relay Marathon, a relay race from Padre Island to Corpus Christi's Cole Park. Fees are $10 for singles and $15 for families. You can get a membership application at Fleet Feet Sports, (361) 225-3338, 514 Everhart Road, Roger Soler's Sports, (361) 992-8397, 5854 S. Staples St., or by leaving a message on the group's answering machine.

Shooting

Corpus Christi Pistol & Rifle Club
F.M. Rd. 763 on Oso Creek, Corpus Christi
• (361) 852-1212

This club on the city's far south side offers sporting clays, skeet, and trap on their outdoor range. Nonmembers shoot for $8.40 a 25-target round for skeet and trap; sporting clays are $10 a round. To shoot a rifle or pistol you must be a member of the club. Dues are $108 a year, and you must go through a 10- to 15-minute safety orientation.

The site is open from 5 PM to 10 PM, Tuesday, 3 PM until sunset Wednesday, 3 PM to midnight Thursday and 9 AM to sunset Saturday and Sunday.

The Sharp Shooter
2033 Airline Rd., Ste. K, Corpus Christi
• (361) 980-1190

The Sharp Shooter offers indoor pistol, rifle, and reactive ranges. It has a total of 15 shooting bays. Fees for both rifles and pistols are $14 an hour per person, not per gun. Two people can shoot in one lane for $21 an hour. The price is the same for all three ranges.

The Sharp Shooter carries a full supply of ammunition, holsters, reloading supplies, gun-cleaning supplies, gun safes, and guns. A top-of-the-line air ventilation system keeps the air clean. You can rent guns, targets, and ear protection. The complex includes a lounge and viewing windows. A retired Texas Ranger—the law enforcement agency, not the baseball team—teaches a one-day concealed-handgun class for $100. Shooting lessons cost $30 per lesson.

The Sharp Shooter is open from noon to 8 PM Tuesday through Friday, 10 AM to 8 PM Saturday and noon to 6 PM on Sunday.

Shuffleboard

Roberts Point Park
Waterfront, Port Aransas
• **(361) 749-5429**

Shuffleboarders can borrow equipment without charge from the harbormaster's office next to Roberts Point Park in Port Aransas. Playing at these outdoor shuffleboard courts will give you a great view of the Corpus Christi Ship Channel and the Port Aransas Harbor. A $20 deposit is required to borrow equipment.

Soccer

Coastal Bend Women's Soccer Association
• **(361) 992-3141**

The Coastal Bend Women's Soccer Association has begun rebuilding in recent years and is now up to about 12 teams. Ages of participants range from 18 to 55 (you have to be at least 16). The spring season begins in February and runs until the beginning of June, while the fall season begins in September and runs until December. Games are played on Sundays at Oso Soccer Field on S. Padre Island Drive near Oso Bay. There are no playoffs. The cost is $17.75 per person. The association holds monthly meetings. For registration information, call the number above or drop by Soccer Etc., 6038 S. Padre Island Drive.

Softball

North Bay Area

Aransas County Softball Association
1300 N. Live Oak St., Rockport
• **(361) 729-4011**

This nonprofit league supports and promotes adult softball (16 years and older) in Aransas County. The association offers co-ed and men's leagues and sponsors a senior citizen's tournament each summer. Games are played between March and November in spring, summer, and fall seasons. Each team plays

about 10 games per season. The men's league has a playoff system. Registration fees are $290 a team for men's teams and $225 for co-ed teams. Games are played at Tiger Field in Rockport.

Corpus Christi

Corpus Christi Softball Association
5230 Kostoryz Rd., No. 17, Corpus Christi
• **(361) 852-8776**

This nonprofit organization promotes a family environment (no alcohol) at its softball games held throughout most of the year. Divisions include 55-and-older men's, 60-and-older men's, church, co-ed, men's open, men's industrial, (players must work 30 hours or more for the company that sponsors them) and church boys and girls. The cost is $295 per team for a seven-game season plus playoffs. The association sponsors four seasons: one each in the spring and fall and two in the summer. The cost for teams in the men's 55-and-older league is $265 and $225 for the men's 60-and-older. Teams must win 50 percent of their games to qualify for the playoffs.

The Grandstands Softball Complex
Saratoga Boulevard and Greenwood Drive, Corpus Christi
• **(361) 854-9994**

The Grandstands' owners discovered a few years ago that you could make money by offering softball lovers a nice place to play. Softball is played here 345 days a year. This facility on the city's far south side has four softball fields, a clubhouse with a full-service concession stand, and a nine-station batting cage.

They offer men's, women's, and co-ed leagues six times a year. Each league lasts seven weeks with playoffs between each session. Teams in the top 25 percent qualify for the double-elimination playoffs. Awards and trophies are awarded in 13 team and individual categories. Come summer, some 200 teams will be signed up to compete.

The registration fee is $300 per team.

Games usually begin at around 6:30 PM and end at 11:30 PM. Batting cages are open 4 PM to 10:30 PM or later Monday through Friday, noon to 8 PM weekends and extended hours during tournaments.

Square Dancing

It all began in the early 1960s when Richard "Blackie" Handy, a new young caller from Corpus Christi, was asked to teach a class for beginners in Aransas Pass. Two couples enrolled in the class loved it so much they decided to organize classes in Rockport. Square dancing flourished in Rockport and continues to do so to this day. The original group adopted the name Paws & Taws, square dancing terms denoting the man, Paw, and the woman, Taw.

In 1965 the group finished the Paws and Taws Convention Center on Fulton Beach Road. Groups from throughout the state hold approximately 14 square-dancing weekends there each year. The building is home to the Ocean Waves Square Dance Club. You can try your hand (or foot) on the center's wooden floor from 8 to 10 PM every Wednesday night. Admission is $2 a person. Call (361) 729-2828 or (361) 729-0745.

In Corpus Christi, check out the Yellow Rockers Square Dance Club, (361) 857-5917 or (361) 850-8812. The Yellow Rockers meet at 8 PM Tuesday at the Jackson Woods Presbyterian Church in Northwest Corpus Christi. The church is located at 10500 Stonewall Boulevard at the intersection of McKinzie Road. Admission is $2 per person.

Swimming

People might go crazy if they didn't have a place to cool off in the middle of the long, hot summer. Fortunately the Corpus Christi area has several swimming pools (not to mention the bays and Gulf of Mexico) in which to escape the heat.

The cities of Portland, Ingleside, and Port Aransas have public swimming pools. Admission to the Portland pool, (361) 777-3301, one block west of U.S. Highway 181 on Moore Avenue, is $1 for children and adults. Admission to the Ingleside pool, (361) 776-7972, 400 Mustang Drive, is $1.50 for children and adults. Admission to the Port Aransas Pool, 700 Clark Parkway, (361) 749-2416, is $2 for adults, $1 for children 2 to 18, $1 for seniors 60 and older, and free to children younger than 2.

The Corpus Christi Park & Recreation Department offers several ongoing swimming programs. They include lap and general swimming, swim league practice, Masters and U.S. Swimming programs, Red Cross and Gus and Goldie swimming lessons, Red Cross lifeguarding and water safety instructors courses, and water aerobics. Pools are also available for private swimming parties.

The department offers swimming for the disabled of all ages, a program that incorporates lessons, water games, and practice. An adult or older sibling must accompany the swimmer in the pool. The program begins in June at Collier Pool, 3801 Harris Street. Call (361) 852-0243.

Corpus Christi has nine swimming pools in all. For information call (361) 880-3481. We've featured two swimming pools in the following entries.

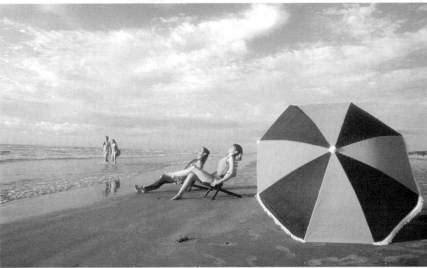

Padre Island offers off-season visitors a peaceful place for relaxation under the sun.

Photo: courtesy of the Greater Corpus Christi Business Alliance

RECREATION

Collier Pool
3801 Harris Dr., Corpus Christi
• (361) 852-0243

This outdoor heated pool in a small city park in the center of the city is open year round. General swim, lap swim, and swim leagues are available. Pools are open all day during the summer season; hours are limited during the off-season. Admission is $2 for adults and $.50 for seniors and youths. Season and annual passes also are available.

Corpus Christi Natatorium
3202 Cabaniss Pkwy., Corpus Christi
• (361) 878-2337

The city's only natatorium is a climate-controlled, indoor state-of-the-art facility with two swimming pools. One is an Olympic-size pool and the other a 25-yard instructional aerobic exercise pool. General swim, lap swim, swimming leagues, and step and splash aerobics are available. Admission is $3.50 for adults, $2 for seniors and $1 for youth. Season and annual passes are available.

Tennis

North Bay Area

Rockport Fulton
Tennis Center and School
5102 Texas Hwy. 35 N., Rockport
• (361) 729-2742

This public tennis facility is a combination tennis center and school. The school is a nonprofit entity that aims to promote tennis among area youth. It raises money, holds youth tournaments, and offers scholarships for those who can't afford to play. The tennis center has six courts, (four lighted) a pro shop, and sponsors tournaments and leagues. The center is open from 8 AM to 8 PM every day. Fees are $4 a day, $15 a week, or $40 a month. It has women's, mixed doubles, men's, and senior leagues.

Corpus Christi

H.E.B. Tennis Center
1520 Shely St., Corpus Christi
• (361) 888-5681, (361) 882-6013

This city-owned facility has 24 outdoor lighted courts and a full-service pro shop. It rents rackets and balls and strings rackets. In-house and citywide leagues are available. Fees

are $2.50 per person for 90 minutes. Six-month permits offering unlimited play are available for $32 for juniors and $72 for adults. Annual permits are $58 for juniors and $140 for adults.

The center also offers private, semiprivate, and group lessons. Civic and corporate tournament rates are $2.50 per court per hour. The whole facility can be rented for $140 for a half-day and $280 for a full day. The center holds about 30 tournaments throughout the year. Hours are 9 AM to 9:30 PM weekdays, 9 AM to 6 PM Saturday and 1 to 6 PM on Sunday.

Al Kruse Municipal Tennis Center
502 King St., Corpus Christi
• (361) 883-6942

This city-owned tennis center in South Bluff Park has 10 courts, a full-service pro shop, equipment rental, professional instruction, and stringing service. In-house and citywide leagues are available. The cost is $2.50 per person for 90 minutes. A six-month permit is $32 for juniors (18 and younger) and $72 for adults. An annual permit is $58 for juniors and $140 for adults. The center is open every day of the year except Christmas, New Year's Day, Easter, and Thanksgiving. It's open from 8:30 AM to 9 PM on weekdays and 8:30 AM to 6:30 PM on weekends.

Volleyball

Roberts Point Park
Port Aransas
• (361) 749-5429

Volleyball equipment is available for use without charge from the Harbormaster's office next to Roberts Point Park in Port Aransas. This sand volleyball court offers a great view of the Corpus Christi Ship Channel and the Port Aransas Harbor. Expect windy conditions. The park is adjacent to the south ferry landing. When you exit the ferry, look to your left. You can't miss it.

Youth Activities

Recreational activities for youth are not hard to find in the Corpus Christi area. Schools, park and recreation departments, little leagues, churches, and youth groups provide a wealth of opportunities for young people. We've accumulated a vast list of groups offering recreational activities for youngsters, but it is by no means all-inclusive.

Many park and recreation departments offer activities for youths. The Corpus Christi Park & Recreation Department, (361) 880-3480, is particularly active. Activities offered by the city include a baseball league for high school boys (registration is by team only). Also available is a summer youth basketball league for boys and girls entering the 7th grade through grade 12. A fast-pitch softball league for girls between the ages of 8 and 18 requires team registration; the season runs from May through July. A slow-pitch softball league for boys and girls between the ages of 9 and 14 holds games on Saturdays for six to eight weeks beginning in March; call (361) 880-3479 for this league.

Youth Groups

The Corpus Christi area has numerous youth groups offering a variety of recreational activities, and we've included many of them in this section.

In the **North Bay** area, contact YMCA of Rockport-Fulton, (361) 790-9622, 644 E. Market Street, Rockport; Aransas Pass Scout Center, (361) 758-7398, 259 S. McCampbell Street, Aransas Pass; and (Portland) Youth Football, (361) 643-1390.

In **Corpus Christi**, contact Boy Scouts of America, (361) 814-4300, 700 Everhart Road, Building A; Boys & Girls Club of Corpus Christi, (361) 853-2505, 3902 Greenwood Drive; Camp Fire Council of Corpus Christi Area, 1601 N. Chaparral Street, (361) 887-1601; Girl Scouts, (361) 883-3611, 1620 S. Brownlee Boulevard; Nueces County 4-H & Youth Development Program, (361) 767-5220, 710 E. Main Street, Robstown; Corpus Christi Youth Football, (361) 852-6992, 3702 Lamont Street; Corpus Christi Youth Football League, (361) 851-8952, 5714 Ayers Street; YMCA, (361) 882-1741, 417 S. Upper Broadway; YMCA Coles Youth In-tramural Program, (361) 882-1741, 924 Winnebego Street; YMCA Crossley Youth Intramural Program, (361) 886-9311, 2512 Koepke; YMCA Flour Bluff Intramural Program, (361) 939-8904, 2505 Waldron Road; and YWCA, (361) 857-5661, 4601 Corona Drive

In **Kingsville**, the Boys & Girls Club of Kingsville, (361) 592-2100, 1238 E. Kenedy Avenue, provides activities for youths.

Soccer

The following organizations are available for youth soccer: Coastal Bend Youth Soccer Association, (361) 992-8299; Padre Soccer League, (361) 994-7810; and Santa Fe Soccer League, 4401 Little John Drive, (361) 857-8217.

Baseball and Softball

Baseball and softball leagues for children are found throughout the Corpus Christi area. The following is a list of the leagues found here.

In the **North Bay** area, contact the Aransas Pass Little League, (361) 758-5644; San Patricio Girls Softball Association, (361) 643-4440; and Portland Little League, (361) 643-1390.

In **Corpus Christi**, contact the International Pony League, (361) 855-3100; National Little League, (361) 993-8862; Oil Belt Little League, (361) 241-8802, 3910 Cliff Crenshaw Road; Oso Pony Baseball Inc., (361) 980-1108; Southside Pony League, 3801 Gollihar Road, (361) 857-5714; Padre Little League, 6869 Yorktown Blvd., (361) 991-5321; Southside Youth Sports Complex, (361) 851-0207; and Universal Little League, (361) 855-4272.

In **Kingsville**, contact the National Little League, (361) 595-1700; and Brush Country Girls Softball, (361) 592-8445, (361) 592-8450.

Spectator Sports

Sports fans are plentiful in the Corpus Christi area, but unfortunately the area has few professional sports teams. Still sports fans will find plenty to hold their interest—you can watch and cheer for everything from windsurfers to college tennis to high school football teams.

Water-based sports, obviously, are going to be as near as the bayfront. You can see windsurfing, sailing, and surfing all year round. High school sporting events are also as near as the closest stadium, and with 10 high schools in Corpus Christi alone, you're likely to have plenty of teenage teams to choose from.

College sports are a little more limited. Texas A&M University-Corpus Christi, which became a four-year institution in the fall of 1994, began adding 14 intercollegiate sports programs in the fall of 1998 and continues through 2001. First on line was women's golf and men's and women's tennis. In the fall of 1999, the university added baseball, softball, and men's and women's basketball, and in the fall of 2000, it added men's and women's cross-country teams and women's volleyball. Men's and women's indoor and outdoor track and field will round out the new programs in the fall of 2001. The teams will participate in the NCAA Division I.

Texas A&M University-Kingsville, about 45 miles from Corpus Christi, also has a strong intercollegiate athletic program. The university's 10 athletic teams draw plenty of spectators from around the Corpus Christi area, particularly for the top-ranked Javelinas football games. The Javelinas—also known as the Hoggies—have been ranked one of the nation's best football teams since the program began in 1925. The Javelinas compete in the NCAA Division II Lone Star Conference and have won seven national titles. More than 100 Javelinas have gone on to the professional ranks, including NFL Hall of Famer Gene Upshaw, Darrell Green, James Jefferson, Johnny Bailey, Heath Sherman, John Randle, and Earl Dotson. Games are played in the 15,000-seat Javelina Stadium, on the northeast corner of the campus.

At Texas A&M University-Kingsville, you'll also find men's teams competing in baseball, basketball, cross-country, and track; women's teams here compete in volleyball, basketball, softball, cross-country, and track. The university's Nolan Ryan Baseball Field was completed in 1994 with fund-raising help from its great namesake pitcher, and a new softball facility was finished in 1997.

The good news for sports lovers is the recent advent of a professional sports team, the Corpus Christi IceRays hockey team. The IceRays finished their first season in 1998-99 with a playoff run, losing in the second round with a 3-to-1 series loss to the Lake Charles Ice Pirates. And South Texas fans—many of whom had never seen a game before—responded with enthusiasm, quickly becoming infected with puck fever. All 35 of the IceRays home games were sellouts, breaking the old Western Professional Hockey League season sellout record of 14 games.

• **185**

However, other professional sports ventures have proved unsuccessful, namely the now defunct Barracudas baseball team and the disbanded Sharks basketball team, which didn't last a single season.

Many Coastal Bend sports fans take to the highways to cheer for their favorite out-of-town professional teams in Houston and San Antonio, about 3½ and 2½ hours away, respectively. In Texas, where football is more than a passion for many folks, it's no big deal to travel hours to see a game played by alma mater Texas A&M University in College Station or The University of Texas at Austin. You can also check out the Houston Astros baseball team, the San Antonio Spurs basketball games or even the Dallas Cowboys and Texas Rangers in the Dallas area—as long as you don't mind the drive.

For information about these out-of-town matchups, check the local newspapers' sports sections. Closer to home, here is the lowdown on some of the more popular local and regional teams and how to go about seeing a game or event.

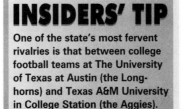

INSIDERS' TIP

One of the state's most fervent rivalries is that between college football teams at The University of Texas at Austin (the Longhorns) and Texas A&M University in College Station (the Aggies).

Auto Racing

CC Speedway
241 Flato Rd., Corpus Christi
• **(361) 289-8847**

Bring your earplugs and watch stock-car racing every Saturday night between April and August at Corpus Christi Speedway, the self-proclaimed fastest quarter-mile asphalt track in Texas. Gates open at 6 PM, with races starting at 8 PM. General admission tickets are $8 and pit passes are $15. Children 12 and younger get in free with a paying adult.

Greyhound Racing

Corpus Christi Greyhound Park
5302 Leopard St., Corpus Christi
• **(361) 289-9333**

This $18 million complex offers year-round parimutuel greyhound racing with 450 race programs—300 evening and 150 matinee programs, with 13 races per program. Post time is 7:30 PM Tuesday through Saturday. Matinees take place at 1:30 PM Wednesday, Friday, Saturday, and Sunday. Odds are available daily at the track. There is also a restaurant here.

Hockey

IceRays
500 N. Water St.,
Corpus Christi (team offices)
• **(361) 814-PUCK**

Corpus Christi's newest sports team is the IceRays, part of the Western Professional Hockey League, which had its inaugural season in 1996. The league has 14 professional teams in four Southwestern states.

The IceRays inked a five-year contract with a five-year option to play in the Igloo, at the city's Memorial Coliseum on Shoreline Boulevard. Head coach is Taylor Hall, a native of Regina, Saskatchewan, who served as head of the New Mexico Scorpions during the 1996-97 hockey season. Hall's playing experience spanned 12 years and included a five-year stint in the National Hockey League with the Vancouver Canucks and the Boston Bruins. He completed his playing career with the Tulsa Oilers of the Central Hockey League as the team's all-time leading scorer, with 269 points, and was first in all-time goals with 124.

The local team played its first game in October 1998, finishing up with a playoff run but lost in the second round. Fans have been extremely enthusiastic about this new-to-South Texas sport—all 35 home games were sellouts, breaking a previous Western Professional Hockey League record of 14 sellout games in a season.

The hockey season usually lasts through April, with playoffs into May. Individual tickets are $12-$20 and season tickets are $458-$781. For more information and sports paraphernalia, check out the team's offices or call the number above. There is also a merchandise store at Sunrise Mall, 5858 S. Padre Island Drive.

Rodeo

Buccaneer Days PRCA Rodeo
Memorial Coliseum, Corpus Christi
• **(361) 882-3242.**

Buccaneer Days is a professional rodeo event

SPECTATOR SPORTS

Seasonal bird hunting is a popular pastime throughout the Corpus Christi area.

Photo: courtesy of the Greater Corpus Christi Business Alliance

held every April in Memorial Coliseum, which is located along the city's bayfront. Rodeo riders from all over the nation come to compete in a variety of events such as roping, bull-riding, and more.

Tuff Hedeman Professional Bull Riders Challenge
J.K. Northway Exposition Center, Kingsville
• **(361) 592-8516, (800) 333-5032**

This professional bull-riding competition began in 1997. The three-day event, held the first weekend in January, attracts professionals from all over the country and is a national final qualifying event. Admission is $10 and $15. For more information, see our Annual Events and Festivals chapter. The J.K. Northway Exposition Center is located at Dick Kleberg Park, which is on the south edge of Kingsville between the U.S. Highway 77 Business and U.S. Highway 77 Bypass.

Running

Beach-to-Bay Marathon
Corpus Christi
• **(361) 225-3338**

Jogging is seldom considered a spectator sport, but Corpus Christi's annual Beach-to-Bay Marathon may be worth watching. Held on the third Saturday in May (Armed Forces Day), this relay marathon draws thousands of runners from all over the state and nation. Each team of six runners must complete a marathon-length course (26.2 miles), with the six runners each logging approximately 4.4 miles. For more information see our Annual Events chapter.

Sailing

Every Wednesday evening, sailors converge on Corpus Christi's downtown marina and yacht basin for their weekly escape—the evening sailboat races. You can watch from the yacht basin or the seawall. Corpus Christi Bay is a great place for sailing because it has protected waters and good breezes.

If you want to sail yourself, small sailboats and catamarans are available for rent in season. You can also rent captained boats and bare-

boat charters. For a list of rental and charter companies throughout the area, contact the Corpus Christi Business Alliance's convention and visitors department at (361) 881-1888.

You can also learn to sail at the Corpus Christi Sailing Center, on the L-Head, (361) 881-8503. A Saturday and Sunday basic course costs $190, a three-day live-aboard course costs $590, and a five-day, live-aboard course costs $990 (see our Beaches and Watersports chapter).

Boating

East-West Powerboat Shootout
Corpus Christi Bay, Corpus Christi
• **(361) 881-1888, (800) 766-2322**

This national racing event is held every June in the Corpus Christi Bay. Lots of noise, fast boats, and plenty of excitement are guaranteed to thrill. Be sure to bring your ear plugs and plenty of sunscreen.

Windsurfing

Drive along Ocean Drive in Corpus Christi any day of the week and you're likely to see windsurfers toting their boards to the water and braving the bayfront waves. Windsurfing—the sport of riding an enlarged surfboard that's equipped with a sail—is an extremely popular sport here. Oleander Point, at Cole Park in the 2000 block of Ocean Drive, is the most common gathering place.

With its mild climate and consistent winds of 15 to 25 mph blowing across the bayfront, the city has positioned itself to become a windsurfing capital.

U.S. Open Windsurfing Regatta
Oleander Point, Cole Park, Corpus Christi
• **(361) 985-1555**

You may want to check out this colorful regatta held on Memorial Day weekend each year. The four-day event, begun in 1987, attracts some of the nation's best windsurfers as well as plenty of enthusiastic amateurs. Winners can receive up to $70,000 worth of prizes during the weeklong competition. For more information see our Annuals Events and Festivals chapter.

Volleyball

Men's
Pro Beach Volleyball Competition
Cole Park Ocean Drive
at Del Mar Boulevard, Corpus Christi
• **(210) 938-8810**

Corpus Christi is a designated stop on the Miller Lite AVP Tour. Catch the action as these awesome athletes show their skills. Tickets range in price from $8 to $30.

Tennis

HEB College Team Championships
H.E. Butt Tennis Center, Corpus Christi
• **(361) 882-6013**

Considered the first of its kind in the United States, this college tennis championship tournament has been held here since 1968. There's a waiting list to enter each year, with the nation's top-ranked university teams lined up to attend more than a year in advance.

Of the 11 conferences represented in the 1998 tournament, most teams were conference champions or runners-up. Participating teams included 1996 champion Southern Alabama, 1997 defending champion Middle Tennessee, Clemson, Tulsa, Virginia Tech, Ball State, Texas Tech, Tulane, University of Washington, Baylor, Minnesota, Colorado, Oklahoma, Southern Methodist, and University of Nevada Las Vegas.

The tournament, which is held annually in March, is free of charge to spectators. All matches are held at the HEB Tennis Center, beginning on Friday and ending with the finals Sunday afternoon.

SPECTATOR SPORTS

Daytrips and Weekend Getaways

Corpus Christi is two to four hours away from several attractive tourist destinations. So if you have the time and want to see other parts of the Lone Star State, hop in the car and hit the road for one of the destinations listed in this chapter.

We've included popular tourist destinations within a reasonable driving distance. Note that this chapter is entitled "Daytrips and Weekend Getaways," which means that some trips can be completed in a single day while others require a more lengthy commitment of time. Our six destinations are San Antonio, South Padre Island, Goliad, Matagorda Island, Austin, Houston, and Laredo. Each write-up contains a brief introduction followed by sections on attractions and restaurants and accommodations when a choice is available. A quick history is included for San Antonio, South Padre Island, and Goliad. The Austin and Houston write-ups include sections on nightlife and the four largest cities include shopping destinations.

San Antonio, home to the beautiful Riverwalk, is the No. 1 tourist destination in Texas. It's also a great place to witness the influence of Mexican and Spanish culture on South Texas. South Padre Island, renowned for its beautiful beaches, is another popular tourist destination, so much so that it's the city's only industry. Goliad is the site of the most fought-over fort in Texas history, while Matagorda Island offers visitors a look at a relatively unspoiled coastal ecology. Austin, the Texas state capital, is one of the fastest-growing cities in the country, while Houston, one of America's largest cities, boasts a varied and sophisticated culture. And, finally, Laredo, on the border across from Nuevo Laredo, Mexico, offers visitors a quick and safe trip to another country.

Enjoy your travels!

LOOK FOR:
- San Antonio
- South Padre Island
- Goliad
- Matagorda Island
- Austin
- Houston
- Laredo

San Antonio

A little more than two hours from Corpus Christi, San Antonio offers a glimpse into the state's history as well as its future. This city of more than a million is one of the nation's 10 most populated and is a major tourist destination. The historic Alamo, the graceful Riverwalk, an array of historic Spanish missions, plenty of theme parks, and a fleet of museums attract thousands of visitors.

You can drive to San Antonio from the Corpus Christi area, taking U.S. Highway 37 N. Or you can travel by air via most major airline carriers.

History

The first settlers here were the Native Americans, who lived along the San Antonio River and called it *Yanaguana*, which means "clear waters." In 1691, a group of Spanish missionaries came upon the river, and since their arrival coincided with the feast day of Saint Anthony, they named the river "San Antonio." The city was actually founded in 1718 with the establishment of Mission San Antonio de Valero—known later as the **Alamo**—where 189 Texas defenders held the old mission against 4,000 Mexican soldiers for 13 days. "Remember the Alamo" became a rallying point for the Texas revolution against Mexico, and the Alamo today is a shrine and museum dedicated to Texas history.

Historical attractions abound here, starting with the downtown area. Check out **La Villita**, one of the original settlements of Spanish soldiers, and the **Spanish Governor's Palace**, which served as the seat of government when San Antonio was capital of the Spanish Province of Texas. You can also visit the **San Fernando Cathedral**, constructed in 1731, and the **José Antonio Navarro State Historical Park**.

Just northeast of downtown is **Fort Sam Houston**, where military greats like Pershing and Eisenhower served. San Antonio was also a training site for the Buffalo Soldiers, famed African-American cavalry fighters who helped bring peace to the western frontier a century ago. Today Fort Sam Houston is headquarters for the Fifth U.S. Army and the Health Services Command and home to the **Fort Sam Houston Museum** and the **U.S. Army Medical Department Museum**.

Attractions

The Paseo del Rio, or **Riverwalk**, is a cobblestone and flagstone-covered path that borders both sides of the San Antonio River downtown. It's 20 feet below street level. There are plenty of European-style cafes, specialty boutiques, and high-rise hotels along the walk, as well as quiet park areas. The scenic walkway is 2.5 miles long, bordered at the north end by the Municipal Auditorium and Conference center and at the south by the King William Historic District.

For sightseeing from the water, take the **Yanaguana Cruise** barge, (210) 244-5700, down the river. You can also dine aboard open-air, candlelit barges as they wind their way along the scenic waterway. The 40-minute, narrated cruises are available Monday through Sunday, 9 AM to 11 PM. Admission is $5.25 for adults, $1 for children 5 and younger and $3.65 for active military and seniors.

The **King William Historic District**, on the south bank of the San Antonio River, is a 25-block area that was zoned as the state's first historic district. This neighborhood, originally settled by prominent German merchants in the 1800s, is still graced by stately mansions. A self-guided walking tour brochure is available from the San Antonio Conservation Society, 107 King William Street, (210) 224-6163. Tours of selected homes are held annually on the Saturday following Thanksgiving Day. For information, call (210) 227-8786. Visitors should be sure to journey to the **San Antonio Missions National Historical Park**, (210) 932-1001, an 819-acre park that retraces the historic Mission Trail. Included in the park are four Spanish Colonial missions—Mission Concepcion, Mission San José, Mission San Juan and Mission Espada—as well as the Rancho de las Cabras in Floresville, the historic ranch site that supplied livestock for the missions. The chain of missions established along the San Antonio River in the 18th century are reminders of one of Spain's most successful attempts to extend its New World dominion northward from Mexico. They were the greatest concentration of Catholic missions in North America. The missions are open daily from 9 AM until 6 PM in the summer, and 8 AM until 5 PM in the winter, except for Thanksgiving, Christmas, and New Year's Day. Admission is free, but donations are accepted.

Don't forget the most famous of all the missions, Mission San Antonio de Valero, or the **Alamo**, (210) 225-1391. After losing San Antonio to the Texans during the siege of Bexar, Mexico's General Santa Anna decided to retake this key location and at the same time impress upon the Texans the futility of further resistance to Mexican rule. When Santa Anna's army arrived in San Antonio in February 1836, some 145 Texans took refuge in the mission under joint command of William B. Travis and Jim Bowie. Over a two-week period, Mexican forces increased to 2,000, while a few Texans managed to enter the Alamo grounds and brought the number of defenders to 189.

Finally, the Mexican army stormed the fortress on the morning of March 6, 1836, and killed all the Texan defenders, sparing only a few noncombatants including Susanna Dickenson, wife of one of the Texans, her baby and a servant of Travis. To reinforce his goal of terrorizing Texan colonists, Santa Anna released this group to spread the word about what had happened. Losses in the battle were placed at 189 Texans to 1,600 Mexicans. In spring and summer, the Alamo is open Monday through Saturday 9 AM to 6:30 PM Sunday from 10 AM until 6:30 PM. It closes at 5:30 PM during the fall and winter months. The Alamo is closed on Christmas Eve and Christmas Day. Admission is free, but donations are accepted.

Also on Alamo Plaza are three popular stops for visitors. The popular **Cowboy Museum**, 209 S. Alamo Plaza, (210) 229-1257, charges $3 admission for adults and $2 for children. It is open daily from 10 AM to 6 PM. The **Plaza Wax Museum** and **Ripley's Believe It or Not!**, (210) 224-9299, can provide hours of entertainment. From likenesses of Joan Crawford, John Wayne, and Humphrey Bogart to the familiar faces of Dorothy and Toto on their way to visit the Wizard of Oz, this place is sure to be a hit with young and old. Admission to the Plaza Wax Museum is $10.95 for adults and $4.95 for children, while admission to Ripley's is $10.95 for adults and $4.95 for children. You can also get a combination ticket to visit both that costs $14.95 for adults and $7.95 for children.

INSIDERS' TIP

The first inhabitants of the San Antonio River were Native Americans, who called the area "Yanaguana" or "refreshing waters." A band of Spanish explorers came upon the river in 1691 and since it was the feast day of St. Anthony, they named the river San Antonio.

For an intense dose of Texas history, plan on a visit to the Imax Theater at the Rivercenter Mall, (210) 225-IMAX. There you can watch The Price of Freedom, a 48-minute film about the battle of the Alamo, on a six-story silver screen. It is open daily 8:30 AM until 10 PM. Admission is $7.50 for adults, $6.75 for senior citizens, and $4.75 for children ages 3 to 11.

For family activities, head to the **San Antonio Zoo**, (210) 734-7183, in Brackenridge Park, a 433-acre refuge in the city's center. The zoo is ranked as one of the nation's best, with more than 3,000 animals in its collection. Admission is $7 for adults and $5 for children ages 3 to 11, free for children under 3. The zoo is open daily from 9 AM until 5 PM. In addition to the mammals, birds, and reptiles, the zoo also offers a 10-minute narrated children's boat ride.

Nearby is the **Witte Museum**, 3801 Broadway, (210) 357-1900, which contains exhibits that explore Texas history and science. Admission is $5.95 for adults and $3.95 for children ages 4 to 11 (3 and under are free). The museum is open 10 AM until 5 PM Monday; 10 AM until 9 PM Tuesday (with free admission from 3-9 PM); 10 AM until 5 PM Wednesday through Saturday; and noon until 5 PM Sunday. It is closed Thanksgiving, Christmas Eve, and Christmas Day.

San Antonio is also home to two major theme parks, **Sea World of Texas**, (210) 523-3900, and **Six Flags Fiesta, Texas**, (210) 697-5000 or (800) 473-4378. Sea World is the world's largest marine life park. Days and hours of operation vary by season. Admission is $32.95 for adults, $22.95 for children ages 3 to 11 and $28.95 for senior citizens. Six Flags is made up of four themed areas, including the Mexican town of Los Festivales, the German village of Spassburg, the 1920 cowboy boom town of Crackaxle Canyon and the small Texas town of Rockville during the golden age of rock 'n' roll. It's open in the spring and summer, but the days and hours vary by season. Admission is $38.78 for those over 48 inches tall, $19.38 for those under 48 inches, and $26.93 for senior citizens. Children ages 2 and under are free.

On a cultural note, be sure to plan a visit to the **McNay Art Museum**, (210) 824-5368, which is set in a Mediterranean-style mansion and has wide-ranging collections (admission is free). Also see the **San Antonio Museum of Art**, (210) 978-8100, housed in the castle-like former headquarters of the Lone Star Brewery. This museum is noted for its antiquities collections, Mexican folk art, modern art, and Spanish colonial art. Admission is $5 for adults, $1.75 for children and $4 for senior citizens. Admission is free on Tuesdays. The museum is open 10 AM until 5 PM Wednesday through Saturday, 10 AM until 9 PM Tuesday, and noon to 5 PM Sunday.

You may also want to check out the action with the **San Antonio Spurs** basketball team, (210) 554-7787, the **San Antonio Dragons** hockey team, (210) 737-7825, and the **San Antonio Missions** minor league baseball team, (210) 675-7275.

DAYTRIPS AND WEEKEND GETAWAYS

Shopping

San Antonio is also a good place to do some serious shopping. There are a number of major malls, including the beautiful **Rivercenter Mall** in the middle of downtown. The largest department stores here are Dillard's and Foley's, while other stores include The Limited, Gap, Victoria's Secret, Banana Republic, Express, Gymboree, Bath and Body Works, the Disney Store, Project Earth, Godiva Chocolatier, Latin Gold Cigar Company, Sports Fantasy, and Brentano's bookstore.

If you want a more colorful shopping experience, be sure to hit **El Mercado**, (210) 207-8600, 514 W. Commerce Street, a Mexican-style market area downtown. Billed as the largest Mexican marketplace outside of Mexico, the area is bustling with shops selling such items as leather goods, blankets, clothing, jewelry, pottery, and other curiosities. Nearby is the **Farmers Market Plaza**, which features food, cafes, and a stage for weekend entertainment.

Restaurants

You won't go hungry in this city, which has a number of notable restaurants and offers Mexican, German, French, Chinese, and American cuisine. The following are just a few of our favorites. All prices listed below are the average cost of a dinner for two, excluding drinks, appetizers, desserts, tax, and tip.

The Barn Door, (210) 824-0116, 8400 N. New Braunfels Avenue, offers real Texas-style steaks in a rustic atmosphere. You can also get quail, pork chops, catfish, or flounder. Dinner for two is about $40.

Casa Rio, (210) 225-6718, 430 Commerce Street, serves Tex-Mex dishes on the Riverwalk. It also offers dining on floating barges along the river. It's open daily. A dinner for two is less than $20.

Earl Abel's, (210) 822-3358, 4200 Broadway Street at Hildebrand Avenue, is an old-fashioned eatery that serves great chicken-fried steak, fried chicken, burgers, and steaks —as well as fabulous homemade desserts such as lemon chess pie, maple pecan pie, and chocolate layer cake. It's open daily. A dinner for two costs about $20.

Drive out to the **Grey Moss Inn**, (210) 695-8301, 19010 Scenic Loop Road, for a romantic evening. About 45 minutes from downtown, this restaurant has an outdoor patio and more than 500 wines. The specialties are mesquite-grilled seafood, steaks, lamb chops, and chicken. Reservations are taken for seating from 5 to 10 PM. Dinner for two is about $50.

La Fogata, (210) 340-1337, 2427 Vance Jackson Road, may be the city's most popular Mexican restaurant. You can dine in the courtyard or inside on delectable Mexican entrees, including a tasty chicken in mole sauce. It's open daily and can be crowded on the weekends, when reservations are recommended. Dinner for two costs about $35.

For a fun after-hours dining experience, try **Mi Tierra Café and Bakery**, (210) 225-1262, 218 Produce Row. This is practically a late-night institution, with its colorful atmosphere and wide-ranging menu. Open 24 hours daily, this restaurant has been serving up Mexican specialties and mariachi music since 1941. Two can dine here for less than $20, and don't forget to pick up some pan dulce or sugary pralines on your way out.

Paesano's Classic Italian restaurant, (210) 227-2782, 111 W. Crockett Street, has traditional Italian specialties served in an old-world ambiance. Especially good are the veal dishes, snapper, and an excellent shrimp Paesano. There are two locations: one on the Riverwalk and another on the city's north side, at 555 E. Basse Road. Dinner for two is about $35.

Restaurant Biga, (210) 225-0722, 206 E. Locust Street, is an elegant restaurant that serves Southwestern and Mediterranean cuisine in a renovated century-old mansion. Seasonal specialties include items such as antelope, pheasant, seared sea bass, and grilled oysters, as well as exotic breads and pastries. It's open for dinner Monday through Saturday. A dinner for two costs $40 to $60. Lunch is by private booking only.

Also downtown is **Schilo's German Delicatessen**, (210) 223-6692, 424 E. Commerce Street. Authentic, old-style German decor and fare are hallmarks of this longtime delicatessen. We recommend the hearty split-pea soup, homemade root beer, Reuben sandwiches, and cheesecake. It's open Monday through Saturday. Two can easily dine here for $20.

Mission Concepcion and other missions are popular stops for tourists in San Antonio.

Photo: courtesy of the San Antonio Convention and Visitors Bureau

Accommodations

San Antonio has a wide array of hotels, bed and breakfast inns, and motels, offering accommodations that can fit into any traveler's budget. A complete listing of the city's hotels is available from the **San Antonio Convention and Visitors Bureau**, (800) 447-3372. Here are a few of the city's most famous and prestigious hotels, as well as several less pricey establishments.

The **Menger Hotel**, (210) 223-4361, 204 Alamo Plaza, offers history and luxury to visitors. Opened in 1859 by W.A. Menger, it offered 19th-century visitors a taste of history and elegance and enjoyed visits from some of the era's most prominent people. O. Henry favored the hotel and included it in several of his works. General Robert E. Lee rode his horse, Traveller, into the lobby. General Ulysses S Grant tipped a few at the Menger Bar. President Dwight D. Eisenhower enjoyed strolling the gardens. It was the San Antonio home of Sarah Bernhardt, Judge Roy Bean's Lilly Langtry, and movie vamp Mae West.

INSIDERS' TIP

Even the name of San Antonio's AA baseball team reflects its history—the San Antonio Missions. To get tickets for a game, call (210) 675-7275.

Today the Menger Hotel is a National Historic Landmark, and it even offers Victorian-style lodging rooms that are available by special request. More modern amenities include in-house movies, room service, valet parking, a spa, and the downtown's largest heated swimming pool. A double room costs $145 per night for one person, and $155 for two people.

Another hotel that offers a taste of history is the **Crockett Hotel**, (210) 225-6500, 320 Bonham Road, near Alamo Plaza. This elegant hotel, which has 206 guest rooms, has a historic flavor, from its frosted-glass lobby paneling to the adobe-colored atrium. A double room costs $89.95–$129.95 per night.

Or try **La Mansion del Rio**, (210) 518-1000 or (800) 292-7300, 112 College St., which overlooks the historic Riverwalk. Built in 1852 as a private boys school, La Mansion has 337 luxury guest rooms, many with balconies and views of the San Antonio River. This graceful hotel is the only four-star hotel in San Antonio and has also been ranked in the top 10 percent of hotels worldwide. A double room costs between $214 and $324 per night, depending on the view and size of the room.

The **Radisson/Market Square**, (210) 224-7155, 502 W. Durango Street, has 250 guest rooms, a swimming pool, and a health center. A double room is $99 to $159 per night, but promotional and off-season discounts can drop the price as low as $69 per night.

The **Days Inn Alamo Riverwalk**, (210) 227-6233, 902 E. Houston Street, has 50 guest rooms and is near many of the city's downtown attractions. A double room costs $85 to $94 per night.

Near the downtown convention center is one of the city's 10 La Quinta hotels, **La Quinta Convention Center**, (210) 222-9181, 1001 E. Commerce Street. It has 190 hotel rooms, and a swimming pool. A double room costs $85 to $119 per night. A continental breakfast is included.

South Padre Island

A 34-mile stretch of beach just a half-hour's drive from Mexico, this community is home to about 2,000 residents and nearly 2.5 million annual visitors. To get there, take Texas Highway 77 south, then take Texas Highway 100 through Port Isabel and over the Queen Isabella Causeway bridge to South Padre Island. It takes about 3½ hours to drive here from Corpus Christi—and you'd better stick to the speed limits, because the small towns along the route strictly enforce them. You can also fly into **Harlingen's Valley International Airport**, 45 minutes away, or **Brownsville/South Padre Island International Airport**, 25 minutes away.

History

According to legend, Caribbean pirates first discovered Padre Island nearly 500 years ago. As they searched for ports to pillage, they were thwarted at the tip of Texas. The coastline that confronted them was actually a 100-mile-long barrier sand dune created by nature to protect the Texas coastline from erosion, wind, storm, and sea. Officially claimed by the Spaniards in 1519, it was named Isla Blanca, or White Island. In the 1800s, the first settlement on the island was named after its founder, Padre José Nicolas Balli.

South Padre Island is a much younger entity, created in 1964 when the Port Mansfield Channel divided Padre Island into two parts, creating a more convenient passage for ships and barges into the Intracoastal Waterway. The move also created a tropical island retreat that had a few hundred permanent residents by 1973 and self-government. Because it was separated from the rest of the big island, this community established its own identity as a coastal resort town focused on fun in the sun. Many residents are transplanted Northerners who came south searching for warmth and stayed to establish businesses, captivated by the Tex-Mex lifestyle and ambiance.

The town itself is totally focused on tourism—that's literally the only industry here. And with 5,000 hotel and condo units, more than 300 varieties of birds and an abundance of fish in the Gulf of Mexico and the Laguna Madre Bay, South Padre Island has plenty to offer tourists. City officials play their welcoming role to the hilt. They recently declared neckties illegal on the island. The penalty for wearing a tie is a written notice and a free South Padre Island T-shirt.

The climate is subtropical, with an average high of 82 in the summer and a low of 65 in the winter, plus an average of 27.6 inches of rainfall each year.

More importantly when planning your trip, remember that South Padre Island is a hugely popular destination for college students on spring break. More than 100,000 students converge annually on the town, bringing with them headliner bands, games, beachside events, basketball and volleyball tournaments, surfing, sumo wrestling, partying, and more. This small community swells at the seams during this rowdy time of year, and if you're looking for a quiet vacation, you might want to select a different time to visit.

Attractions

Fishing is a major draw here, with 800-pound marlins in the Gulf of Mexico. The Laguna Madre Bay is filled with speckled trout, redfish, and flounder. Check out fishing guides and charter boats to get the best fishing information and guidance. For information call the **South Padre Island Convention and Visitors Bureau**, (956) 761-6433 or (800) SO-PADRE.

Surfing on South Padre Island is considered the best on the Texas coast. Fall through spring is the best time of year for the biggest waves, while summer offers smaller waves that are good for

The 2.6-mile Queen Isabella Causeway links South Padre Island to the mainland.

Photo: courtesy of the South Padre Island Convention and Visitors Bureau

DAYTRIPS AND WEEKEND GETAWAYS

newcomers. Surfboard sales, rentals, and lessons are available at Isla Blanca Park and at a variety of shops along Padre Boulevard.

Windsurfing is increasingly popular here, with plenty of rentals and lessons available at local shops. You can also rent sailboats, personal watercraft, paddleboats, and bumper boats. Bicycling, pedal-powered buggy rides, miniature golf, shuffleboard, horseback riding, and sandcastle building are among other recreational opportunities.

Golfers have plenty of courses from which to choose. Several are in Brownsville, about 25 minutes from South Padre Island, while others are in Harlingen, about 45 minutes away. Among courses open to the public is the newly opened **South Padre Island Golf Club**, (956) 943-5678, in Laguna Vista about 20 minutes from South Padre Island. It has an 18-hole, par 72 championship course. In Brownsville, golf courses open to the public are the **Brownsville Golf and Recreation Center**, (956) 541-2582; **Fort Brown Municipal Golf Course**, (956) 541-0394; and the **Riverbend Golf Course**, (956) 548-0191.

Peek into the **Coastal Studies Laboratory**, (956) 761-2644, at the southern end of the island in Isla Blanca Park. This laboratory, operated by the University of Texas-Pan American, features aquariums of fish and native marine life, as well as a vast shell collection. It's open 1:30 until 4:30 PM Sunday through Friday and admission is free.

Camping, picnic pavilions, jetty fishing, and RV hookups are available at **Isla Blanca Park**, (956) 761-5493. The day-use fee is $4 per vehicle.

Laguna Atascosa National Wildlife Refuge, (956) 748-3608, 25 miles northwest of South Padre Island, is a 45,000-acre refuge filled with birds, nature trails, and wildlife. Tour roads, including a 15-mile bayside drive, are accessible from sunrise to sunset. The refuge is open from sunrise to sunset daily. Admission is $2 per vehicle.

The **Port Isabel Lighthouse**, on the mainland near the foot of the Queen Isabella Causeway, offers a panoramic view of the Laguna Madre. The 1853-era lighthouse is open 10 to 11:30 AM and 1 to 5 PM daily.

You should also visit the **Port Isabel Historical Museum**, (956) 943-7602, in one of the area's oldest structures which is famous for its fish murals. The two-story museum contains interactive exhibits that teach about the area's colorful past, including archaeological findings of coins that date back to before 1810 and both the Mexican and Civil wars. Admission is $3 for adults, $1 for students, $.50 for children ages 3 to 5, and $2 for senior citizens. It's open 10 AM until 4 PM Wednesday through Saturday, and 1 to 4 PM Sunday.

Sea Turtle Inc., (956) 761-1720, 6617 Padre Boulevard, a sea turtle conservation group, offers educational shows featuring endangered sea turtles cared for by organization members. Shows are at 10 AM Tuesday and Saturday, with a requested donation of $2 for adults and $1 for children.

Internationally known environmental artist Wyland painted his 53rd Whaling Wall—the only one in Texas—on the exterior of the South Padre Island Convention Centre, 7355 Padre Boulevard. The wall features whales frolicking in an undersea environment. Wyland intends to paint 100 such walls to educate people about marine conservation.

INSIDERS' TIP
Diving, skydiving, dolphin watching, and deep sea fishing are among the most popular recreational activities for visitors to South Padre Island, Texas.

Restaurants

In addition to a vast array of fast-food eateries, the island offers several options for fine dining. Many restaurants specialize in fresh seafood, while others offer Mexican fare. Here is a listing of some of the most popular restaurants in town. All prices listed below reflect the average cost of a lunch or dinner for two, excluding drinks, appetizers, desserts, tax, and tip.

Amberjack's Bayside Bar & Grill, (956) 761-6500, 209 W. Amberjack Street, serves seafood, steaks, pasta, hamburgers, and sandwiches in a casual setting. The Rasta-style shrimp is a house specialty, featuring shrimp in a tasty cream-of-coconut and curry sauce. It's open daily for lunch and dinner during the season, and closed on Mondays during the winter months. A dinner for two costs about $25.

Blackbeard's, (956) 761-2962, 103 E. Saturn Street, serves seafood, burgers, and steaks in a pirate-themed, casual setting. It's open daily. Two can dine here for about $25.

Browse among the Harley-Davidson accessories and funky clothing while you're waiting for your food at **Blue Rays Diner**, (956) 761-7297. Located at 410 Padre Boulevard, the restaurant is open for lunch and dinner and specializes in burgers and other diner-style fare. Dinner for two costs about $20.

When you want to get out of those beach clothes and have an elegant dining experience, head for the **Lantern Grill**, (956) 761-4460, 3109 Padre Boulevard. It features seafood and steaks served with Mediterranean flair. A dinner for two costs about $40.

For a bayside buffet, check out **Louie's Backyard**, (956) 761-6406, 2305 Laguna Boulevard. This is a popular summertime stop for many visitors and residents, who swear by Louie's seafood and prime rib. It's closed in the winter. The average cost of a buffet dinner for two is $35.

You can get premium handcrafted beer at the **Padre Island Brewing Company**, 3400 Padre Boulevard, (956) 761-9585. The kitchen serves pizza, sandwiches, seafood, and burgers. It's open for lunch Tuesday through Sunday and dinner every day. A dinner for two costs about $25.

Try the **Palmetto Inn**, (956) 761-4325, 1817 Padre Boulevard, for Mexican specials and seafood. The Carrasco family has been serving up steaks and nightly specials, such as fresh red snapper and fajitas, since 1956. This is the oldest restaurant on the island, and it's open daily. Two can dine here for less than $20.

Kids love to watch the electric train travel around the front room at **Rovan's Restaurant and Bakery**, (956) 761-6972, 5300 Padre Boulevard. This longtime restaurant is known for homestyle breakfasts, baked goods and mesquite-pit barbecue. A breakfast for two costs about $10; dinner for two is about $15.

For elegant bayside dining, try **Scampi's Restaurant and Bar**, (956) 761-1755, 206 W. Aires Street. You can get seafood, pasta, and prime steaks at this upscale restaurant, which offers an extensive wine list. It's open for dinner only, and a meal for two costs about $32.

202 Bayside Bar & Grill, (956) 761-8481, 202 W. Whiting Street, is a casual, open-air eatery where you can munch on gourmet pizza, grilled appetizers, and entrees. Dinner for two will cost about $20 to $25.

Accommodations

There are more than 5,000 hotel, motel, and condo units in South Padre Island, and it would be impossible to list every establishment here. However, a comprehensive list is available from the local **chamber of commerce**, (956) 761-6433 or (800) SO-PADRE. Bear in mind that room prices vary with the season: Hotels will be cheapest here between the off-season fall and winter months. In addition, many hotels require damage deposits and key deposits, particularly during spring break, when thousands of college students converge on this town.

Bahía Mar Resort, (800) 99-PADRE, 6300 Padre Boulevard, is a 15-acre resort with a 12-story hotel, condominiums, and meeting rooms. It's also the official hotel for contestants in the Miss Texas USA Pageant. You can walk down to the beach, play tennis, lounge by either of two large pools, and eat in the Bahía Breeze Restaurant. The nightly rate for a standard room with two queen beds is $85 to $134, depending on what time of year you visit.

Many national hotel chains offer accommodations here: The **Holiday Inn Sunspree Resort**, (956) 761-5401 or (800) 531-7405, 100 Padre Boulevard; **Radisson Resort**, (956) 761-6511 or (800) 333-3333, 500 Padre Boulevard; **Sheraton Fiesta Beach Resort**, (956) 761-4913 or (956) 761-6551 or (800) 222-4010, 310 Padre Boulevard; **Best Western Fiesta Isles**, (800) 528-1234, 5701 Padre Boulevard; **Days Inn South Padre Island**, (956) 761-7831 or (800) 329-7466, 3913 Padre Boulevard; and **Ramada Limited**, (956) 761-4097 or (800) 2-RAMADA, 4109 Padre Boulevard.

Goliad

Head over to the town of Goliad and the **Goliad State Historical Park**, (361) 645-3405, for a look at one of the most fascinating and bloody chapters in Texas history. The **Presidio La Bahía**, designated a National Historic Landmark, is considered the world's finest example of a

Spanish frontier fort. It is also the most fought-over fort in Texas history, having been a participant in six national revolutions and wars for independence.

To get to Goliad from Corpus Christi, take U.S. Highway 77 north, then take Texas Highway 183 north to Goliad. Driving time is about 1½ hours. The park has wheeled camper sites with electricity, water, and sewage facilities; primitive camping sites; and screened shelters. There are also toilets, showers, a playground, picnic sites along the San Antonio River, and a restored museum/interpretive center, the **Mission Espíritu Santo**.

Goliad, with a population of 2,026, has several fast-food restaurants and about a dozen cafes and restaurants. Many campers like to bring their own food and cook outdoors.

History

Strategically situated on an elevation overlooking the surrounding area, this site was established by the Spanish, who arrived in 1749. They found evidence of an Indian village they named Santa Dorotea. The Spanish settlers founded the town around the protection of the fort, renaming it La Bahía, (The Bay).

This town was the original Goliad. Its name was changed in 1829 as an anagram for Hidalgo, in honor of the patriot priest of the Mexican Revolution, Father Miguel Hidalgo, who sounded the famous "Grito de Delores" in 1810 for Mexican Independence from Spain. Goliad became the second-largest populated settlement in Spanish Texas.

In 1721, the Royal Presidio La Bahía was established in response to encroachment by the French. Built on the banks of the Garcitas Creek, the fort was later moved inland near Mission Valley, and in 1749, relocated to its present position.

The Royal Presidio La Bahía became the only fort responsible for the defense of the coastal area and eastern province of Texas. Soldiers from Presidio La Bahía assisted the Spanish army fighting the British along the Gulf Coast during the

INSIDERS' TIP

An annual memorial service is still held in the town of Goliad to honor those Texans who were murdered in the Goliad Massacre in 1836.

American Revolution. This action gives Goliad the distinction of being one of the only communities west of the Mississippi River to have participated in the American Revolution.

It's also considered the birthplace of the Texas Revolution. On October 9, 1835, a group of Texas citizens attacked the Mexican garrison stationed at the presidio and seized the fort. This action followed the incident at Gonzales, Texas, one week earlier. It was at the presidio that the first Declaration of Texas Independence was drawn up on December 20, 1835, signed by 92 citizens and distributed throughout Texas. Along with it flew the first flag of Texas independence. Nothing short of full independence from Mexico would satisfy those who had suffered under the injustices of a dictatorial government led by the self-styled "Napoleon of the West," General Antonio Lopez de Santa Anna.

The darkest day in Texas history, the Goliad Massacre, took place here on Palm Sunday, March 27, 1836, when Col. James Walker Fannin and 341 men under his command were executed a week after their capture at the Battle of Coleto, under Santa Anna's orders. Twice as many people died at Goliad than the Alamo.

Nothing touched the raw nerve of the American character as the news of the large numbers of men who were slaughtered in one execution. As grim details reached the United States, volunteers streamed forth for Texas. This one single event, the Goliad Massacre, more than any event in the Texas Revolution, proved to the people of the United States what manner of warfare confronted the Texans.

Attractions

The **Presidio La Bahía (Fort of the Bay)** is the oldest fort in the western United States and the only Texas Revolution site that has retained its original 1836 appearance. Nine flags have flown over the presidio, and it was the site of the saddest chapter in Texas history, the massacre of Fannin's troops—the single largest loss of life during the war for Texas's independence.

The presidio was restored in the 1960s to stand as a memorial for Texans, along with its sister shrines, the Alamo and San Jacinto. Local artisans supplied the labor for the project, and the noted restoration architect, Raiford L. Stripling, directed the project to its completion. It is today considered one of the most authentic restoration projects in the United States. The presidio compound is a self-sustaining private institution operated under the administration of the Diocese of Victoria Catholic Church. Tax deductible contributions are accepted and can be given through the fund-raising campaign, "Friends of the Fort." The fort is open daily from 9 AM until 4:45 PM, and admission is $3 for adults, $2.50 for those ages 60 and over, $1 for children ages 6 to 11, and free for children age 5 and younger. To arrange guided tours for large groups or schools, call (361) 645-3752.

Visit the **Our Lady of Loreto Chapel**, the oldest building in the old fort compound, which has been in continuous use since the 1700s. Although the presidio is a fort, not a mission, a chapel was erected inside the quadrangle for the sole use of the soldiers and Spanish settlers living in the town of La Bahía surrounding the fort. The religious needs of the Indian tribes were served by the missions of Rosario, Espíritu Santo, and Refugio.

One of the oldest churches in America, it is also one of the only buildings in existence to retain its groin-vaulted ceiling. The striking fresco at the back of the altar was created in 1946 by the "Michelangelo of South Texas," Corpus Christi artist Antonio Garcia. In the niche above the chapel entrance is the statue of Our Lady of Loreto made by Lincoln Borglum, of Mount Rushmore fame.

This centuries-old chapel was where Fannin's men were held for part of their captivity before they were massacred. The First Declaration of Texas Independence was signed inside the chapel on December 20, 1835.

Another attraction is the **Mission Espíritu Santo**, which was founded in 1722 near Matagorda Bay to serve the Karankawa Indians and their allies. The Indians abandoned the mission in 1724, however, and two years later the missionaries moved to Mission Valley near modern Victoria, in the territory of the Aranama and Tamique Indians.

In 1749 the mission was relocated to its present site on the San Antonio River near modern Goliad. Mission Espíritu Santo was granted jurisdiction over all land between the Guadalupe and San Antonio as far north as Capote Hills near modern Gonzales. On this land grazed the mission's cattle herds, which soon grew to approximately 40,000 head. The first large cattle ranch in Texas, Mission Espíritu Santo supplied its own needs and those of Spanish colonial settlements as far away as Louisiana. Destruction and theft by civilians and hostile Indians eventually depleted the herds.

Espíritu Santo served as a mission for 110 years, longer than any other Spanish colonial mission in Texas.

Yet another mission nearby is **Mission Nuestra Señora del Rosario**. This one was founded in 1754 by Franciscan missionaries from Mexico in an attempt to colonize the Karankawa Indians. The Rosario ruins are about 4 miles west of Goliad State Historical Park headquarters and 6 miles west of the city of Goliad off U.S. Highway 59. In 1776 the superior of Franciscan missions in Texas, Father José De Solis, reported of Mission Rosario: "As far as the temporal goods are concerned, it is in a flourishing condition. It possesses two droves of asses, forty tame horses, thirty tame mules, twelve teams of oxen, five thousand head of cattle, two hundred milk cows, and seven hundred sheep."

This temporal success, which was only momentary, did not guarantee spiritual success. When secularization of Texas missions was ordered in 1794, missions Espíritu Santo and Rosario were permitted to continue because their Indians had not yet adapted to civilized life. The missionaries feared that they would return to nomadic life, fears that were well grounded. Later, the Indians deserted the mission, and its lands were distributed to colonists.

General Ignacio Zaragoza's birthplace, across from the presidio, is another stopping point during your visit to this state historical park. Zaragoza was born at this site in 1829 and lived in the area as a child. Educated in Mexico, he joined the Mexican army and worked his way to the rank of general. At the Battle of Pueblo, Mexico, on May 5, 1862, Gen. Zaragoza's outnumbered forces defeated a French army of intervention. To commemorate the event, May 5—or *Cinco de Mayo*—became a Mexican national holiday and is celebrated each year in Goliad.

Also at the park, you can take a nature trail that heads from the mission buildings and picnic grounds and traverses typical South Texas brushland, or chaparral. The brushland contrasts sharply with the woodlands of the San Antonio River floodplain. Bird life along the trail is especially varied due to the proximity of diverse habitats and to the mild regional climate.

You'll find the ruins of an old quarry, thought to date to the early mission period, in the park. Stone from the quarry was used in construction of the mission church, granary, priests' quarters, workshop, the exterior compound wall, and other structures. Other buildings of wood and adobe also once existed inside the compound wall. A brick kiln, which can be seen from the nature trail, was built in the late 1930s during reconstruction of the mission. Near it is an older kiln, probably used for making lime for mortar or for firing bricks and tiles.

The workshop is a reconstruction of a previous structure. Here, under supervision of the missionaries, the Indians learned cattle-raising, farming, spinning and weaving, carpentry, and blacksmithing.

In the granary, a display of Indian and Spanish colonial artifacts and interpretive exhibits is of special interest. In addition, slide and film presentations on the history of the area after the Spanish period, together with artifact exhibits, can be seen in the park headquarters.

Once you've finished with the park, be sure to head into the town itself for another dose of historical attractions. The **county courthouse** in Goliad is listed on the National Register of Historic Places. The Second Empire Style-style courthouse, designed by noted Texas architect Alfred Giles, was completed in 1894. Limestone used in the construction was hauled from Austin by oxcart. Restored and enlarged in 1964, the courthouse is also a Recorded Texas Historic Landmark.

Other 19th- and 20th-century buildings, many of which are in the National Registry, can be seen downtown as well. The **Market House Museum**, which was designated a State Archaeological Landmark in May 1981, was built by the city in the early 1870s. It contained stalls, which were rented to farmers for the sale of meat and produce. Firehouse hooks and ladders were added in the 1880s. Today it is a museum and houses the Goliad County Chamber of Commerce.

On the north courthouse lawn is the **Hanging Tree**, an oak tree that served as the site of court sessions between 1846 and 1870 and is now a Recorded Texas Historic Landmark. Death sentences pronounced by the court were carried out immediately with a rope and a strong limb. During the 1857 Cart War, in which Texan freighters perpetrated a series of vicious attacks against Mexican cart drivers along the Indianola–Goliad–San Antonio Road, this site witnessed a

Learn more about President Lyndon B. Johnson at his presidential library on the UT campus.

Photo: Peter A. Silva

number of unauthorized lynchings before the conflict was ended by Texas Rangers. Approximately 70 men lost their lives during the conflict, some of them on this tree.

Accommodations

Goliad State Park, (361) 645-3405, is open all year with facilities for picnicking, hiking, tent and trailer camping, and both history and nature study. The campsites range from primitive to those with water, sewer, and electrical connections. Restrooms are in picnic and camping areas; showers are included in the camping area restroom.

Screened shelters with electricity, water, tables, and cooking grills are available. Fishing and boating are permitted in the San Antonio River. A playground and two miles of hiking trail provide further activities. You can get entrance and camping permits from park headquarters. The park entrance fee is $2 per person 12 and older; children younger than 12 get in free.

For overnight stays, the cost is $12 a night for RV hookups. Screened shelters are $18 per night. Other nightly fees include those for trailer sites, including water and electricity, $10; water-only sites, $8; and primitive sites, $4. A group dining area with a complete kitchen, a grill, microwave, refrigerator, picnic tables, and a large fireplace rents for $65 a day.

If you want lodging in an 18th-century Spanish colonial fort, try staying at **The Quarters**, within Presidio La Bahía, (361) 645-3752. The price is $150, and the fort accommodates up to four people. It has a fully equipped kitchen, bathroom with shower, master bedroom with queen bed, a second bedroom with twin beds and a living-dining area with a table, chairs, and a couch.

You can also stay at the **Budget Inn Goliad,** (361) 645-3251, 105 S. Jefferson. A room for two people costs $38 per night.

Matagorda Island

One of the wildest sites maintained by the state of Texas is the **Matagorda Island State Park and Wildlife Management Area**, (361) 983-2215, 16th Street and Intracoastal Canal in Port O'Connor. Separated from the mainland by San Antonio and Espíritu Santo Bays, Matagorda Island is one of the barrier islands that borders the Gulf of Mexico. It also protects the mainland from the great tides and strong wave action of the open Gulf.

With Gulf beaches, uplands, and tidal marshes, the island serves as home to more than a dozen species of endangered and threatened wildlife. There is no daily user fee, and the facilities are open year round.

To get to Port O'Connor from Corpus Christi, take U.S. Highway 181 north to Texas Highway 35 and continue north to Texas Highway 185, then head east through Seadrift to Port O'Connor.

The island is accessible only by boat and has no telephone, electricity, food concession, or drinking water. The state ferry from Port O'Connor runs Thursday through Sunday and costs $10 for adults, $5 for children younger than 12. It is strongly recommended that all visitors call for ferry reservations, as space is limited.

Camping is $4 per night for four people. Visitors must bring an ample personal water supply.

Although the southern tip of this Gulf of Mexico barrier island is privately owned, the remainder—about 51,000 acres—is state and federal land administered by the Texas Parks and Wildlife Department. The island's primary management goal is preservation and conservation, with emphasis on endangered and threatened species. Within the wildlife management area, a 36,568-acre area offers limited recreational use such as nature study, birding, and fishing. Supervised hunts are held here, and fishing is permitted under state regulation. All of the activities can be restricted or prohibited if state authorities decide they are endangering the species.

In the park area, there are 2 miles of beach open to year-round picnicking, fishing, hiking, beach combing, nature study, swimming, and primitive camping. All access to the island is by chartered or private boat. Pit toilets and an outdoor shower are also available. However, visitors are warned that shade is limited and you should bring sun protection, as well as insect repellent.

For several years, beginning in 1942, a portion of Matagorda Island was used for practice bombing by the U.S. Air Force. Now, as a state park, the 7,325-acre area has largely returned to its natural state as a haven for migratory waterfowl and deer. The park is seven miles south of Port O'Connor, separated from the mainland by Espíritu Santo and San Antonio bays.

Attractions

Wildlife is abundant here, and visitors can glimpse 19 species that are on state or federal endangered lists, including the whooping crane, brown pelican, piping plover, peregrine falcon, Eskimo curlew, and the Kemp's ridley sea turtle.

More than 300 species of migratory and resident waterfowl, shorebirds, songbirds, raptors, and other birds inhabit the island at various times throughout the year. Every spring and fall, the area serves as a critical stopover site for numerous migrating birds. Matagorda Island is also an important wintering home for many avian species, including the whooping crane.

Alligators also reside here, as do 19 species of snakes, including the western diamondback rattlesnake. The island's marshes provide habitat and nourishment for shrimp, oysters, crabs, and a wide variety of sportfish. Bottle-nosed dolphins frolic in the Gulf.

INSIDERS' TIP

In the 1850s, a health resort named Saluria was established on Matagorda Island but it was destroyed by a tropic hurricane.

There's plenty to do on Matagorda Island in addition to **observing nature**. **Historical sites** range from an 1852 lighthouse to an abandoned air base. Human habitation here goes back to the time of the Karankawa Indians, whose height, giant bows and mosquito repellent—a coating of alligator grease and dirt—impressed European settlers.

Eighty miles of beach, roadway, and mowed paths are available for hiking and biking. **Surfing**, **swimming**, and **beach combing** are all popular. Bicycles and surfboards can be brought over on the state ferry.

Anglers come for a wide variety of sportfish, including redfish, trout, flounder, and whiting.

The island has **two campgrounds**. A 2-mile stretch of Gulf beach open for primitive camping is served by a shuttle vehicle making the 3.5-mile connection to the boat dock. The cost of being ferried in this truck by the park rangers is included in the state ferry fee you already paid to get to the island. At the boat dock is the Army Hole Campground, equipped with pit toilets, a cold-water shower and other amenities. There are also a 14-bed group barracks and a smaller overflow barracks. The campground is open Fridays and Saturdays only, and an overnight stay costs $12 per person. To make reservations call (361) 983-2215.

Austin

Austin is a 3½-hour drive from Corpus Christi via interstate highways. You'll begin on Interstate 37 to San Antonio where you'll connect with Interstate 35, which will take you to Austin. Traffic from Corpus Christi to San Antonio is generally light. You'll find highways in San Antonio more congested but manageable. However, once you reach the northern outskirts of San Antonio you'll find the going a bit slower. Traffic between San Antonio and Austin has doubled in the past decade, making it the most congested and accident-prone section of Interstate Highway 35 between Mexico and Canada.

An alternative route you might want to consider is more scenic and takes you through several small towns. Driving time is about the same, but you won't get as bored or frustrated. To get there take U.S. Highway 181 across the Harbor Bridge. Stay on U.S. 181 as you head northwest, passing through Sinton, Beeville, Kenedy, and, finally, Karnes City. At Karnes City take Texas Highway 123 north through Stockdale and Seguin until you connect with IH-35 in San Marcos. From there, follow IH-35 until you reach Austin.

Austin, the capital of Texas, is home to the University of Texas at Austin, a thriving technology industry and one of the best live music scenes in the country. The city recently surpassed Seattle as the 22nd-largest city in the nation, with a population of 540,000, and, by the end of 1998, census figures project Austin's population will have outstripped those of Boston and Washington, D.C.

As the state capital, Austin has always had more than its share of government employees and buildings. The most prominent structure is the Texas Capitol Building, which opened in 1888 and is designed after the U.S. Capitol. You'll find it in the center of Austin just north of downtown. A few blocks north of the capitol is the University of Texas at Austin, one of the largest universities in the nation with an enrollment of more than 48,000. Its 357-acre campus is home to the Lyndon Baines Johnson Library and Museum, the Harry Ransom Humanities Research Center and the Archer M. Huntington Art Gallery. See Attractions, below, for tour details of these sites.

Austin calls itself the "Live Music Capital of the World," and although that may be a stretch, it's fair to say that few cities can match it for the quality and quantity of music. The late Janis Joplin earned her stripes in Austin clubs before hitting it big. So did Willie Nelson and the late blues-rock guitarist Stevie Ray Vaughan.

Austin is home to Dell Computer Corporation, maker of personal computers, and founder and chairman Michael Dell, who at $4 billion and growing is the wealthiest person in Texas, surpassing Ross Perot. More than 900 software companies occupy Austin and its suburbs—the largest concentration of microchip plants outside California's Silicon Valley.

Despite the city's booming growth, it's still a great place to enjoy the outdoors. The Colorado River (known as Town Lake inside the city) weaves its way through Austin on its way to the Gulf of Mexico, and the Texas Hill Country provides a lush backdrop on the city's west side. From atop Mount Bonnell (a large hill overlooking the Colorado River) you can see the UT campus, the Texas Capitol, downtown, Lake Austin, and the Texas Hill Country. Take a scenic drive on Loop 360 and enjoy the view or head out on Farm-to-Market Road 2244 (also known as Bee Cave Road) or Farm-to-Market Road 2222 and enjoy the Lake Austin scenery. Better yet, take a short drive (or walk if you're staying nearby) to Town Lake, where you can walk or ride a bike along the 11.5-mile hike-and-bike trail.

History

Austin is named for Stephen F. Austin, one of the state's founding fathers, who contributed greatly to Texas winning its independence from Mexico and, later, joining the United States. A

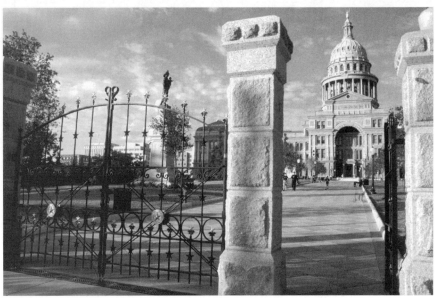

The door is always open to visitors at the Texas State Capitol.

Photo: Peter A. Silva

man named Jake Harrell is often given credit for founding what would later become Austin when he pitched a tent at what would later become the corner of 1st Street and Congress Avenue in 1838.

That fall, Mirabeau Bonaparte Lamar, vice president of the Republic of Texas, visited the site and declared it "the seat of future empire." After succeeding Sam Houston as Texas's president, Lamar recommended the site for the state's capital. It's prime location, and a yellow fever epidemic in Houston, convinced the selection committee to choose Austin for the fledgling republic's capital.

Work on the new capital began in May 1839. A year later the city had 856 residents and two newspapers. With Mexico's armed forces threatening the capital, government leaders packed up and moved to safer quarters in Houston, where they stayed until 1844.

The city got its first telegraph line in 1865, and the first train arrived in 1871. Construction on the University of Texas began in 1882. The city has grown steadily over the years, fed by University of Texas graduates who couldn't bear to leave the city. The city's population has boomed in the past decade as high-tech companies from around the world have set up shop here.

Attractions

Austin has its share of fun things to do and see. Start with a tour of the **Texas Capitol Building**, (512) 463-0063, at the northern end of Congress Avenue and downtown Austin. It was built in the 1880s out of pink granite from a quarry in nearby Marble Falls. An $81 million restoration project completed in 1995 returned the building to much of its original state. Free daily tours of the 26-acre complex and its grounds are available from 8:30 AM to 4:30 PM. Tours leave every half hour. And as long as you're in the area why not tour the nearby **Governor's Mansion**, (512) 463-5518, 1010 Colorado Street, home of the state's highest officeholder since 1856. Free tours are given Monday through Friday from 10 AM to noon. Each tour lasts 20 minutes.

Barton Springs Pool, (512) 476-9044, 2201 Barton Springs Road, is a great place to cool off in the summer. This 1,000-foot-long, spring-fed pool is a constant 68 degrees year round. It's an ideal spot to catch some rays, bodywatch, and marvel at nature's handiwork (we're talking about the pool here) without straying far from the big city. Admission on summer weekdays is $2.50 for adults, $1 for youths ages 12 to 17 and $.50 for children younger than 12. Weekend admission is $2.75 for adults, $1 youths and $.50 for children. You'll be charged a $3 parking fee on weekends if you park near the north gate. Parking adjacent to the south gate is free, although there are plans to charge for parking there in the future.

The **Town Lake Greenbelt** serves as a meeting place for runners, walkers, and cyclists. This 11.5-mile hike-and-bike trail circles a portion of Town Lake. You can rent a mountain bike at the **Bicycle Sport Shop**, (512) 477-3472, 1426 Toomey Road (Lamar Boulevard at Riverside Drive). A free hiking and biking guide is available from Austin Parks and Recreation, (512) 499-6700, 200 S. Lamar Boulevard.

The **Lyndon Baines Johnson Library and Museum**, (512) 916-5136, 2313 Red River Street on the UT campus, houses more than 36 million personal and official documents and historical and cultural exhibits pertaining to the former president. The library and museum chronicle Johnson's rise from obscurity to the American presidency.

Shopping

For an interesting culinary shopping experience try **Central Market**, (512) 206-1000, 4001 N. Lamar Boulevard, a warehouse-sized grocery store specializing in health and exotic foods. While you're there, walk a few paces over to the **Clarkesville Pottery** store, (512) 454-9079, in the same shopping center, and take a look at the selection of plates, glasses, jewelry, and pottery. Prices tend to be high here, but you can still find earrings for less than $20.

And, finally, nothing sums up the Austin experience more than a visit to the corner of N. Lamar Boulevard and Sixth Street. Here you'll find a **Whole Foods Market**, (512) 476-1206, a popular natural food grocery store chain, and the **Book People Bookstore**, (512) 472-5050. Book People, a locally owned store, has managed to capture the small-bookstore feel and place it inside one of the largest bookstores in Texas. Inside you'll find thousands of books and magazines, comfortable antique chairs for sitting and reading, gift items like candles and jewelry, CDs, and a coffee shop. Give yourself plenty of time. You could easily spend an entire day here.

Restaurants

Austin has a good mix of restaurants for a town of its size.

For good Italian food try **Mezzaluna**, (512) 472-6770, 310 Colorado Street, in the downtown area, where dinner for two averages around $50.

Those wanting to sample the local Tex-Mex cuisine will want to visit **Matt's El Rancho**, (512) 462-9333, 2613 S. Lamar Boulevard. Matt's has been in business since 1952, serving what it claims is the "best Mexican food and Margaritas in the world." Dinner for two ranges anywhere from $15 to $25.

If Thai jungle salsa and spicy peanut sauce are more to your liking, try **Satay**, (512) 467-6731, 3202 W. Anderson Lane, where you'll find more than 100 dishes from Singapore, Indonesia, Cambodia, Laos, Vietnam, and the Philippines. Dinner for two averages around $30 to $40.

If you're looking for hot chili set in a rustic atmosphere, duck into the **Texas Chili Parlor**, (512) 472-2828, 1409 Lavaca Street, not far from the Texas Capitol. Here you'll find great burgers, cold beer and some of the best chili around, with a choice from mild to very hot. Dinner for two is $20 or less.

Nightlife

Austin isn't short on nightlife, either. Downtown's E. Sixth Street is the city's center for live music venues, dance clubs, restaurants, bars, and lounges that tend to appeal to the college crowd. You'll find plenty to do there every night, and if you like crowds you'll love Sixth Street on the weekend. While you're there, check out **Esther's Follies**, (512) 320-0553, 525 E. Sixth Street, for a lighthearted spoof of local, Texas, and national events.

Antone's, (512) 320-8424, 213 W. Fifth Street, is a legendary Austin blues club, booking well-known blues musicians from around the country. **La Zona Rosa**, (512) 472-2293, 612 W. Fourth Street, is known for booking big-name acts into its fairly small venue, attracting a variety of artists from Sarah Hickman to David Byrne. The music varies quite a bit here, including rock, blues, country, modern folk, and conjunto.

The **Warehouse District** west of Congress Avenue and south of Sixth Street has in recent years become a hot spot for nighttime fun, featuring clubs, bars, and upscale restaurants that appeal to an older, professional crowd. **Speakeasy**, (512) 476-8017, 412 Congress Avenue, is a sophisticated jazz lounge featuring the best in local jazz musicians. At Speakeasy you'll find people dressed to the nines, smoking cigars and drinking martinis.

Accommodations

Austin has a wealth of accommodations to meet just about any budget. And because Austin is still fairly small, no matter where you stay you're not far from the city's main attractions. Austin has the usual chains as well as a few locally owned lodgings and several bed and breakfasts. Prices listed are for two adults. Add a 15 percent hotel/motel tax to all room prices.

For first-class accommodations try the **Driskill Hotel**, (512) 474-5911, 604 Brazos Street, in downtown. Cattle baron and businessman Jesse Driskill built the hotel in 1886 for the then-lofty sum of $400,000. Politicos and other VIPs have made the Driskill their home away from home ever since. Room prices are around $225 a night.

For economical accommodations try **The Habitat Suites**, (512) 467-6000 or (800) 535-4663, 500 Highland Mall Boulevard, where you'll find a family atmosphere for families on a budget. The Habitat Suites has 96 suites with kitchens, a breakfast buffet and a free happy hour of beer, wine, and light hors d'oeuvres every afternoon excluding Sundays. Room prices are around $127 a night.

Wellesley Inn & Suites on Town Lake, (512) 326-0100 or (800) 444-8888, 1001 IH-35, offers efficiencies and suites at even lower prices. Close to downtown and Town Lake, Wellesley offers 143 efficiencies, six suites, and eight disabled-equipped rooms. Room prices range from $79 to $109.

The **Miller-Crockett House**, (512) 441-1600, 112 Academy Drive, is a bed-and-breakfast two blocks from downtown Austin. It offers three large rooms with private baths and balconies, two bungalows, and spectacular views of the Austin skyline. Wake up to a full gourmet breakfast amid the beautiful live oak trees that grace the grounds. Room prices range from $89 to $139 per night. Rates for extended stays are available.

Want to stay in a funky old hotel where touring musicians like to hang out? Then try the **Austin Motel**, (512) 441-1157, 1220 S. Congress Avenue, south of the Congress Avenue Bridge. You'll discover interesting shops and restaurants all along this section of Congress Avenue. Inside the hotel restaurant you'll often find runners recuperating from their trek around the Town Lake hike-and-bike trail. Room prices range from $57 to $123 per night.

Houston

Driving to Houston from Corpus Christi takes about three hours depending on how fast you drive (the speed limit is 70 now in many areas) and whether you run into heavy traffic as you near the nation's fourth-largest city. To get there take U.S. Highway 181 across the Harbor Bridge and veer to the west through Taft and Sinton. In Sinton take a right on U.S. Highway 77, which will take you through Refugio to the outskirts of Victoria. There you'll connect with Loop 175, which will take you to U.S. Highway 59. Follow U.S. 59 until you reach Houston.

Houston has several major highways running through and around it. U.S. 59 (known as the Southwest Freeway in Houston) will take you into the heart of the city, inside Loop 610. Downtown Houston and many of the city's major attractions are inside the loop.

Houston is twice the size of Rhode Island and home to more than 4.1 million people of more than 100 nationalities. This international flavor has led more than 60 nations to set up consular offices in this city, whose residents speak more than 90 languages.

Houston also is home to headquarters for America's manned space flight effort (Space Center Houston), the world's largest medical center (The Texas Medical Center), the world's richest rodeo (the Houston Livestock Show and Rodeo), and the international energy industry. Museums, art galleries, the symphony, and the Theatre District add a touch of class to this rough-and-tumble oil town. Houston is one of few cities to have permanent theater, opera, symphony, and ballet companies. You'll also find hundreds of city parks, more than 8,000 restaurants, the Houston Zoological Gardens, Enron Field (the nation's first retractable roofed stadium), the Astrodome, and Six Flags AstroWorld and WaterWorld among the attractions. Houston in recent years has spent around $1 billion in renovation and new construction projects in the downtown area designed to make it an attractive entertainment and residential district.

History

This former capital of Texas began life as a marketing ploy by entrepreneurs John and Augustus Allen, who purchased land along Buffalo Bayou and decided to start a city. They named it for Sam Houston, hero of the Texas war for independence, drew up a map and convinced the legislature to make it the new country's capital.

Yellow fever and an almost impenetrable link to the Gulf of Mexico later convinced authorities to move the capital to Austin, but because the bayou was the only east-west waterway in the area the city took root and began to flourish.

Several railroads brought lines to Houston, making it an economic hub for shipping and receiving goods. The city competed with Galveston for many years for the distinction of being the largest city in Texas until the 1900 hurricane destroyed Galveston. Investors fled the island city, fearing their investments would be wiped out by future hurricanes, and Houston took the top spot for good.

The discovery of oil at Spindletop cemented Houston's fate as the state's largest city, and by 1906 more than two dozen oil companies called the city home. The Houston Ship Channel opened in 1914, a 51-mile circuitous route linking Houston to the Gulf of Mexico.

By 1948, Houston's port was second only to New York in size. In the 1960s, the Texas Medical Center became a leader in cancer treatment and heart surgery, and the city became home to the nation's manned space program. The oil bust in recent years forced Houston to diversify its economy, a task that appears to be complete. Houston is now the fourth largest city in the nation.

Attractions

Here are some of our favorite things to do and see in the city.

The **Museum of Fine Arts, Houston**, (713) 639-7300 or (713) 639-7379 (Spanish), 1001 Bissonnet, houses the largest art collection in the Southwest. Permanent exhibits include Renaissance, impressionist, and post-World War II American art. Admission is $3 for adults, $1.50 for college students and seniors 65 and older and children ages 6 to 18, and free for children younger than 6. Admission is free on Thursday. The museum is closed on Monday.

Learn about manned space flight and more at **Space Center Houston**, (281) 244-2105 or (800) 972-0369, 1601 NASA Road 1. Activities include tours of NASA's Johnson Space Center, interactive exhibits, IMAX films, and live demonstrations exploring the past, present, and future of manned space flight. While you're there you can land the space shuttle, cruise the surface of the moon, or touch a moon rock. Admission is $13.95 for adults, $12.95 for seniors, $9.95 for children ages 4 to 11, and free for children younger than 4.

Experience Chinese culture, history, and landmarks at **Forbidden Gardens**, (281) 347-8000, 23500 Franz Road in Katy. Forbidden Gardens is a 40-acre outdoor museum with miniaturized exhibits of the Forbidden City, the merchant city of Souzhou, and the tomb of the first emperor of China. Admission is $10 for adults, $5 for seniors and children.

The **Houston Museum of Natural Science**, (713) 639-4600 or (713) 639-4603 (Spanish), One Hermann Circle Drive, houses a museum, planetarium, IMAX Theater, and three-level butterfly tropical rain forest. The nation's fourth most visited museum is near Hermann Park. Admission to the museum is $4 for adults, $3 for seniors and children ages 3 to 11, and free to children younger than 3. Admission to the planetarium is $4 for adults, $3 for seniors, and children ages 2 to 11. Admission to the planetarium's laser light show is $6. The shows, scheduled during nighttime hours, are recommended for people 13 and older. Admission to the IMAX Theater is $6 for adults, $4 for seniors and children ages 3 to 11, and free to children younger than 3. Admission to the butterfly rain forest is $4 for adults, $3 for seniors and children ages 3 to 11, and free for children younger than 3.

Moody Gardens, (409) 744-4673 or (800) 582-4673, One Hope Boulevard in Galveston, offers visitors a variety of experiences ranging from a tropical rain forest to a ride on a paddlewheel boat. Build sandcastles on a white-sand beach, experience a jolting adventure in the IMAX Ridefilm Theater, or watch butterflies hatch in the Butterfly Hatching Hut. Admission is $7.50 per adult per attraction, $6.25 for children, and $5.25 for seniors. Tickets to the aquarium are $11 for adults, $9.25 for seniors and $6.25 for children. You also can purchase a ticket for a single admission to each attraction for $21.95 each.

Now more than 30 years old, the **Astrodome**, the world's first domed stadium, is still worth a visit. Its history is outlined in a high-tech video as part of a tour of the dome. The Astrodome, (713) 799-9595, 8400 Kirby Drive and Loop 610 S., was once dubbed the "eighth wonder of the world." Tours are given at 11 AM and 1 PM Tuesday through Saturday. Admission is $4 for adults; $3 for military, seniors 65 and older and children ages 4 to 11; and free to children younger than 4. You must be part of a tour to go inside. Parking is $5.

Six Flags Houston AstroWorld and **WaterWorld**, (713) 799-8404, is next to the Astrodome. The more than 100 rides and attractions and 15 acres of water rides are among the reasons it's the most visited amusement park in the Southwest. It features the most roller coasters and rides of any theme park in Texas. It also has shows and water rides, including the Edge, an 83-foot slide, a wave-pool, beach, and rushing stream. A recent addition is the Serial Thriller, a suspended, looping roller coaster. Admission to Six Flags Houston AstroWorld is $40.96 for people

DAYTRIPS AND WEEKEND GETAWAYS

48 inches and taller and $20.49 for anyone less than 48 inches tall. Admission to WaterWorld is $21.47 for people 48 inches and taller and $16.14 for anyone less than 48 inches tall. All prices include tax.

Shopping

You would be hard-pressed to find a city with more shopping opportunities than Houston. Shoppers have more than 30 malls to choose from. The place to start is the Post Oak-Galleria area, at Westheimer Road and Post Oak Boulevard.

The Galleria, 5075 Westheimer Road, has more than 300 stores and restaurants offering mostly upscale merchandise. Stores include Lord & Taylor, Macy's, Neiman Marcus, and Saks Fifth Avenue. Other amenities include an ice skating rink and two hotels.

Across the street from the Galleria is the **Centre at Post Oak**, featuring such stores as FAO Schwarz, Barnes & Noble Booksellers, and Old Navy.

The Montrose area west of downtown offers shoppers more offbeat choices, while the immense **Antique Center**, (713) 688-4211, 7200 Katy Road, is a don't-miss destination for antique lovers.

Bargain hunters need not fear: Houston has something for you, too. Reduced prices on clothing and other merchandise are available at several area outlets: the **Conroe Outlet Center**, (936) 756-0999, 45 miles north on IH-45; **The Strand Outlet Shops**, (409) 765-7199, on Galveston Island; and the **Sealy Outlet Center**, (979) 885-3200, west on IH-10.

And because Texas is known for its cowboys, no trip to the Lone Star State would be complete without visiting a western-wear store. **Cavender's Boot City**, (713) 952-7102, 9525-B Westheimer Road, and **Stelzig's of Texas Western Store**, (713) 629-7779, 3123 Post Oak Boulevard, will have the duds needed to turn you into a real live cowpoke.

Restaurants

Houston has more than 8,000 restaurants offering every sort of food imaginable. We've chosen several established restaurants with good reputations to meet a variety of budgets.

Brennan's, (713) 522-9711, 3300 Smith Street, combines Louisiana Cajun with Texas-style cooking to produce spicy and creative dishes. Try the mesquite-grilled veal chop, complimentary pralines and Ramos gin fizz and milk punch. Jacket is required. Dinner for two excluding drinks is $65 to $90.

Houston's rich and powerful can often be found at **Tony's**, (713) 622-6778, 1801 Post Oak Boulevard. Don't miss out on Tony's wonderful desserts. Jacket and tie are required. Dinner for two excluding drinks is $80 and up.

Butera's, (713) 523-0722, 4621 Montrose Boulevard, is an open-air cafe offering patrons traditional deli food along with a few unusual items. Dinner for two is $45 or less.

D'Amico's Italian Market Cave, (713) 526-3400, 510 Morningside Street, is a combination deli and specialty store offering great food at low prices. Don't miss the fish of the day and the crab claws. Dinner for two is $40 or less.

Ninfa's, (713) 228-1175, 2704 Navigation Boulevard, is the original restaurant in what has become a successful chain of Mexican-food restaurants. Ninfa Laurenzo, the restaurant's founder, now owns several restaurants, but the original is still considered the best. Dinner for two is $40 or less.

Take an hour-long drive from downtown Houston to **Gaido's of Galveston**, 3800 Seawall Boulevard in Galveston, (409) 762-9625. Galveston is on an island with the same name 50 miles southeast of Houston. To get there take IH-45. Look for the giant crab on top of the building. Gaido's has been in business since 1911 and continues to pack customers into its cavernous dining room. Take in the ocean view as you dine on Gulf seafood. Dinner for two will run you $30 to $50.

At **Brenner's Steakhouse**, (713) 465-2901, 10911 Katy Freeway, you can enjoy a great view of the garden and pond while dining on steaks and other offerings. Try the homemade salad dressings. Order wine and you'll get a trip to the wine cellar to select your choice. Dinner for two costs $75 to $100.

Nightlife

For the greatest number of entertainment options in the smallest area, you'll want to try the **Richmond Avenue entertainment district**, which runs from the 5600 block to the 6500 block of Richmond Avenue, west of Loop 610. This dining and entertainment district offers food, dancing, and live entertainment at some of Houston's most popular nightspots. Restaurants in this area range from casual to elegant, the food from steaks to Lebanese cuisine.

Club hopping along Richmond Avenue will expose you to the range of musical genres, everything from rock 'n' roll to blues to country. Shopping and accommodations are here, too. And while you're in the area, pop into **Dave and Buster's**, (713) 952-2233, 6010 Richmond Avenue. Here you'll find 50,000 square feet of billiards, shuffleboard, bowling, play-for-fun blackjack, golf, Skeeball, and a midway filled with more electronic games than you've ever seen in one place. For more information on the Richmond Avenue area, call the Richmond Avenue Merchants Association at (713) 974-4686.

Accommodations

Houston has more than 38,000 hotel/motel rooms to offer. Choosing from among the many fine hotels isn't easy. The major hotel and motel chains are represented here—Comfort Inn, Hilton, Days Inn, Holiday Inn, Omni, Hyatt, and others—as well as a number of locally owned lodgings. Following are a few we think you'll like. Remember to add a 15 percent hotel/motel tax to all prices.

Shoppers will enjoy our first listing, which is really two hotels in one. The **Westin Galleria & Westin Oaks Hotels**, (713) 960-8100 or (800) 228-3000, 5060 West Alabama, are in the renowned Galleria shopping center. The Westin Galleria has 485 rooms; the Westin Oaks, 406. All rooms have private balconies; penthouse suites are available. Room prices range from $109 to $255 a night.

Radisson Astrodome Hotel, (713) 748-3221 or (800) 333-3333, 8686 Kirby Drive, is across the street from the Astrodome. It's also close to the Texas Medical Center, Hermann Park (where the zoo and other attractions are located), and the Museum District. This nine-story building and three additional buildings hold 631 rooms, including 44 suites. Room prices range from $99 to $149 a night.

The **Houstonian Hotel, Club & Spa**, (713) 680-2626 or (800) 231-2759, 111 N. Post Oak Lane, is Houston's only member of Preferred Hotels & Resorts Worldwide. Nestled amid 18 wooded acres in the Galleria area, the Houstonian provides seclusion from big-city stress yet is near shopping and restaurants. Room prices range from $149 to $295 a night.

The 12-story white-marble **Park Plaza Warwick Hotel**, (713) 526-1991 or (800) 670-7275, 5701 Main Street, was built in 1926, and, although fully updated, still retains its earlier charm. This 308-room hotel is next to the Museum of Fine Arts and Natural Science Museum. Rooms range from $139 to $185 a night.

Homestead Village, (713) 797-0000 or (888) 782-9473, 7979 Fannin Street, offers an apartment-like setting for people planning to stay a night, a week, or longer. Rooms come with a fully equipped kitchen and free local calls. Laundry facilities are on the premises. Homestead Village is across the street from the Astrodome. Room prices are about $55 a night or around $280 weekly.

Laredo

Laredo is really two cities: Laredo on the U.S. side of the Río Grande and Nuevo Laredo on the Mexico side. Los dos Laredos (the two Laredos), as they call themselves, work closely to promote international trade and tourism. Three international bridges link the two cities, providing access to tourists and business people alike. Laredo feels larger than its population warrants because of international trade and the large Mexican population across the border. Laredo's population in 1996 stood at 166,000, while the population of Nuevo Laredo was 575,000.

Laredo is a 2½-hour drive from Corpus Christi via two-lane highway through South Texas brush country. To get there take N. Padre Island Drive (Texas Highway 358) to Texas Highway 44 W. Stay on Texas 44 through Robstown, Agua Dulce, Alice, and Freer. When you get to Freer, Texas 44 joins with U.S. Highway 59, which takes you through 65 miles of desolate cactus and brush country to the border town of Laredo. Its sister city—Nuevo Laredo, Mexico,—lies across the Río Grande.

You'll quickly understand why the town of Freer adopted the rattlesnake as its school mascot: The brush and cacti that cover the area are the perfect habitat for the venomous rattler. When you reach Laredo, stay on U.S. 59, which becomes Saunders Street inside the city limits, until you reach IH-35.

You'll know you're near the border when you hear all the horn honking. Laredo and Nuevo Laredo residents seem to find lots of reasons to lean on their horns, a practice most Texans frown on. Maybe it's the narrow streets in both downtowns that lead so many drivers to vent. Whatever the reason, don't take it personally. You may find that the traffic in Laredo moves at a snail's pace in certain areas and at certain times of the day. You should also remember that the best times to visit weatherwise are in the winter and spring when temperatures are bearable.

INSIDERS' TIP

Taxis in Nuevo Laredo should be approached with caution: They are not metered, and fares can get expensive. Make sure you and the driver agree on a price before you get in a cab.

Laredo is one of the oldest cities in the United States and the oldest independent city in Texas. Today it is one of the fastest growing cities in the nation. The North American Free Trade Agreement and cross-border production sharing (known as *maquiladoras*) have spurred Laredo's growth. A *maquiladora* uses inexpensive Mexican labor to assemble items that are then returned to the country of origin, where they are sold or exported. More than 100 are in the Nuevo Laredo area. They've contributed to making Laredo the nation's largest commercial inland port, handling 35 percent of all U.S. exports into Mexico. At the southern end of IH-35, the port marks the entrance to the Panamerican Highway, which extends through Central and South America. It's also the distribution point for 190 *maquiladoras* in neighboring Mexican states.

Laredo is part Texan, part Mexican, with a large, bilingual Hispanic population that speaks English as a second language. Tourists flock to the two Laredos from both sides of the border. U.S. citizens are drawn to Nuevo Laredo to find bargains on furniture, artwork, liquor, jewelry, prescription drugs, silver, and Mexican curios. Mexicans cross into Laredo to buy electronics, perfume, and clothes at rates 20 percent to 30 percent below normal, and to shop at the upscale **Mall del Norte**, where they can buy items unavailable in Mexico.

The downtowns of the two cities are connected by a pedestrian bridge (International Bridge No. 1) at the south end of Convent Street. U.S. citizens can visit within a 26-mile area inside Mexico for as long as 72 hours with no paperwork. You must carry proof of U.S. citizenship such as a birth certificate or a drivers' license.

International Bridge No. 2 is a few blocks to the east at the end of Interstate 35. A third bridge is on the far west side of Laredo and is used mostly by trucks carrying cargo across the border. Both downtown bridges are open to vehicular traffic, and both collect a toll each way. Tolls are $1.50 on the U.S. side and $1.55 on the Mexico side, or $2.95 for a round trip. If you're planning to drive across the border, it's a good idea to buy Mexico insurance from a company in Laredo.

To walk across from Laredo, park in the free public lot below International Bridge No. 1 on Salinas Avenue and Water Street. Pedestrians pay $.35 to enter Nuevo Laredo and another $.25 to return to Laredo. The bridge connects Convent Street with Avenida Vicente Guerrero on the Nuevo Laredo side. This is the city's main tourist attraction with shops along either side.

These days it's not necessary to change your money into pesos. Most Nuevo Laredo retailers accept U.S. currency, and many post prices in dollars. Credit cards and travelers checks are widely accepted. Most merchants speak English, and many will haggle with you over prices. Each visitor to Mexico can bring back as much as $400 worth of duty-free (tax-free) retail items for personal use every 30 days. The next $1,000 is taxed at a flat rate of 10 percent. You can bring into the United States one carton of cigarettes and one quart or liter of alcohol per adult every 30 days.

IRS tax and a federal duty will be collected on quantities over the one duty-free quart. Some prescription drugs may be purchased in Mexico (often at much lower prices) and brought into the United States, provided you have a valid U.S. doctor's prescription for a reasonable amount.

Calling into and out of Mexico requires the use of certain access numbers. When calling from Mexico to Laredo, dial 95-956 and then the Laredo number. Local calls within Nuevo Laredo from public phones require Mexican pesos or a phone card that can be purchased at pharmacies. To call Nuevo Laredo from the United States you must dial international code 011, country code 52, city code 87 and then the Nuevo Laredo number. Each city has a different code. The Laredo area code is 956.

History

Three Spanish families first settled Laredo in 1755, led by army officer Don Tomas Sanchez de la Barrera y Gallardo, who named the city for one in Spain. The city was one of the first settlements in Texas not established as either a mission or a fort.

After the Texas Revolution of 1836, and an earlier one in Mexico, Laredo's population stood at around 2,000, with ranching and farming the dominant way of making a living in the area. Laredo lay smack dab in the middle of a disputed territory, with Mexico claiming the boundary between the two countries to be much farther north at the Nueces River, while the Texans claimed it to be along the Río Grande.

In 1840, Mexican citizens in the area formed a coalition of three northern Mexican states and southwest Texas and set up an independent Republic of the Río Grande, with Laredo as the capital. Laredoans are proud of this aspect of their history. The flags of seven countries have flown over Laredo as opposed to six for the rest of the state.

The rebellion lasted 283 days before being crushed by the Mexican Army. The boundary dispute was eventually settled by the Mexican War, which established the Río Grande as the border. After the war, many Laredo residents moved to the southern section of the city south of the river in order to preserve their Mexican citizenship. They renamed the area Nuevo Laredo.

Attractions

Of course there's more to do in Laredo than shop, eat, and drink (although some people do nothing else). It should come as no surprise that the Spanish influence extends to other areas as well.

Been to a bullfight lately? Then cross the border to Nuevo Laredo for an old-fashioned *corrida* (bullfight). Traditional bullfights in which the bull is killed are held at the **Plaza de Toros Lauro Luis Longoria**, (52) (87) 12-71-92, (52) (87) 12-71-93 or (888) 240-8460. *Toreadores* (bullfighters) from throughout Mexico and Spain appear here. Ticket prices range from $3 to $17 depending on the view and whether you sit in the sun or the shade.

If you're in Laredo between mid-March and late July or early August take in a baseball game featuring the only binational sports franchise in the world. The **Tecolotes de los dos Laredos** (the Owls of the two Laredos), (956) 795-2350, is a Mexican League AAA baseball team that plays half its home games in Laredo and the other half in Nuevo Laredo.

INSIDERS' TIP

Tolls to enter Laredo from Nuevo Laredo, Mexico, tend to fluctuate based on the value of the peso to the U.S. dollar.

Laredo prides itself on having lived under seven flags during its history: Spain, Mexico, Texas, the Republic of the Río Grande, the Confederacy, the United States, and France. Laredo served as the capital of The Republic of the Río Grande when Federalist leaders proclaimed independence from Santa Anna's Centralist Mexican government. The republic lasted a mere 283 days, but Laredoans have commemorated the moment with the **Republic of the Río Grande Museum**, (956) 727-3480, 1003 Zaragoza Street. Admission is $1 for all ages. It's open from 9 AM to 4 PM Tuesday through Saturday and 1 to 4 PM on Sunday.

To learn more about Laredo's history take the **Heritage Trolley Tour**, (956) 727-0977, from 9 AM to 11 AM on Tuesday and Thursday and 10 AM to noon on Saturday. Tickets are $8 for adults and $4 for children younger than 12, students with valid ID and guests in wheelchairs. A turn-of-the-century trolley will pick you up at the Río Grande Museum and take you on a two-hour tour of the 242-year-old city's historic district.

Shopping

Laredo is home to two shopping malls: **Mall del Norte**, the ninth-largest in Texas, an upscale mall that caters to Americans and well-to-do Mexicans, and **Riverdrive Mall**, near the border. You'll find many of the usual chains—Dillard's, The Gap, Victoria's Secret—represented at Mall del Norte, on Interstate 35 north of U.S. Highway 59. Shoppers looking for bargains should head to Riverdrive Mall near the border where you'll find chains like JCPenney, Bealls, and lower-end stores. While you're there, check out Laredo's downtown shops, which one local resident described as "the largest urban outlet mall in America." They may not look like much from the outside, but inside you'll find bargains on many of the same items you'd find at the malls. Try **La Fama**, (956) 726-3636, 404 Convent Street, for a wide variety of cosmetics and name-brand clothing.

In Nuevo Laredo, shopping opportunities are plentiful. Vendors ply their wares along busy streets, and children offer everything from necklaces to gum.

Among those shopping experiences you won't want to miss are **El Mercado**, a two-story outdoor market on Avenida Vicente Guerrero, four blocks from International Bridge No. 1. You'll find all sorts of Mexican art and curios in these small, jam-packed shops, which open up on a courtyard. Here you'll find everything from gaudy sombreros and fake designer watches to authentic Mexican artwork and Tiffany-style lamps.

Be sure to visit **Marti's**, 12-33-37, Avenida Vicente Guerrero 2923. Marti's is known locally as the Neiman Marcus of the border, and its selection and prices bear that out. This three-floor shop carries everything from designer clothing and jewelry to furniture and home decorations.

Another shop to check out is **Rafael**, Avenida Vicente Guerrero at Sonora Street. You can tell this is a great place by the fact that it's so hard to find. Owner Rafael Costilla hasn't bothered to put up a sign advertising his store nor installed a business phone. That's because his reputation is so great people find him anyway. Inside you'll find lanterns, hand-blown glass, carved masks, and metal furniture stacked to the rafters. You'll also find a plentiful supply of doors made from weathered mesquite, punched-tin lampshades, and hand-forged metal drawer pulls.

Restaurants

When it comes to dining out, Mexican food is the specialty on both sides of the border, but you'll also find many popular chain restaurants such as Tony Roma's, Pelican's Wharf, and Tokyo Gardens. Restaurants serve everything from Tex-Mex (a form of Mexican food eaten by Mexican immigrants living in Texas) to offerings from Mexico's interior.

Victoria's 3020, 13-30-20, at the corner of Victoria and Matamoros streets in Nuevo Laredo, offers a good representation of food from throughout Mexico. The glass-walled restaurant overlooking a lush, Spanish-style courtyard is a hotspot for food, drinks, and socializing 2½ blocks from the border. Dinner for two, including appetizers, dessert, and coffee, ranges from $50 to $75.

Laredo Bar and Grill, (956) 717-0090, 102 Del Court, serves steaks, chicken, seafood, burgers, salads, and other American and international food in a quiet dining atmosphere. The food is prepared and presented well. Dinner for two, including appetizers, dessert and coffee, costs around $35.

Toño's Bar & Grill, (956) 717-4999, 120 W. Del Mar Boulevard, combines dishes native to Mexico with original recipes concocted by Toño himself. The menu includes typical Mexican foods—enchiladas, tacos—as well as more exotic meats such as pheasant and dove.

For nightlife try **Señor Frog's**, 13-30-31, 351 Ocampo Street, Nuevo Laredo. Señor Frog's can best be described as Mexico's version of The Hard Rock Cafe, with trendy videos playing on screens throughout the restaurant/bar. The restaurant portion is open throughout the week. The bar is open Thursday through Saturday, attracting a younger crowd.

El Dorado, 12-00-15, Beldon and Ocampo streets, Nuevo Laredo, has been in business since 1922, operating until recently as the Cadillac Bar. The restaurant portion of this restaurant/bar offers interesting specialties like frog legs, quail, cabrito (goat), and traditional Mexican food. El Dorado's bar claims to make the best Margaritas in the world and touts its "famous Ramos Gin Fizz."

On the U.S. side try **Guapos Sports Cafe**, (956) 791-5918, 107 Calle Del Norte. Guapos serves food and drinks at its popular restaurant and bar. It has music, a live deejay, and several TV monitors tuned to sports programs.

Accommodations

Laredo has a variety of accommodations available, most within a few minutes' drive of the border. A 14 percent hotel/motel tax will be added to the rates quoted.

La Posada Hotel/Suites, (956) 722-1701 or (800) 444-2099, 1000 Zaragoza Street, is the most renowned hotel in the area. The 208-room Spanish-style building overlooks the Río Grande River and downtown Nuevo Laredo, one block from International Bridge No. 1. The former 19th-century Spanish-Colonial convent offers a tropical courtyard, swimming pool, fitness center, and free airport transportation. Nightly rates range from $199 for a standard room to $146 for a deluxe suite.

The **Red Roof Inn**, (956) 712-0733 or (800) 843-7663, 1006 West Calton Road, is one of the most recent additions to the city's accommodations offerings. Rooms are comfortable if unspectacular and offered at a reasonable price. Amenities include a swimming pool, lighted work area, and sitting area. This 150-room hotel is a short drive from the border and Mall del Norte. Prices range from $53 to $59 a night.

The **Best Western Fiesta Inn**, (956) 723-3603 or (800) 460-1176, 5240 San Bernardo Street, is 2.5 miles from the border and across Interstate 35 from the Mall del Norte. Amenities at this 151-room motel include a free continental breakfast, swimming pool, courtesy van, lounge, and meeting rooms. Rooms are around $59 a night.

As the name suggests, **Family Gardens Inn**, (956) 723-5300 or (800) 292-4053, 5830 San Bernardo Street, caters to families with decent, moderately priced rooms, a general store and free hot dogs, nachos, popcorn, lemonade, and beer in the evenings. Some rooms come with a living room and small kitchen. This 192-room hotel offers a swimming pool, playground, courtesy van, and meeting rooms. It's a two-minute drive from Mall del Norte and a five-minute drive from the border. Room prices are around $54 to $61 a night.

The Military

Evidence of the Corpus Christi area's close ties with the military is as near as the skies and seas, where you'll find a multitude of aircraft and ships used by our armed forces.

Residents and visitors become accustomed to seeing the distinctive orange-and-white training aircraft overhead. The sounds, too, are different from that of commercial aircraft—you'll likely hear the drone of propeller-driven planes used by beginning student aviators at Naval Air Station Corpus Christi and the deeper roar of training jets flown by advanced students at Naval Air Station Kingsville.

Boaters and fishers may encounter some of the more than two-dozen mine warfare ships stationed here. The mine warfare ships are ported at Naval Station Ingleside, across the bay from Corpus Christi, as part of the Navy's recently established mine-warfare headquarters here.

And with the Corpus Christi Army Depot (the Army's largest helicopter repair and maintenance facility) here, you're also likely to see several different types of helicopters. The Depot, as it is called, is one of South Texas' largest industrial employers, with 2,772 civilian employees. Its steady workforce and good wages have been credited with establishing a Hispanic middle class in this region.

As the chamber of commerce puts it, "South Texas is Navy country." That sentiment was never more heartfelt as when city leaders and state politicians battled successfully to retain their military presence in the light of recent Defense Department downsizing. After three rounds of base closures, the Corpus Christi area lost one air-training base but gained a mine-warfare center and strengthened its missions at several existing bases.

Some credit the Corpus Christi area's long-standing loyalty to the armed forces, particularly the Navy, with helping to preserve its military presence through the decades. The relationship has certainly benefited both the community and the military—the military's arrival helped foster development and growth of the region, particularly the city of Corpus

A T-45 Goshawk on final approach.

Photo: courtesy of the Naval Air Station Kingsville

Christi itself. The Corpus Christi area, with its unique geographic and meteorological assets, has aided the Navy's task of training student pilots.

The roots of this relationship can be traced back more than half a century. In 1938, as America became increasingly involved in the ongoing war in Europe, a Navy survey team came to South Texas to scout possible locations for a pilot-training base.

The sleepy fishing town of Corpus Christi (then-population 60,000) caught the attention of Navy planners because of three key assets: a moderate year-round climate, miles of available land for future expansion and plenty of open, uncluttered air space.

In June 1940, President Franklin D. Roosevelt, an avid supporter of aviation and former secretary of the Navy, signed a bill approving funds for construction of the $100-million Naval Air Station Corpus Christi.

INSIDERS' TIP

The first military presence in the Corpus Christi area came in August 1843, when Gen. Zachary Taylor arrived in the fledgling town and set up camp for his troops.

It was to be the single biggest economic boost that the city had ever known, transforming a sandy expanse of snake-infested flatlands and fishing shacks into a busy complex of runways, barracks, seaplane hangars and paved roads.

Construction began immediately, and planes began flying at the newly built base an astonishing nine months after the first spadeful of dirt had been turned. Originally planned for completion in three years, the base was finished in two years—due at least in part to the U.S. government's haste to get pilots in the air after the December 1941 bombing of Pearl Harbor.

During World War II 600 pilots per month completed their training and received their wings at what was known as "The University of the Air." More than 35,000 naval aviators graduated from this base during the war. At that time Corpus Christi was the only primary, basic and advanced training base in the nation—and the largest pilot training facility in the world.

The local newspaper used to devote entire pages to publishing the photographs and names of every new graduate, in recognition and support of the war-bound young men whose smiling faces were pictured wearing leather aviators' caps and goggles. Among the more well-known people who trained as pilots at Corpus Christi are former president George Bush, game show host Bob Barker, and astronaut John Glenn.

The military's arrival changed the complexion of the community, transforming it almost overnight from a rural outpost to a major city. Hotels, restaurants, stores, and entertainment halls were created to meet the demands of the energetic new arrivals.

Celebrity visits became a matter of course. Among the most prominent during the war years were President Franklin D. Roosevelt, Rear Adm. Chester W. Nimitz, and heads of state including King Ibn Saud of Saudi Arabia.

There were even celebrities-turned-naval aviators among those stationed at the base. For example, Ted Williams, the Boston Red Sox star hitter, was a physical fitness instructor at Corpus Christi after he received his wings. Hollywood film star Tyrone Power was at the base for months while learning to fly. Entertainers such as Bob Hope, Frank Sinatra, Louis Armstrong, Ginger Rogers, Rita Hayworth, and Katherine Hepburn came to the new base to entertain the young recruits.

The growth extended to neighboring communities, as auxiliary naval air stations were built in the nearby towns of Kingsville and Beeville to assist in pilot training.

After the war, the Navy's need for pilots decreased dramatically, and the Corpus Christi base was downgraded to a smaller facility. The bases in Kingsville and Beeville were shut down until 1948, when the Navy decided to use the South Texas complex, which includes Corpus Christi, Beeville, and Kingsville, as headquarters for its air training command and for teaching jet pilots to fly.

Today, there are an estimated 11,000 military and civilian employees at South Texas' four military facilities in Corpus Christi, Ingleside, and Kingsville.

The Corpus Christi base continues to teach beginning naval aviators how to fly, and has gained increasing importance as a headquarters for joint training of students from the Navy, Marine Corps, Air Force, Coast Guard, and foreign countries.

The auxiliary training base in Beeville was shut down by the Base Closure and Realignment Commission in 1991, but the Kingsville base continues to train the Navy's advanced students to fly high-tech combat jets.

THE MILITARY

Lexington Ghost

One of the most famous nicknames given to USS *Lexington* is "Blue Ghost," a reference to the venerable warship's seeming invulnerability to enemy attack.

During World War II, this aircraft carrier participated in nearly every major operation in the Pacific Theater. The Japanese reported her sunk four times, but each time she returned to fight again. That led propagandist Tokyo Rose to call her the Blue Ghost, a moniker she and her crew wore with pride.

But there are other kind of ghosts aboard this decommissioned aircraft carrier, which now serves as a floating museum in Corpus Christi Bay. Many visitors have reported amazing encounters with apparent apparitions.

There's a neatly dressed young sailor with piercing blue eyes who has been seen in the engine room. There have been footprints seen when no one was around, rustling noises in hallways where no one was supposed to be, and some tourists have said they felt that someone was watching them—but turned around and found no one there.

Even museum employees tell tales of strange encounters—hearing footsteps behind them while walking through deserted areas of the aircraft carrier, or seeing the figure of a Japanese aviator in the hallway. A painting crew once stopped for a break and returned to find their work completed—in a very short time for such a large job.

Some folks speculate that some of the ghosts are sailors who were killed aboard the ship, particularly the 50 seamen who died in a Japanese kamikaze attack on Nov. 5, 1944. Others say that the empty spaces of an old ship tend to echo with strange, unnatural noises that lead some people to think of spirits.

These mysterious occurrences seem to bewilder both staff and visitor—and add yet another dimension to visiting the historic ship. So keep in mind that the ghosts aboard the Blue Ghost may turn your museum visit into a supernatural adventure.

Also in 1991 the Corpus Christi area gained another military mission when the Navy decided to base its mine-warfare operations at Ingleside. The base at Ingleside now serves as home to more than two-dozen mine-warfare ships and is used as a centralized location to train and deploy the Navy's mine-warfare fleet and personnel.

The Ingleside base, with its fast-growing population and modern facilities, is one of the Navy's most progressive installations. In 1997 the base won the Commander-in-Chief's Installation Excellence award for its innovative programs, conservation of natural resources, and partnering programs with the local community.

Today the Corpus Christi area continues to nurture its relationship with its military neighbors, considered key economic assets for the region. A local task force remains vigilant in its efforts to protect local bases from closing.

For its part, the military cherishes its relationship with the community as well. Aviators and sailors are active in the community and often serve as volunteers at local schools and charitable events. Navy officers say the Corpus Christi area is one of the most welcoming destinations for personnel, and there are plans to establish the Corpus Christi-Ingleside area as a fleet concentration area, similar to San Diego, California, and Norfolk, Virginia.

The Navy has also expanded its operations here, sending a squadron of mine-hunting helicopters to the Corpus Christi base and building the first two projects in an ongoing series of joint-partnership housing ventures—which pair Navy funds with private money—in the Corpus Christi area.

A detailed description of each of the military bases, their missions and availability of access to the public follows.

Naval Air Station Corpus Christi
19 Ocean Dr., Corpus Christi
• **(361) 939-3420 public affairs office**

The primary mission of this 4,400-acre naval base is pilot training, overseen by the Chief of Naval Air Training. Beginning flight students come to Corpus Christi to start their training and, depending on their performance, to determine which aircraft they will eventually fly on active duty in the Navy.

Three training squadrons, overseen by Training Air Wing Four, teach students the various stages of flight—VT-27 and VT-28, used for training primary students in a single-engine turboprop; and VT-31, where students do advanced flying in a larger, twin-engine turboprop. Students train for approximately 18 months before they receive their wings, and approximately 400 students graduate from the program each year.

The base is also home to one of the Navy's two mine-warfare helicopter squadrons, Helicopter Mine Countermeasures Squadron 15, which uses massive Sea Dragon helicopters to sweep the seas for underwater mines.

Other tenants at the base are the Commander of the Navy's Mine Warfare Command; the U.S. Coast Guard; the Corpus Christi Army Depot; U.S. Customs; and the U.S. Naval Hospital.

There are 1,619 active-duty personnel on base, 2,500 reservists and 5,404 civilians. The estimated annual economic impact of the base is $333 million.

The base has two entrances, one at the southernmost end of Ocean Drive and the other from South Padre Island Drive. There are security guards posted at each entrance, and though the base is open to the public, unchaperoned sightseeing is not permitted. The base, however, is available for pre-arranged tours and for special events, such as concerts and the occasional air show that features the Navy's flight demonstration team, the Blue Angels. Call the public affairs office for more information.

Naval Air Station Kingsville
554 McCain St., Ste. 309, Kingsville
• **(361) 516-6146 public affairs office**

The best and brightest flight students are assigned to this air training base, on nearly 4,000 acres about 45 miles south of Corpus Christi.

During their yearlong training stint, Navy

INSIDERS' TIP

The weather is one of the reasons that the Coastal Bend was chosen as a home for three Navy bases—clear skies are the norm an average of 328 to 345 days per year.

and Marine Corps students learn to fly jets, to engage in air-to-air combat, to drop bombs and—most crucially—to land on the Navy's principal warships, aircraft carriers.

There are two training squadrons, VT-21 and VT-22. Both use the same syllabus and same aircraft, the T-45A Goshawk, to train student pilots. When the students graduate and receive the wings of gold that mark them as naval aviators, they go to the fleet for further training in fighter jets such as the F-14 Tomcat and the FA/18 Hornet.

Established in July 1942, the base first provided a home for four squadrons that trained pilots in fighter and bomber tactics and a gunnery school for combat aircrew men. After World War II, training was reduced and the land leased to Texas A&I College in Kingsville for use as an agricultural station.

In 1951 the base was reopened as an auxiliary station, and in 1969, it was redesignated as a naval air station.

The base boasts four 8,000-foot runways, an auxiliary landing field in nearby Orange Grove and a target range in McMullen County. Its assets are valued at more than $300 million.

Tenant commands are the Naval Oceanographic Command Detachment, the Naval Air Maintenance Training Group Detachment, the Mobile Mine Assembly Group Detachment, the Relocatable-Over-the-Horizon Radar, and U.S. Border Patrol sector offices and headquarters.

There are 786 officers and enlisted personnel on base, and 1,042 civilians.

Again, this base is not open for general sightseeing. There are special events during which the public is invited aboard the base, including a Fourth of July celebration with aircraft flybys and static displays of vintage aircraft. You can also arrange a tour for your school or tour group by calling the public affairs office in advance.

Naval Station Ingleside
1455 Ticonderoga Rd., Ingleside
• **(361) 776-4206**

Located on the northern shore of Corpus Christi Bay, this base sits astride the Corpus Christi ship channel, a deep-water artery linking the city to the Gulf of Mexico. Originally planned as a Navy homeport, the base had its groundbreaking in February 1988. The area was first chosen to serve as home for the battleship

USS *Wisconsin* and the aircraft carrier USS *Lexington*. However, in April 1991, the Navy changed its plans for the base and instead designated it as the headquarters for the Navy's mine-warfare fleet.

The change in its mission came as Navy leaders increased attention on mine warfare in the wake of the Persian Gulf War, when the United States' feeble minesweeping capabilities forced cancellation of planned amphibious landings.

The base was officially dedicated on July 6, 1992, and the first mine-countermeasures ship, USS *Scout*, arrived in June 1992. The ship has the distinction of being the first U.S. Navy ship homeported in Texas since World War II.

Since then, Navy officials have consolidated their mine-warfare assets—ships, aircraft, divers and training headquarters—at Ingleside so personnel can train and work nearby to improve their capabilities. Recent international mine-hunting exercises have allowed the U.S. Navy to demonstrate its new prowess in the field of mine warfare.

There are 3,650 personnel assigned to Ingleside, including 3,300 military personnel and 350 civilians. The base boasts a state-of-the-art 4,600-foot waterfront with a 1,100-foot double-deck pier.

Tenant commands include the Regional Support Group, which provides maintenance and training for the ships at Ingleside; Mine Countermeasures Squadrons One and Two, deployable squadrons sent to mine-warfare ships overseas; Shore Intermediate Maintenance Activity, which makes special and advanced ship repairs; and a branch medical and dental clinic.

There are now 22 mine countermeasures ships at the base, including the Navy's first command and control ship, USS *Inchon*; 12 Avenger-class mine countermeasures vessels; and nine Osprey-class coastal mine hunters. A total of 25 ships is scheduled to be stationed here by 1999.

This is an open base—you can drive onto it at any time. Also, the public affairs office offers a free "windshield" tour of the base at 1:30 PM every Tuesday. Reservations are not required.

Once a month, usually on a Saturday, a ship is designated for free public visitation. The ships are also available for pre-arranged tours for groups and organizations.

Corpus Christi Army Depot
308 Crecy St., Corpus Christi
• (361) 939-2749

In the 1940s the Navy operated an aircraft overhaul and repair facility to maintain the seaplanes and carrier-based aircraft used to teach World War II-era pilots. The operation was shut down on June 30, 1959, putting 3,000 people out of work.

The facility sat idle for two years, until the Army took over the large hangars and other buildings and opened its U.S. Army Aeronautical Depot Maintenance Center in 1961. The facility began by repairing fixed- and rotary-wing aircraft. In 1967, the fixed-wing aircraft repairs were phased out because of increased demand for helicopter service.

By 1968 the depot was repairing more than 400 helicopters per year; in 1974, its name was changed to Corpus Christi Army Depot.

Today the depot has more than 100 production shops and 2,772 civilian employees. Though the facility began with employees working mostly on Army helicopters, today's employees work on rotary wing aircraft from all branches of the armed services, including Air Force, Marine Corps and Navy.

The 154-acre depot runs on $600-million worth of facilities at Naval Air Station Corpus Christi.

The Corpus Christi depot is the Army's largest helicopter repair depot and, as such, is considered a key player in the country's military readiness.

The depot is not open to the public; however, organizations and clubs can schedule prearranged tours of the facility. Call the public affairs office for more information.

Naval Air Station Corpus Christi is the home of Naval Air Training Command and Corpus Christi Army Depot.

Photo: courtesy of the Naval Air Station Corpus Christi

THE MILITARY

Retirement

The Corpus Christi area, as you will discover in the pages that follow, has plenty to offer retirees. As in other Sunbelt regions, one of the main attractions here is the warm weather. Each year thousands of "winter Texans" close up their homes in the Midwest or other cold locales, climb into recreational vehicles and begin their long journey to the Corpus Christi area in search of sunshine and streets free of ice and snow. Some stay in the many campgrounds and RV parks in the area (see our Campgrounds and RV Parks chapter), while others prefer to stay in one of the many condominiums available here (see our Weekly and Long-Term Rentals chapter).

And while many spend only their winters here, others decide to make the Corpus Christi area their full-time homes, including many retired military who were stationed at one of the local military bases at some point during their careers (see our Military chapter).

Retirees who decide to live in Corpus Christi-area communities full time will find many fine neighborhoods from which to choose. Rockport is an especially popular home for retirees, who enjoy its small-town lifestyle, art galleries, fishing, watersports, and attractive views of Aransas Bay. Corpus Christi is another popular retirement area. "Corpus," as many locals call it, has many of the amenities people enjoy in larger towns—restaurants, museums, the arts—without sacrificing its small-town appeal. Retirees (and anyone else tired of the rat race) will enjoy the ease with which one can move around in Corpus Christi. Both the Aransas Pass and Corpus Christi housing authorities can help low-income retirees find subsidized housing (see the listings that follow).

Kingsville also draws its share of military retirees. Many retired jet pilots settle here; two have served as mayor in recent years, while seven former chamber of commerce presidents have been retired aviators.

Other retirees will want to look into the several independent and assisted living facilities in the area, several of which we describe in the "Housing" section of this chapter. Assisted living facilities and home-healthcare providers have increased tremendously in the Corpus Christi area during the past few years. Their growth is a response to the growing number of seniors here and their desire to stay out of nursing homes as long as possible.

Organizations, agencies, and senior centers do more to bolster the quality of life for older adults here. Seniors will find several chapters of the American Association of Retired Persons (AARP) meeting in the Corpus Christi area. The Area Agency on Aging of the Coastal Bend provides a wide range of services to seniors in a 12-county area. The Corpus Christi area has numerous senior centers, including eight in Corpus Christi, each offering activities for older adults along with daily lunches. Call (361) 883-5743 or (800) 817-5743.

Following is a description of agencies that help retirees and seniors meet their needs, including a breakdown of the American Association of Retired Persons (AARP) chapters in the area. They're listed in alphabetical order instead of by geographic region because many are regional or statewide resources. Sections on area senior centers and housing options follow.

LOOK FOR:
- **Organizations and Services**
- **Agencies and Programs**
- **Senior Centers**
- **Housing**

Organizations and Services

American Association of Retired Persons (AARP)

The AARP serves the needs and interests of people 50 and older through legislative advocacy, research, informative programs and community services provided by local chapters and volunteers throughout the country. However, to join an AARP chapter you must first join the national organization. National dues are $10 a year or $28 for three years. You do not have to belong to a chapter to join the national organization.

Members can receive free tax assistance by calling (361) 985-8230. During tax season volunteers staff 15 sites throughout the Corpus Christi area, helping seniors and others prepare income tax forms. The AARP also administers the Prescription Drug Program, (800) 456-2277, which provides prescription and nonprescription products at discount prices.

In this section we fill you in on the AARP chapters in the Corpus Christi area.

Rockport-Fulton AARP Chapter No. 1536
Paws & Taws Convention Center, 400 Fulton Beach Rd., Fulton
• **(361) 729-1026**

This active group meets at 10:30 AM on the second and fourth Thursday of each month. The first monthly meeting is reserved for busi-

ness, and the second is set aside for a covered-dish lunch. Entertainment is included at both meetings. The group's board of directors meets on the first Thursday of the month.

Chapter members play bridge at 1 PM every Thursday and hold a country-and-western dance every Thursday night except during summer months. Although the chapter doesn't meet in June, July, and August, bridge players still get together on Thursdays at Wells Fargo Bank, One Broadway Plaza. Members collect trash along a 2-mile stretch of Texas Highway 35 as part of the state's litter control program and visit a local nursing home on the first Saturday of each month to play bingo with residents. Proceeds from the dances and bridge games go toward college scholarships and local charities. Dues are $3 per year.

AARP Senior Citizens Group Chapter No. 1855
Senior Citizens Center, 720 E. Lee Ave., Kingsville
• **(361) 592-8049**

The 35 to 40 seniors who belong to this group meet at 6:30 PM on the third Thursday of each month. They bring sandwiches, cake, and coffee or have a covered-dish supper. Speakers are often invited to address the group on current issues.

Portland AARP Chapter No. 2901
Senior Citizens Center, Wildcat and Fifth Ave., Portland
• **(361) 643-3132**

The Portland AARP chapter is active in fund-

The white pelican is a resident water bird along the Gulf Coast.

raisers to support such worthy causes as the public library, emergency medical services, the Portland Police Department and drug prevention programs. They also collect food and clothes for the needy, especially around Thanksgiving and Christmas. The group meets at 6 PM on the fourth Friday of the month. The chapter's program usually includes AARP affiliated business, entertainment, speeches and, occasionally, bingo.

Southeast AARP Chapter No. 2939
Garden Senior Center, 2133 Greenley St., Corpus Christi
• (361) 855-5827

Southeast AARP members meet at 1 PM on the first and third Wednesday of each month. A covered-dish lunch and bingo are featured at the first monthly meeting; cookies and bingo are on the agenda for the second monthly meeting. Business is discussed at both meetings. Guest speakers and entertainment are common. The group regularly contributes a part of its budget to charity.

Greenwood AARP Chapter No. 4386
Greenwood Senior Center,
4040 Greenwood Dr.
• (361) 853-8404, 854-4628

This group strives to live up to the AARP motto: "To serve and not to be served." They do this by being self-sufficient and helping the needy whenever possible. They meet at 10 AM on the first and third Thursday of each month. Members discuss chapter business, community activities, and volunteer opportunities. They socialize, eat sweets, and drink coffee.

Agencies and Programs

Adopt A Nursing Home Volunteer Program
• (361) 878-3546

This program uses volunteer groups of at least three people to visit nursing homes four times a year. They take residents on outings, help them with arts and crafts, play table games, and visit them in their rooms.

Adult Protective Services
• (800) 252-5400

This state-licensed agency investigates reports of abuse, neglect, or exploitation of elderly or disabled people.

American Red Cross— Coastal Bend Texas Chapter
1721 S. Brownlee St., Corpus Christi
• (361) 887-9991, (800) 656-9991

The local chapter of this nationwide group offers a 20 percent senior discount on first aid, CPR, and other classes. It also offers two classes for the price of one for seniors and their spouses or caregivers.

American Red Cross "I'm OK" Program
1721 S. Brownlee St., Corpus Christi
• (361) 887-9991, (800) 656-9991

Volunteers in this program call seniors once or twice a week and sometimes visit them in their homes if no relative lives in the area. The service is free; bilingual volunteers are available.

Area Agency on Aging of the Coastal Bend
2910 Leopard St., Corpus Christi
• (361) 883-5743, (800) 817-5743

One of the most dynamic forces for senior services in the region, this agency plans, coordinates and funds nutrition and other support services for residents 60 and older in 12 Corpus Christi-area counties. Services include meals, transportation, senior center activities, legal services, and Alzheimer's support services.

Area Agency on Aging Case Management
2910 Leopard St., Corpus Christi
• (361) 883-5743, (800) 817-5743

This program buys in-home services for the elderly including personal care, homemaker, personal response units, and bathroom safety bars from home health agencies when all other avenues of help are exhausted.

Arthritis Foundation— South Texas Chapter
• (713) 529-0800, (800) 364-8000

Warm water therapy and arthritis self-help courses are two of the services the Arthritis Foundation provides to arthritis sufferers. It also provides brochures and videos and organizes fund-raisers and memorials for people who have passed away from arthritis.

Coastal Bend Legal Services Metro Corpus Christi
• (361) 883-3623, (800) 840-3379

Low-income seniors receive assistance with problems that cannot be handled without legal expertise, such as appealing denied Medicare or

Medicaid benefits, reviewing insurance or pension benefits and preparing wills. This agency also conducts community education programs on legal rights and responsibilities.

Corpus Christi
Central Library Career Center
805 Comanche St., Corpus Christi
• **(361) 880-7004**

Employment is a vital aspect in the lives of many older adults, and this center, at the Corpus Christi Central Library, provides local job listings for those seeking jobs, along with resources to explore careers, prepare resumes, write cover letters, and hone interviewing skills. The center, which serves the general population as well as older adults, offers free workshops to help job hunters and people changing careers.

Corpus Christi
Retired Teachers' Association
• **(361) 852-6763**

This group of former teachers holds monthly meetings to give seniors the chance to socialize and remain informed on topics related to teaching and the teacher retirement system. Members also perform community service projects. National, state, and local dues are $30 per year.

Del Mar College
Senior Education Program
Harvin Center, Baldwin and Ayers Sts.
• **(361) 698-1298**

This community college program encourages lifetime learning for older adults by allowing people 65 and older to audit classes without paying tuition. The program also offers free, volunteer-taught classes of interest to persons 55 and older as well as enrichment seminars for seniors.

Eldercare Locator
• **(800) 677-1116**

This national information and referral service helps find community resources for elderly individuals throughout the United States. Call between 8 AM and 7 PM (CST) Monday through Friday.

Elderhostel Programs National office
• **(617) 426-7788**

This worldwide program provides noncredit courses, lodgings, and meals for people 55 and older. This educational program offers participants the chance to combine study and the exploration of new places in an academic environment. In addition to calling the national office, above, you can call Del Mar College at (361) 698-1514; Texas A&M-Corpus Christi at (361) 994-5967; and Texas A&M-Kingsville at (361) 593-2861.

Foster Grandparent
Program
• **(361) 844-7625**

This federally funded program sponsored by the Corpus Christi State School provides volunteer opportunities for seniors 60 and older who meet federal income guidelines. Volunteers are matched with individuals ages 1 month to 21 years to provide one-on-one companionship. Volunteers receive an hourly stipend for 20 hours a week as well as transportation to the work site, training, and insurance.

Hearing Aid Helpline
• **(800) 521-5247**

Callers to this helpline receive information on signs of hearing loss and can request a free consumer kit that answers questions about hearing aids, including how to shop for them and what to look for. The helpline also puts callers in touch with a reputable, qualified hearing-aid specialist in their area.

Home Provider Program/Community
Care for Elderly and Disabled
• **(361) 855-9924**

This service is designed to provide in-home assistance with personal care and household tasks to seniors who are unable to perform those tasks themselves. Personal care may include help with bathing, dressing, and meal preparation. Housekeeping may include tasks like washing dishes, doing laundry, cleaning, and shopping. Other services include home-delivered meals, respite services, emergency response systems, and adult day care.

Housing and Community
Development Program
1201 Leopard St., Corpus Christi
• **(361) 880-3010**

A city of Corpus Christi initiative, the Housing and Community Development Program provides loans and grants to rehabilitate owner-occupied housing for low-income, elderly, and

---

INSIDERS' TIP

North Bay Hospital in Aransas Pass is the home base for the National Association of Senior Friends—Aransas Pass Chapter, a club so exclusive "it takes 50 years to become a member."

disabled people. It also runs a grant program for emergency repair services for the elderly and disabled.

Jewish Community Council of Corpus Christi
750 Everhart Rd., Corpus Christi
• (361) 855-6239

This Corpus Christi-based group provides basic computer instruction, low-impact aerobics, and counseling for seniors. They have facilities available for social activities, and provide speakers who can discuss issues important to seniors. The council's services are available to people of all faiths.

Medicare
•(800) 442-2620 for claims
• (800) 772-1213 for eligibility
• (800) 269-0271 for fraud/abuse

The federal Medicare program provides insurance for both hospital and medical coverage to people who are disabled or 65 and older and who have paid into the Social Security System. The government has put several resources at the disposal of older adults, including numbers to call for the status of pending claims and general information on eligibility. In cases of suspected fraud and abuse related to health and human services for Medicare recipients, a special arm of the program will evaluate and process complaints.

National Association of Retired Federal Employees
Sparkling City by the Sea Chapter 91
Lindale Senior Center, 3135 Swantner Ave.
• (361) 852-6658

This organization strives to preserve federal retirement benefits for civilian employees and retirees. Officers help members and non-members with insurance, payment or the filing out of documents when a spouse dies. The local chapter meets from 1:30 to 3:30 PM on the first Tuesday of each month. Every Wednesday from 10 AM to 2 PM it operates a service center to help federal retirees or their survivors. The service center is held at the Corpus Christi Army Depot, Building 1727, Room 102A, 308 Crecy Street, Naval Air Station-Corpus Christi. Call (361) 961-3112 for information. You can also email the local chapter at Hvsalinas@aol.com.

National Health Information Center
• (800) 336-4797

Information on general health, Lyme disease, cancer, health insurance, Medicaid, Medi-

care, and more is available by calling this toll-free number. Callers can also receive a list of health publications.

North American Senior Citizens Association
Lindale Senior Center, 3135 Swanter Rd., Corpus Christi
• (361) 884-3410

This senior advocacy group's goals include better housing, healthcare, services, economic conditions, and education for all senior citizens. They hold a dance from 1 to 4 PM every third Saturday of the month and a business meeting from 5 to 7 PM on the Friday before each dance.

Ombudsman Long-Term Care Program
• (361) 883-5743, (800) 817-5743

This program sponsored by the Area Agency on Aging investigates and acts on complaints by nursing home residents or their families. Volunteers who staff this program go through special training and certification. The Blue Angel Volunteer Program works in conjunction with the ombudsman program. Blue Angel volunteers visit nursing home residents on a weekly basis.

Operation Heat Help
• (361) 885-6910

This program run by the city of Corpus Christi Gas Department helps low-income seniors pay their winter gas bills.

Port Aransas Meals on Wheels
710 W. Ave. A, Port Aransas
• (361) 749-4111

This program run by the city of Port Aransas provides meals delivered to seniors' homes.

Retired and Senior Volunteer Program
1201 Leopard St., Corpus Christi
• (361) 880-3149

RSVP provides volunteer opportunities for people 55 and older, retired or still working. RSVP volunteers serve with nonprofit, private, and public community organizations in Corpus Christi and rural Nueces County.

Salvation Army Home League
1507 Mestina St., Corpus Christi
• (361) 884-9497

These meetings for older women consist of fellowship, community service, education, and worship. The Home League meets at 5 PM Thursday in the Fellowship Hall of The Salvation Army Church, 1802 Buford Street.

RETIREMENT

Senior Community Services
1201 Leopard St., Corpus Christi
• **(361) 814-1681**

This city-sponsored program is designed to foster independence for individuals 60 and older who are homebound and isolated. Staff members provide hot lunches to seniors Monday through Friday at eight different senior centers in Corpus Christi.

Senior Companion Program
• **(361) 880-3154**

This program is designed to help adults maintain their independence by providing volunteers to give them a hand with their daily needs. Assistance includes housekeeping, meal preparation, respite care, social recreation, and home management. Volunteers receive an hourly stipend for a 20-hour work week, meal, and mileage money, insurance, and training.

Senior Employment Project
• **(361) 880-3304**

This federally funded program sponsored by the city of Corpus Christi provides employment training for economically disadvantaged senior citizens over 55. Services include temporary part-time, minimum-wage work, job-search counseling, and educational opportunities.

Senior Friends
Sunrise Mall, 5858 S. Padre Island Dr., Corpus Christi
• **(361) 993-4288, (800) 445-5280**

This seniors association is designed to meet the special needs of older adults, such as insurance claims counseling, physician referral and regular health screenings. The organization provides exercise, computer and Spanish classes, guest speakers, social events, travel, volunteer opportunities, and a bimonthly newsletter.

Senior Friends also is available in northwest Corpus Christi, 3151 McKinzie Road, (361) 241-4407, and in Aransas Pass, 1560 W. Wheeler Avenue, (361) 758-8585, extension 222.

Senior Link/Elder Link
• **(361) 937-3965**

The Senior Link is a group of nonprofit services for seniors, their families, and professionals in the aging field. Services include the *Gray Gazette,* a newspaper published each month; and Elder Link, a program designed to help older adults stay in their homes.

Seniors Assisting Seniors
3312 Wayside Dr., Corpus Christi
• **(361) 886-2782**

This program operated with the assistance

Rockport-Fulton is home to many retirees, artists, boaters, and fisherman— anyone who wants a peaceful, relaxing place to call home.

Photo: courtesy of the Corpus Christi Convention and Visitors Bureau of the Corpus Christi Police Department gives seniors 55 and older the chance to help seniors whose homes have been burglarized. Members conduct a free home safety check to deter future burglaries.

Seniors Awareness & Safety Facts Education
• (361) 887-2260

This educational program sponsored by the Nueces County Sheriff's Department makes presentations before groups of 10 and more on crimes against the elderly, travel safety, frauds and scams, 911 education, and personal safety in the home.

Service Corps of Retired Executives Association
615 N. Upper Broadway, Room 654
• (361) 888-4322, (361) 888-3331

Retired corporate and business managers serve as volunteers providing free counseling to people planning to start a new business and to business owners who need help to make their business grow. They conduct monthly seminars on topics such as business plans, sources of capital, insurance, and marketing, which are presented by people with fine-tuned expertise in these areas.

Silver Haired Legislators
• (361) 883-5743, (800) 817-5743

This senior advocacy group convenes in Austin to discuss issues important to senior citizens. Members 60 and older elect four representatives from the Corpus Christi area. The group debates issues and establishes priorities for consideration by the Texas Legislature.

Spohn Healthwise 55
• (361) 881-3733, (800) 451-3631

Healthwise 55 is a club for seniors sponsored by Spohn Health System. Healthwise 55 benefits include trips, 24-hour membership infoline, exercise and strengthening classes, lectures, dances and socials, club calendars, health screening and seminars, and membership luncheons. Members receive discounts on items such as eyewear, hearing aids, medical equipment, prescriptions, and gifts. Seniors also benefit from discounts at local restaurants and area florists.

State Long-Term Care Ombudsman
• (800) 252-2412

Provides assistance with those needing an ombudsman (someone who assists in investigating and solving complaints) to deal with long-term care needs. It also provides local numbers seniors may call for help.

Texas Department on Aging
• (512) 424-6840, (800) 817-5743

This is the state-level focal point for all activities related to the needs and services of older persons throughout Texas. It provides funds for local aging services through Title III of the Older Americans Act. Call for information on elderly services at the Area Agency on Aging nearest you.

Texas Department of Human Services Bureau of Long-Term Care
• (800) 458-9858

This regulatory agency surveys and investigates compliance of long-term care facilities with Medicare and Medicaid standards. Call for information on facilities or to voice a complaint. They cover all nursing homes, private and nonprivate.

United Way INFO•LINE
• (361) 882-4636, (800) 421-4636

The United Way of the Coastal Bend operates this information and referral service for people needing help from health and human service agencies in the Texas Coastal Bend. With assistance from local volunteers, the service has helped seniors get their lawns mowed and obtain wheelchair ramps.

Vineyard Employment Ministry
• (361) 888-5161

Corpus Christi Metro Ministries runs this employment program to help anyone seeking employment, including seniors. It provides networking with other agencies to develop job opportunities and other support services.

Volunteer Center
505 S. Water St., Corpus Christi
• (361) 887-8282

The Volunteer Center places people of all ages as volunteers for 250 agencies throughout the Corpus Christi area. Volunteers are assigned according to their interests, abilities, and skills they would like to develop.

Workforce Development Corporation
• (361) 882-7491

This federally funded program helps economically qualified Corpus Christi–area residents 55 and older find a job. They provide job leads, employer incentives, workshops, resume

RETIREMENT

services, computer training, GED classes, and testing. They also offer physicals, eye exams, glasses, and uniforms. All services are free of charge.

YMCA
417 S. Upper Broadway, Corpus Christi
• **(361) 882-1741**

The YMCA offers wellness programs for people of all ages. Senior activities include water exercise classes, as well as fitness evaluations, aerobic fitness classes, and personalized exercise programs.

YWCA
4601 Corona Dr.,
Corpus Christi
• **(361) 857-5661**

The YWCA has a variety of low-impact aerobic and water fitness classes. Classes are designed to increase flexibility, fitness, toning, and endurance. The Y also offers classes designed for arthritis sufferers and people concerned about osteoporosis.

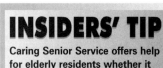

INSIDERS' TIP

Caring Senior Service offers help for elderly residents whether it be for two hours or around the clock. Services include everything from respite care (giving loved ones a break) to grocery shopping, light cleaning, and companion care. This for-profit company can be reached in Corpus Christi at (361) 883-9494.

Senior Centers

Corpus Christi-area senior centers offer activities designed to benefit the health and well being of adults 60 and older. Activities vary from center to center, but all focus on providing nutritionally balanced meals on weekdays. Activities include health screenings, benefits counseling, recreation, health promotion programs, physical fitness, legal assistance, and transportation.

Senior centers in the area, excluding those in Corpus Christi (see subsequent information), include: Council on Aging Senior Center, 912 S. Church Street, Rockport, (361) 729-5352; Kleberg County Human Services, 720 E. Lee Avenue, Kingsville, (361) 595-8572; Ricardo Senior Center, (361) 595-8572, U.S. Highway 77 S., Ricardo; Ingleside Senior Center, Avenue E and Seventh Street, Ingleside, (361) 776-3136; Senior Citizens Community Center, 250 S. 13th Street, Aransas Pass, (361) 758-2939; and Portland Senior Center, (361) 643-6501, extension 258, 601 Wildcat, Portland. In Corpus Christi, Senior Community Services, (361) 814-1681, a division of the Corpus Christi Park and Recreation Department, provides recreational programs for seniors at eight senior centers. Activities include fitness classes, dances, senior group meetings, community organization meetings, and arts and crafts classes. Staff members are available to help with benefits counseling, housing, letter writing and reading, volunteer opportunities, home visits, telephone reassurance, nutrition education, and health screening. The centers also host local speakers.

Adults 60 and older may eat lunch at the centers Monday through Friday. The department publishes a monthly activity calendar detailing activities, including classes, at the city's senior centers. To receive a calendar call Senior Community Services at the number above. To register for classes, call or drop by the center offering the class.

These programs are available at all Corpus Christi senior centers: Briarwood Senior Center, 1701 Thames Drive, (361) 991-8081; Broadmoor Senior Center, 1651 Tarlton Street, (361) 888-7012; Ethel Eyerly Senior Center, 654 Graham Road, (361) 937-3218; Greenwood Senior Center, (361) 854-4628, 4040 Greenwood Drive; Lindale Senior Center, 3135 Swanter Road, (361) 854-4508; Northwest Senior Center, 9725 Up River Road, (361) 241-3956; Oveal Williams Senior Center, 1414 Martin Luther King Drive, (361) 887-7633; and Zavala Senior Center, 510 Osage Street, (361) 882-1561.

Housing

North Bay Area

Carriage Inn
401 Northshore Blvd., Portland
• **(361) 777-0303**

The Carriage Inn opened its doors in August 1998, offering a unique blend of 110 efficiencies, 1- and 2-bedroom apartments and 1- and 2-bedroom cottages designed for independent living. These ground-floor apartments and cottages are across the street from the Northshore Country Club.

Amenities include three meals a day in an elegant dining room, trash pickup at your door, free basic cable, weekly housekeeping including linens, transportation in a white stretch limousine, free laundry facilities, utilities, large whirlpool and spa, enclosed courtyard, covered patios and apartment maintenance. They also offer crafts, recreation, and planned social activities.

Pets are allowed. Each unit is linked via an alert system to a computer at the front desk, which is staffed 24 hours a day. Monthly prices range from $1,495 to $2,195.

Lostin Meredith Apartments
250 S. 13th St., Aransas Pass
• (361) 758-3032

Eighty family units and 38 units for elderly or disabled individuals are available through the Housing Authority of Aransas Pass. The authority also has close to 200 units available through a federally funded program to supplement rental payments of low-income families.

Corpus Christi

The Esplanade
5813 Esplanade Dr., Corpus Christi
• (361) 991-9600

This exclusive retirement community on the city's southside offers independent and assisted living in an attractive, homey apartment-like setting near Spohn Hospital South. The Esplanade has 51 studio suites and one-bedroom apartments and all suites have private bathrooms. Amenities include three meals a day in its formal dining room, an atrium with 30-foot ceiling, a courtyard, library, beauty salon, barber shop, cable television, utilities, transportation, and 24-hour emergency response. Weekly housekeeping and linen service are other conveniences. Activities include bingo and other games, Bible study, church group meetings, parties, dances, and field trips to local attractions. Ice cream socials welcome new residents.

Monthly fees range from $995 to $1,650 depending on the size of the room. These prices do not include additional personal care services.

The Grand Court Retirement Community
2709 Cimarron Blvd.
• (361) 980-8200

The Grand Court opened its doors in 1998, offering luxuri-

ous living in 142 independent and assisted living apartments. They offer studio and one- and two-bedroom apartments, paid utilities and three meals a day in their elegant restaurant-style dining room.

Amenities include planned social activities, an exercise room, scheduled transportation, emergency call systems, 24-hour staffing and security, fully equipped kitchens and weekly housekeeping, church services, and a full-time activities director. Other amenities include laundry service, daily trash removal, beauty shop, in house home health and rehabilitation, enclosed courtyards, barbecue pavilions, convenience store, library, complimentary washers and dryers, covered parking, card-key entry, billiard room, and two card rooms.

Monthly prices range from $1,300 to $2,400 depending on the size of the apartment and the level of care needed.

Housing Authority of Corpus Christi
3701 Ayers St., Corpus Christi
• (361) 884-3801

This housing authority serving Corpus Christi was established in 1938 to provided help to low-income families seeking a place to live. The authority operates low-rent public housing developments and facilitates a federally funded program to supplement rental payments of low-income families.

Homewood Residence at Corpus Christi
6410 Meadowvista Blvd., Corpus Christi
• (361) 985-0555

This retirement community offers independent living for seniors in an apartment setting. It offers one-bedroom apartments in two floorplans as well as two-bedroom apartments.

Area retirement communities offer retirees in the Corpus Christi area a safe, structured living environment.

Photo: Daniel Fielder

Homewood Residence offers unfurnished apartments with all utilities included. It also offers a dining service, courtyards, private patios and housekeeping and linen services. Homewood offers an emergency alert system, kitchen and laundry appliances, transportation, a hair salon, and advocacy and social activities. Other amenities include covered parking and maintenance and staff on site 24 hours a day.

Monthly rates for one-bedroom apartments are $1,390 a month, $1,490 for large one-bedroom apartments and $1,890 for two-bedroom apartments.

Heartland of Corpus Christi
202 Fortune Dr., Corpus Christi
• (361) 289-0889

Heartland provides more hands-on care to residents than many senior facilities in the Coastal Bend area. This assisted living and skilled-nursing facility is near West Oso High School in northwest Corpus Christi. Heartland has a high number of residents in need of personal care, along with several who need the round-the-clock care required for skilled-nursing residents.

Residents eat three meals a day in a restaurant-style dining room, and staff administers all medications. Heartland's director of assisted living is a registered nurse who can make working with doctors easier.

Activities include exercise classes, church services, Bible study, bingo and other games and field trips to movies, lunch, shopping or more distant destinations such as Sea World in San Antonio. Heartland has 50 one-bedroom, private apartments with 321 square feet of space, a full bath and large closet. Most apartments are private, but the complex recently began offering companion living. Amenities include a coin laundry, beauty salon, barbershop, and cable television. The cost is $1,250 to $2,500 a month for an assisted living private room.

Mount Carmel Home
4130 S. Alameda St., Corpus Christi
• (361) 855-6243

This assisted living home is run by the Carmelite Sisters in an attractive mission-style building in central Corpus Christi. It is not affiliated with the Diocese of Corpus Christi and welcomes residents of all faiths. Mount Carmel has 70 private one-bedroom, one-bath apartments. Some have living areas, too. Residents must be recommended by a doctor and be able to perform personal care services or arrange for a home-health agency to provide them. The staff does not perform nursing procedures.

Residents eat three times a day in the Mount Carmel dining room, and residents are free to come and go as they please. The staff provides housekeeping, clean linens, and towels. Activi-

The Rockport-Fulton RV Association has more than 1,500 RV sites to accommodate visitors.

ties include exercise classes, sing-a-longs, Bible classes, church services, and crafts classes.

Monthly fees range from $700 to $1,200.

Trinity Towers
101 N. Upper Broadway, Corpus Christi
• (361) 887-2000

You won't find a better view than the one offered by Trinity Towers. This 19-story high-rise in downtown Corpus Christi offers views of Corpus Christi Bay from each of its 170 units. Three blocks from the bay, Trinity Towers allows residents to choose from 10 floor plans ranging from a studio efficiency to 1,500-square-foot, two-bedroom apartments. It also offers three levels of care: independent living, assisted living, and residence in its skilled nursing unit.

The Holmgreen Center, a five-story addition completed in 1998, connects to the main facility via a skywalk. It's home to assisted living and skilled-nursing units. For those who choose the independent-living arrangement, one meal a day in Trinity Towers' dining room is included in the cost, and residents can pay for additional meals as needed. Others receive three meals a day. Amenities include transportation,

a beauty salon, library, billiard room, health club, and 24-hour security. Activities include musical programs, book reviews, art demonstrations, fashion shows, and games.

Monthly fees for independent living range from $1,275 to $3,000.

Villa Residential Care Homes
4834 Yorktown, Corpus Christi
• (361) 991-3252
2822 Robby, Corpus Christi
• (361) 242-9446

These apartments for assisted living residents are studios with or without kitchenettes. The studios without kitchenettes have 330 square feet, while the deluxe studios have 440 square feet. Living plans come with three meals a day and all bills, including cable but not telephone service, are paid.

Villa Residential provides assisted living until residents need skilled nursing services.

Amenities include activities, exercise classes, and transportation to and from the doctor, the bank, Wal-Mart, and the grocery store.

Prices range from $850 to $2,000 a month depending on the apartment size and care level.

Neighborhoods and Real Estate

LOOK FOR:
• Real Estate
  Companies in the
  various areas

The sun and saltwater work their magic on many visitors, who decide that they want to make their stay in the Texas Coastal Bend permanent. If you're one of those who choose to adopt South Texas as a home, you're in for good news. The real estate market here is booming, and it is rich with variety. Realtors say there truly is something for every taste, and the price ranges vary tremendously—meaning there will likely be something to suit your budget as well.

Annual statistics from the Corpus Christi Association of Realtors and Multiple Listing Service indicate that the number of homes sold has been on a steady increase—and so has the average price of those homes. The real estate market did $332 million worth of business in 1999, and 2000 promised to be even better.

The caveat here is that the rental market is not quite as upbeat. Although there is an increase in apartment construction, prices remain relatively high and in some areas apartment vacancies are scarce to non-existent. Many people find they are better off renting a home than an apartment—the price may be about the same, and you'll end up with more space and more options.

Before you set out in search of that "For Sale" sign sitting in front of your dream house, take a minute to get acclimated to the vagaries of the region. First, let's explain why the real estate market is doing so well. Realtors say that recent years have recorded an increasingly large number of home sales here. Why? Well, the economy is very good, not only nationally but locally. There are lots of jobs, and the U.S. Navy's increasingly large presence has helped to not only bring more people to the area, but also to supply additional work for local industry, retailers, and service professionals.

Secondly, interest rates are extremely good, hovering in the 7- to 8-percent range. Realtors say that interest rates are the same as they were 25 years ago.

Thirdly, the city has provided some incentive programs to first-time buyers, such as low down payments, low interest rates, and other financial bonuses.

And finally, the tight apartment market means that many would-be renters have chosen instead to purchase. Newcomers figure that if they're going to pay $800 a month in rent, they might as well put that money into a mortgage payment.

For many newcomers, the Coastal Bend real estate market also offers an important advantage: low prices, particularly for waterfront property. The down side is that homeowner's insurance rates can be higher than in other areas because the area is subject to hurricanes and storms.

If you do decide to become a permanent resident of the Coastal Bend, there are a few peculiarities of the local real estate scene that you should be aware of. Obviously, any house you select should undergo several inspections: for termites, which are a common menace in this moist,

Kings Crossing Country Club is an exclusive south Corpus Christi neighborhood, complete with 18-hole golf course, tennis court, pool, and dining facilities.

Photo: Daniel Fielder

warm climate; for plumbing problems, which can be particularly important if you're looking at an older house; and for structural concerns, which are also an issue here because of the soil and area climate conditions.

The plumbing test is important because the cast-iron pipes in older houses tend to rot, at least partly because of the salt in the soil. A plumbing static test should be part of any inspection before you purchase a house because it tells you whether the pipes leak and if any need to be replaced. Replacement means taking out the cast-iron pipes and replacing them with the more lasting PVC pipes—another costly job.

All these concerns are certainly workable and can be overcome by thorough inspections and investigations on your part or the part of your broker. Doing the necessary homework before you buy a house here will pay off in the long run.

We've provided you with a description of towns and neighborhoods, plus listings of real estate professionals in each area. Remember, these listings are not all-inclusive but should give you a good place to begin your home hunting here. So, come on. Join the many other transplanted Texans who have decided to settle in the Coastal Bend, where the climate, the economy, the quality of life, and the housing prices combine to entice thousands each year.

North Bay Area

Rockport

The Rockport-Fulton area sits on the coastline and has long been known as a haven for vacationers and nature lovers. Increasingly popular with birders, the area also attracts retirees who want to make their stay here a permanent one.

One of the most popular and well-known areas is **Key Allegro**, an island of canal-front lots with vacation/resort homes. Established about 30 years ago, this development now has about 700 homesites. The homes are usually stucco with tile roofs, most of them two-story with upstairs living areas, waterfront views, and boats docked in the back for quick access to fishing and birding. Prices can range from $100,000 to $1 million.

Another popular part of town is the **Rockport Country Club Estates** subdivision, where oak trees abound and the golf course is the neighborhood's centerpiece. There are many new homes here, with more under construction. Prices range from $130,000 to $1 million.

Old Rockport neighborhoods display classic Victorian beach-style architecture, including high ceilings, crown molding, and large open windows originally designed to permit the cooling sea breezes through the houses. Many of these homes line Fulton Beach Road, which overlooks Aransas Bay, and range in price from $50,000 to $400,000, depending on age and condition.

Among real estate publications available for buyers are Rockport's *Property Previews*, which is published eight times a year. Another is *Corpus Christi Homes*, published weekly. Both publications are free and available from real estate offices as well as at many local businesses and restaurants. You can also scan the real estate sections of the town's weekly newspapers, the *Rockport Pilot* and *The Herald*.

Real Estate Companies

Century 21-Emery Real Estate
501 S. Austin St., Rockport
• **(361) 790-9500**
Owner Barbara Emery has been running this company since 1991. It has six full-time agents and specializes in waterfront properties.

Coldwell Banker Myers-Gallagher
3002 N. Texas Hwy. 35, Ste. D, Rockport
• **(361) 729-6060**
This is a branch office with 10-12 agents, managed by broker Joe Myers.

Key Allegro Real Estate Co.
1798 Bayshore Dr., Rockport
• **(361) 729-2333, (800) 348-1627**
With 14 full-time agents, this is the city's largest real estate company. Owned by Carla Krueger Rinche, it has been in business for about 35 years and was the original developer of the Key Allegro Island subdivision. This firm handles residential property in Aransas County and Live Oak Peninsula and is known for handling some of the larger, pricier homes in the area.

Ledbetter's Key Allegro Sales
1809 Bayshore Dr., Rockport
• **(361) 729-2772**
Established in 1978 on Key Allegro, this firm is headed by principal broker Jerre Ledbetter. It has seven agents and specializes in property on Key Allegro Island, although it is not limited to this subdivision.

Sipe Real Estate
546 Texas Hwy. 35 S., Rockport
• **(361) 729-2603, (800) 232-7187**
Established in 1945 by Winnie Sipe, this is the oldest real estate company in Aransas County. It has been owned since 1966 by Juanita Wagley, Mrs. Sipe's daughter. With five full-time agents, this company specializes in channel and waterfront homesites, but it sells property all over the county.

Aransas Pass, Ingleside, Gregory, and Portland

Continuing in a southerly direction toward Corpus Christi on Texas Highway 35, you come to the communities of Aransas Pass, Ingleside, Gregory and Portland. Many of the real estate

firms in this area serve all these towns, so it seems logical to include them together. Still, each town has its own flavor.

Aransas Pass, a town built on the shrimping industry, is a waterfront community of mostly modest homes. Obviously, the residences on the waterfront are more costly and more exclusive. One of the newer and more popular neighborhoods here is **Pelican Cove**, a waterfront community of new homes that are approximately 2,000 square feet. These residences are on the upscale side, ranging from $120,000 to $300,000.

Nearby Ingleside has seen a steady growth in its population since the expansion of the naval mine warfare base here. That has meant an increased demand for housing—and a corresponding increase in the number of new homes and developments that have been built in the past five years. Among the newer subdivisions are **Lakeview** and **Parkside Terrace**, both of which offer new homes of approximately 1,200 square feet. These homes tend to sell for $60,000 to $80,000. Nearby is the separate community of **Ingleside on the Bay**, which has older waterfront homes. The prices here go from $60,000 to $200,000. A two-bedroom, canal front home was listed recently for $75,000, while a four-bedroom was listed for $155,500.

The Gregory-Portland area shares a public school district and many of the same real estate characteristics. Newcomers, particularly those from the military and outlying areas, tend to move here because of the quality reputation of the school district. One of the most popular subdivisions is **Northshore**, which is a country-club neighborhood of large, new homes, usually in excess of 2,000 square feet. A brand-new three-bedroom, two-bath brick home here was listed for $148,900, while a house with four bedrooms, five bathrooms, a fireplace, cathedral ceilings, and a swimming pool was listed for $389,000.

Newcomers can find a listing of properties available in *The Real Estate Book*, which is published quarterly, and *Corpus Christi Homes*, a newspaper published every two weeks. Both publications are free and available from real estate agents as well as at local businesses and restaurants.

Real Estate Companies

Associated Brokers Group
614 Eighth Ave., Portland
• **(361) 643-3031**
Established in 1985, this firm is owned by

John Thomas and has eight full-time agents. They handle mostly residential properties in Portland, Ingleside, and Aransas Pass, as well as some commercial properties.

Century 21 Bay Area Realtors
1559 S. Commercial St., Aransas Pass
• **(361) 758-7506, (800) 234-9112**

With four agents, this office sells properties in Rockport, Portland, Port Aransas, Aransas Pass, and occasionally Ingleside. Co-owners Ivah Mircovich and Virginia Bufkin have been in the real estate business for more than 25 years, and this office has been affiliated with Century 21 since 1992.

Century 21 Myers-Lee Real Estate
921 Houston St., Portland
• **(361) 643-2591**

Co-owned by Joe Myers and Phyllis Lee, this office has 23 agents. They sell properties in Aransas, Kleberg, Nueces, and San Patricio counties. The agency was established more than 25 years ago and is one of the largest real estate firms in the North Bay area. Myers-Lee also has a branch office in Ingleside.

Coldwell Banker Myers Gallagher
264 S. Commercial St., Aransas Pass
• **(361) 758-7534**

Formerly Aransas Real Estate, this is a branch office affiliated with the Corpus Christi main office. It has seven agents and covers the North Bay area.

McAllister and Associates
2605-A Amarillo St., Ingleside
• **(361) 776-3550**

A husband-and-wife team, Billie and Shirley McAllister, operates this seven-agent real estate office established in 1993.

Muti-million-dollar homes line Corpus Christi's famous Ocean Drive.

Photo: Daniel Fielder

North Bay Properties
720 Dallas St., Portland
• **(361) 643-8525**

Owned by Eileen Morris, this office has six agents. They handle residential properties, rentals, and commercial properties. This company was established in 1997, but Morris has been handling real estate in Portland since 1978.

Port Aransas to Padre Island

Port Aransas

This area is a resort vacation community with many neighborhoods inhabited by both full-time and part-time residents. The lifestyle is extremely casual here, and it shows in the architecture: the homes are simple, many offering views of the waterfront and the wetlands.

The **Port Aransas Private Marina** is a neighborhood near the beach and adjacent to the Corpus Christi Ship Channel, and residents enjoy waterfront views of the channel and nearby St. James Island. These wood-frame homes were built in the late 1950s and 1960s and are on the canal with a boat slip at each address. An on-site manager controls access to the marina. A five-bedroom, three-bath home here is listed for $550,000.

Island Moorings is another popular neighborhood, 2 miles south of town on the canal. Many homes have a Southwest flavor, with stucco and tile roofing. And the residents are strict about adhering to this style—an architectural committee has to review all new home construction. Prices in this neighborhood range from $230,000 for a three-bedroom, two-bath home to $549,000 for a four-bedroom, five-bathroom house.

Channel Vista neighborhood is south of the ferry landing and near the ship channel, providing convenient access to town and schools. Mostly permanent residents live here, and a new city park and swimming pool are under construction nearby. A three-bedroom, three-bath home was listed for $129,900.

A new development is **Beachwalk**, which offers

homes that are less than a year old but are modeled after Victorian cottages. The homes feature wide porches and picket fences, and residents have amenities that include a boardwalk to the beach, swimming pool, and clay tennis court. A three-bedroom, two-bath home is listed for $150,000.

Port Aransas's brokers have their own listing service, called Port Aransas Listing Service, and the real estate offices produce brochures on available listings. Usually the brochures are divided by price and type of property, such as residences, condominiums, and lots. The real estate market is strong, but it is mostly a seller's market: little inventory and high demand. New construction is ongoing, so there should be more properties available soon.

Real Estate Companies

Coldwell Banker Island Realtors
821 Alister St., Port Aransas
• **(361) 749-6000, (800) 580-6600**

This is the only franchise company in the city, offering eight full- and part-time agents. The owner is Jack Ponton, who has been in the real estate business for more than 25 years.

Mark R. Grosse Real Estate
211 W. Cotter Ave., Port Aransas
• **(361) 749-6603**

One of the oldest real estate companies on the island, this firm was established in 1978. It's owned by Mark and Carolyn Grosse and has two additional full-time agents.

Port Aransas Realty
111 E. Cotter Ave., Port Aransas
• **(361) 749-4000, (800) 242-3480**

This is the city's largest real estate company, with two locations and 11 full-time agents. One office is in the city harbor, while the other is at Island Moorings. It is known for its service and professionalism.

Whitten Real Estate
2106 Texas Hwy. 361, Port Aransas
• **(361) 749-0001, (800) 460-4557**

Established in 1980, this agency has three agents and is owned by Bill Whitten. They list and sell resort properties, as well as handling real estate auctions and estate auctions.

Padre Island

If you continue through Port Aransas and head to Corpus Christi along the coastline, you'll arrive at Padre Island. This area offers fairly expensive waterfront homes, with $109,000 being the lowest price you'll likely find. The homes here are more costly at least in part because the residences require sturdier construction because they're on the coastline and therefore will bear the brunt of a tropical storm or hurricane. The area tends to attract a lot of retirees, particularly those who enjoy fishing or boating.

That said, Realtors also point out that these waterfront homes are among the most reasonably priced in the United States. You can buy a lot on the waterfront, with a bulkhead already built in, for $30,000 or so. We were told by one real estate broker that the prices are good because the company that originally developed the island went bankrupt. An increasing number of foreign investors, particularly Canadians, have come to buy property here—and, again, many retirees look at the prices and decide this is where they'll locate their retirement home.

The **Padre Isles Property Owners Association**, (361) 949-7025, is a very strong and active organization here, and they do have architectural restrictions for new construction.

A popular island neighborhood is **Point Tesoro**, where we found a listing for a two-story, three-bedroom waterfront home for $125,000. A four-bedroom stucco home on the main channel was listed for $219,000.

Real Estate Companies

Coldwell Banker Island Realtors
14945 S. Padre Island Dr., Corpus Christi
• **(361) 949-7077**

With 17 full-time agents, this company has been in operation since 1985. Owner Terry Cox specializes in sales on the island.

Prudential Real Estate Center
14200 S. Padre Island Dr., Corpus Christi
• **(361) 949-7033**

The oldest real estate company on the island, this firm has 15 full-time agents. It is owned by Jacqueline Svoboda.

Corpus Christi

The region's largest city, Corpus Christi has the most diverse real estate offerings in the area. You can buy an older frame home and remodel it, or you can opt for a brand-new house in

Home building is currently experiencing a boom on the canals of Padre Island.

Photo: Daniel Fielder

what passes for the suburbs—new developments on the south side of town. You can choose to live in an older, quiet, oak tree-shaded neighborhood or in a modern subdivision built around a golf course and tennis courts.

Among the city's most opulent residences are the mansions that line **Ocean Drive**, the city's showcase street that fronts Corpus Christi Bay. It was once described by *Texas Monthly* magazine as the most beautiful street in Texas. These are the area's multimillion-dollar homes, and although there are other areas that attract the city's wealthy, this is the most well known neighborhood for the very affluent.

The rest of the city offers a wide variety of price ranges, depending on the size, location, and condition of the home you select. It's probably best to make some decisions before you begin your search. For example, do you want to live near the waterfront? Would you prefer an older home or a new one? This can help you and your Realtor narrow the search and focus on the type of residence you want.

The local board of Realtors divides the city into six areas, each with a distinct personality and attractions: the southside, near southside, central city, northwest, Flour Bluff, and Padre Island. We discussed homes on Padre Island in the section that includes Port Aransas and Padre Island, so we won't repeat that information here.

Of all the city's neighborhoods, the southside has the largest number of new homes. A variety of new developments attract many of the mid- to upper-income home buyers. The area's largest neighborhood is **Country Club**, a golf course-centered neighborhood with large homes that were built in the 1970s. Most of them are ranch-style residences, many in excess of 2,000 square feet. A three-bedroom, two-bath brick

home was listed for $109,900. A four-bedroom, 3½-bath, two-story brick home was listed for $139,900.

Another well-known southside neighborhood is **King's Crossing**, another golf-course neighborhood with a lot of new construction, large homes, and contemporary designs. We found a three-bedroom, two-bath home with a swimming pool, fireplace, built in 1995, listed for $215,000. A four-bedroom, 2½-bath, two-story brick home was listed for $139,900.

Yet another popular southside neighborhood is **The Lakes**, with artificial lakes, lots of new construction and large residences aimed at an upper-middle income population. A four-bedroom, 2½-bath home, built in 1990, with a fireplace was listed for $143,900. A three-bedroom, four-bath waterfront home with a swimming pool was listed for $329,500.

Not all the southside neighborhoods are so pricey. In **Bear Creek** subdivision, established about a decade ago, you'll find new homes that are smaller and more affordable. A three-bedroom, two-bath brick home was listed for $78,400, while another with three bedrooms and two baths was selling for $97,900.

The area known as the near southside extends from the outskirts of downtown to the city's main throughway, S. Padre Island Drive. This area includes the mansion-lined Ocean Drive homes as well as some of the city's older, historic neighborhoods. Many of the homes, while not on the waterfront, are within a few blocks of Corpus Christi Bay. And, obviously, the price of real estate does tend to go up with proximity to the bayfront.

One of the most popular neighborhoods in this area is the **Del Mar** subdivision, which contains some of the city's oldest homes, built in the 1930s and 1940s. These homes, mostly wood-frame structures, are flanked by large live oak trees and characterized by hardwood floors, high ceilings, and expansive windows. There is very little new construction here, although several Realtors noted a trend of young professionals who purchase old homes and renovate or tear them down and rebuild. An English Tudor-style home with three bedrooms, two baths, fireplace, and hardwood floors was listed for $104,900, while a two-story, three-bedroom with 1½-baths was listed for $139,900. At the higher end, we found a lovely Austin stone two-story with four bedrooms, two baths on three lots that was listed for $310,000.

NEIGHBORHOODS AND REAL ESTATE

Adjacent to Del Mar is the **Morningside** neighborhood, another one that features mostly older homes. We found a two-story, three-bedroom, two-bath house on a corner lot for $109,900.

Other popular and long-time neighborhoods in this area are **Bessar Park** and **Aransas Cliffs**, close to the bayfront and featuring older homes, lots of trees and mostly spacious lots. Many of these homes have been renovated and are quite beautiful; just a few blocks away, you'll find homes that are badly in need of renovation. We found a two-bedroom that listed for $66,500; we also found a Colonial-style three-bedroom, two-bath advertised here for $149,000.

One of the more exclusive addresses in this area is **Hewitt Drive**, where the city's millionaires dwell in houses that take up several lots and sit well back from the roadway. A four-bedroom, five-bath home on Hewitt was recently listed for $525,000, while a five-bedroom, four-bath residence was listed at $835,000. This area also includes the elaborate waterfront homes along the city's showpiece street, Ocean Drive, which also tend to be pricey. We found a three-bedroom for $695,000 and a four-bedroom for $649,000.

Lamar Park is another well-known and pricey area of town, although not nearly as exclusive as Ocean Drive. The homes here were built in the 1950s and are generally one-story brick or stone residences with spacious yards. Prices range from $129,900 for a modest three-bedroom, two-bath home with fireplace to $375,000 for a four-bedroom, four-bath home with a swimming pool.

South Shores is another high-priced neighborhood that borders the bayfront, with homes that tend to be newer, more elaborate and larger than other homes in this part of town. A four-bedroom, three-bath home was listed for $205,000; a five-bedroom, four-bath house was listed for $498,500.

The downtown area of the city has very few residences for sale. It includes central city housing for low- to moderate-income residents as well as a lot of older homes that once were beautiful but now need a lot of work. Realtors say this is a fairly inactive market, meaning that few homes come up for sale here.

An exotic plumeria shows its brilliance.

Photo: MaryJane Crull

The city's northwest area is often known by the names of the two school districts out here, **Calallen** and **Tuloso-Midway**. The area has a fair amount of new construction and is considered the city's more rural section, with many of the homes on large lots or acreage. People often move out here for the school districts, which are small but affluent, with a tax base that includes the city's petrochemical plants. Prices range from $62,000 for a two-bedroom country home on a half-acre with a horse barn to $349,000 for a four-bedroom, two-story brick home with 5,728 square feet and an acre lot.

The northwest area's crown jewel neighborhood is **Wood River**, with a golf course, hills, and lots of native mesquite trees. A three-bedroom, two-bath brick home on a cul de sac here was listed for $104,900. We also found a 5,000-square-foot, two-story Colonial-style mansion on the golf course that has four bedrooms, 3½ baths, a swimming pool, and an exercise room. It was listed for $395,000.

Another subdivision out here is **Solar Estates**, which is not quite as expensive. We found a brick three-bedroom, two-bath home for $92,900 and a four-bedroom, two-bath for $105,900.

The area of the city to the south, past the shopping malls, is known as **Flour Bluff**. This area has its own school district, like the northwest neighborhoods, but it is more eclectic. There are some very low-income residences here as well as some very expensive homes. Bordered on one side by the Laguna Madre and on the other by Oso Creek, this area offers a sort of waterfront or rural lifestyle for folks who don't want to live in the city. Some people buy homes with acreage out here so they can keep horses; others buy canal lots with boat slips in the back.

One neighborhood in the Flour Bluff area is **Tropic Isles**, which offers houses on the water that range from $73,000 to $398,000. A three-bedroom, two-bath home facing the waterfront was listed for $89,900. We also found a four-bedroom, three-bath home with a fireplace listed for $115,500.

Another established area is **Roscher Estates**, where we found listings that included a custom-built, three-bedroom, three-bath brick home on an acre lot offered for $265,000 and a huge five-bedroom, 3½-bath brick home listed for $398,900.

Real Estate Companies

Berney Seal Co. Realtors
601 Everhart Rd., Corpus Christi
• (361) 992-9000

This company is owned by Berney Seal, a Realtor who has been selling property since 1965. His company has 20 full-time professional Realtors. The company specializes in residential property in all price ranges.

Century 21—Best of the Best
7110 S. Staples St., Suite B, Corpus Christi
• (361) 994-0204

This is the largest of several Century 21 offices here, with about 30 agents. Owner Lowell Gaut has been in the real estate business since 1990, and the office became affiliated with Century 21 in 1997. The agency specializes in relocation and residential property, although it also handles commercial, farm, and ranch listings. Gaut says his company deals a lot with military newcomers and offers in-house mortgage financing.

Garron Dean and Associates
453 Robert Dr., 7 Corpus Christi
• (361) 992-4182

Established in 1972, this firm is owned by Garron Dean. It has 20 agents and serves all of Corpus Christi as well as the neighboring communities of Portland and Rockport.

Alfred Edge Realtors
4466 S. Staples St., Corpus Christi
• (361) 993-3343

Owner Alfred Edge marked his 53rd year as a broker in 2000, so he definitely has plenty of experience in the real estate business. At one time, Edge had 10 offices throughout this area; now he runs just one office with 32 agents. They handle residential, farm and ranch, and some industrial properties, focusing primarily on the southside of the city.

ERA Windward Properties
5801 S. Staples St., Corpus Christi
• (361) 994-1089

This company advertises a sale guarantee— if it doesn't sell your house, then the company will purchase it (at a discounted price). Owner David Wallace says it's an example of the company's service-oriented attitude. Wallace has 25 agents at this company, which was es- tablished about five years ago. It handles residential properties throughout the city and is one of the 200 top-selling ERA companies in the United States.

Group One Real Estate
5302 Everhart Rd., Corpus Christi
• (361) 991-9111

Owner Sarah Graham runs one of the city's largest real estate firms. Group One Real Estate employs approximately 20 agents. Graham has been in the business for more than 32 years, and her company handles residential, farm and ranch, and commercial properties throughout the city.

Holtzclaw Herrmann
4250 Five Points Rd., Suite 8,
Corpus Christi
• (361) 241-5363

This firm, which specializes in property on the city's northwest side, is owned by Judy Herrmann, Darlene Holtzclaw, and Doug Holtzclaw. Established in 1992, it has 11 agents and sells mostly residential properties as well as some farm, ranch, and commercial land.

Main Realty
1601 S. Alameda Ave., Corpus Christi
• (361) 883-9209

Established in 1975 by Mary and Sam Main, this father-daughter company handles both residential and commercial property. Mary conducts the residential portion of the business, and her father, Sam, deals with the commercial properties.

Coldwell Banker
Pacesetter Steel Realtors
6116 S. Staples St., Corpus Christi
• (361) 992-9231, (800) 338-0493
5525 S. Staples St., Corpus Christi
• (361) 993-3317
12349 Leopard Ave., Corpus Christi
• (361) 242-9799

This company represents the merger in January 2000 of two companies, Pacesetter Realtors—the city's largest real estate company— and a local agency, Arlene Steel Realtors. At the same time, the company joined with Coldwell Banker, which has clients nationally and internationally. Today, the resulting firm has more than 80 associates, and offers services in relocation, residential property, commercial property, as well as property management. April Magnuson is the president of the company. Coldwell Banker Pacesetter Steel has three offices in the city.

RE/MAX Metro Properties
5890 Everhart Rd., Corpus Christi
• **(361) 994-9393**

This is one of the city's largest companies, with 44 agents. Owner Tim Teas says the company handles mostly residential property as well as some commercial, farm, and ranch listings. Property listings range from all over town to Padre Island and Ingleside.

Kingsville

Local Realtors describe this community as one in transition. Its economy was originally centered on ranching and railroads but is now driven by the U.S. Navy's largest jet training facility and one of the world's largest petrochemical plants. The city is in the midst of some of the finest recreational areas in the United States, yet its land value and cost of living remain comparatively moderate.

Kingsville is home to Texas A&M University-Kingsville, the aforementioned Naval Air Station and an increasing number of manufacturing facilities. The city is poised for growth, and a housing task force has set a goal to build an average of 20 new homes a year through the year 2000. The military's growing presence, the expanding number of manufacturing facilities and the increase in U.S. trade with Mexico mean that there is a need for housing here. That said, there are still homes to be purchased and rented. The apartment market remains tight, and many newcomers, particularly those from the military, prefer to rent or buy a house, even if they are here for only a short time.

Many people come here for the recreational opportunities of fishing and hunting. Other newcomers are winter Texans who buy property here or retired military folks who decide to settle down in South Texas.

Housing options vary widely here. You can find a historic Victorian-style home in town or a newly built ranch house with acreage right outside the city limits. Prices are just as varied. We found a one-story, three-bedroom brick house in town for $72,000 and a four-bedroom new home with a fireplace for $83,500.

In the more rural areas around Kingsville, including **Riviera** and **Ricardo**, we found a three-bedroom, two-bath home on 30 acres for $148,000. Another rural home was a three-bedroom, 2½-bath house with a screened porch, hot tub, and Italian tile floors for $169,000.

Real Estate Companies

Betty Haas Realtors
1921 E. King Ave., Kingsville
• **(361) 592-3321**

Formerly Alfred Edge Realtors, this firm is now owned by Betty Jo Haas. It has six agents and handles residential and commercial properties as well as property management.

Century 21 Myers Real Estate
2701 U.S. Hwy. 77 S., Kingsville
• **(361) 595-7653, (800) 333-9318**

Owned by Joe Myers and Linda Quandt, this office has 18 agents. They offer full-service real estate marketing for buyers, sellers, builders, investors, and renters. The company handles properties throughout the Coastal Bend, from Rockport to Kingsville.

Coldwell Banker Homestead Properties Inc.
515 E. King Ave., Kingsville
• **(361) 592-4343**

This firm is the one of the largest real estate companies in Kingsville, with 11 full-time agents whose combined experience totals more than 185 years. Established in 1960, the firm became affiliated with Coldwell Banker in 1985. Their motto is to "Make Real Estate Real Easy" for their clients and they specialize in offering state-of-the-art technology, such as computerized listings. Co-owners are manager Patti Wolfe and broker Ricki Cunningham.

Kingsville Realtors Group
1314 E. King Ave., Kingsville
• **(361) 592-8282**

Formerly Kingsville Real Estate, this office is run by a trio of broker-owners who have more than 30 years in the business. Odis Michalk, Bev Nielsen, and Julia Wade specialize in residential properties, although they also handle farm and ranch land, and investment properties. Two of the owners are natives of Kingsville, while the third has lived here 20 years, so they know the area well.

Childcare and Education

The Corpus Christi area offers many options for childcare and education, from daycare facilities to universities. Not only does the region have more than a dozen public school districts, it also has a host of private schools. We've separated the school districts by geographic region, as we've done with other categories in this book, to make it easier for you to find a school in a particular area or city. We end the chapter with the three universities in the region, which offer more than 200 degree programs.

LOOK FOR:
• Childcare Facilities
• Public Schools
• Private and
  Parochial Schools
• Colleges and
  Universities

Childcare

The Corpus Christi area has four childcare centers that are accredited by the National Academy of Early Childhood Programs. The accreditation program, run by the National Association for the Education of Young Children (NAEYC), ensures that participating centers have met national standards that include curriculum, interaction between children and adults, safety, child-to-teacher ratio, nutrition, and communication with parents. Centers that have received the accreditation in Corpus Christi are First Presbyterian Church Day School, First United Methodist Church Vincent Morris Children's Center, and Naval Air Station Corpus Christi's Child Development Program. In Kingsville, Naval Air Station Kingsville's Child Development Center has also been accredited by the NAEYC. For more information about these centers, including addresses and phone numbers, see the listings in the "Education" section of this chapter.

The area has many excellent, nonaccredited daycare homes that provide warm, safe environments for just a few kids. There are also many topnotch facilities and preschools that haven't gone through the fees, paperwork, and visits required for official accreditation. As always, your best sources are friends, neighbors and others whose judgment you trust. Talk to the people you know, ask them about the places you want to visit, and then go in person to check it out.

You can obtain a free list of licensed daycare facilities by calling the Texas Department of Protective and Regulatory Services in Corpus Christi, (361) 854-2011. Licensed facilities are listed by county.

For low-income families, Corpus Christi has several well-established daycare facilities that are licensed by the state. The Mary McLeod Bethune Day Nursery, 900 Kinney Street, (361) 882-7326, takes infants through school-age children for full- and part-time care. Open since 1942, it also offers summer camp programs, before- and after-school care and transportation. It is open 7:15 AM to 5:30 PM Monday through Friday.

Two other well-respected, low-income facilities include Dos Mundos Day School, 849 Erwin, (361) 884-7062; and Brooks Chapel Early Childhood Development Center, 1517 Winnebago Street, (361) 884-8861.

When you're looking for a school or daycare center, be sure to make several visits. Meet with the teachers and inquire about the student-to-teacher ratio. Ask about accreditation, programs, staffers' backgrounds, and activities. Trust your instincts and don't be afraid to ask questions. You, better than anyone else, know what your child needs.

We have included childcare listings in the Early Childhood section of this chapter because so many of the programs are also for school-age youngsters.

Education

In the arena of higher education, the outlook here is far brighter than it has been in past decades. For many years, community leaders had complained that the state gave short shrift to higher education in South Texas, which translated to a lack of funding and political support. A legislative study in 1988 showed that the state spent $43 per college student in South Texas, compared with $103 per college student in the rest of the state. As a result of these studies, attorneys for the Mexican American Legal Defense and Educational Fund (MALDEF) filed suit against the state on behalf of the League of United Latin American Citizens. A judge ruled that the state had discriminated against South Texas residents in its distribution of higher educational funding and initiatives. In 1993, lawmakers passed several bills that began the process of sending more dollars to South Texas colleges and universities. Officials with MALDEF have estimated it will take 10 years and $2 billion to bring the area's higher education institutions up to par with the rest of the state; however, many see the progress made so far as a good starting point.

The area has two four-year universities, Texas A&M University-Corpus Christi and Texas A&M University-Kingsville, as well as one junior college, Del Mar College.

Texas A&M University-Corpus Christi and Texas A&M University-Kingsville both have some history in this region; both have grown since becoming affiliated with the prestigious Texas A&M University System in 1989. Both universities also changed their names in 1993 to reflect their affiliation with the Texas A&M

INSIDERS' TIP

When choosing an early childhood program for your youngster, make several visits to the facility and be sure to meet with and talk to the teachers. Getting a list of programs licensed by the state, or those accredited by a national agency, is a good starting point.

University System. It's also worth noting that TAMU-Corpus Christi became a four-year university in 1994, which means it's undergoing expansion in many areas, including academics and sports.

Del Mar College, a junior college in Corpus Christi, often serves as a starting point for youngsters who want to begin their college education in an affordable setting, then continue their degree program at a larger university. Del Mar also offers a number of vocational programs that are quite popular.

Our listings are by no means all-inclusive, particularly when it comes to private daycare facilities, but they give you a good starting point for recommendable centers and schools.

Early Childhood

Corpus Christi

Central Christian Children's Academy
6301 Weber Rd., Corpus Christi
• (361) 851-8747
This Christian daycare program, open since 1980, averages about 110 children daily, ages 6 months to kindergarten. The program includes chapel time, one Montessori class, a latchkey program, and a Mother's Day Out program. It's open 7:30 AM to 6 PM for the daycare program and 9:30 AM to 2:30 PM for the Mother's Day Out program.

Early Childhood Development Center
Texas A&M University-Corpus Christi,
6300 Ocean Dr., Corpus Christi
• (361) 980-3366
Opened in August 1996 as a venture between the city's largest public school district and Texas A&M University-Corpus Christi, this center enrolls 132 children ages 3 through the 3rd grade. It emphasizes dual-language learning, multi-age grouping, and team teaching. It is open to all students in the Corpus Christi Independent School District; applicants are chosen through a lottery system.

First Baptist School
3115 Ocean Dr., Corpus Christi
• (361) 884-8931
With approximately 225 students, this pri-

vate daycare/school offers Christian-based education for preschoolers through the 8th grade. The curriculum is A-Beka, a Christian-based educational program, and classes include music, computer, Bible, and chapel. The school has been in operation for almost 25 years.

First Christian Day School and Childcare Center
3401 Santa Fe St., Corpus Christi
• (361) 854-1241

This school has been operating for nearly 30 years and enrolls approximately 160 students, ages 2 through kindergarten. Officials pride themselves on their teacher-to-student ratio: 1-to-8 for the 2-year-olds; 1-to-12 for the 3-year-olds; 1-to-14 for the 4-year-olds; and 1-to-16 for the kindergartners. The school also offers special programs for music, science, and cognitive skills development.

First Presbyterian School
430 S. Carancahua St., Corpus Christi
• (361) 887-7116

This popular daycare program enrolls approximately 72 students, ages 2 through 5. The program is half-day and is accredited by the NAEYC. Registration for the fall is held in March, and some classes fill up fast.

First United Methodist Church Vinson Morris Children's Center
900 S. Shoreline Blvd., Corpus Christi
• (361) 884-9211

This is a full-time church-run facility that enrolls 82 children, ages 18 months to 5 years. The daycare center offers both half-day and full-day programs, and it is open from 6:30 AM to 5:45 PM. It has been in operation since 1965 and is NAEYC-accredited. Like the facility listed above, there can be a waiting list for some classes, particularly the 18-month-old group. Student-to-teacher ratios are way below the state requirement, and the teachers tend to have a lot of longevity here.

Jewish Community Council of Corpus Christi
750 Everhart Rd., Corpus Christi
• (361) 855-6239

As many as 150 students are enrolled at this 25-year-old school, which offers a manipulative-based program for youngsters ages 2 through 5. Each class has a teacher and an assistant, and the student-to-teacher ratios tend to be lower than the state requirements. The school is open in the morning and offers a structured enrichment program and free play in the afternoons. Only a third of the students are Jewish; the remainder are from other religions and varying nationalities.

Montessori School of Corpus Christi
2205 16th St., Corpus Christi
• (361) 883-9306

This year-round school, opened in 1981, enrolls about 70 students in a Montessori-based curriculum where the emphasis is on individualized learning within a prepared environment. Children can progress through the curriculum at their own pace, in multi-age classrooms. The school also offers creative arts courses, such as art, music, drama and song, and field trips.

In addition, there is an extended care program, summer camp, and day care during the school's break.

Naval Air Station Corpus Christi Child Development Center
Ninth and E Sts., Blg. 1782
• (361) 939-7843

Open to military personnel only, this NAEYC-accredited facility has the capacity to care for 117 youngsters. It enrolls children ages 2 through school age. The center is open daily from 6:45 AM to 5:15 PM.

Naval Air Station Kingsville Child Development Center
742 Rosendahl St., Ste. 101, Kingsville
• (361) 516-6176

This facility is open to military personnel and civilian employees at this Navy base, south of Kingsville. It has the capacity to care for 63 youngsters, ages 6 weeks to 6 years. It also offers family childcare, where youngsters are taken care of in private homes; an after-school program for children ages 6 to 12; and a summer camp program. The center is accredited by the NAEYC.

Public Schools

North Bay Area

Aransas County Independent School District
1601 Pirate Blvd., Rockport
• (361) 790-2212

The Aransas County Independent School District is a 4-A school system serving a 280-square-mile area including the communities of Holiday Beach, Lamar, Fulton, Rockport and a small portion of northern Aransas Pass. The district serves approximately 3,500 students on six campuses: one early childhood, two elementaries, one intermediate, one junior high, and one high school, encompassing more than 73 acres. Among special programs are gifted/talented, special education, GED, vocational, high school honors, advanced placement, and community education.

Aransas Pass
Independent School District
244 W. Harrison Blvd., Aransas Pass
• (361) 758-3466

This school district serves 2,231 children residing in the eastern end of San Patricio County, a 53.1-square-mile area. The system is composed of five campuses that encompass kindergarten through grade 12, including three elementary schools, one intermediate school, and one high school.

The public school system curriculum includes not only special programs for students who plan to attend college, but also courses and training for those planning to enter the work force immediately after graduation from high school. These include correlated vocational academics and vocational office education. Other special programs offered include: all University Interscholastic League (UIL) academic and extra curricular activities, a gifted and talented program, art, speech and hearing therapy, all levels of special education, band, choir, and all sports.

Gregory-Portland
Independent School District
308 N. Gregory, Gregory
• (361) 643-6566

Students from the neighboring communities of Gregory and Portland attend schools in this district north of Corpus Christi.

The district enrolls about 4,300 students and includes four elementary schools (grades pre-K through 4); one intermediate school (grades 5 and 6); one junior high school (grades 7 and 8); and one high school (grades 9 through 12).

Ingleside Independent School District
2807 Mustang Dr., Ingleside
• (361) 776-7631

Approximately 2,000 students attend the district's two elementary schools, one junior high, and one high school. The district is bordered on the south and west by Corpus Christi Bay and includes several petrochemical plants as well as the Naval Station Ingleside, the Navy's Mine Warfare Center. The district has a gifted and talented program, a special education program, and a Tech-Prep program designed to give

high school graduates job-entry, college, or trade-school skills.

Port Aransas to Padre Island

Port Aransas Independent School District
100 S. Station St., Port Aransas
• (361) 749-5500

Situated on the island, this school district has one elementary school, one junior high, and one high school, serving about 530 students. It has a staff of 80 employees. The district has received awards for academic excellence and for meeting the needs of parents. In addition to academics, the Port Aransas Marlins are competitive in a number of extracurricular areas, including girls and boys basketball, tennis, and drama. It is one of the few school districts in the area that does not boast a football team—a testimony to the part that watersports, particularly surfing, play in the lives of the community's students.

Corpus Christi

Corpus Christi
Independent School District
801 Leopard St., Corpus Christi
• (361) 886-9200

This is the largest of five public school districts within the city limits of Corpus Christi as well as the largest in the Coastal Bend. It has 63 campuses with approximately 41,000 students in prekindergarten through grade 12. An instructional staff of more than 2,800 teachers is complemented by a support staff of 2,500.

The district has five senior high schools, 12 middle schools, 40 elementary schools, and six special campuses. The high schools all have regular and honors programs. Roy Miller High School was revamped as the Miller High School Center for Communications and Technology in 1996 and now offers course work that focuses on engineering and computer science, technology and business, and communications.

The middle schools contain grades 6 through 8. Baker Middle School is part of the Athena Program for gifted and talented students, with enrollment determined by scores on tests administered each spring, summer, and fall, and by teacher recommendation. Wynn Seale Middle School Academy of Fine Arts is for students interested in the arts as well as academics, with a curriculum that integrates band, orchestra, art, dance, choir, piano, and theater arts with the general curriculum of math, science, English, and social studies.

One of the elementary schools, Windsor Park, also has a program for the gifted and talented. Admittance, again, is by test scores and teacher recommendation. Another elementary school, Chula Vista Academy of Fine Arts, emphasizes art, music, and drama in addition to reading, mathematics, and composition. Students must demonstrate interest in the arts and apply for admission.

There are also seven special-emphasis schools, based on the belief that some students do best in a highly structured curriculum, with emphasis on basic skills, good citizenship, and discipline.

Other special campuses include the Adult Learning Center, Human Development Center, Teenage Mothers School, and the Student Learning and Guidance Center.

Flour Bluff
Independent School District
2505 Waldron Rd., Corpus Christi
• (361) 937-2681

The approximately 5,200 students enrolled in this district attend classes on five campuses, including an early childhood center for prekindergarten and kindergarten, a primary school for grades 1 and 2, an elementary school for grades 3 and 4, an intermediate school for grades 5 and 6, a junior high for grades 7 and 8, and a high school for grades 9 through 12. The district also has two alternative centers, one to educate students who are behind in credits and need extra assistance to graduate with their class and another for students with disciplinary problems. The district includes the southern portion of Corpus Christi, near Naval Air Station Corpus Christi.

Calallen Independent School District
4205 Wildcat Dr., Corpus Christi
• (361) 241-9321

This district in the northwestern part of the city has six campuses, including four elementary schools, one middle school and one high school. It enrolls approximately 4,706 students. The district's 75-member jump rope team, the Calallen Hop-A-Longs, has won state, national, and international awards, traveled to 10 foreign countries and served as a state demonstration team for the American Heart Association.

Tuloso-Midway
Independent School District
9760 LaBranch St., Corpus Christi
• (361) 241-3286

This district has four campuses: one elementary, one intermediate, one middle, and one high school. It is in the city's northwestern end and enrolls approximately 3,000 students. This district has received state recognition for its academic achievements.

West Oso Independent School District
5050 Rockford Dr., Corpus Christi
• (361) 855-3321

This district has five campuses, including three elementary schools, one junior high, and one high school. It is on the city's west side and enrolls 1,900 students.

Kingsville Area

Kingsville Independent School District
207 N. Third St., Kingsville
• (361) 592-3387

This is the largest of four public school districts in the area and serves approximately 5,000 students. Facilities include six elementary schools, one intermediate school, one middle school, one traditional high school, and an alternative high school. There is also a Life and Academic Skills Education Reinforcement (LA-SER) School that provides services to students who would normally be expelled.

In addition to standard academic courses, the high school offers a strong vocational program with seven career pathways that include agricultural science and technology, business and marketing, health science technology, industrial and engineering technology, automotive/aircraft technology, law enforcement, and home economics. The high school was also the first in the nation to offer a jet maintenance class, using a Navy jet housed at the school.

The system also offers a Challenge program, open to gifted and talented students.

Ricardo Independent School District
W. County Rd. 2160, Ricardo
• (361) 592-0471

This district south of Kingsville educates children through the 8th grade. Students then can transfer to high schools in Kingsville or nearby Riviera. Riviera Independent School District, in the southern part of Kleberg County, goes through the 12th grade and has a 2-A high school.

Santa Gertrudis
Independent School District
King Ranch, Texas Hwy. 141, Kingsville
• (361) 592-7582

This small school district takes the ranch's students through the 8th grade. The Learning Academy, established in the 1994-95 school year, is a joint venture between Santa Gertrudis Independent School District and nearby Driscoll Independent School District. The Academy, on the campus of Texas A&M University-Kingsville, began with 9th grade and will expand to a four-year high school as the students progress. The system serves 135 students beginning in prekindergarten.

Private and Parochial Schools

The largest group of private schools in the Corpus Christi area are the parochial campuses run by the Catholic Diocese of Corpus Christi, 3036 Saratoga Boulevard, (361) 814-0444. The diocese operates 26 private Catholic schools in an area that extends from Victoria in the north all the way south to Laredo. Approximately 6,000 students attend these schools, many of which use a year-round schedule.

Corpus Christi has nine Catholic elementary schools: Central Catholic, Christ the King, Holy Family, Incarnate Word Academy Elementary, St. Patrick's, St. Pius, Most Precious Blood, Our Lady of Perpetual Help and Saints Cyril & Methodius. There are also two middle schools, Bishop Garriga Middle School and Incarnate Word Academy Middle School, and one high school, Incarnate Word Academy High School.

In Kingsville, there are two Catholic elementary schools. These schools are St. Gertrude and St. Martin.

Other Catholic elementary schools in the area include St. Anthony's in Robstown and Sacred Heart in Rockport, as well as seven schools in Laredo, on the Texas-Mexico border.

All these institutions are known for their emphasis on Catholic education, as well as for their smaller class size and a high level of parent involvement. Several schools have won national recognition for their programs, including St. Patrick's Elementary in Corpus Christi, which is one of only 15 schools in the nation to have twice received the prestigious Blue Ribbon Award from the U.S. Department of Education, in 1986 and 1997.

The three campuses at Incarnate Word Academy, (361) 883-0857, 2910 S. Alameda Street, Corpus Christi, attract students from throughout the area. Although they are considered part of the diocesan school system, they are actually owned by the Sisters of the Incarnate Word and Blessed Sacrament, a religious order that started in 1625 in Lyon, France. The school, founded in 1871, began as an all-girl high school; it later expanded to include elementary students, both boys and girls. The high school became coeducational in 1975. Today, the academy is composed of three campuses: one elementary school that has a Montessori program, a middle school for students in grades 6 through 8, and a high school.

The following listings describe some of the other private schools in the city and area.

St. James Episcopal School
602 S. Carancahua St., Corpus Christi
• (361) 883-0835

Near downtown, this private school has a reputation for academic excellence. It enrolls about 348 students, ages 2½ through 8th grade. Class sizes run around 18 in middle and lower school and 12 in the preschool. Founded in 1946, the school was separated and incorporated in 1995 but remains affiliated with the Episcopal Church of the Good Shepherd. Students start each day with spiritual reflection. In 1992, the school won the nation's Blue Ribbon of Excellence Award.

Kingsville Area

Epiphany Episcopal School
206 N. Third St., Kingsville
• (361) 592-2871

This is a nondenominational Christian private school that has been in operation since 1950. It enrolls children ages 3 through the 5th grade for a total enrollment of 150 students. After-school care is also available, from 3:15 to 5:30 PM.

Presbyterian Pan American School
U.S. Hwy. 77 and F.M. Rd. 772, Kingsville
• (361) 592-4307

A fully accredited college prep school, this facility has boarders as well as day students enroled in grades 9 through 12. A self-described "community of worship, study, and work," it has gained a reputation for recruiting international students who are interested in an American education. Originally founded in 1918 as a

INSIDERS' TIP

Del Mar College in Corpus Christi is the only community college in Texas with a nationally accredited art program. The college in also established the state's first criminal justice degree program.

missionary school for Mexican boys, it became coeducational in 1957. It now enrolls local and area students as well as a number of international students. The enrollment is approximately 100 students.

Colleges and Universities

Del Mar Community College
Baldwin and Ayers Sts., Corpus Christi
• **(361) 886-1254 admissions/registrar**

This is a technical and junior college with two campuses and outreach programs that provides academic, occupational and continuing education classes to more than 28,000 students each year. Founded in 1935, the college was originally under the control of the Corpus Christi Independent School District and designed to provide two years of post-secondary education. It started with 154 students in borrowed classrooms. The college became an independent political subdivision in 1951.

As one of the state's most affordable colleges, Del Mar allows students to take a full-time course load for about $300 in tuition and fees each semester. The college also distributes more than $8 million in financial aid each year.

The Dr. Hector P. Garcia Plaza is a focal point on the campus of Texas A&M University-Corpus Christi.

Photo: Daniel Fielder

Del Mar offers programs to earn associate degrees in art, science and applied science; certificates of achievement; and enhanced skills certificates in more than 100 fields of study. More than 75 percent of students who plan to transfer and complete their bachelor's degree do so within one year. The average passing rate for Del Mar graduates in licensed occupational programs is 92 percent.

Texas A&M University-Corpus Christi
6300 Ocean Dr., Corpus Christi
• **(361) 994-2624, (800) 4TAMUCC**

Situated on a 240-acre island campus that fronts Corpus Christi Bay, this four-year university specializes in business, education, science, and the arts. It is a member of the Texas A&M University System, enrolls approximately 6,000 students and employs 250 full-time teachers. Nicknamed the Island University, it was ranked one of the nation's best public regional universities by *U.S. News and World Report*, in the magazine's 1998 guide to America's Best Colleges. It is also a fast-growing university: It was expanded from a two-year to four-year university in 1994, and student enrollment has nearly doubled. The university is also now looking to add intercollegiate athletics to its roster of recreational activities. Still, classes tend to be small, with an average 15-to-1 student–teacher ratio.

The university is on Ward Island, which was used as a top-secret radar installation during World War II. The Defense Department was persuaded to relinquish the island so it could be used as the site of a university, sponsored by the Baptist General Convocation of Texas. The first university on Ward Island, called University of Corpus Christi, was a private, liberal arts college that opened in 1947. Through the years, its name was changed to Texas A&I University-Corpus Christi and Corpus Christi State University. It joined the Texas A&M University System in 1989, and changed its name to Texas A&M University-Corpus Christi in 1993. Today, it offers more than 50 degree programs.

Among its well-known efforts are those in environmental research, particularly appropriate because of the school's location along the coast. In 1997, the university's $10 million Center for Environmental Studies opened with 18 state agencies and research organizations. The building provided a new home for the university's Center for Coastal Studies, which has specialized in research on the coastal environment and with state and federal regulatory agencies. Among research projects that have been conducted at the center are a study of the environmental effects of oil spills and the resulting cleanup, and a study on the invasion of brown mussels along the Texas coast and marshes.

Texas A&M University-Kingsville
Office of School Relations, MSC 116, 700 University Blvd., Kingsville
• **(361) 593-3907, (800) 687-6000**

This longtime four-year university is devoted to educating students from South Texas,

CHILDCARE AND EDUCATION

and offers 56 undergraduate degree programs in subjects including engineering, business, science, agriculture and education. Its mission is to foster the growth of a middle class in South Texas; currently 65 percent of its students are Hispanic, and many are first-generation college students, which means that the university experience is new to them as well as to their families.

The campus consists of 1,625 acres on five sites in South Texas, including a main campus, a university farm, a Citrus Research Center in Weslaco and buildings in Baffin Bay and Kleberg County. It also offers 57 graduate degrees in 40 areas, including three doctorates. Among its more renowned activities are agricultural research—its citrus center developed the well-loved Rio Red and Star Ruby varieties of grapefruit—and athletic achievement, having produced a football program that has won seven national titles and sent more than 100 players to the pros, including Darrell Green, Earl Dotson, John Randle and Jermane Mayberry.

Established in 1925 as South Texas State

INSIDERS' TIP

The John E. Conner Museum at Texas A&M University-Kingsville features a display of a 1910-era kitchen that includes period utensils such as a butter churn and a hand-cranked washing machine.

Teachers College, it joined the Texas A&M University system in 1989. Texas A&M University-Kingsville enrolls more than 6,000 students annually and specializes in developing programs for minority students in agriculture, science and engineering. The university is also one of the community's major employers, with 815 employees, including 260 faculty members, 450 staff members and more than 100 part-time employees, most of whom are instructors.

The university is also known for research into wildlife science, conducted at the Caesar Kleberg Wildlife Research Institute. Ongoing research focuses on such topics as big cats, including ocelots and mountain lions, in South Texas, and on helping ranchers manage habitats so they can utilize the wildlife as an economic resource.

A final claim to fame: The university says it is the only one in the United States with the javelina as its mascot. The javelina, also called the collared peccary, is a sort of wild pig that is known for its aggressiveness.

Healthcare

Corpus Christi serves as the healthcare center for the area in and around Corpus Christi, including many rural counties without advanced healthcare facilities. Fourteen of the 16 hospitals listed in our four geographical areas are in Corpus Christi. The Christus Spohn Health System and Columbia/HCA Healthcare Corporation, dominate the local industry, operating all but five of the 16 hospitals.

Corpus Christi has seen an explosion of hospital mergers, expansions, and new construction during the past few years. And now a nationwide trend to open new hospitals devoted to specific healthcare needs has led both Christus Spohn and Columbia/HCA to open cardiology centers.

Christus Spohn Health System has four major hospitals—Christus Spohn Hospital Shoreline, Christus Spohn Hospital South, Christus Spohn Hospital Memorial and Christus Spohn Hospital Kleberg—in our coverage area, along with 13 primary-care centers and several medical, educational, and wellness services. Established in 1905, Christus Spohn is a member of Christus Health which is a nonprofit healthcare system based in Dallas.

Columbia/HCA is one of the largest hospital networks in the United States. It operates six full-service and specialty hospitals in our four geographical areas, along with one psychiatric center. In the past few years it has expanded facilities at three hospitals and built two new ones. Four of its hospitals—Bay Area, Bayview Psychiatric Center, Doctors Regional, and The Heart Hospital of South Texas—operate as campuses for one entity, the Corpus Christi Medical Center Family of Hospitals.

Both Christus Spohn and Columbia/HCA say they're expanding to provide needed healthcare services to the area, a region that traditionally has been underserved by the healthcare industry. Their recent emphasis

LOOK FOR:
- **Hospitals**
- **Specialty Hospitals**
- **Referral Services**
- **Walk-In Clinics**
- **Mental Health**
- **Hospices**
- **Alternative Healthcare**

Corpus Christi's Driscoll Children's Hospital offers specialty care in a variety of neonatal pediatric areas.

Photo: Daniel Fielder

on cardiovascular care is in response to the needs of an aging population that is experiencing more heart problems.

In this chapter, along with write-ups on full-service and specialty hospitals, you'll find information on physician referral services, telephone numbers to call in a medical emergency or when you need medical information, walk-in clinics, mental health facilities, hospices and alternative healthcare.

Our listings are divided into the four geographical areas and are then listed alphabetically within those areas.

Hospitals

North Bay Area

North Bay Hospital
1711 W. Wheeler Ave., Aransas Pass
• **(361) 758-8585, (800) 400-3742**

North Bay Hospital, owned by Columbia/HCA Healthcare Corporation, is the only fully accredited acute-care hospital in San Patricio and Aransas counties, serving the communities of Aransas Pass, Rockport, Fulton, Ingleside, Port Aransas and Portland.

The hospital's emergency room averages 1,400 visits a month. North Bay recently expanded its emergency room space and has doctors trained in emergency medicine available 24 hours a day.

The hospital's more than 55 physicians provide outpatient and inpatient care for people needing surgery, orthopedics, urology services, complete diagnostic laboratory services, cardiology and radiology services, including MRI, CAT-scan, ultrasound and American College of Radiology accredited mammography.

Recent additions in services include an Outpatient Cardiac Rehabilitation Center, a medical detoxification program, psychiatric services, and a Pain Management Center.

Corpus Christi

Bay Area-
Corpus Christi Medical Center
7101 S. Padre Island Dr., Corpus Christi
• **(361) 985-1200, (800) 265-8621**

Bay Area, another Columbia/HCA hospital, is a full-service, acute-care hospital with an adjacent three-story medical office building. It provides a full range of healthcare services, including specialized areas such as the Breast Center of South Texas, the Corpus Christi Cancer Center, a new orthopedics unit dedicated to reconstructive knee and hip surgery, and a women's services department with gynecological surgery, labor-delivery-recovery-postpartum suites, and comprehensive nursery services.

Bay Area also is home to Corpus Christi Bay Area Surgery, a full-service ambulatory surgery center and a medical education residency clinic.

Christus Spohn Hospital Shoreline
600 Elizabeth St., Corpus Christi
• **(361) 881-3000, (800) 247-6574**

Licensed for 432 beds, Christus Spohn Hospital Shoreline is the largest hospital in the region. A recent $28.8 million addition, Christus Spohn Shoreline Pavilion, provides patients with state-of-the-art diagnostic, surgical, and cardiac services. The pavilion connects with the main hospital via a skybridge across Elizabeth Street. The pavilion also is home to the Christus Spohn Heart Institute.

Christus Spohn Hospital South
5950 Saratoga Blvd., Corpus Christi
• **(361) 985-5000, (800) 247-6574**

Christus Spohn Hospital South opened in 1994 to meet the medical needs of Corpus Christi's fast-growing Southside area. This 98-bed hospital offers diagnostic, surgical, obstetrical, gynecological, emergency, geropsychiatric, and orthopedic services. Christus Spohn Wellness Services, located in the Christus Spohn South Health Plaza, provides classes, health screenings, health and fitness programs, and senior programs.

Christus Spohn Hospital Memorial
2606 Hospital Blvd., Corpus Christi
• **(361) 902-4000, (800) 247-6574**

Christus Spohn Hospital Memorial, the second largest in Corpus Christi, is a teaching hospital affiliated with the University of Texas Health Science Center in San Antonio. This 387-bed hospital offers psychiatric, obstetrical, orthopedic, cancer, cardiac, surgical, diagnostic, and ophthalmology services.

The hospital also is the lead emergency facility in the area with one of only four Level III trauma centers in Texas. The hospital is staffed with nurses trained in advanced trauma care and board certified emergency physicians in all major specialties 24 hours a day. The hospital also is equipped to treat burn victims and maintains the only civilian burn center in South Texas.

Corpus Christi Naval Hospital
**10651 E St., Naval Air Station,
Corpus Christi**
- **(361) 961-2688**

Situated on Naval Air Station Corpus Christi, this ambulatory care facility serves active-duty military and their family members as well as military retirees and their dependents. Built in 1974, this five-story hospital employs approximately 400 military personnel and civilians. The hospital houses outpatient clinics on two floors and administrative offices.

A snack bar, store, and optometry shop are in the basement.

Doctors Regional—
Corpus Christi Medical Center
3315 S. Alameda St.
- **(361) 857-1400, (800) 442-2361**

Doctors Regional is a full-service, acute-care hospital offering a range of inpatient and outpatient services, including a 24-hour emergency room, a Cardiac Cath Lab, and a neuroscience program that offers stereotactic procedures for noninvasive brain surgery.

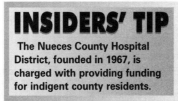

INSIDERS' TIP

The Nueces County Hospital District, founded in 1967, is charged with providing funding for indigent county residents.

This Columbia/HCA hospital provides care for high-risk obstetrical patients, as well as critically ill newborns. Its Level III neonatal intensive care unit allows mother and baby to remain in the same facility following childbirth.

Two office buildings, Physicians Medical Plaza and the Dr. Charles S. Clark, Sr. Medical Tower, and two multilevel parking garages are adjacent to the hospital. The Doctors Regional complex includes a MRI Diagnostic Center, a conference center, and The Women's Pavilion. The Women's Pavilion houses offices for obstetricians and gynecologists, a diabetes management program, and women's health education resources.

Northwest Regional Hospital
13725 F.M. Rd. 624, Corpus Christi
- **(361) 241-4243**

Northwest Regional Hospital, owned by Columbia/HCA, is the only acute-care medical facility in northwest Corpus Christi. The hospital's service area includes Nueces County and several surrounding counties.

Last year, Northwest Regional Hospital completed a $15 million expansion that added 47,000 square feet, doubling the hospital's size.

The addition allows the hospital to provide improved emergency care, outpatient surgery, and diagnostic treatment.

The hospital provides 24-hour emergency services, sports and rehabilitative medicine, cardiac nuclear testing, angiography, cancer care, and cystology services.

Kingsville Area

Christus Spohn Hospital Kleberg
1311 E. General Cavazos Blvd.
- **(361) 595-1661, (800) 247-6574**

This Kingsville hospital is a general acute care hospital licensed for 100 beds, providing inpatient and outpatient services to residents in Kleberg and surrounding counties. A new three-story facility houses a birthing center. The first floor has six labor-delivery-recovery-post-partum rooms, two labor rooms, a newborn nursery, a Cesarean-section room, and a waiting area.

The second floor houses the Cissy Horlock-Taub Diagnostic Center, a 2,500-square-foot facility, featuring state-of-the-art equipment for women's health needs, among them, certified mammography and a chronic disease counseling unit.

Specialty Hospitals
Corpus Christi

Corpus Christi
Warm Springs Rehabilitation Hospital
2606 Hospital Blvd., Corpus Christi
- **(361) 888-4458, (800) 500-0107**

Although on the first and eighth floors of Christus Spohn Hospital Memorial, Warm Springs is a separate medical facility specializing in treating catastrophic neurological injuries. It provides inpatient and outpatient services to people with brain injuries, burns and strokes, and neurological and orthopedic disorders. The hospital is part of the nonprofit Warm Springs Rehabilitation System, which also operates hospitals in Gonzales, Victoria, and San Antonio.

The treatment method at Warm Springs is

HEALTHCARE

an interdisciplinary team approach involving physical and occupational therapy, physical medicine and rehabilitation physicians, rehabilitation nursing, speech therapy, social services, and rehabilitation psychology. The hospital employs about 75 people.

Driscoll Children's Hospital
3533 S. Alameda St., Corpus Christi
• **(361) 694-5000**

This 188-bed hospital is a private, nonprofit tertiary-care referral center serving children in a 32-county South Texas area. Its philosophy is that children are not small adults, and therefore have health needs requiring different services, care, and resources.

It maintains 128 acute-care beds, 40 intensive-care beds for premature newborns, and 20 intensive-care beds for children with a wide variety of medical and surgical abnormalities. Driscoll was the first hospital in South Texas to provide emergency services exclusively for children. The hospital's critical-care transport service provides immediate 24-hour-a-day response, transferring children who need specialized medical and surgical care by airplane, helicopter, or ground transport vehicle to Driscoll's emergency room and intensive care units.

Driscoll employs more than 1,200 people in its hospital and adjacent rehabilitation center. It offers a three-year pediatric residency program offering training for physicians specializing in pediatric medicine. It is fully accredited by the American Council of Graduate Medical Education.

Driscoll Children's Rehabilitation Center of South Texas
3511 S. Alameda St., Corpus Christi
• **(361) 694-4380**

This hospital, adjacent to Driscoll Children's Hospital, began in 1939 as the Ada Wilson Children's Center for Rehabilitation and operated independently until merging with Driscoll. It offers outpatient services for children and young adults ranging from those with mild developmental delays to people with multiple handicaps.

The facility houses Driscoll's rehabilitation department, day surgery unit, and Neuromuscular Institute, which includes orthopedics, neurology, and neurosurgery. Outpatient services include physical therapy, occupational therapy,

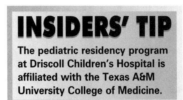

INSIDERS' TIP

The pediatric residency program at Driscoll Children's Hospital is affiliated with the Texas A&M University College of Medicine.

speech therapy, audiology, hyppotherapy, medical specialty clinics, and case management services.

Integrated Health Services
1310 Third St., Corpus Christi
• **(361) 888-4323**

Integrated Health Services provides both complex-acute medical care and comprehensive physical rehabilitation services to inpatients. It's licensed by the state of Texas as a long-term acute-care hospital, and it's the only facility of its type in the area.

The 31-bed hospital takes patients from hospital intensive-care units and other patients needing acute care. The staff provides ventilator care, in-house dialysis and wound care. Specialty Hospital has more than 75 employees and 50 physicians specializing in individualized care and complements services offered by other hospitals.

The Heart Hospital of South Texas
7002 Williams Dr., Corpus Christi
• **(361) 980-1800**

The Heart Hospital, adjacent to the Bay Area campus, specializes in treating heart disease. This Columbia/HCA hospital offers comprehensive diagnostics, treatment and surgical procedures at its 72-bed facility. The Heart Hospital features cardiac catheterization laboratories, coronary care beds, operating rooms, telemetry beds, noninvasive diagnostic facilities, and a fully equipped fitness center.

Surgicare Specialty Hospital
718 Elizabeth St., Corpus Christi
• **(361) 882-3204**

Surgicare is an ambulatory surgery center equipped with four operating rooms and an emergency treatment room. The six-bed hospital offers dentistry, general surgery, gynecology, ophthalmology, orthopedics, pain therapy, podiatry, plastic surgery, and urology.

Surgicare, which employs more than 50 people, is part of the Columbia/HCA network.

Referral Services

Corpus Christi has several medical referral services, which provide callers with information on physicians and services available in the area. These include **Driscoll Physician Re-**

ferral, (361) 694-5437; **DoctorSource Physician Referral Service**, (361) 242-3031; and **Christus Spohn Healthline**, 5920 Saratoga Boulevard, Corpus Christi, (361) 881-3103 or (800) 247-6574.

Walk-In Clinics

The only thing worse than getting sick while on vacation is not knowing where to find a doctor. For emergencies, you can turn to any of the full-service hospitals in the area. But what if your ailment doesn't warrant a trip to the emergency room? For those occasions you might, instead, turn to one of the Corpus Christi area's walk-in clinics, which handle minor emergencies and illnesses.

Walk-in clinics generally can treat minor injuries like sprains, cuts, minor burns, whiplash and flu-like symptoms. Many have X-ray equipment and on-site diagnostic labs.

Most operate during typical business hours, although a few offer evening and weekend hours. They accept insurance, credit cards, cash, Medicare, and Medicaid. Below you'll find the names, addresses, phone numbers, and office hours of several walk-in clinics in the area. Because hours often change, be sure to call the clinic to confirm the information or to ask additional questions.

North Bay Area

Rockport Health Clinic
1704 Jenkins, Rockport
• **(361) 790-9047**
Hours are 8 AM to 4:30 PM Monday through Friday.

Corpus Christi

Bayside Family Medicine Associates and Minor Emergency Center
3817 S. Padre Island Dr., Corpus Christi
• **(361) 857-0178**
Bayside is open 8 AM to 8 PM Monday through Friday and 8 AM to 5 PM on weekends. Bayside Family Medicine also operates a 24-hour answering service.

Urgent Care Clinic
3434 Saratoga Blvd., Corpus Christi
• **(361) 852-0852, ext. 60**
The clinic is open from 9 AM to 6 PM weekdays except on Thursdays, when the clinic is

open from 2 to 6:30 PM. On Saturday, hours are 8 AM to noon.

Port Aransas to Padre Island

Christus Spohn
Family Health Center—Padre Island
14202 S. Padre Island Dr., Corpus Christi
• **(361) 949-7660**
This family care center is open 8 AM to 6 PM Monday through Friday.

Kingsville Area

Christus Spohn
Family Health Center—Bishop
301 W. Main St., Bishop
• **(361) 584-2563**
The Bishop clinic is open from 8 AM to 5 PM Monday and Friday, 9 AM to 9 PM Tuesday and Thursday and from 8 AM to noon Wednesday. The clinic is closed from noon to 1 PM and on weekends.

Christus Spohn
Family Health Center-Kingsville
915 S. Ninth St., Kingsville
• **(361) 592-6456**
This clinic is open Monday through Friday from 8 AM to 5 PM. It's closed on weekends.

Mental Health
Corpus Christi

Nueces County
Mental Health and Mental Retardation Community Center
1630 S. Brownlee Blvd, Corpus Christi
• **(361) 886-6900**
The Nueces County Mental Health and Mental Retardation Community Center provides services for children and adults with severe mental illnesses, mental retardation, and other developmental disabilities. The organization operates facilities in both Corpus Christi and Robstown, located in western Nueces County.

The Robstown outpatient clinic is located at 102 N. 4th St., (361) 387-3588. Nueces County MHMR also operates a 24-hour jobline at (361) 886-6918.

Hospices

North Bay Area

Aim Hospice
703 E. Concho St., Rockport
• **(361) 729-0507, (800) 854-2674**

This nonprofit hospice has been in business here for about 10 years, serving people with terminal illnesses with a life expectancy of six months or less. All hospice care is provided in the patient's home or nursing home, with family, friends, or paid caregivers caring for them.

The hospice staff teaches families to provide assistance and provides a social worker, pastoral worker, and bereavement counseling for a year after the death. Aim Hospice serves clients within a 70-mile radius of Rockport.

Corpus Christi

Christus Spohn Hospice
1660 S. Staples St., Corpus Christi
• **(361) 881-3159**

Christus Spohn Hospice, in business since 1983, provides home care for terminally ill patients who prefer to die at home surrounded by loved ones instead of in a hospital hooked up to medical equipment. To qualify, patients must have accepted their impending death and stopped all curative treatments. Christus Spohn Hospice provides a team of nurses, a medical director, nurses aids, a social worker, chaplain, and a counselor who work together to keep the patient comfortable at home or in the nursing home in which they reside.

The staff works to control symptoms and pain and help the family deal with the sorrow of losing loved ones. They help the family get their finances in order and prepare for death. They strive to keep patients at home and pain-free and work with their doctor and family in caring for them.

Christus Spohn Hospice serves clients within a 100-mile radius of Corpus Christi.

VistaCare Hospice
5656 S. Staples St., Ste. 350 Corpus Christi
• **361) 854-1540, (888) 878-1540**

VistaCare, based in Arizona, has 16 locations in Texas, including one in Corpus Christi. This Medicare-certified hospice program provides a full range of comfort care to people with terminal illnesses and their loved ones. This includes skilled nursing, certified nurses aids, spe-cially trained volunteers, chaplains, social workers, and 13 months of bereavement follow-up for families. The staff works in conjunction with their primary-care physician and the VistaCare medical director. They serve clients within a 50-mile radius of Corpus Christi.

People receiving hospice care elsewhere who wish to move to or visit the Corpus Christi area can do so without losing benefits. Call VistaCare's toll-free number for a free video.

Alternative Healthcare

Corpus Christi

Angel Light
Healing Arts and Yoga Center
5301 Everhart Rd., Corpus Christi
• **(361) 854-6563**

Angel Light is an alternative health and education center providing products with an angelic theme. Its mission is "to create a safe place of beauty and light where one can enlighten one's mind, whole one's body, and renew one's spirit."

Here you'll find self-help and transformational books, tapes and CDs, candles, herbs, beauty products, art and jewelry. Angel Light features practitioners in massage, herbology, energy work, and card reading. It also hosts classes in yoga, reiki, belly dancing, and meditation. Yoga classes are held twice a day, once in the morning and once at night. Retail business hours are 10 AM to 7 PM Monday through Friday and 10 AM to 4 PM on Saturday.

Delos Mind-Body Institute
525 S. Carancahua St., Corpus Christi
• **(361) 882-9355**

The institute offers a combination of conventional and alternative medical treatments including acupuncture, homeopathy, herbal medicine, bioenergetics, counseling, psychotherapy, biofeedback, and massage. Their staff includes medical doctors, naturopathic doctors (specialists in preventative medicine and nonevasive healing methods such as herbs and homeopathy) a registered massage therapist, psychologist, and licensed acupuncturist.

The Delos Mind-Body Institute has been in business for eight years in Corpus Christi. It operates The Wellness Center, a training site for students from the University of Texas School of Medicine.

HEALTHCARE

Numbers to Call

When an emergency arises or you need general information or direction to community resources, refer to this list. For emergencies requiring ambulance, police, or fire departments, call 911.

AIDS Information Hotline .... (800) 590-2437
AIDS Services of the Coastal Bend 24-Hour Hotline .... (361) 814-7001
AIDS Testing-Fast .... (800) 584-8183
Area Agency on Aging of the Coastal Bend .... (361) 883-5743
Coast Guard Marine and Air Emergency (Search and Rescue) .... (361) 937-1898
Corpus Christi-Nueces County Health Department .... (361) 851-7200
HIV Testing Center .... (800) 584-8183
Medic Alert Foundation .... (800) 432-5378
National Child Abuse Hotline .... (800) 422-4453
Nueces County Community Action Agency .... (361) 883-7201
Nueces County Medical Society .... (361) 884-5442
Nueces County Psychological Association .... (361) 991-5915
Poison Center .... (800) 764-7661
Problem Gamblers Helpline .... (800) 522-4700
Texas Aged and Disabled Services .... (361) 878-3452
Texas Mental Health and Mental Retardation Department .... (361) 888-5301
Tri County Emergency Medical Service .... (361) 776-0025
United Way Info-Line .... (361) 882-4636

HEALTHCARE

Media

LOOK FOR:
- Publications
- Local TV Stations and Networks
- Cable Providers
- Radio

One large daily newspaper, several weekly and biweekly newspapers, seven TV stations, and about 30 radio stations serve the Corpus Christi area. Local news coverage ranges from good to comical depending on the source, and hard-hitting investigative pieces are less common than in urban areas. The *Corpus Christi Caller-Times* is the only daily newspaper published in the area, although the *San Antonio Express News*, *Houston Chronicle* and *Dallas Morning News* can be purchased from newspaper racks here.

As in most rural areas, weeklies and biweeklies abound, with one or more newspapers published in small towns throughout the area. Corpus Christi lacks a city magazine of the sort found in many urban areas as attempts at establishing one over the years have failed. Instead the market is blanketed with specialty publications (aimed at lawyers, Catholics, and seniors, for example) and publications targeted at tourists. Most publications are available in grocery stores, convenience stores, and restaurants in the areas they serve.

Publications

Daily Newspapers

Corpus Christi Caller-Times
- 820 Lower N. Broadway, Corpus Christi
- (361) 884-2011

It seems only fitting to begin our section on the media with the area's primary source for news. Although the San Antonio, Houston, and Dallas newspapers can be purchased here, and five local TV stations and several radio stations broadcast local news reports, the *Caller-Times* leads the way in local coverage. Like many newspapers with hyphenated names, the *Caller-Times* began as two newspapers, first as competitors and later as partners in a joint-operating agreement for the same company.

The *Corpus Christi Caller*, at the time a weekly, rolled off the presses for the first time on January 21, 1883, on a rare below-freezing day. The birth of triplets to Mrs. Mark Downey was among the breaking stories of the day, and the 849 subscribers in the town of 3,257 read all about it.

The *Corpus Christi Times* (operating as the *Corpus Christi Democrat* until 1917) was founded in 1911 by J.W. Bauerfeind and a man named O'Flaherty. (As far as is known, history has not recorded his first name.) For years the two papers battled for subscribers, with the *Caller* having the advantage of a larger staff and greater resources. Although the *Times* operated with only one reporter for many years, it benefited from the ability to steal stories from its morning competitor.

In 1924 Bernard Hanks, publisher of the *Abilene Reporter-News*, and Houston Harte, publisher of the *San Angelo Standard-Times*, formed a partnership to buy newspapers. They bought the *Corpus Christi Times* in 1928 and the *Corpus Christi Caller* in 1929. For the next 58 years the two papers operated jointly but published separate newspapers. The *Caller* served morning readers, and the *Times* kept afternoon readers informed. On May 29, 1987, the *Times* published its last afternoon edition.

On June 1, 1987, the first edition of the new combined morning paper, the *Corpus Christi Caller-Times*, hit the streets. During the past several years the paper has won numerous journalism awards. On May 20, 1997, longtime publisher and media conglomerate E.W. Scripps Company announced plans to buy the *Caller-Times* after the paper's parent company decided to concentrate on shopper publications and direct marketing. The sale became final in October 1997.

The *Caller-Times* usually publishes stand-alone local, sports, and classified sections. The "Weekend" section published every Friday details recreational and entertainment activities throughout the area, and the Sunday edition includes the *TV Channels* magazine, advertising inserts, and an expanded "Help Wanted" section. Other features include: a section each Monday on financial planning, a tabloid focusing on local people published each Thursday, and a monthly tabloid devoted to senior issues.

Weekly and Biweekly Newspapers

Weekly and biweekly newspapers are available by subscription or can be purchased at convenience stores, grocery stores and, occasionally, newspaper racks in their coverage areas. Generally speaking, a weekly or biweekly devoted to a particular town cannot be found in other towns.

Ad Sack
- **3040 S. Padre Island Dr., Corpus Christi**
- **(361) 854-0137, (800) 659-0137**

The *Ad Sack* has been a Corpus Christi institution since 1971, offering bargain-hunters and those looking to sell something a place to buy and sell wares. This 16- to 24-page newspaper is published every Friday and the 50,000 or so copies are distributed throughout the Corpus Christi area. The *Ad Sack* publishes classified and display advertisements.

Aransas Pass Progress
- **346 S. Houston St., Aransas Pass**
- **(361) 758-5391**

The *Aransas Pass Progress*, one of the oldest businesses in the area, was founded in 1909 for the sole purpose of promoting a land sale. It all began when J.W. Vernor, a 24-year-old printing equipment salesman from Dallas, moved to Aransas Pass at the request of a local real estate firm to promote a land auction involving hundreds of acres of city lots. Vernor's duty was to attract prospective buyers by touting the auction.

When the auction was over, Vernor continued publishing the *Progress* until 1911. The current publisher is Richard P. Richards, whose father, J.G. Richards, purchased a half interest in the paper in 1946. The *Progress*, published every Wednesday, has approximately 2,600 paid subscribers. The Progress usually publishes around 14 pages, and, like most small-town newspapers, concentrates coverage on local issues such as fishing, the shrimping industry, local residents, and Aransas Pass schools.

Each year the *Progress* and its sister paper, *The Ingleside Index*, publish *The North Bay Area Visitors & Newcomers Guide*.

Christian Metro Times Newspaper
- **Corpus Christi**
- **(361) 855-5343**

Publisher Belma Fussell describes the *Christian Metro Times Newspaper* as providing local, national, and international news on issues important to Christians that would otherwise be unavailable. The *Metro Times* also provides a forum for local ministers to share their ministries' events with other Christians and provides information on Christian-owned businesses in the area. The *Metro Times* publishes in the middle of each month. Between 10,000 and 15,000 free copies are distributed to churches, stores, and restaurants throughout the Corpus Christi area.

The Coastal Bend Herald
- **1114 Main St., Rockport**
- **(361) 729-1828**

The *Coastal Bend Herald* may well be the most ambitious weekly in the area, covering an area from Rockport to the north side of Corpus Christi. Publisher Kerry Riley bought the paper, established in 1976, in October 1996. *The Herald* and its more established competitor, *The Rockport Pilot*, compete for advertisers and readers in an old-fashioned newspaper war. *The*

Herald strives to cover a broader area than *The Pilot*, which focuses its reporting on the Rockport/Fulton area.

The Herald is published on Thursdays and is distributed to more than 4,000 paid subscribers. It usually runs about 18 pages, with news and sports in separate sections. *The Herald* also publishes a weekly TV listing.

Coastal Bend Sun
• **427 Naval Air Station Dr., Corpus Christi**
• **(361) 937-4584**

Seventy-eight-year-old publisher Marie Speer has three area publications in her fold, including the *Coastal Bend Sun*, which she began publishing in 1994. Her other publications are the *Flour Bluff Sun* and the *Seaside Sun*. Published each Saturday, the *Coastal Bend Sun* is a general-interest tabloid that reports on municipal and state issues affecting area residents.

By virtue of the weekly's size and location, coverage tends to focus largely on Corpus Christi. (Many stories that appear in the *Coastal Bend Sun* also can be found in the *Flour Bluff Sun*.) The *Sun's* slogan—"We tell the truth"—is a not-so-subtle jab at the *Corpus Christi Caller-Times*, which Speer believes often slants its coverage to support its opinion on a particular issue. "We don't give any window dressing," she says. "We tell it like it is." The *Coastal Bend Sun* has a circulation of about 2,500.

Corpus Christi Homes Newspaper and Real Estate Guide for the Coastal Bend
• **4639 Corona St., Ste. 2, Corpus Christi**
• **(361) 854-6494, (877) 854-6470**

This free publication published every other Friday runs photos of Corpus Christi-area homes with brief descriptions, along with listings of homes, apartments, and condominiums for lease. It usually publishes 12 to 16 pages and distributes about 10,000 copies to more than 200 spots throughout the area. The Real Estate Guide is published bimonthly by Master's Publishing Company.

Corpus Christi Jobs
• **4639 Corona St., Ste. 2, Corpus Christi**
• **(361) 854-6494, (877) 854-6470**

The name pretty much says it all. This biweekly newspaper—published by Master's Publishing Co.—lists job openings in the Corpus Christi area. Publishing every other Friday, *Corpus Christi Jobs* usually runs eight to 12 pages and prints 10,000 copies. Although it focuses mostly on job openings, it also contains articles, most of which are employment related.

Flour Bluff Sun
• **427 Naval Air Station Dr., Corpus Christi**
• **(361) 937-4584**

The *Flour Bluff Sun*, another Speer publication (see the third previous listing), is the community newspaper for Flour Bluff, a Corpus Christi neighborhood on the city's south side.

The *Flour Bluff Sun*, which began publishing in 1976, publishes each Friday and is delivered to its 2,500 subscribers in Flour Bluff, Padre Island, and Naval Air Station-Corpus Christi.

Flightline/Aircraftsman Newspaper
• **4455 S. Padre Island Dr., Ste. 116, Corpus Christi**
• **(361) 814-0866**

The *Flightline/Aircraftsman Newspaper* is the general-interest newspaper for Naval Air Station Corpus Christi and the Corpus Christi Army Depot (on the naval air station) on the city's south side. Articles cover base news and news from the Navy. The paper is distributed at Naval Air Station Corpus Christi, Naval Air Station Kingsville, Naval Station Ingleside and some nearby restaurants.

The Flying K
• **554 McCain St., Ste. 309, Kingsville**
• **(361) 516-6146**

Training squadrons and other departments at Naval Air Station Kingsville submit articles for this 1,500-circulation newspaper. Published every other week, it is produced by the public affairs office and distributed free on the base.

The Foc'sle
• **1455 Ticonderoga Rd., Ingleside**
• **(361) 776-4206**

Featuring articles of interest to the Navy's mine warfare community, this newspaper at Naval Station Ingleside has a circulation of 10,000 active duty and retired military readers here as well as overseas. It is produced by the base public affairs office every other week, and is distributed free at Naval Station Ingleside, Naval Air Station Corpus Christi, and the Family Service Center at Bay Vista Shopping Center, 2370 Texas Highway 361.

The Ingleside Index
• **346 S. Houston St., Aransas Pass**
• **(361) 758-5391**

In contrast to its nearest neighbor, *The Aransas Pass Progress*, the *Ingleside Index* is a relatively young creature, having sprung into existence in early 1951 at the hands of local newspapermen Carter Snooks and Bill Kennedy.

The duo operated *The Index* until J.G. Richards, publisher of *The Aransas Pass Progress*, bought it on March 21, 1973. *The Index* and *The Progress* share similar layouts, news philosophies, staffs, and facilities. *The Ingleside Index* focuses on Ingleside people and issues and military stories of interest to the many people stationed at Naval Station Ingleside, the center for the Navy's mine warfare fleet and equipment.

Published on Thursdays, *The Index* usually runs about 10 pages. It has more than 900 paid subscribers. Each year the *Index* and *Progress* publish *The North Bay Area Visitors & Newcomers Guide*.

The Kingsville Record and Bishop News
• **105 S. Fifth St., Kingsville**
• **(361) 592-4304**

The Kingsville Record and Bishop News is one of the largest small-town newspapers in the Corpus Christi area. Published on Wednesdays and Sundays, *The Record* boasts an average of 20 to 30 pages per issue. The paper is owned by the King Ranch Inc. and has been in business since 1906 when the Kingsville Publishing Company formed *The Kingsville Record*. Recently it merged with another newspaper, *The Bishop News*, expanding its coverage area to include the town of Bishop.

The Kingsville Record and Bishop News now has about 6,200 paid subscribers and covers news in Kingsville, Bishop, Riviera, Driscoll, Ricardo, and surrounding areas. The paper is divided into several sections—news, sports, society, classified, and a Sunday entertainment tabloid with articles on restaurants, music, and other entertainment-related subjects. It also includes local TV listings and a page devoted to subjects of interest to children.

Port Aransas South Jetty
• **141 W. Cotter Ave., Port Aransas**
• **(361) 749-5131**

The *South Jetty* began in 1971 with a shoestring budget and a cause. Publishers Suzanna Reader and Steve Frishman convinced Reader's father to donate $1,000 to start up a newspaper to fight a proposed deepwater port near Port Aransas that would allow tankers to dock and unload crude oil for refining in Corpus Christi. Reader and Frishman, along with others fond of Port Aransas's laid-back lifestyle, railed against the proposal in the *South Jetty*'s pages. So far, their efforts have paid off: The deepwater port, now labeled Safe Harbor, has yet to be built.

Current editor Mary Judson thinks the *Jetty*'s history is special. In the old days, before newspapers became profit centers and journalists claimed to be objective, newspapers generally were started by non-journalists to promote a cause. The *South Jetty*, Judson says, was founded in that same spirit. Judson and her husband, publisher Murray Judson, bought the *South Jetty* in 1981 and published their first edition in January of that year. The paper is published every Thursday.

As evidence of the city's status as a tourist destination, about 2,500 of the *South Jetty*'s 4,700 subscribers live outside Port Aransas. The *South Jetty* is mailed to subscribers in 49 states and several foreign countries. Its 16- to 18-page editions boast more fish photos than any newspaper in the area. Deep-sea fishing is big business in Port Aransas, so it's not unusual to see the *South Jetty*'s pages plastered with photos of smiling tourists displaying their catches.

The *South Jetty* covers Mustang Island and Port Aransas and publishes visitors guides in August, November, February, and May.

Portland News
• **101 Cedar Pl., Ste. G, Portland**
• **(361) 643-1566**

Several Portland newspapers bit the dust in the hundred or so years before the Guthrie Publishing Company founded the *Portland News* in 1964. In 1971 Guthrie Publishing sold the *News* to James F. Tracy Jr., who now publishes the weekly with his son, John H. Tracy. The *News* focuses its coverage on Portland, a few miles from Corpus Christi on the north side of the Nueces Bay Causeway. The *News* has about 2,500 paid subscribers and publishes about 12 pages each week.

The Rockport Pilot
• **1002 Wharf St., Rockport**
• **(361) 729-9900**

The Rockport Pilot is one of the older publications in the area and more than a century older than its Rockport rival, *The Coastal Bend Herald*. *The Pilot*, which publishes on Wednesdays and Saturdays, started in 1869 and is owned by Hartman Newspapers with Mike Probst as publisher.

More than 5,700 people subscribe to *The Pilot*, which normally runs about 16 pages. *The Pilot* covers Rockport and Fulton schools and city governments, along with the Aransas County government and the Aransas County Navigation District. It's interesting to note that back editions of this and other area newspa-

MEDIA

pers are rare because hurricanes and other storms have destroyed them.

Seaside Sun
- **427 Naval Air Station Dr., Corpus Christi**
- **(361) 937-4584**

A third Marie Speer publication, the *Seaside Sun*, has been guiding Corpus Christi-area tourists to a good time since 1976. This small tabloid gives tourists information on local fishing, entertainment, and tourism-related activities in the area. The *Seaside Sun* is free and published every other Thursday.

Thrifty Nickel
- **1308 Airline Rd., Corpus Christi**
- **(361) 980-0008, (888) 980-0008**

The *Thrifty Nickel* published in Corpus Christi is one of about 120 franchises throughout the United States. This free weekly newspaper publishes classified and display advertisements catering to bargain-hunters. The *Thrifty Nickel* usually runs about 28 pages and distributes around 41,000 copies throughout the Corpus Christi area. It's published every Thursday.

Specialty Newspapers

South Texas Catholic Monthly
- **620 Lipan St., Corpus Christi**
- **(361) 882-6191**

The Catholic community keeps up to date on news of the Diocese of Corpus Christi through this monthly newspaper published by the diocese and circulated to church members. Topics include official diocesan news, local news about the Catholic community, and national and international news from a Catholic news service. The *South Texas Catholic Monthly* is a mixture of news stories and columns of interest to Catholics in Corpus Christi and the surrounding area that is served by the diocese. It's available by paid subscription or free at local Catholic churches. It's published on or near the last Friday of the month.

Magazines and Other Print Media

Explore the Texas Coastal Bend 2000 Information Guide
- **13041 Pond Springs Rd., Austin**
- **(512) 249-0086, (800) 330-8069**

This glossy tourist guide is produced by Anaqua Publishing Inc. in Austin for the Texas Coastal Bend Regional Tourism Council. Its small pages are stuffed with all sorts of Corpus Christi-area tourism information, including a calendar of events, tours, and a buyer's guide. This annual publication is available free all over the Corpus Christi area, including local chambers of commerce.

South Texas Women's World
- **Corpus Christi**
- **(361) 949-2348**

Publisher Mary Weaver describes *South Texas Women's World* as a publication with a "positive outlook that gives readers something enjoyable to read." As the name suggests, this monthly tabloid focuses on women and women's issues. Already in its sixth year, this free publication is published on the 10th of each month and has a circulation of about 40,000.

The Real Estate Book
- **4942 Arlene Dr., Corpus Christi**
- **(361) 851-9250**

Chances are you've seen the local version of *The Real Estate Book* in your hometown or some other city you've visited. That's because the Atlanta-based publisher has more than 400 franchises throughout the United States. The concept is straightforward enough:

CBS affiliate KZTV-TV is located in uptown Corpus Christi.

Photo: Daniel Fielder

MEDIA

Take pictures of homes for sale throughout the Corpus Christi area and put them in a small book with brief descriptions and prices. Tom Dunovan, owner of the local franchise, has produced the local book since 1984. Twenty-five thousand copies of the publication are available every four weeks for free at retail outlets throughout the area.

TRAVELHOST
of Corpus Christi Magazine
• 4455 S. Padre Island Dr., Ste. 116, Corpus Christi
• (361) 814-0866
• www.travelhost.com

This tourist-oriented publication is available free of charge in many Corpus Christi-area hotel rooms. This four-color glossy magazine features travel-related articles on area attractions along with a dining guide, shopping guide, and activities listing.

This monthly publication also includes a map of the area.

Local TV Stations and Networks

Take our advice: Get cable. Without it you'll spend most of your time trying to decipher a fuzzy screen. Only one of the seven local TV stations comes through clear enough to make TV viewing enjoyable without cable.

Because five cable companies serve the area, (see the following section for information on cable providers) you'd be wise to consult the cable conversion chart in the *Caller-Times*'s *TV Channels* magazine. Find your city, locate the network you want to watch and follow your fingers to find the correct number to which to tune your set. To avoid confusion, ignore the numbers broadcast by the local TV stations because they won't coincide with the number on your TV dial. For instance, KIII-TV, the ABC affiliate in Corpus Christi, promotes itself as Channel 3, which is where you'd find it if you didn't have cable. Cable subscribers in Corpus Christi will find the station on Channel 5; cable subscribers in other areas will find it on channels 2, 3, or 4.

Corpus Christi is the 128th-largest TV market in the United States. The five major networks—ABC, CBS, NBC, PBS, and Fox—each has an affiliate here. Two Spanish-language TV stations serve as affiliates to the Spanish-language networks Telemundo and Univision. All

TV stations and the one network listed here are based in Corpus Christi.

Catholic Communications Network
• 1200 Lantana St., Corpus Christi
• (361) 289-6437

You need no more evidence of the influence of Catholicism in the Corpus Christi area than the existence of the Catholic Communications Network, a product of the Diocesan Telecommunications Corp. (DTC), a nonprofit entity that operates radio station KLUX 89.5 FM and the Catholic Communications Network. Network is perhaps too strong a word for what the DTC does. The DTC airs programming provided by the Eternal Word Television Network over Channel 27 to Heartland Cable Television subscribers.

Programs cover topics pertaining to and of interest to Catholics. Most programming comes from Eternal Word Television with a few locally produced shows thrown into the mix. The DTC has the right to inject its own programming whenever it wants. Local shows include the Sunday Mass from Corpus Christi Cathedral and the Spanish-language Mass from San Fernando Cathedral in San Antonio.

KLUX 89.5 FM, an easy listening station, consistently ranks among the top three stations in the area with the much-sought-after 35-and-older audience. This non-profit station does not run commercials. It instead runs inspirational pieces and disseminates emergency information from the city.

KIII-TV, Channel 3
• 4750 S. Padre Island Dr., Corpus Christi
• (361) 854-4733

KIII-TV is the No. 1 TV station in the area, having topped the news ratings for the past 17 years. Mike McKinnon, who has headed the station since it went on the air in 1964, owns the ABC affiliate. Much of KIII's success is attributed to the appeal of anchorman Joe Gazin, who joined the station in 1977 after working as a news anchor in Madison, Wisconsin. His easy-going style and smooth delivery appeal to area viewers, who have tuned in to Joe night after night for years.

KZTV-TV, Channel 10
• 301 Artesian St., Corpus Christi
• (361) 883-7070

KZTV-TV, the local CBS affiliate, runs a distant third to the top-two stations in the local news ratings and shows no signs of climbing out of the cellar. The station began in 1956

MEDIA

as KSIX-TV, with Vann M. Kennedy as the station's president, a title he continues to hold today. In the days before cable, the station dubbed itself "the clear channel" because of its unfuzzy signal. For years its newsroom was in Corpus Christi while its studio and transmitting tower remained in Robstown, which meant anchormen had to spend 30 minutes before each newscast on the road.

Kennedy is known as a conservative businessman who runs a tight ship, budget-wise. News reporters are generally young, and production quality is sometimes lacking.

KEDT-TV, Channel 16
• 4455 S. Padre Island Dr., Ste. 38, Corpus Christi
• (361) 855-2213

KEDT is the Corpus Christi area's Public Broadcasting System affiliate. It went on the air on October 15, 1972, after a local grocery store tycoon took a liking to Public Broadcasting System programs during his travels. He said the programs inspired and challenged viewers to be participants in their communities. He and another Corpus Christi resident decided to bring public broadcasting to the city.

The station had its share of problems in the beginning, namely the fact that most local residents didn't know it existed. But Richard Nixon saved the day when he got into trouble and KEDT decided to televise gavel-to-gavel coverage of the Senate Watergate hearings. The public (most of whom voted Democratic) responded wholeheartedly.

Like many public TV stations, KEDT has experienced its share of struggles related to funding. A few years ago the TV station and its sister radio station, KEDT-FM, were on the brink of shutting down. The TV station owed creditors $1.1 million and some bills were even running 90 days past due. A new station manager, who has since left for greener pastures, substantially reduced the debt and moved the station into larger, more attractive offices. Outdated equipment has been replaced and staff morale repaired. The station is now a stable PBS affiliate. KEDT airs PBS and local instructional programs.

KORO-TV, Channel 28
• 102 N. Mesquite St., Corpus Christi
• (361) 883-2823

Corpus Christi's first Spanish-language TV station went on the air on April 19, 1977. It broadcast a San Antonio TV station's signal and gradually inserted local ads and programs

as they came along. The station has grown along with the Spanish-language market nationwide. KORO is now an affiliate of Univision, a Spanish-language network based in Miami. KORO airs both a 5 PM and 10 PM local newscast in Spanish.

KDF-Fox, Channel 47
• 409 S. Staples St., Corpus Christi
• (361) 881-6100

KDF-Fox, as the name suggests, is the local affiliate of the Fox Broadcasting Company. It became the 143rd Fox affiliate on April 10, 1994, despite Fox's reservations about KDF's status as a low-power TV station. A Fox official said at the time that only two other low-power stations had been chosen as Fox affiliates. She said KDF's aggressive programming and the addition of a nightly newscast helped convince them to take KDF on as an affiliate.

Paloma Broadcasting Corp., whose stockholders included the Catholic Diocese of Corpus Christi's Diocesan Telecommunications Corp., originally owned the station, but financial troubles and Chapter 11 bankruptcy forced Paloma to sell the station to a group of KRIS-TV executives under the name Miramar Broadcasting Company. Miramar then sold KDF to the South Carolina-based Evening Post Publishing Co. in February 1998. The company also owns KRIS-TV, Channel 6 and KAJA-TV, Channel 68.

The Fox affiliate broadcasts a 30-minute news program at 9 PM Monday through Friday.

KAJA-TV, Channel 68
• 409 S. Staples St., Corpus Christi
• (361) 881-6100

KAJA is the sister station of KDF-TV, operating out of facilities in the same building and owned by Evening Post Publishing Co. of South Carolina. KAJA is an affiliate of the Spanish-language network, Telemundo. Like KDF, KAJA was previously owned by Paloma Broadcasting Corp. and was sold to Miramar Broadcasting Company when Paloma ran into financial problems.

KAJA is a low-power station distributed mostly by cable systems in Nueces and San Patricio counties. Telemundo, the nation's second-largest Spanish-language TV network, took KAJA on as an affiliate in October 1993. Programming includes talk shows, soap operas, variety shows, dramas, comedies, and news. A majority of Telemundo's programs are produced in the United States. The rest come mainly from Latin America and Spain.

KRIS-TV, Channel 6
- **409 S. Staples St., Corpus Christi**
- **(361) 886-6100**

The perennial bridesmaid among Corpus Christi TV stations is KRIS-TV. Although ratings for its newscasts have seldom topped KIII-TV during the past 17 years, the NBC affiliate's hard work and a willingness to try new things has narrowed the gap between the No. 1 and No. 2 stations. KRIS prefers cleanly written, well-reported TV news stories to the flashier style favored by so many local news teams. Former longtime owner T. Frank Smith Jr. sold the station to South Carolina-based Evening Post Publishing Co. in February 1998, making it one of three stations in Corpus Christi to be owned by the same company.

Cable Providers

Five cable television providers, including two in Corpus Christi, serve the Corpus Christi area. Prices and packages vary from company to company and even from city to city. Call the cable company that serves your area of interest for information on prices and services.

Cable One
- **316 S. Commercial St., Aransas Pass**
- **(361) 758-7621, (800) 242-2039**

Cable One serves Aransas Pass, Ingleside, and Gregory. It offers 44 channels on its standard basic service. Cinemax 1 and 2; HBO 1,2, and 3; Showtime 1,2, and 3; The Movie Channel, and pay-per-view services are available at additional cost.

Charter Communications
- **415 S. Sixth St., Kingsville**
- **(361) 595-5726**

Charter Communications in Kingsville serves residents within the city limits of Driscoll, Kingsville, and Agua Dulce. It offers basic service with 12 channels in Kingsville and 17 basic service channels in Agua Dulce and Driscoll. The company offers expanded service with 32 channels in Kingsville only. Cinemax, HBO, Showtime, and The Disney Channel are available at additional cost. The Disney Channel is not available in Agua Dulce and Driscoll.

Charter Communications
- **822 Market St., Portland**
- **(361) 643-8588, (800) 873-9395**

Charter Communications provides service in Port Aransas, Portland, Sinton, and Rockport.

Port Aransas residents receive standard basic service with 33 channels. Cinemax, Encore, HBO, Showtime, and The Movie Channel are available at additional cost.

Portland residents can choose from standard basic with 39 channels and extended basic with 43 channels. Cinemax, Encore, HBO, The Playboy Channel, Showtime, and The Movie Channel are available at additional cost.

Rockport residents can choose from standard basic service with 40 channels or extended basic with 46 channels. Cinemax, HBO, The Playboy Channel, Showtime, and The Movie Channel are available at additional cost.

Heartland Cable Television
- **5541 Bear Ln., Corpus Christi**
- **(800) 880-0292**

Heartland Cable Television is Corpus Christi's wireless cable television company. Its signal is broadcast via the airwaves to antennas placed atop subscribers' homes. Their signal covers a 25-mile radius of downtown Corpus Christi. Heartland offers basic service with 28 channels. Cinemax, HBO, and HBO Plus are available at additional cost.

TCI Cablevision
- **4060 S. Padre Island Dr., Corpus Christi**
- **(361) 857-5000**

TCI Cablevision offers basic service with 18 channels and expanded basic with 35, including The Disney Channel. Cinemax, Encore, HBO, Showtime, and Starz are available at additional cost.

Radio

The Corpus Christi radio market is surprisingly diverse for a relatively unpopulated area. About 30 radio stations broadcast here compared to about 20 in the much larger Austin area. Rock 'n' roll, country, Christian, and Spanish-language stations dominate.

One company owns six stations in the Corpus Christi market. Gulfstar Communications Inc. of Austin owns stations KRYS 1360 AM, KRYS 99.1 FM, KMXR 93.9 FM, KSAB 99.9 FM, KUNO 1400 AM, and KNCN 101.3 FM.

Contemporary
KKBA 92.7 FM (Adult Contemporary)
KKPN 104.5 (Modern Adult Contemporary)
KLUX 89.5 FM (Easy listening)
KMXR 93.9 FM (Adult contemporary)
KZFM 95.5 FM (Contemporary hits)

MEDIA

Children
KRYS 1360 AM (Radio Disney)

Christian
KBNJ 91.7 FM
KCTA 1030 AM
KFGG 88.7 FM
KINE 1330 AM (Spanish Christian)

Classical
KEDT 90.3 FM (Jazz, blues, NPR news)

Country
KFTX 97.5 FM
KOUL 103.7 FM
KRYS 99.1 FM

International (Spanish Top 40)
KUNO 1400 AM

News/Talk
KEYS 1440 AM
KCCT 1150 AM (24-Hour Sports Talk)

KSIX 1230 AM (CBS Radio Network,
Astros baseball)
KTKY 106.1 FM
KTSA 550 AM (From San Antonio)
WOAI 1200 AM (From San Antonio)

Nostalgia
KCCG 107.3 FM

Rock
KBSO 94.7 FM (Classic Rock)
KFLZ 106.9 FM (Alternative Rock)
KBTE 102.3 FM (Rhythmic Contemporary)
KLTG 96.5 FM (Soft rock hits: '70s, '80s, '90s)
KNCN 101.3 FM (Album-oriented rock)
KRAD 105.5 FM (Alternative/
Modern Rock)

Tejano
KLHQ 98.5 FM
KMIQ 105.1 FM
KNDA 102.9 FM
KSAB 99.9 FM

Worship

Take a spin down Corpus Christi's Shoreline Boulevard and you'll soon realize the importance religion plays in the lives of Corpus Christi area residents. A 15-foot, 6-inch statue of Jesus entitled *It Is I* towers over the roadway and Corpus Christi Bay in front of First United Methodist Church. Standing in the bow of a boat in rough waters, arms uplifted, the scene depicts the story of how Jesus calmed his disciples' fears amidst a storm on the Sea of Galilee. (For more information on the statue and artist, see the Close-up in this chapter.) Many city residents had long dreamed of erecting such a statue somewhere along the city's bayfront. After all, the city takes its name from the Latin phrase for "Body of Christ," a name given by Alonzo Álvarez de Piñeda, who is said to have discovered Corpus Christi Bay on the Roman Catholic Feast Day of Corpus Christi.

Geographically, Corpus Christi is a long way from the center of the Bible Belt, but ideologically it's smack dab in the middle, albeit with a more Catholic slant than most Bible Belt states. Religion pops up in all sorts of places here. For instance, it's common to begin public meetings— city council meetings, commissioners court meetings, school board meetings, etc.—with a prayer. You'll also hear them before some high school football games and other school-related events, although recent court decisions have sought to put an end to that practice. The Hispanic influence on the Corpus Christi area, which touches so many aspects of life here, is especially evident in the region's religious makeup. A 1995 poll conducted by the *Corpus Christi Caller-Times* newspaper revealed that half the city's residents were Catholic compared with 27 percent statewide. The strong showing among Catholics in Corpus Christi is due in part to the area's large Hispanic population and its ties to Roman Catholicism. According to the *Caller-Times* poll, 63 percent of the city's Catholics, or 80,000 people, are Hispanic.

In 1995, approximately 35 percent of the population were Protestant, including 13 percent Methodist, 6 percent Presbyterian, 3 percent Lutheran, 3 percent Episcopalian and 1 percent Church of Christ.

In Corpus Christi the Catholic Church influences religion, politics, social issues, and entertainment. The city is home to the Catholic Diocese of Corpus Christi, founded as a mission field in 1874 and established as a diocese in 1912. It includes all or part of several South Texas counties from Corpus Christi to Freer, not including the Rio Grande Valley in far South Texas. According to church estimates, the diocesan population totals more than 350,000 people.

Before it became a republic, the area that is now Texas belonged to Mexico. The government encouraged Roman Catholics to settle the area by awarding them land. Impresarios were people who contracted with the Mexican government to bring Roman Catholic settlers to Texas in exchange for 23,000 acres for each 100 families. Their descendants (many of whom are no doubt Catholic) inhabit the area today.

The Bishop of Corpus Christi is the Most Rev. Edmond Carmody, who serves as pastor of the Corpus Christi Cathedral, an architecturally and historically significant church that sits on a bluff overlooking Corpus Christi Bay (see our Attractions chapter). Carmody succeeded the Most Rev. Roberto Gonzalez, who was named Archbishop of Puerto Rico.

Kent Ullberg and the Christ Statue

For more than 65 years, the Christian community in Corpus Christi, which means "body of Christ" in Latin, had discussed the possibility of a Christ statue overlooking Corpus Christi Bay. Several memorials were proposed, including the commissioning of Gutzon Borglum, the sculptor of Mount Rushmore, to create such a piece. None of the projects succeeded.

Retired schoolteacher Dorothy McCoy prompted interest again when she searched for ways to memorialize her son, Bob, who was killed in a 1991 auto accident. She sent a check to the First United Methodist Church, 900 S. Shoreline Boulevard, and a letter outlining her vision for a Christ statue "stilling the waters."

With McCoy's initial contribution, a fund drive was started to make the statue a reality. In 1993, Corpus Christi sculptor Kent Ullberg was commissioned by the church to produce the statue.

Unveiled in October 1995, Ullberg's $100,000 sculpture depicts Christ with uplifted arms standing in the bow of a boat in rough waters. The scene represents the time Jesus calmed his disciples' fears amidst a storm on the Sea of Galilee by rebuking the wind and stilling the waters. The details were researched for historical accuracy, including the sandals Jesus is wearing and the boat's design.

Called *It is I*, the bronze sculpture is 15 feet, 6 inches tall and rests on an 8-

Artist Kent Ulberg stands next to the 15¹/₂-foot sculpture of Jesus he created for the First United Methodist Church in Corpus Christi.

Photo: courtesy of the First United Methodist Church

foot granite base. The statue is outside the entrance to the church sanctuary, facing the bay.

Ullberg has created and installed more than 40 monumental sculptures worldwide. His work has been shown at the National Museum of Natural History in Stockholm, Sweden; the Exhibition Hall in Beijing, China; and the Salon d'Automne in Paris, France.

His other sculptures in the Coastal Bend include *Leaping Marlin* at the entrance to Padre Island and *Spring Plumage* at the Texas State Aquarium.

Carmody is a native of Ireland who came to Corpus Christi from the diocese in Tyler, Texas. He was installed as Corpus Christi's seventh bishop on March 17, 2000.

The diocesan offices are located throughout the city. The chancery office, (361) 882-6191, is at 629 Lipan Street in the city's uptown region. Diocesan facilities include retreat centers, a newspaper and TV network, and a Catholic school system. The Diocese of Corpus Christi is known as a conservative diocese, especially under the direction of former Bishop René Gracida, who in 1990 became the nation's first and only Catholic bishop to excommunicate several Catholics who administered abortion clinics or performed abortions.

In recent years anti-abortion protests have led to pickets, lawsuits, and arrests when anti-abortion activists (made up of Catholics and Protestants alike) blocked access to abortion clinic entrances.

Catholic Social Services, (361) 884-0651, which operates as an affiliated corporation of the diocese, runs several charitable programs in Corpus Christi. It provides emergency aide for poor and indigent individuals and families with immediate needs that cannot be met by state or federal assistance. Help includes cash, food, clothing, furniture, and other household goods. Each year the agency serves about 20,000 people in Corpus Christi.

The Jewish Community Council of Corpus Christi, (361) 855-6239, 750 Everhart Road, serves the area's Jewish community as well as people of other faiths. It operates the Jewish Community Center and a preschool program for children age 2 through kindergarten age. It also provides meeting space for the community and maintains a swimming pool. Anyone can become a member of the Jewish Community Center for a fee ranging from $100 to $190 a year. Membership entitles you to pool privileges, school discounts, a newsletter, and retail discounts.

Corpus Christi's small Muslim community worships at 7341 McArdle Road. Members, who built the mosque in 1998, raised construction funds from local and out-of-town sources. The organizational wing of the mosque, the Islamic Society of South Texas, can be reached at (361) 992-8550.

The Christian Business Men's Committee, (361) 851-1605, 5205-A Embassy Drive, Corpus Christi, is a Christian outreach to the business community. The committee, one of about a thousand throughout the country, hosts monthly speaker luncheons at the Holiday Inn-Padre Island Drive, 5549 Leopard Street, and weekly scripture studies. Scripture studies are held five times a week at various times and sites. Although the committee is Protestant in terms of teachings and interpretation of scripture, participation is open to people of all faiths. The committee hosts an annual Leadership Prayer Breakfast in which members pray for local elected officials.

The Corpus Christi Baptist Association, (361) 853-2555, 4301 Ocean Drive, Corpus Christi, helps Southern Baptist Churches in the Corpus Christi area with religious education and weekday ministries (helping the poor, fighting illiteracy, etc.). It also helps start new churches and directs callers to a Southern Baptist Church that is right for them.

You won't find many mosques or Buddhist or Hindu temples in the area, but you will find a surprising variety of churches and temples here. For a complete list of churches and services in Corpus Christi turn to the Saturday religion page of the *Corpus Christi Caller-Times*. Many newcomers to the area say the extensive listing of worship services in the newspaper helped guide them in choosing a church. For a list of churches and services in other parts of the Corpus Christi area, check the weekly newspaper serving the area in which you are staying. See our Media chapter for information on newspapers.

WORSHIP

Index

INDEX

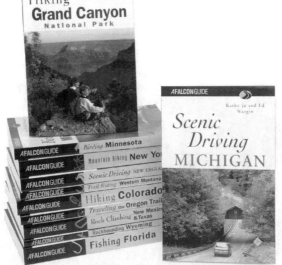